Emotion in Early Christianity

Emotion in Early Christianity

Andrew Crislip

William B. Eerdmans Publishing Company
Grand Rapids, Michigan

Wm. B. Eerdmans Publishing Co.
2006 44th Street SE, Grand Rapids, MI 49508
www.eerdmans.com

Published 2026
Printed in the United States of America

32 31 30 29 28 27 26   1 2 3 4 5 6 7

ISBN 978-0-8028-8426-8

Library of Congress Cataloging-in-Publication Data

A catalog record for this book is available from the Library of Congress.

Contents

Abbreviations

AB	Anchor Bible
ABD	*Anchor Bible Dictionary*. Edited by David Noel Freedman. 6 vols. New York: Doubleday, 1992
ACW	Ancient Christian Writers
AHR	*American Historical Review*
ANF	*Ante-Nicene Fathers*
BDAG	Bauer, Walter, Frederick W. Danker, William F. Arndt, and F. Wilbur Gingrich. *Greek-English Lexicon of the New Testament and Other Early Christian Literature*. 3rd ed. Chicago: University of Chicago Press, 2000
BibInt	*Biblical Interpretation*
BibInt	Biblical Interpretation Series
BR	*Biblical Research*
CBQMS	Catholic Biblical Quarterly Monograph Series
CRB	Cahiers de la Revue Biblique
CS	Cistercian Studies
DSM	Diagnostic and Statistical Manual
ECL	Early Christianity and Its Literature
FC	Fathers of the Church
GCS	Die griechischen christlichen Schriftsteller der ersten [drei] Jahrhunderte
GRBS	*Greek, Roman, and Byzantine Studies*
HTR	*Harvard Theological Review*
JBL	*Journal of Biblical Literature*
JBRec	*Journal of the Bible and Its Reception*
JECS	*Journal of Early Christian Studies*

JNES	*Journal of Near Eastern Studies*
JSNT	*Journal for the Study of the New Testament*
LCL	Loeb Classical Library
LNTS	The Library of New Testament Studies
LSJ	Liddell, Henry George, Robert Scott, Henry Stuart Jones. *A Greek-English Lexicon*. 9th ed. with revised supplements. Oxford: Clarendon, 1996
NHC	Nag Hammadi Codex
NHMS	Nah Hammadi & Manichaean Studies
NHS	Nag Hammadi Studies
NovT	*Novum Testamentum*
NovTSup	Supplements to Novum Testamentum
NPNF	*Nicene and Post-Nicene Fathers*
NTOA	Novum Testamentum et Orbis Antiquus
NTS	*New Testament Studies*
OLA	Orientalia Lovaniesia Analecta
OTP	*Old Testament Pseudepigrapha*. Edited by James H. Charlesworth. 2 vols. New York: Doubleday, 1983, 1985
PG	Patrologia Graeca [= Patrologiae Cursus Completus: Series Graeca]. Edited by Jacques-Paul Migne. 162 vols. Paris, 1857–1886
PIMS	Pontifical Institute of Mediaeval Studies
RBS	Resources for Biblical Study
SBL	Society of Biblical Literature
SC	Sources chrétiennes
SD	Studies and Documents
SECA	Studies on Early Christianity Apocrypha
SNTSMS	Society for New Testament Studies Monograph Series
STAC	Studien und Texte zu Antike und Christentum
StPatr	Studia Patristica
SUNT	Studien zur Umwelt des Neuen Testaments
SymS	Symposium Series
TDNT	*Theological Dictionary of the New Testament*
TENTS	Texts and Editions for New Testament Study
TS	Texts and Studies
TU	Texte und Untersuchungen
VB	Lefort, L.-Th. *S. Pachomii vita bohairice scripta*. Corpus Scriptorum Christianorum Orientalium 89. Paris: Reipublicae, 1925
VC	*Vigiliae Christianae*
VCSup	Vigiliae Christianae Supplements Series

VS	Lefort, L.-Th. *S. Pachomii vitae sahidice scriptae*. Corpus Scriptorum Christianorum Orientalium 99–100. Paris: Reipublicae, 1933
WBC	Word Biblical Commentary
WUNT	Wissenschaftliche Untersuchungen zum Neuen Testament
ZAC	*Zeitschrift für Antikes Christentum*

1

Finding Emotion in Early Christianity

From all the hours spent in United Methodist Sunday school, summer camps, and youth fellowship in the 1980s, I vividly remember one hymn as a favorite: "They'll Know We Are Christians by Our Love," also known as "We Are One in the Spirit." Apart from "Kumbaya" or "Amazing Grace," it is the only hymn from my youth whose melody I can instantly recall. It's not an altogether surprising song to remember, since it stands out in the UMC hymnal. Not a Protestant hymn at all, it was written by the Catholic priest Peter Raymond Scholtes, first published in 1966, and inspired by the liturgical transformation of Vatican II.[1] This minor-key folk song based on John 13:35 reflects the ferment of Christian music in the 1960s, a harmonious counterpoint to the emerging rock and roll revivalism.[2]

When I used to sing it, I heard the song's evocation of Christian love as a call to action in the world. This is the clear message of the lyrics, which share broadly in the 1960s' revolutionary ideas of justice and reconciliation: Christians "work with each other," "work side by side," "guard each one's dignity and save each one's pride," "walk with each other," and "pray that all unity may one day be restored." The lyrics state not only that such actions are incumbent on Christians, but that by these actions and mindsets outsiders ("they") will recognize the Christian *as Christian*. All of these community and self-identifying actions manifest the distinctive Christian emotional concept of "love."

1. Here and the following is indebted to Joshua Taylor, "History of Hymns: 'They'll Know We Are Christians by Our Love,'" *Discipleship Ministries*, June 26, 2019, https://www.umcdiscipleship.org/articles/history-of-hymns-theyll-know-we-are-christians-by-our-love.

2. See Randall Stephens, *The Devil's Music: How Christians Inspired, Condemned, and Embraced Rock 'n' Roll* (Cambridge, MA: Harvard University Press, 2018).

This confluence of action, thought, and community points to an important observation in the study of emotions. As much as it might feel like it, emotions are not feelings inflicted on us, which we as individuals suffer (hence the term "passion"). Rather, emotion is a form of practice, a way of being, a stance, an orientation, an action to be cultivated, which can transform the self and the world.[3] In this way, emotion as a practice can be as important to Christian life as ritual, prayer, and creed. It spreads no less than the vibrations of sound, the movements of dance, or the virality of memes among bodies and communities.[4] Love, thus, forms a core of Christian identity and practice, as a way of life and a universal philanthropy that the Christian sends out into the world. One could find this understanding of Christian love preached in any number of churches today, and many have experienced such feelings spread almost contagiously in physical gatherings.

Yet, love (*agapē*) in John's Gospel, the text from which the hymn draws its inspiration, takes on a different form, the sort of difference that historians of emotion are always on the lookout for and that translation and sheer familiarity of emotional concepts like "love" can disguise. Leading into his farewell discourse, Jesus instructs his disciples that they will not be able to follow where he is going. Instead, as something of a consolation, they are to love one another: "I give you a new commandment, that you love one another. Just as I have loved you, you also should love one another. By this everyone will know that you are my disciples, if you have love for one another" (John 13:34–35).[5] There are four important interrelated points in this passage. First, this love is new and differs from the other familiar forms of love; the novelty of this love emblematically expresses the fulfillment of the new covenant between God and his people.[6]

3. As argued from several perspectives by Monique Scheer, "Are Emotions a Kind of Practice (and Is That What Makes Them Have a History)? A Bordieuian Approach to Understanding Emotion," *History and Theory* 51 (2012): 193–220; Lisa Feldman Barrett, "The Conceptual Act Theory: A Precis," *Emotion Review* 6 (2014): 292–97; and Steven J. Kraftchick, "Πάθη [*Pathē*] in Paul: The Emotional Logic of 'Original Argument,'" in *Paul and Pathos*, ed. Thomas H. Olbricht and Jerry L. Sumney, SymS 16 (Atlanta: SBL Press, 2001), 39–68.

4. Emotional contagion is well established in anthropology and observable in experimental psychology. I have benefited from Elaine Hatfield and Richard L. Rapson, "Emotional Contagion: Religious and Ethnic Hatreds and Global Terrorism," in *The Social Life of Emotions*, ed. Larissa Z. Tiedens and Colin Wayne Leach (Cambridge: Cambridge University Press, 2004), 129–43; and Teresa Brennan, *The Transmission of Affect* (Ithaca, NY: Cornell University Press, 2004).

5. Unless otherwise noted, Scripture references are from the NRSV. In some cases, I substitute my own or other translations when needed.

6. Raymond E. Brown, *The Gospel According to John (XIII–XXI)*, AB 29A (New York: Doubleday, 1970), 614.

Second, although Jesus's love for his disciples manifests in his willing death and God's love manifests in giving his son to the world (3:16), Jesus does not mandate this love to be exteriorized as charitable action. It is emotional, a feeling, "affective," "intimate," and "interiorized."[7] To belong to Christ demands not just acting in this new way or believing in this new way but feeling in this new way. Third, quite in contrast with its 1960s reception, Christians do not direct this new covenantal love toward the world or to outsiders but to other disciples of Jesus (*agapēn echēte en allēlois*, 13:35) and against the world. Fourth and finally, by this interiorized, affective love of other disciples, they will be recognized by others as distinct and different, recognized as who they are.[8]

John, thus, envisions his community defined by a distinctive way of feeling. The emotion of love constitutes a new commandment, directed toward other members of the community, even "constitutive of the community."[9] Their peculiar love distinguishes Christians from the emotion of outsiders, so distinct that even outsiders perceive the difference and recognize Christians immediately not by their creed or their actions but their emotion. This foundational gospel urges its readers to identify themselves as an "emotional community," to use a concept from the history of emotions.[10] To be a Christian is to feel like a Christian.

In this book I show how Christians from the time of Paul to late antiquity came to understand and define themselves, their communities, practices, and identity through the experience of emotion. From the earliest Christian writings (even before the term "Christian" had been coined), authors promoted the self-understanding that Christians could, should, and even must experience different emotions or experience emotions differently than outsiders. Christian reflection on emotion and passion was surely compounded and complicated by their unique theology of an impassible yet incarnated, fully human, and suffering God and extended to their understanding of the nature of humanity, even the origin of the created world. To grapple with the complexity of emotion is an important part of the social, intellectual, and institutional history of

7. As Brown puts it. He further notes the intersection of salvation and emotion: "The love that Jesus has for his followers is not only affective but also effective: it brings about their salvation" (*Gospel According to John*, 612).

8. Brown writes that "even outsiders will recognize the distinctiveness of Christian love" (*Gospel According to John*, 615).

9. "Yet, while for Qumran love is a duty consequent upon one's belonging to the community, for John, Jesus' love for men is constitutive of the community" (Brown, *Gospel According to John*, 613).

10. A concept proposed and developed by Barbara H. Rosenwein, *Emotional Communities in the Early Middles Ages* (Ithaca, NY: Cornell University Press, 2006); and described succinctly in Barbara H. Rosenwein and Riccardo Cristiani, *What Is the History of Emotions?* (Cambridge: Polity, 2018), 39–45.

early Christianity, as well as an important indicator of the experience of being Christian in the ancient world.

Recent cognitive science insists that emotions are far more than irrational impulses or evolutionarily conditioned responses triggered by external stimuli. Emotions fundamentally determine the contours of human experience and are inseparable from the senses and our embodiment. They shape the way it feels to move through the world. More radically, it is through emotions that we construct our lived reality, the lens through which we perceive the world that we live in.[11] To understand what it meant to be a Christian in the ancient world and how Christians understood their community, behaviors, and identity, the historian must attend to more than propositional knowledge or assertions of group affiliation or difference but to the ways that Christians moved through the world around them and made sense of their world as embodied beings. It is through emotions, both as concepts and as practices, that humans make sense of the world around them.[12]

I write as a historian of early Christianity, so I am concerned with identifying changes in emotional norms and emotional language as well as continuities. Emotions have a history and influenced history in the centuries between the emergence of Christians as an identifiable movement and the dissolution of the greater Roman Empire. Historians and theologians have long asked a perennial and important question—What difference did Christianity make?—toward which one might assess all sorts of historical topics, such as gender, wealth, charity, morality, textuality, and so on.[13] When it comes to emotions, Christianity made quite a bit of difference. Christianity could offer a very dif-

11. As discussed by Lisa Feldman Barrett, *How Emotions Are Made: The Secret Life of the Brain* (Boston: Houghton Mifflin Harcourt, 2017), e.g., 134. The connections between emotion, embodiment, sensation, and the emergent history of experience are explored by Rob Boddice and Mark Smith, *Emotion, Sense, Experience*, Cambridge Elements: Histories of Emotions and the Senses (Cambridge: Cambridge University Press, 2020).

12. "Concepts" here, from the perspective of contemporary neuroscience, are cognitive, embodied, and constructed. Helpful overviews are in Barrett, *How Emotions Are Made*; Lisa Feldman Barrett and James A. Russell, eds., *The Psychological Construction of Emotion* (New York: Guilford, 2014); and Lisa Feldman Barrett, "The Theory of Constructed Emotion: An Active Inference Account of Interoception and Categorization," *Social Cognitive and Affective Neuroscience* 12 (2017): 1–23, which along with the following responses gives an overview of the current debate. See also Scheer, "Are Emotions a Kind of Practice?," for a different perspective.

13. See, for example, how Virginia Burrus poses the question regarding sexuality and morality in *The Sex Lives of Saints: An Erotics of Ancient Hagiography* (Philadelphia: University of Pennsylvania Press, 2004), 2.

ferent way of feeling compared to the standards promoted by Greco-Roman moral philosophy. Even within that diverse category that we call Christianity (or Christianities), writers and communities furthermore modeled different and often conflicting ways for how to feel. Sometimes emotions themselves formed crucial disjunctions between competing groups. While there was no single way to feel like a Christian, many early Christian authors agreed in citing the emotions as a principal marker of their community, practice, and identity as Christians and the peculiarity of their experience as Christians.

In this introductory chapter, I lay out some concepts and debates, returning to these in later chapters, but more often they run silently in the background as perspectives which have shaped the way I think about emotions as a historical topic. First, I discuss the terminology and definition of emotion and specify how I use the concept and the terminology in the book. Second, I outline three theories from the cognitive and affective sciences and more interdisciplinary cultural studies, which have influenced contemporary humanities scholarship, including biblical studies and early Christian studies. Third, I place this book within the context of the history of emotions. I also relate the study of emotion to the formation of social identity, which has become such an important theme in the study of early Christianity. Finally, I provide an overview of the six chapters that follow, each of which addresses an emotion or constellation of emotion concepts through which Christians queried and defined themselves as Christians and as humans: joy, sadness, anger, disgust, envy, and (by way of conclusion) love.

"Emotion" and Emotion Words

"Emotion" has become a nearly inescapable feature of contemporary global culture, in schools, workplaces, pulpits, and therapy. Yet the term itself is of recent vintage and is far from a universal concept. Some languages and cultures (ancient and contemporary) have no word or concept that approximates the modern "emotion," categorizing certain feelings or embodied experiences ("qualia") into a class of embodied thoughts. Among these is biblical Hebrew, notwithstanding the growing bibliography on ancient Jewish emotions.[14] Cop-

14. F. Scott Spencer, "Getting a Feel for the 'Mixed' and 'Vexed' Study of Emotions," in *Mixed Feelings and Vexed Passions: Exploring Emotions in Biblical Literature*, ed. F. Scott Spencer, RBS 90 (Atlanta: SBL Press, 2017), 5. This whole essay provides a useful survey of recent scholarship of emotions in biblical studies, and the essays therein include current approaches to ancient emotions in Hebrew sources. See further discussion in Françoise

tic also lacks a native word close to that of "emotion."[15] Coptic translations of philosophically inclined Greek originals and some native authors sometimes preserve the term *pathos* for emotion, but *pathos* more often signals "passion" as it does today, referring to sinful desire. Some contemporary languages also lack such a concept, such as Akan and other west African languages, Tahitian, and others.[16] Other cultures and languages show this phenomenon by describing feelings that seem naturally emotional in the modern West, such as depression, in principally somatic or bodily terms.[17]

Greek and Latin, however, have well-developed concepts that point to a class of experiences similar to those included in the modern "emotion," even if we are cognizant that they are not identical.[18] Among the Greek sources that will dominate the following chapters, it is passion (*pathos/pathē*; sometimes *pathēma/pathēmata*) that normally translates to emotion.[19] Passion points to rather different semantics for ancients writing about emotions, an expanded range of experience that includes suffering, experience, and illness. Latin writers like Cicero, or the much later Augustine, had their own ways of speaking about emotion, under influence of the Greek, with terms like *perturbatio*, *affectus*, or even *motus*, which lies at the root of the modern neologism "emotion."[20] While I will return to the emotions or passions in Greek and Roman antiquity when relevant in the following chapters, I wish simply

Mirguet, "What Is an 'Emotion' in the Hebrew Bible? An Experience That Exceeds Most Contemporary Concepts," *BibInt* 24 (2016): 442–65.

15. Andrew Crislip, "Emotion Words in Coptic: Reflections on the Evidence from Shenoute the Great," *Journal of the Canadian Society for Coptic Studies* 10 (2018): 45–57.

16. Andrew Beatty, *Emotional Worlds: Beyond an Anthropology of Emotion* (Cambridge: Cambridge University Press, 2019), 242; similarly emotions in some west African languages are generally "somatized," rather than categorized abstractly into a group of distinct and discrete feelings; see Vivian Afi Djokoto and Sumie Okazuki, "Happiness in the Eye and Heart: Somatic Referencing in West African Emotion Lexica," *Journal of Black Psychology* 32 (2006): 117–40.

17. Arthur Kleinman and Joan Kleinman, "Somatization: The Interconnections in Chinese Society Among Culture, Depressive Experiences, and the Meanings of Pain," in *Culture and Depression: Studies in the Anthropology and Cross-Cultural Psychiatry of Affect and Disorder*, ed. Arthur Kleinman and Byron Good (Berkeley: University of California Press, 1985), 429–90.

18. Literature covering this problem is extensive, so I will not attempt to replace or recreate it here. See the studies by David Konstan, *The Emotions of the Ancient Greeks: Studies in Aristotle and Classical Literature* (Toronto: University of Toronto Press, 2006), 3–40; and Simo Knuuttila, *Emotions in Ancient and Medieval Philosophy* (Oxford: Clarendon, 2004).

19. On *pathēmata* as passions, see the Neoplatonist Iamblichus. William V. Harris, *Restraining Rage: The Ideology of Anger Control in Classical Antiquity* (Cambridge, MA: Harvard University Press, 2001), 124.

20. Rosenwein, *Emotional Communities*, 32–56, covers Greek and especially Latin emotion

to note here, as others have more comprehensively, that the modern concept of emotion is not the same as the ancient concepts of *pathos*, *perturbatio*, and so on.[21] Among the more salient differences is the common use of passions in moralizing discourse and to describe suffering. The *pathē* for Christians, thus, overlap semantically with experiences that contemporary psychologists would not describe as emotions, such as sins, lusts, and desires, or more positively as enduring or suffering, most notably the *passio* of the incarnate God-man Jesus Christ, a unique emotional exemplar for the early Christian experience.[22]

The very ubiquity of Christian critique of passions as sinful desires or diseases of the soul drove the invention of the modern concept of emotion as an alternative to pious Christian moralizing.[23] The fact that this moralizing connotation is still present in much contemporary use of the word "passion" is also a reason that scholars of ancient passions frequently prefer the neutrality of "emotion," in spite of its very modern lineage. Although its usage goes back to the seventeenth century, "emotion" as it is used today may be traced most proximally to Scotland in the 1820s, where philosophers intended to displace concepts such as affections or passions that were too theologically freighted as well as too diffusely applied to cognitive and bodily phenomena.[24] Historians have regularly commented on the incommensurability of the word to ancient and non-European contexts and urged historians to be wary of anachronism, which are significant points to keep in mind.[25]

In the end, however, historians of the ancient and medieval worlds, as well as the modern one that gave birth to the word, have generally settled on this conventional term as indispensable if imperfect.[26] "Emotion" remains a useful

---

words through late antiquity; also Damien Boquet and Piroska Nagy, *Medieval Sensibilities: A History of Emotions in the Middle Ages*, trans. Robert Shaw (Cambridge: Polity, 2018), 18–25.

21. A comprehensive account may be found in Thomas Dixon, *From Passions to Emotions: The Creation of a Secular Category* (Cambridge: Cambridge University Press, 2006). That said, important work has traced this philosophical lineage without overly problematizing the word, as in Richard Sorabji, *Emotion and Peace of Mind: From Stoic Agitation to Christian Temptation* (Oxford: Oxford University Press, 2000).

22. As emphasized by medieval historians, Bouquet and Nagy, *Medieval Sensibilities*, 16–18. See also the older but useful entry by Wilhelm Michaelis, "πάσχω κτλ," *TDNT* 5:904–39.

23. Thomas Dixon, "'Emotion': The History of a Keyword in Crisis," *Emotion Review* 4 (2012): 339.

24. Dixon, "Emotion"; also Jan Plamper, *The History of Emotions: An Introduction*, trans. Keith Tribe (Oxford: Oxford University Press, 2015), 9–25.

25. E.g., Mirguet, "What Is an 'Emotion'?"; and Rob Boddice, *The History of Emotions* (Manchester: Manchester University Press, 2018), 41–46.

26. Dixon, "Emotion," 343, cited in Spencer, "Getting a Feel," 29–30. For a biblical studies

term, for all its imprecision and potential for anachronistic thinking, as a sort of master category, which like "religion" or "magic" has resisted many valiant attempts to kill it off.[27] Despite its modernity, and although psychologists, cognitive scientists, anthropologists, and historians still lack consensus as to precisely what it is, emotion has become a concept that allows specialists in these fields to talk with one another. From a historical perspective, it allows for comparison and observation of change. Furthermore, it is hardly necessary (or practical) to avoid translation of ancient emotional concepts, whether that be *passio* (emotion), *orgē* (anger), or *phthonos* (envy). Especially for common concepts like these, translations helpfully convey their meaning in the vast majority of instances.[28] In those places where the English translation fails to capture the sense of feeling (as frequently is the case with ancient concepts of *lypē* [sadness] and *agapē*), such differences and discontinuities provide useful points for historical analysis.

I use "emotion" with these historical caveats in mind and in line with its broad adoption among historians. Part of this approach means attending to the specific words used by the early Christians, whether identifying a category of experience, such as *pathos*, *logismos* (thought), or *epithymia* (desire), or the specific emotions (*chara* [joy], *lypē*, and so on) that the following chapters address, in line with the approaches of historians of ancient and medieval emotions.[29] This is not a matter of philological pedantry or antiquarianism but points toward the interdisciplinary study of emotion, as currents in neuroscience "encourage" historical analysis of emotions, especially that which engages with the history of emotion words.[30] At the same time, in the interest

perspective see Stephen C. Barton, "'Be Angry but Do Not Sin' (Ephesians 4:26a): Sin and the Emotions in the New Testament with Special Reference to Anger," *Studies in Christian Ethics* 28 (2015): 21.

27. Boddice, *History of Emotions*, 41–46, who, although he critiques others for their use of "emotion," arrives at the same place or something very close to it; also for "emotion" as an etic category for comparing Christian and Stoic perspectives, see Katherine M. Hockey, *The Role of Emotion in 1 Peter*, SNTSMS 173 (Cambridge: Cambridge University Press, 2019), 56.

28. Ed Sanders, *Envy and Jealousy in Classical Athens: A Socio-Psychological Approach* (Oxford: Oxford University Press, 2014), 5–7. He suggests 95 percent for *orgē*.

29. See Rosenwein, *Emotional Communities*, 1–31, for a methodological discussion. Recent studies of individual emotions or emotional constellations representative of the history of ancient emotions include Françoise Mirguet, *An Early History of Compassion: Emotion and Imagination in Hellenistic Judaism* (Cambridge: Cambridge University Press, 2017); and Laurel Fulkerson, *No Regrets: Remorse in Classical Antiquity* (Oxford: Oxford University Press, 2013).

30. Boddice, *History of Emotions*, 46.

of covering a range of sources from the first to the fifth century in a relatively brief space, I have tried to avoid excessively detailed word studies.

What Are Emotions?

Many have observed the past two decades' rapid proliferation of interest in emotions in psychology and brain science, literary studies, anthropology, philosophy, sociology, geography, archaeology, and cultural studies.[31] The turn to emotion is indeed remarkable, not least considering that not very long ago even psychologists hardly took emotions seriously as an object of study.[32] No doubt this is part of larger trends of the past seventy years, including the major social and intellectual movements of the 1960s and '70s, as well as more recent trends, such as the long-predicted and now consummated "triumph of the therapeutic" or the wide-ranging embrace of "the body" in various strands of scholarship.[33] Emotion has become a significant topic of historical and religious studies as well, and several synthetic studies now survey the various approaches to emotions and situate them within the disciplines of neuroscience and cognitive science, the social sciences, and philosophy.[34]

While this richness of emotional historiography frees me from providing yet another analysis of the historiography of emotions, I still wish to lay out briefly the basic methodological approaches. In presenting work at conferences

31. E.g., Boddice, *History of Emotions*, 1–2; and Ruth Leys, "The Turn to Affect: A Critique," *Critical Inquiry* 37 (2011): 434–35.

32. As in the heyday of behaviorism, in which emotions "were redefined as mere behaviors for survival: fighting, fleeing, feeding, and mating," Barrett, *How Emotions Are Made*, 171. The period between 1900 and 1959 has been called the "Dark Ages" of the study of emotion by Maria Gendron and Lisa Feldman Barrett, "Reconstructing the Past: A Century of Ideas About Emotion in Psychology," *Emotion Review* 1 (2009): 316–39.

33. Emotions research "increased exponentially" in the 1960s and beyond, which Plamper connects to a variety of important social and intellectual currents in the late twentieth century, *History of Emotions*, 201–2, here quoting Gendron and Barrett, "Reconstructing the Past," 335. Philip Rieff, *The Triumph of the Therapeutic: Uses of Faith After Freud* (New York: Harper & Row, 1966); Ruth Leys, *The Ascent of Affect: Genealogy and Critique* (Chicago: University of Chicago Press, 2017); and Ruth Leys, *Trauma: A Genealogy* (Chicago: University of Chicago Press, 2000).

34. E.g., Rosenwein and Cristiani, *What Is the History of Emotions?*; Plamper, *History of Emotions*; Boddice, *History of Emotions*; and Rob Boddice, *A History of Feelings* (London: Reaktion, 2019). The fundamental debates in philosophy of emotion are discussed by Peter Goldie, "Emotion," *Philosophy Compass* 2.6 (2007): 928–38.

and in print, one often encounters radical differences in approaches to emotion, down to the very meaning of the word. Part of this is because everyone intuitively knows what an emotion is (at least in Anglo-American culture). Every day we feel a whole range of positive and negative emotions. From our infancy we have been trained to name feelings and express them ("Use your words," we parents have learned to say). For most of us, we need no more think about the nature of emotion than about "thought" or "pain."

Yet for all their intuitive facticity, there still is little professional consensus on what emotions are. Even the cognitive and neurological sciences have not come to a consensus about the most basic questions and premises of their fields: where emotions are located, how many there are, whether they exist as natural kinds or biological reflexes (or not at all), or how they function.[35] Given the intensity of scientific, social scientific, and humanistic research on emotions in the past two generations, it is rather shocking that there is so little that can be fundamentally agreed upon.[36] In the decade that I have been actively reading emotions research, consensus opinions about emotions have changed considerably, and I have no reason to expect that this field will be any more unified in the near future. Still, it is incumbent on even us humanists to engage critically and humbly with the interdisciplinary study of emotions, even with the risk that the terrain we tread upon might look very different in the (even near) future.

I address this in the following three sections: (1) basic emotions, (2) affect theory, and (3) psychological construction. While basic emotions theory and the affect theory that depends on it represent important currents in the study of emotions in various historical contexts, I have found the current neuroscientific approach of psychological construction to be the clearest way of grounding the history of emotions in dialogue with cognitive science, which allows for the change of emotions over time and the existence of sometimes radically different emotions across cultures, while at the same time insisting on the reality of emotions as embodied, evolutionary processes central to culture, cognition, and the construction of reality.[37]

35. The wide diversity in affective science is reflected in Lisa Feldman Barrett, Michael Lewis, and Jeannette M. Haviland-Jones, eds., *Handbook of Emotions*, 4th ed. (New York: Guilford, 2016); also see the various articles in "Special Section: On Defining Emotion," in *Emotion Review* 2.4 (2010): 363–85.

36. See the critical discussion in Leys, *Ascent of Affect*.

37. See Barrett and Russell, *Psychological Construction*. On the reality of emotion (and what that means for the psychological construction approach), see Lisa Feldman Barrett, "Emotions Are Real," *Emotions* 12 (2012): 413–29.

Basic Emotions

Contemporary scientific approaches to emotion may be broadly divided into two main schools of thought, the basic emotions approach and the constructed emotions approach.[38] The basic emotions school is the most widely known and influential approach to emotions and dominates much of the funding for emotions research. It understands emotions intuitively and in some ways close to the folk psychology that predominates in contemporary culture in North America and Europe.[39] Furthermore, through a rather circuitous and contested genealogy of influence, the universalism of basic emotions research lies behind much work in emotions in religious studies, biblical studies, and the humanities more broadly from the perspectives of affect theory.[40]

As the name implies, the basic emotions school posits a core set of basic emotions shared by all humans. There might be six or seven or eight or nine, but an influential list counts six basic emotions: anger, fear, disgust, sadness, happiness (or pleasure), and surprise.[41] Crucial to this approach is that these emotions exist as natural kinds; they exist independently of our knowledge or observation of them, and they can be localized to areas in the brain and body, like the elements or the human appendix.[42] These emotions are something like neural circuits, or "affect programs," that have evolved in humans over many millennia and are shared in various degrees by nonhuman animals.[43] A snarling dog feels anger like we do; a cat fleeing under a car feels fear; a spinner dolphin flipping above the water feels pleasure or happiness.[44] Basic emotions psychologists find compelling evidence for the universality of this corpus of basic emotions in facial expression studies, carried out worldwide,

38. As the neuroscientist Lisa Feldman Barrett presents it in *How Emotions Are Made*, 1–55.

39. Lisa Feldman Barrett and James A. Russell, "An Introduction to Psychological Construction," in Barrett and Russell, *Psychological Construction*, 1.

40. Leys, *Ascent of Affect*.

41. Barrett, *How Emotions Are Made*, 5; Plamper, *History of Emotions*, 153–54; and chronicled in detail by Leys, *Ascent of Affect*, 26–128.

42. For critiques of this, see Lisa Feldman Barrett, "Are Emotions Natural Kinds?," *Perspectives on Psychological Science* 1 (2006): 28–58.

43. On emotions as, or at least overlapping with, affect programs, see Paul E. Griffiths, *What Emotions Really Are* (Chicago: University of Chicago Press, 1997).

44. Barrett assesses the existence of emotion in nonhuman animals (negatively) in *How Emotions Are Made*, 252–77; and Barrett et al., "'Of Mice and Men': Natural Kinds of Emotions in the Mammalian Brain? A Response to Panksepp and Izard," *Perspectives on Psychological Science* 2 (2007): 297–312.

which claim to show that while words and display rules may change among cultures, humans the world over reliably recognize the facial markers of the core emotions, such as disgust, sadness, and anger.[45]

Such emotions are adaptive responses encoded into our DNA and our very being. While they have evolved to help us survive, in our society such primitive circuits may prove maladaptive. The anger that helped early humans defend themselves and hunt might now be diagnosed in North America as toxic masculinity. The sadness that appears in times of loss and humiliation to diffuse conflict and preserve the self for the future now may be overactive in our capitalist postmodernity, leading to an epidemic of depression. Our seemingly ubiquitous anxiety may be a maladaptive manifestation of fear, once useful for avoiding physical danger but now hypervigilant and out of control in a digitally connected global village.

This view suffuses popular understanding of emotions in North America. It informed the Disney/Pixar film *Inside Out* (2015) and its sequel (2024), to take a familiar example.[46] Emotions (in the original just five: joy, sadness, disgust, anger, and fear, joined by anxiety, embarrassment, envy, and ennui in the sequel) exist as animated homunculi within the film's protagonist, ontologically independent of her awareness of them, autonomic affect circuits that react to stimuli so quickly that Riley (the protagonist) cannot be conscious of what her emotions are doing. But she feels them, nonetheless, and at her lowest points is at their mercy. Each of these emotions (like a body part) has its function. Even an unpleasant emotion like sadness has evolved for its utility over the millennia. Psychological health lies in identifying and optimizing these emotions. The story resolves with Riley's recognition that even a painful emotion like sadness has its own role to play in mental health and should not be repressed (a self-realization that the homunculus Sadness shares). As primitive evolutionary forces, emotions control us, but emotional well-being can be achieved by recognizing these forces and channeling and optimizing them.

This influential model of emotional life echoes many a folk psychology, pointing to the intuitive facticity of the basic emotions approach: Who has not felt at the mercy of emotions that come or go unbidden? Emotions, in very current jargon, can be "triggered" by external stimuli as if they were reflexes.[47]

45. For discussion, see Leys, *Ascent of Affect*, 76–128; Leys, "Turn to Affect," 438–39; and Barrett, *How Emotions Are Made*, 1–55. Notably, complex or compound emotions (such as regret, guilt, envy, and Schadenfreude) lack any distinctive facial expression.

46. Barrett, *How Emotions Are Made*, xii.

47. Leys, "Turn to Affect," 438.

Our perceived passivity and vulnerability to these forces is writ into the terms by which ancients, too, described emotions as passions ("sufferings," "happenings," or "illnesses"), spirits, and demons. This is one of the great draws of the basic emotions approach—it *feels* right.

Ultimately, all humans, in all cultures in all times, the thinking goes, share these basic emotions; it is an explicitly universalist account of emotions, rooted in decades of clinical research. A universal or basic emotions theory offers space for historical or cross-cultural analysis mostly through the study of display rules. Some cultures encourage the expression and valuation of certain emotions and repress and stigmatize others, and these values and norms can and do change. A method of emotions history, which developed in the 1980s and 1990s in a series of significant studies, works well with a universalist understanding of emotions (see more below), as it limits its purview to the changes in emotional expression and cultural values and discourses about emotions ("emotionology"), none of which necessarily impinges on underlying biological reality.[48] But ultimately, the basic six or seven or eight emotions of the modern West are the same everywhere and in all times; only the labels and rules for expression change.

Affect Theory

The basic emotions trajectory of psychology has influenced the humanistic and social scientific study of emotion as well, most profoundly in "affect theory," a loosely held constellation of voices and approaches embraced most prominently among cultural and literary theorists but also in anthropology, geography, biblical studies, and early Christian studies. This influence might seem unexpected given that basic emotions theory's universalist, essentialist (even ethnocentric), ahistorical, and nonlinguistic assumptions run counter to a number of trends in the humanities, such as relativism, historicism, textuality, and the "linguistic turn." The strangeness of this confluence in affect theory has been noted by critics, as an anthropologist observes, "The irony of mixing outré *post*-poststructuralist rhetoric with wide-eyed scientism is inescapable.

48. This is the approach of Peter N. Stearns, who reflects on the history of the history of emotions in his own "Modern Patterns in Emotions History," in *Doing Emotions History*, ed. Peter N. Stearns and Susan J. Matt (Urbana: University of Illinois Press, 2014), 17–40; an overview of Stearns's "emotionology" is in Rosenwein and Cristiani, *What Is the History of Emotions?*, 29–34. The prolegomenon to this method was published by Peter N. Stearns and Carol Z. Stearns, "Emotionology: Clarifying the History of Emotions and Emotional Standards," *AHR* 90 (1985): 813–36.

It is as if the New Atheists—Dawkins, Hitchens, and Grayling—had adopted Mother Teresa as their mascot."[49] While even its ardent advocates admit that it is difficult, even impossible, to reduce the field to a clear list of propositions, underlying the varying approaches to affect is the presupposition that affects are nonrational forces and drives within the human (body) that influence all of us prior to cognition, awareness, and language.[50]

A primary foundation for affect theory is the basic emotions research of Silvan Tomkins, also an early innovator in the psychology of facial recognition. In the case of affect theory, however, this mid-twentieth-century neuroscience is filtered through the emergent trajectories of cultural studies and queer theory, rather dramatically repurposing Tomkins's research "for understanding the role of embodiment in (queer) identity formation and change."[51] Affects are not (necessarily) the same as emotions, and affect theory jettisons the reductive lists of six, seven, or eight basic emotions or affect programs for a creative and multiplying cast of affects, which range from the familiar yet freshly problematized (happiness, depression, trauma) to the

49. Beatty, *Emotional Worlds*, 206.

50. Beatty, *Emotional Worlds*, 205–8, critiques affect theory to good effect. I have benefited also from the incisive analysis by Steve Pile, "Emotions and Affect in Recent Human Geography," *Transactions of the Institute of British Geographers* n.s. 35 (2010): 5–20, who concludes that affect theory "is not a theory, but a chain gang of metaphors (or resources or assumptions)" (17). A much-cited introduction to affect theory is Gregory J. Seigworth and Melissa Gregg, "An Inventory of Shimmers," in *An Affect Theory Reader*, ed. Gregory J. Seigworth and Melissa Gregg (Durham, NC: Duke University Press, 2010), 1–25. A very sympathetic presentation of affect theory and the history of early Christianity is in Maia Kotrosits, *Rethinking Early Christian Identity: Affect, Violence, and Belonging* (Minneapolis: Fortress, 2015), 1–32. In embracing affect theory in search of "national haunting and ongoing and transgenerational trauma" and "ambivalent kinds of forgetting," Kotrosits writes that "one of the bigger gifts of affect theory is an attention to felt forces that can't be contained (by language or other symbolic systems, by our subjective boundaries, etc.) and offer of [*sic*] a little bit of a reprieve from linguistic analysis" (1, 17).

51. Ruth Leys, "Turn to Affect," 440–41. Especially see Silvan Tomkins, *Shame and Its Sisters: A Silvan Tomkins Reader*, ed. Eve Kosofsky Sedgwick and Adam Frank (Durham, NC: Duke University Press, 1995); and Eve Kosofsky Sedgwick, *Epistemology of the Closet* (Berkeley: University of California Press, 1990). Leys traces the genealogy of affect theory to the basic emotions research of Tomkins and Paul Ekman, fully described in her *Ascent of Affect*. Anthropologist Beatty does not draw the connection as closely as Leys but agrees that affect theorists' "favoured emotion scientists" work in the universal or basic emotions tradition (*Emotional Worlds*, 205, with more bibliography on affect theory and its intellectual history). A different genealogy is proposed by Donovan O. Schaefer, *The Evolution of Affect Theory: The Humanities, the Sciences, and the Study of Power*, Cambridge Elements: Histories of Emotions and the Senses (Cambridge: Cambridge University Press, 2019).

newly theorized ("cruel optimism," "stuplimity," "diasporic grief").[52] Such affects bubble beneath the surface of consciousness and language and exist in queer interstices within and between bodies. They are typically described by the affectively inclined in an evasive manner, apophatically gesturing toward affect's unknowable, unquantifiable, yet ineluctable influence on bodies.[53] An oft-cited passage from the *Affect Theory Reader* gives a sense of the style and focus of affect theory:

> Affect arises in the midst of *in-between-ness*: in the capacities to act and be acted upon. . . . That is, affect is found in those intensities that pass body to body (human, nonhuman, part-body, and otherwise), in those resonances that circulate about, between, and sometimes stick to bodies and worlds, *and* in the very passages or variations between these intensities and resonances themselves. Affect, at its most anthropomorphic, is the name we give to those forces—visceral forces beneath, alongside, or generally *other* than conscious knowing, vital forces insisting beyond emotion—that can serve to drive us toward movement, toward thought and extension, that can likewise suspend us (as if in neutral) across a barely registering accretion of force-relations.[54]

The descriptive excess evokes a quasi-scientific (trans- or post-) humanism, on the one hand, rooted in the physical or mechanical but, on the other, disconnected from any sort of observable or reproduceable science. Affect theorists write in a tension between mechanical or digital metaphors and metaphors of fantastically messy embodiment. We move through "thickly textured, magnetized worlds," with bodies that "are complex, chunky genealogies, bricolages of existing forms," "under the pressure of a complex welter of affects"—affects

52. E.g., Sarah Ahmed, *The Promise of Happiness* (Durham, NC: Duke University Press, 2010); Lauren Berlant, *Cruel Optimism* (Durham, NC: Duke University Press, 2011); Sianne Ngai, *Ugly Feelings* (Cambridge, MA: Harvard University Press, 2007); and Kotrosits, *Rethinking*, 1, 121.

53. Quoted from Beatty, *Emotional Worlds*, 208, referencing Patricia Ticineto Clough's description in the introduction to *The Affective Turn: Theorizing the Social*, ed. Patricia Ticineto Clough with Jean Halley (Durham, NC: Duke University Press, 2007), 2.

54. Seigworth and Gregg, "An Inventory of Shimmers," 1. This passage is something of a locus classicus and is cited as representative of affect theory's favored discursive style by critics like Beatty, *Emotional Worlds*, 208, and those more sympathetic to the program, such as Spencer, "Getting a Feel," 25–26; the volume as a whole is "field-consolidating," according to Stephen D. Moore, "Why the Johannine Jesus Weeps at the Tomb of Lazarus," in Spencer, *Mixed Feelings and Vexed Passions*, 290.

whose "felt lines between bodies and worlds are thick, living, pulsing veins, not a grid of wires."[55] Such descriptions would not be out of place in speculative science fiction or horror, venturing into an almost Lovecraftian alternative physics. How can an intensity pass between human bodies or between humans and nonhuman objects? How can a "resonance . . . stick to bodies" or "stick to . . . worlds" for that matter? Where can one observe such intensities and stickiness, or "shimmers," or "thick, living, pulsing veins"? Furthermore, if affects are visceral forces "other than conscious knowing," "hovering around" consciousness, prelinguistic and precognitive, how can we access them, share these observations with others, represent them discursively, and assess whether we have interpreted them correctly?[56]

While affect theory is playfully scientistic, and "draws freely, if haphazardly, on biology and neuroscience, . . . its practitioners are not scientists, they are mostly unaware of—or show no interest in—the range of . . . emotion theory, and their line of argument is often hostile, or at least orthogonal, to scientific methods and reasoning."[57] Historian Ruth Leys has excavated how affect theorists incorporated basic emotions research into their work, approaches often cited approvingly by scholars of early Christianity and the Bible.[58] In

55. Donovan O. Schaefer, *Religious Affects: Animality, Evolution, and Power* (Durham, NC: Duke University Press, 2015), 28, 9, 13, 103.

56. Quotation from Schaefer, *Religious Affects*, 28. Others note a basic incoherence in affect theory: "Though affect cannot be presented or *re*presented, affectual geographers, drawing upon non-representational theory, constantly evoke moments when affect is evident. . . . Apologies for being blunt, but this is a straightforward hypocrisy. It continually does what it says cannot be done: it cannot help but re-present and represent *affect—*and *in language*" (Pile, "Emotions and Affect," 17). It is little surprise that affect theorists are especially attracted to film and visual culture for their analysis, which offers the "reprieve from linguistic analysis" praised by Kotrosits, above. Sarah Ahmed is fond of the 2002 *Bend It Like Beckham* (*Promise of Happiness*) and Schaefer the *Jesus Camp* documentary (*Religious Affects*), while *Psycho* features in Eugenie Brinkema, *The Forms of the Affects* (Durham, NC: Duke University Press, 2014).

57. Beatty, *Emotional Worlds*, 205.

58. Leys, *Ascent of Affect*. Examples of such recent scholarship include Kotrosits, *Rethinking*, the scholarship surveyed in Spencer, "Getting a Feel," 25–28, and the essay by Moore included in the volume; along with the special issue of *Biblical Interpretation* 22 (2014), edited by Jennifer L. Koosed and Stephen D. Moore. At times, Leys finds in affect theory "appropriations and uses that amount to straightforward endorsements" of basic emotions research. Yet, a theorist like Massumi also "comes across as a materialist" who posits a mind/body dualism at odds with foundations of embodied emotions research, such as the work of William James; see Leys, "Turn to Affect," 467–68. Barrett shows how James's theory of emotion was fundamentally mischaracterized first by John Dewey, "one of the great mistakes

reviewing affect theory's cooption of affective neuroscience, Leys wonders whether affect theory is playfully intervening in scientific studies "to stir things up," or whether, more problematically, affect theory (here the influential Brian Massumi) is "not only unfair to [neuroscience researchers], but . . . willfully or otherwise misreads the data in order to create paradoxes where there were none."[59] I suspect she favors the latter.

Leys's scorched-earth critique of affect theory strikes some as overstating the case or failing to differentiate scholarly trajectories.[60] Some within affect theory distinguish between the kind of approach above (the more "Deleuzian," after the philosopher Gilles Deleuze) and a more "phenomenological" approach, focusing on the complexities of embodied sensation and "the way things feel."[61] This latter approach still engages creatively with some scientific discourses but accommodates itself more to cultural analysis and does not nitpick terminology, for example, showing a greater comfort with moving between language of affect and emotion (which "falls under the purview of affect theory").[62] This phenomenological approach "is interested in the animality of embodied experience," positing that nonhuman animals have affective or emotional lives, since affects are prelinguistic and circulate around, through, and under "linguistic determination."[63] The decentering of language travels with queer theory, postcolonial studies, and a decentering of humanity and the Anthropocene (often with activist subtexts), whether that be through exploring the affective lives

in modern psychology," which has influenced for the worse the basic emotions school and their adaptors to this day (*How Emotions Are Made*, 160–61).

59. Leys, "Turn to Affect," 467.

60. In a very useful introduction to a collection of essays on emotions in the Bible, Spencer dismisses Leys in a footnote as "overstat[ing] her critique" but focuses only on a minor point in Leys's critique ("Getting a Feel," 26). A detailed critique is in Schaefer, *Evolution of Affect Theory*. I have found her genealogical explication of the methods and foundations of affect theory convincing, along with Andrew Beatty's critique from an anthropologist's perspective and Steve Pile's review of affective geography.

61. Schaefer, *Religious Affects*, 5. Gilles Deleuze's influence in affectively oriented biblical and early Christian studies is considerable, but his oeuvre is challenging and ethically ambiguous. The literary theorist Terry Eagleton's comment on Frederick Jameson's recent survey of "theory" is apropos: "Jameson praises Deleuze as 'one of the most marvelous thinkers of the 20th century', while going on to claim that he turns all the thinkers he deals with into himself. That doesn't seem all that marvelous to admire, any more than there's much to admire about the squalid idealizing of schizophrenia to which his work gave rise." Terry Eagleton, "The Excitement of the Stuff," *London Review of Books* 46.19 (October 10, 2024): 28.

62. Schaefer, *Religious Affects*, 24.

63. Schaefer, *Religious Affects*, 39.

of animals, the environment, or objects.[64] This phenomenological approach shifts between great seriousness of purpose, understandable given its focus on current activist concerns about queerness, feminism, environmentalism, white nationalism, and Islamophobia (just to name some persistent interests), and a scholarly jouissance that recalls its origins in early literary deconstruction.[65] Argumentation embraces ambiguity and contingency (and even opacity),[66] much as affects themselves (as "queer") "frustrate the insistence on a chain of intelligible *whys* at the heart of carno-phallogocentric metaphysics and lead to more complex accounts of the operation of power."[67] Affect theory positions itself as a queer expression of play and pure being that exists not for a purpose but for itself ("autotelic"), in a performative rebuke of the economic imperatives of late capitalism, recognizing the "non-functionalist affective economies" that link animal bodies and environments.[68]

In practice, these branches of affect theory (Deleuzian and phenomenological) are frequently merged in the work of affect theorists, and any definitive differences between them may be hard to observe.[69] Both trajectories focus on very present-day concerns and sources; and while the language of "histories" and "historical significance" occurs, affect theorists show little interest in historical method or serious engagement with older sources.[70] And for all of

64. Schaefer, *Religious Affects*; and Schaefer, *Evolution of Affect Theory*. The latter interests may be seen in Virginia Burrus, *Early Christian Ecopoetics: Cosmologies, Saints, Things* (Philadelphia: University of Pennsylvania Press, 2019); Maia Kotrosits, *The Lives of Objects: Material Culture, Experience, and the Real in Early Christianity* (Chicago: University of Chicago Press, 2020); and Georgia Frank, *Unfinished Christians: Ritual Objects and Silent Subjects in Late Antiquity* (Philadelphia: University of Pennsylvania Press, 2023).

65. See Schaefer, *Religious Affects*, 150–55, on the influence of Derrida for affect analysis.

66. Affect theories tend to be very comfortable with speculative and tentative phrasings like "allow for the possibility," "may not be," "explores the possibility," "offers the suggestion," and "what if?," to take just a few examples from Schaefer, *Religious Affects*, 3, 9.

67. Schaefer, *Religious Affects*, 17.

68. Schaefer, *Religious Affects*, 17, 194. Kotrosits characterizes this project as liberationist self and mutual pleasure, "engaging reparative, accretive, and pleasure-seeking impulses" alongside a hermeneutics of suspicion (*Rethinking*, 6), drawing on Sedgwick. She writes, "What I find so appealing about [affect theory] is that one can enjoy the allure of heightened theoretical language with the added gratification of closer contact between readers and writers" (*Rethinking*, 19).

69. Schaefer, *Religious Affects*, 34; the trajectories receive a longer treatment in Schaefer, *Evolution of Affect Theory*, 6–53.

70. E.g., Schaefer, *Religious Affects*, 6, 93, 192; Ahmed (*Promise of Happiness*, 17) claims to "aim to give a history to unhappiness," without any real attention to historical subjects. This makes sense given the epistemological privileging of the writer's lived experience;

affect theory's positionality as radical cultural critique, it is strangely deferential to authorities, often constructed as a string of summaries and citations of other theorists, a postmodern commentarial tradition of mutual admiration. As among the early humanists, it is worth it to go *ad fontes*, since sometimes the commentarial intermediaries are not fully reliable. The recent turn to animal religious affects, for example, depends on renowned primatologist Jane Goodall's observations of a chimpanzee "waterfall dance," which allegedly demonstrates animal religion and spirituality.[71] But, while she has near-saintly authority, some of Goodall's writing is marred by well-documented plagiarism and lack of scholarly rigor, which makes it a slender reed on which to build a novel theory of the very nature of religion.[72] Although I generally take a different approach, affect theory has exerted a major influence on the study of emotions within biblical and early Christianity studies, and the following chapters will have opportunities to engage productively with this important mode of scholarship.[73]

Psychological Construction

The other main postwar approach to emotions differs considerably in its methods, terminology, and perspective, as well as its potential to contribute to the

---

as Ahmed writes, "So my archive is also my world, my life-world, my past as well as my present, where the word *happiness* has echoed so powerfully" (19). Though still writing through autoethnographic reflection, Ann Cvetkovich is an outlier in engaging with some historical perspectives on melancholia, as in *Depression: A Public Feeling* (Durham, NC: Duke University Press, 2012), 85–101.

71. Schaefer, *Religious Affects*, 1–4, 178–205. Elements of the dance are available on YouTube. While I delight in watching chimpanzees play in the jungle, my affective response to the "dance" differs from Goodall's and Schaefer's.

72. Documented by Michael Moynihan, "Jane Goodall's Troubling, Error-Filled New Book, 'Seeds of Hope,'" *Daily Beast*, March 26, 2013 (updated July 11, 2017), and reported and confirmed elsewhere. Unfortunately, though his argument hinges on Goodall's work, and her plagiarism and research misprisions were exposed years before, Schaefer never addresses these concerns in *Religious Affects* or *Evolution of Affect Theory* (though based on her earlier publications).

73. While affect theory has found avid disciples within biblical studies, classicists writing on emotion have hewed toward a more cognitivist approach, perhaps since ancient theories of emotion, such as of Aristotle or the Stoics, were generally cognitive and appraisal-based theories, unlike the anti-intentionalist prelinguistic interests of affect theory. Thus, modern cognitive theories of emotions have been a more natural method for classicists, such as in Martha Nussbaum's neo-Stoic philosophy in *The Therapy of Desire: Theory and Practice in Hellenistic Ethics*, Martin Classical Lectures 2/2 (Princeton: Princeton University Press, 1994); and Sorabji, *Emotion and Peace of Mind*. The classicist emphases on philology and the precise attention to words and their changing meaning also invite a different approach.

study of emotions in early Christianity. While the basic emotions program posits a set of discrete, universal emotions as evolutionarily selected faculties that can be triggered without our knowledge or understanding, and affect theorists posit ontologically independent intensities of feeling that pass between and through human and nonhuman bodies, the theory of psychological construction (or constructed emotion) has taken the evolutionary insights of early psychologists in a different direction.[74] The theory of constructed emotion denies that there are any innate, discrete, or universal emotions. Emotions cannot be localized to any part of the brain, notwithstanding the many studies undertaken and millions of dollars spent in search of them through fMRI (functional magnetic resonance imaging) or other imaging techniques. While there is no doubt that the brain "makes" the emotions or that the emotions we feel are "real"—and constructed through the interplay of neurological connections, bodily sensation, and conscious thought—there remains no evidence that the brain (or any other part of the body) contains dedicated circuits or loci for affect or emotions, individually or as a group.[75] However hard one looks for basic emotions by their physiological markers, their circuits or networks—or their shimmers, intensities, and stickiness, in the jargon of affect theory—there simply are no "emotions" to be found.[76] Emotions, the theory of constructed emotion claims, are not *things* in the world or in our bodies or brains but *concepts*.

But what of another pillar of basic emotions research, the decades of facial recognition studies, which are said to show the universality of evolutionarily selected basic emotions? Doesn't the universal recognizability of facial expression show the biological nature of the basic emotions? After all, everyone knows how to read a smile or a frown or a raised eyebrow.

Perhaps not. As influential and lucrative as the facial recognition research program has proven, cognitive scientists have criticized the program for a

74. On the Darwinian roots of psychological construction, see Lisa Feldman Barrett, "Psychological Construction: The Darwinian Approach to the Science of Emotion," *Emotion Review* 5 (2013): 379–89; and Lisa Feldman Barrett, "Was Darwin Wrong About Emotional Expressions?," *Current Directions in Psychological Science* 20 (2011): 400–406. On William James, see Lisa Feldman Barrett, *How Emotions Are Made*, 160–61, and for the history of emotion science contrasting the two approaches, Gendron and Barrett, "Reconstructing the Past."

75. Barrett, *How Emotions Are Made*, 12–22.

76. As Barrett notes, "Despite tremendous time and investment, research has not revealed a consistent bodily fingerprint for even a single emotion" (*How Emotions Are Made*, 15).

generation, fundamentally undermining its conclusions.[77] By replicating the experiments and at the same time uncovering shortcomings in the experimental methods unreported in the scientific literature, researchers have shown that when the facial expression interviews are reproduced without "forced choice" questionnaires, the supposed universality of emotions disappears.[78] That is, instead of showing an image of a smiling person and asking, "Is this emotion 'happiness' or 'sadness'?," the interviewer shows the same sort of picture and asks, "What is this person feeling?" When deprived of forced choices and a list of approved emotion words (often translated from English into supposed native equivalents), informants from different cultures and even within the same country and language do not reliably or consistently describe facial expressions as representing basic emotions.[79]

Further complicating universal facial expression theories, none of the paradigmatic facial expressions, as photographed in standard emotional arrays, express felt emotions, nor do they represent the facial expressions normally made by humans, even in the studies' normative North American culture.[80] In brief, the iconic expressions of surprise, disgust, and so on are made by paid actors, coached by researchers into making facial expressions that represent an ideal and exaggerated example of an emotional expression, a smile, scowl, frown, upturned nose, etc. That is, none of the actors was actually feeling anger, sadness, and so on; therefore, when an informant identifies the upturned nose as "disgust" or the furrowed brow as "anger," they are not identifying any emotional experience of the actor but a stereotyped visual and lexical representation of the concept of disgust. More significantly, the facial expressions—artificial and exaggerated—do not reflect the various, multitudinous ways that people, even in North America, make communicative facial expressions.[81] It is hard to imagine encountering any of the classical emotional facial expressions in the field, any more than the classic tragic and comedic masks

77. Ruth Leys, *From Guilt to Shame: Auschwitz and After* (Princeton: Princeton University Press, 2007), 133–50; summarized in Leys, "Turn to Affect," 439–40.

78. Barrett, *How Emotions Are Made*, 43–55; the failure of published research to report the provision of coaching about the meaning of emotion words in the experimental setting is described on 49–50.

79. Barrett, *How Emotions Are Made*, 43–55. The influence of emotion words in interpreting facial expression is assessed further in Maria Gendron et al., "Emotion Words Shape Emotion Percepts," *Emotion* 12 (2012): 314–25.

80. The classic facial expressions are published in Paul Ekman and W. V. Friesen, *Pictures of Facial Affect* (Palo Alto, CA: Consulting Psychologists Press, 1976); and Barrett, *How Emotions Are Made*, 5. The images and many like them are easily found by an internet search.

81. Leys more fully chronicles the interesting and sometimes comical history of facial

represent how humans normally (let alone universally) express sorrow and joy. For all its influence in the academic study of emotions, as well as its intuitive correlation with folk psychology, facial expressions do not provide evidence for a set of basic, universal emotions. Most of us, myself included, mistakenly presume we can more or less reliably read emotional states on others' faces, but we're actually terrible at it.

Yet, even if they don't exist apart from our awareness or as "natural kinds," nevertheless, "emotions are real."[82] In fact, emotions are far more consequential in shaping human experience than even the basic emotions theory would allow.[83] This approach posits two main components of the process we think of as emotion.[84] The first is affect. The second is emotion.

Affect in this model is neither the ingrained affect programs of basic emotions research nor the prelinguisitic and precognitive feelings and drives of affect theory. Affect (or core affect) is indeed a process in our biological system that functions quickly, without our awareness, always running, though always changing, and "not necessarily directed at anything."[85]

This core affect is a "neurophysiological state that is consciously accessible as a simple, nonreflective feeling that is an integral blend of hedonic (pleasure—displeasure) and arousal (sleepy—activated) values." One's momentary affect, the feeling of being alive in the moment, falls somewhere on these basic axes, pleasant to unpleasant "valence" and high to low arousal.[86] Experience can be pleasant and low intensity (perhaps sitting on the couch watching a familiar television program) or unpleasant and high arousal (you are crossing the street and suddenly a car runs a stop sign toward you). Something can be pleasant and high arousal (sex, playing a masterful round of golf) or unpleas-

---

expression emotions research in *Ascent of Affect*, 76–128, which covers some of the major critiques of the program, including coming from Ekman's own former adherents.

82. Barrett, "Are Emotions Natural Kinds."

83. Barrett, "Emotions Are Real"; on the centrality of emotion to human experience, see Barrett, *How Emotions Are Made*, e.g., 104, 126.

84. This approach to emotions shares some features with ancient Stoicism with its two emotional "movements" in the feeling of passion, first movements or pre-passions and passions proper (Sorabji, *Emotion and Peace of Mind*). Leading basic emotions researcher Antonio Damasio also posits a binary (with opposite terminology to the above) between emotion (which I call affect) and feeling (which I call emotion) in, e.g., *The Feeling of What Happens* (New York: Mariner, 2000).

85. James A. Russell, "My Psychological Constructionist Perspective, with a Focus on Conscious Affective Experience," in Russell and Barrett, *Psychological Construction*, 183–208, at 196.

86. Barrett, *How Emotions Are Made*, 72–74.

ant and low arousal (waiting on a delayed bus). These variations of affect can be observed in all sorts of living creatures and drive our "body budget," how we use energy, constantly adapting to meet our goals most efficiently: heart rate falls or rises, breathing changes, blood pressure goes up or down, muscles tighten or loosen, cortisol and other hormones get released, and we modify our access to and use of glycogen. These are all autonomic changes of which we are normally not conscious and would not want to be.

But psychological construction rejects mind- (or brain-) body dualism. Affect is not the body's precognitive reaction to stimuli, subliminal or otherwise, occurring too fast for the mind/brain to make sense of them, as humanistic affect theory would have it.[87] The brain, instead, is very much involved, not in a (belatedly) reactive sense but in a predictive sense. The brain constantly makes predictions about the phenomenal world, which can be validated or proved false and then revised.[88] This all happens without our conscious knowing but is important in minimizing or economizing the brain's already enormous cost to the body's energy budget, 20 percent or more of the entire body's energy.[89] So the brain is always economizing by predicting rather than reacting to reality. This is how someone can hit a baseball moving ninety miles per hour with a 2.5-inch-diameter bat, which would simply be impossible were the brain merely reacting to stimuli.[90] Our brain—developed by varying levels of experience—learns to predict where the ball will be before we even see it. We often feel we know what someone will say before they say it. We instinctively (or so it feels) push a child out of danger before we even have thought about what is happening. Of course, predictions can be wrong, and frequently are; we perceive, intuit, sense, and see things that are not, and fail to see things that are. The baseball is faster/slower/curvier than we expected. The person did not say what we think they would (or did) say. The child was not in danger. The brain, unbeknownst to the conscious mind, is constantly offering up new predictions with the goal not only of reacting to acute threats and stimuli but predicting and more fundamentally budgeting for our bodies' needs and

87. Affect theories commonly draw on Brian Massumi's reading of a 1985 experiment in his article, "The Autonomy of Affect," *Cultural Critique* 31 (1995); critiqued in Leys, "Turn to Affect," 444–58. Leys notes the "constant tendency among the new affect theories . . . to adhere to this same false opposition between the mind and body" (458).

88. Barrett, *How Emotions Are Made*, 59–72.

89. The average human brain uses 20 percent or more of the body's energy, while is only 2 percent of its weight. Marcus E. Raichle and Debra A. Gusnard, "Appraising the Brain's Energy Budget," *Proceedings of the National Academy of Sciences* 99 (2002): 10237–39.

90. Barrett, *How Emotions Are Made*, 63–64, on the baseball analogy.

adjusting to affect, the general feeling of pleasantness and intensity, the steady state of the feeling of existence.

This affect, with partial similarity to its usage in affect theory, exists prior to consciousness, cognition, and language. As such, affect does not have a history or an anthropology, apart from an extraordinarily "deep history," which might chart a glacial change over many millennia.[91] It is universal among human bodies and shared with nonhuman animals.[92] Although we cannot measure the heartrate, blood pressure, and skin conductivity of people in the ancient world, in this understanding of core affect, the affects of the early Christians were quite like our own, a neurophysiological blend of valence and intensity.

The difference in the usage of "affect" among these current approaches to emotion may be seen in the contemporary phenomenon of "trigger warnings," a trend which has spread through schools, universities, and arts organizations. The idea is that disturbing themes and material (running the gamut from war atrocity and sexual violence to racism and cultural appropriation) are likely to be so distressing to people who have experienced such phenomena first- or secondhand that it will automatically trigger distressing affective responses, unconscious and nonlinguistic reflexes that can harmfully catch people unaware. Such warnings give people the opportunity to avoid the media and the trigger or to prepare themselves for the hurt, like tensing one's arm before being punched. If affects function as basic emotions or affect theory claim, this theory makes sense. But in practice, trigger warnings do the opposite. Instead of lessening subjects' distress by allowing them to steel themselves for impact, subjects report increased distress after receiving trigger warnings.[93] This is because affect, and the emotions it forms the basis for, function as the theory of psychological construction claims: predictively, not reactively. When authoritative figures teach people that to encounter disturbing themes and images in media is so likely to cause such serious distress or harm that they should prepare themselves emotionally for pain, they prime them to feel in-

91. The term "deep history" is from Daniel Lord Smail, who falls more on the universal or "basic emotions" theory of emotions, *On Deep History and the Brain* (Berkeley: University of California Press, 2007); as discussed in Leys, "Turn to Affect," 434–45.

92. Barrett, *How Emotions Are Made*, 56–57, 252–77.

93. Benjamin W. Bellet, Payton J. Jones, and Richard J. McNally, "Trigger Warning: Empirical Evidence Ahead," *Journal of Behavior Therapy and Experimental Psychiatry* 61 (2018): 134–41; and Greg Lukianoff and Jonathan Haidt, *The Coddling of the American Mind: How Good Intentions and Bad Ideas Are Setting Up a Generation for Failure* (New York: Penguin, 2018).

creased levels of distress, not because a response has been *triggered* but because it has been predicted and made real, that is, it has been *constructed*, socially, psychologically, and neurologically. This works for pleasant feelings as it does for unpleasant ones.

While this feeling is often running beneath our awareness, core affect is accessible to conscious knowing, as the previous example suggests; it is made meaningful in relation to the world through the process of conceptualizing and categorizing instances of affect as emotions. An emotion in this perspective is thus not a feeling or affect lurking beneath our conscious knowing, waiting to be aroused by a free-floating intensity. Nor is it a circuit in the brain or nervous system, activated or triggered by some stimulus. Nor is an emotion an identifiable amalgam of physiological changes (heartrate, blood pressure, cortisol and hormonal release, skin conduction, muscle tension). Rather, an emotion is a concept constructed by humans to make meaning out of the complex interaction between bodily affect and the experience of perceiving and predicting the world. It is as concepts—and especially as concepts that humans use to do things—that emotions have a history.[94]

Emotional concepts, like other concepts, can have very real effects on the world, notably on our bodies. Research has shown that the conceptual categories applied to food change the body's physiological response to it, for example how test subjects metabolize items labeled as an "indulgent" milkshake or a "healthy" smoothie. While the items tested are nutritionally identical, test subjects' bodies will treat the milkshake as higher in calories and less healthy and thus release different levels of hormones in response.[95]

Emotional concepts work the same way. Perhaps I am "anxious" or "worried," "stressed" or "nervous." Or perhaps I am "hopeful" or "happy" or "giddy" or "excited." All these emotions are differently meaningful in my native American English and demonstrate a type of "emotional granularity" that is learned and socialized over a lifetime, beginning from infancy. All are real, yet all are constructed out of bodily affect. The word we attach to a feeling makes a difference cognitively, socially, and physiologically. This is "how emotions are made" in the theory of psychological construction. Over time, from my earliest experiences as an infant until just now, I have been learning and ap-

94. The connection between emotion's conceptualization and action is clear in another term for emotional construction, the conceptual act theory (Barrett, "Conceptual Act Theory").

95. Barrett, *How Emotions Are Made*, 38–39; and Alia J. Crum et al., "Mind Over Milkshakes: Mindsets, Not Just Nutrients, Determine Ghrelin Response," *Health Psychology* 30 (2011): 424–29.

plying concepts to make meaning out of my affective states. When I feel a range of bodily states of valence and intensity, formed by factors I may be unable to isolate consciously (like blood pressure, skin conduction, cortisol levels, glycogen production, etc.) and some of which I may be very conscious of (the "butterflies" in my stomach or a general lethargy), I may classify those feelings as "anxiety" if I am facing a tense situation with my boss or reclassify it as "nervous excitement" as I'm strapped into a roller coaster. Or I may have learned about depression or melancholia, ennui or malaise, and recognize in the new emotion concept what I am *really* feeling. Each concept entails a different meaning and social understanding and function.

For example, I had been suffering from what I thought was depression for some time during my later graduate school years, so much so that I was ready to seek professional help, which for me—like many men—would be a pretty radical step. I'm sure that if I had gone to a doctor I would have walked away with an SSRI (selective serotonin reuptake inhibitor) after fifteen minutes. That is, until I read an article about a different, newly theorized feeling—"burnout"—which described my experiences to a T.[96] When I realized I was not depressed but feeling burnout, it completely changed the way I interpreted my thoughts and bodily affects, and enabled me to make practical changes in my life. My "depression" disappeared, and I approached the stress of my work differently. But there was never any depression or burnout in my body, and the feeling of the two emotional states was the same. It was the concepts—both historically contingent and of recent invention—that helped me find meaning in my experience and change the way I perceived and predicted the world around me. Being able to identify an affective state as an emotional concept is something humans do all the time and is metabolically efficient, enabling the brain to use its predictive power to fill in the context for one's feeling and thus prepare for the future.[97]

In this perspective, emotions are the way that humans make sense of themselves as embodied beings in the world, and what's more, they are humanity's "constructions of the world."[98] Emotions enable selfhood, as some philosophers have argued: "The πάθη [*pathē*] connect the self to its world; they enable it to be in and integrated with the world. Without them the self ceases to be

96. The history and culture of burnout is analyzed by Jonathan Malesic, *The End of Burnout: Why Work Drains Us and How to Build Better Lives* (Oakland: University of California Press, 2022).

97. Barrett, *How Emotions Are Made*, 121, 132–33.

98. Barrett, *How Emotions Are Made*, 104; and for emotions as meaning, 126.

a self, because it is not differentiated from and still engaged with its world."[99] While all humans share the same basic biology and same affectivity of valence and intensity, each society develops its own concepts of emotion, and these concepts change and evolve, which we can easily observe in recent history. Some recent emotion concepts include "trauma," "exhaustion," and "emotional labor," widely recognizable across professional and colloquial discourses.[100] Yet these are concepts, social and linguistic constructions, not innate biological properties, notwithstanding the professional trend to universalize and institutionalize such recent, largely bourgeois, North American concepts.[101]

The "basic emotions" are no different, simply more widespread and of much older vintage. And while there are many similarities in emotional concepts among cultures and languages, this is not because they are natural kinds, interpreter-independent components of our biological and neurological makeup. It is because, whether in a small-scale preindustrial group or the late capitalist global village, humans in society share similar drives, desires, and conflicts, along with their same embodied core affect. Emotions are so important to our biological nature and to history because it is through emotions that we perceive and create the world around us, how we make meaning of ourselves and the world.

A cognitive science approach like the theory of constructed emotions has limitations for historians. It is an experimental science, based on testing hypotheses on living subjects. We lack almost all the evidence in our historical sources that a scientist would need to test a hypothesis, and our ancient informants are extremely uncooperative in giving us the specific data we ask of them. Yet this approach's emphasis on the transformative power of concepts

99. Kraftchick, "Πάθη [*Pathē*] in Paul," drawing on the phenomenological work of P. Christopher Smith and through him Martin Heidegger.

100. Leys, *Trauma*; Anna Katarina Schaffner, *Exhaustion: A History* (New York: Columbia University Press, 2016); and Arlie Hochschild, *The Managed Heart: Commercialization of Human Feeling*, updated with new preface (Berkeley: University of California Press, 2012).

101. An example of the move to render emotional concepts as biological and universal may be seen in the rise of "trauma," which among affect theorists functions much like the affects as a precognitive and prelinguisitic response, which may be epigenetically transmitted across generations; the manifold problems with this approach to trauma are related to the general difficulties with affect theory more generally, as traced by Leys, *Trauma*. In clinical applications, the ethnocentric assumption of the biological universality of a concept like trauma can have very serious negative impacts on health, as shown by journalist Ethan Watters in his reporting on the influx of Western-trained trauma counselors into post-tsunami Sri Lanka. Watters, *Crazy Like Us: The Globalization of the American Psyche* (New York: Free Press, 2010), 65–125.

and words and the dynamic intersection of body, mind, and society and its allowance for the authentic change of emotional experience over time comport well with a historical approach to emotions. And indeed, historians of emotion have recognized the potential for taking this understanding of "how emotions are made" into consideration when applying the various historical methods for the study of emotions.[102]

Emotions, Experience, and Theory

Among the advantages of psychological construction is its compelling consilience with other trajectories in emotions research in the social sciences and history, including cultural anthropology and history. In contrast, it is hard to reconcile the universalism of basic emotions with the diversity of emotional language and behavior historically and in contemporary societies.[103] But the constructionist model of emotion is productive for exploring emotions in ancient texts. It provides the undeniable diversity of emotional words and experiences, as well as the relativism of emotions that becomes apparent across cultures and times, with a cognitive, biological, and evolutionary foundation based in a large body of experimental evidence. More generally it complements trends in religious studies and history, including early Christian studies, which have embraced cognitive science as a relevant method.[104] Much like other cognitive approaches, psychological construction's emphasis on the world-

102. Beatty, *Emotional Worlds*, 201–5; and Rosenwein and Cristiani, *What Is the History of Emotions?*, 107.

103. Such as the ethnography of Catherine A. Lutz, *Unnatural Emotions: Everyday Sentiments on a Micronesian Atoll and Their Challenge to Western Theory* (Chicago: University of Chicago Press, 1988), which takes aim at the universalism (and ethnocentrism) of basic emotions research. The relativism of such a social construction approach is a methodological concern in the history of emotions approach of William M. Reddy, *The Navigation of Feeling: A Framework for the History of Emotions* (Cambridge: Cambridge University Press, 2001), 40–50.

104. The historiography is reviewed by Lynn Hunt, "The Self and Its History," *AHR* 119 (2014): 1576–86. A range of cognitive science perspectives are represented by Petri Luomanen, Ilkka Pyysiänen, and Risto Uro, eds., *Explaining Christian Origins: Contributions from Cognitive and Social Science*, BibInt 89 (Leiden: Brill, 2007); István Czachesz and Risto Uro, eds., *Mind, Morality and Magic: Cognitive Science Approaches in Biblical Studies* (London: Routledge, 2014); Colleen Shantz, *Paul in Ecstasy: The Neurobiology of the Apostle's Life and Thought* (Cambridge: Cambridge University Press, 2009); and Inbar Graiver, *Asceticism of the Mind*, PIMS Texts and Studies 213 (Toronto: PIMS, 2018).

creating and world-maintaining power of emotion complements the long-standing interest in applying the sociology of knowledge to early Christianity, such as in understanding issues of identity.[105]

Perhaps most distinctively among the diverse cognitive approaches to early Christianity (and certainly distinctive among approaches to emotion), psychological construction emphasizes the centrality of *words* for emotional experience. Words matter deeply and are not simply arbitrary approximations for universal feelings (nor creatively invented for newly discovered feelings), and they matter both as concepts and as part of an emotional lexicon, the mastery of which is called emotional granularity.[106] Words, furthermore, not only create meaning; they provide tools by which the mind predicts the future and changes the body's neurophysiological process to adapt.[107] Words also have the power to create very real illness and suffering, as well as healing, as amply demonstrated in medicine, anthropology, and psychology.[108] Words thus create reality and change bodies, as also demonstrated in recent advances in the history of emotion.[109] Here I will give a brief overview of how I situate my work within the major approaches of emotions history, focusing on elements of three intersecting approaches.[110]

One early and important strategy in the history of emotions focuses on the discursive nature of emotions and the standards for emotional expression that societies set in different times and places.[111] This approach differentiates the experience of emotions and the question of the authenticity of emotions from

105. Petri Luomanen, "The Sociology of Knowledge, the Social Identity Approach, and the Cognitive Science of Religion," in Luomanen, Pyysiänen, and Uro, *Explaining Christian Origins*, 199–229.

106. Words are a "secret ingredient" for creating mental concepts like emotions (Barrett, *How Emotions Are Made*, 97, and further at 103–8).

107. Barrett writes, "Likewise, the words and concepts of your culture help to shape your brain wiring and your physical changes during emotion" (*How Emotions Are Made*, 38–39).

108. Darian Leader and David Corfield, *Why People Get Sick: Exploring the Mind-Body Connection* (New York: Pegasus, 2008), 94–117. This is a component of the well-established and powerful "meaning effect" (or placebo effect), described by Daniel Moerman, *Meaning, Medicine, and the 'Placebo Effect'* (Cambridge: Cambridge University Press, 2002).

109. Noted in recent historiographical introductions to the field, e.g., Boddice, *History of Emotions*, 146; and Rosenwein and Cristiani, *What Is the History of Emotions?*, 119.

110. A useful overview of the work of the three is Jan Plamper, "The History of Emotions: An Interview with William Reddy, Barbara Rosenwein, and Peter Stearns," *History and Theory* 40 (2010): 237–65. For more detailed introductions, see Rosenwein and Cristiani, *What Is the History of Emotions?*; Plamper, *History of Emotions*; and Boddice, *History of Emotions*.

111. The following section is adapted and revised from Crislip, "Emotion Words in Coptic" (see note 15 above), with permission from Lockwood Press.

the emotional standards and the choices of emotional terminologies promoted by society. The former are hard for the historian to access, perhaps only available through private diaries (if one presumes that private diaries offer direct access to authentic emotional experience beyond the influence of society's emotional norms, which is not necessarily the case). In the 1980s Peter Stearns and Carol Zisowitz Stearns promoted a method of history of emotions that addressed such limitations; they argued that the most profitable object of study for the historian lay not in the subjective experience of historical agents (that is, emotions) but in the ways that society talks about emotions, above all the rules and standards that people promote for displaying and evaluating emotions, which they called "emotionology," or the study of emotional discourse.[112] Such a method works best when sources directly address and prescribe rules for emotional display, such as modern self-help literature; the historian could compare emotional norms against private diaries (where such sources exist) to assess historical change.[113] Historians working in this tradition have, thus, tended to focus on the recent past, working within the tradition of American and European social history.

While it is hard to imagine a culture that does not use emotion words in its literature (even if it lacks an abstract category of emotion), not every time and culture leaves behind private first-person narratives which could witness to any sort of "authentic" emotional experience. It is hard to claim that any such unmediated insight into authentic personal feelings could survive from the ancient world. We have no private diaries, and even the important remains of epigraphy or the private correspondence that survive among the documentary papyri of Egypt are still highly regularized and conventionalized.[114]

Furthermore, not every culture has a tradition of prescriptive emotionology, instructions on emotional norms. But the Greco-Roman Mediterranean certainly did; a significant component of Greco-Roman philosophy was devoted to something like emotionology.[115] Platonists, Peripatetics, and Stoics all devoted

112. First outlined in Stearns and Stearns, "Emotionology," and continued through a series of books and articles, such as their book *Anger: The Struggle for Emotional Control in America's History* (Chicago: University of Chicago Press, 1986).

113. Discussed by Plamper, *History of Emotions*, 57–59, 304. Also Rosenwein and Cristiani, *What Is the History of Emotions?*, 29–34.

114. E.g., Angelos Chaniotis, ed., *Unveiling Emotions: Sources and Methods for the Study of Emotions in the Greek World* (Stuttgart: Franz Steiner Verlag, 2012).

115. Greek, Roman, Jewish, and early Christian approaches to the passions as part of moral philosophy are treated in the essays collected by John T. Fitzgerald, ed., *Passions and Moral Progress in Greco-Roman Thought* (London: Routledge, 2008).

considerable effort toward identifying, defining, and taxonomizing the passions (*pathē*), evaluating them as more or less desirable, and prescribing methods for suppressing or cultivating them—that is, rules of emotional display. Outside of the boundaries of more academic philosophy, we have examples not unlike our own self-help literature, such as the physician Galen's treatises *On the Passions and Errors of the Soul* and *On Freedom from Grief*, which instruct elite Roman men how to monitor their own *pathē* and eliminate those considered inappropriate, including anger, grief, and anxiety.[116] Some Christians were interested in such prescriptive literature. The *Shepherd of Hermas* was written in Rome contemporaneously with Galen, and parts of this lengthy collection of visions give practical advice on emotional management.[117] Hermas's focus on emotional management is not typical of all early Christian authors, but he represents an early, influential, and distinctively Christian approach to emotions that will be an important component to this book.[118] Early Christians would follow Hermas in a robust tradition of sentimental education through episcopal sermons and ascetic treatises on the passions.

But how do we approach material from writers who do not offer the explicit emotional guidance of an author like Hermas and later moralists? And is it possible to go beyond the level of discourse to understand whether people in the past felt differently? The former question is addressed by historian Barbara Rosenwein, who, in her work on the early medieval West, is faced with sources much like those from early Christianity: letters, sermons, lives, narratives, and occasional inscriptions and ephemera that employ emotion words without directly reflecting on them or their normativity.[119] Rosenwein proposes that we examine emotions as deployed within communities, which could be closely bound, such as

116. Galen's treatise *De indolentia* or *Peri alypias* has been recently recovered; for discussion see Claire K. Rothschild and Trevor W. Thompson, eds., *Galen's "De Indolentia,"* STAC 88 (Tübingen: Mohr Siebeck, 2014).

117. Andrew Crislip, "*The Shepherd of Hermas* and Early Christian Emotional Formation," StPatr 83 (2017): 231–50; and Petra von Gemünden, *Affekt und Glaube: Studien zur Historischen Psychologie des Früjudentums und Urchristentums*, NTOA/SUNT 73 (Göttingen: Vandenhoeck & Ruprecht, 2009), 309–38.

118. While the *Shepherd* is a second-century composition, papyrological records suggest that it was extremely popular in late antiquity, in fact better represented than any other ante-Nicene text in the papyri. It was also included in early biblical manuscripts. See Malcolm Choat and Rachel Yuen-Collingridge, "The Egyptian Hermas: The Shepherd in Egypt Before Constantine," in *Early Christian Manuscripts: Examples of Applied Methods and Approach*, ed. T. J. Kraus and T. Nicklas, TENTS 5 (Leiden: Brill, 2010), 191–212.

119. Rosenwein, *Emotional Communities*, 57–189, comprises case studies of emotions history as applied to a range of types of evidence; she summarizes her methods in *Genera-*

a monastery, or purely literary, such as a bishop corresponding with suppliants, subordinates, and friends across a region. What is important is that different communities privilege certain types of emotional expression and neglect or suppress others, often without formal prescription of emotional display. Individuals will frequently belong to multiple communities at once and over a lifetime. And communities also differ and change in how emotions are connected with other emotions, which she calls "sequences."[120] Such privileged emotion words, and their sequences, scripts, and conjunctions, differ dramatically among communities in early medieval Europe, for example among various cemeteries or in the courts of successive Merovingian monarchs. The sources that Rosenwein draws on, as a medievalist, are almost exclusively textual (although visual culture and even music can offer their own evidence); therefore, an important component of this method is to take account of the emotion words available.[121]

This phenomenon, the ways that communities police and mimetically cultivate ways of feeling and emotional expression, is especially significant for assessing early Christian identity, what Christians felt it meant to be Christian. Ancient Christians reflected on the passions, their propriety, their meaning, and even their place within the cosmos and history. As early as Paul, Christians advocated a "conversion of the emotions" along with faith in a risen messiah—ways of feeling that distinguished the community from their neighbors, connected its members in spirit and ritual, and linked the members to God no less than they were connected as members of one collective body.[122] When Paul wrote to his communities he wanted them to change "not just in mind, but in feeling."[123]

But how can the historian know whether people in the past meant it when they expressed emotions or whether these were just rhetorical commonplaces?

---

tions of Feeling: A History of Emotions, 600–1700 (Cambridge: Cambridge University Press, 2016), 3–10.

120. Rosenwein, *Generations*, 8; see also Carol Barr-Zisowitz, "'Sadness': Is There Such a Thing?," in *Handbook of Emotions*, 2nd ed., ed. Michael Lewis and Jeannette M. Haviland-Jones (New York: Guilford, 2000), 612–18.

121. On the relevance of art history for medieval emotions see Rosenwein, *Generations*, 4–5; also Barr-Zisowitz, "Sadness," 616. Rosenwein discusses the importance of attention to words, individually and as part of an emotional lexicon in *Emotional Communities*, 32–56.

122. Recognition of this in New Testament studies is in the important work of Stephen C. Barton, from whom I have adopted the phrase "conversion of the emotions." "Eschatology and the Emotions in Early Christianity," *JBL* 130 (2011): 571–91. In addition to Barton's essays on the emotions in the New Testament, to which I will refer throughout this book, see Ian Y. S. Jew, *Paul's Emotional Regime: The Social Function of Emotion in 1 Thessalonians and Philippians*, LNTS 629 (New York: T&T Clark, 2021); and Hockey, *Role of Emotion in 1 Peter*.

123. Kraftchick, "Πάθη [*Pathē*] in Paul," 44.

For critics from the perspective of affect theory this is not so much of a problem; they have confidence that they can read beneath, through, and around words to grasp the authentic emotional transcript, which will often be hidden by surface commonplaces and misdirecting emotional symptoms. Historians of emotions take a different approach. In fact, the problem of the "reality" of emotions is not so different from other areas of historical inquiry: "That texts may be insincere, make things up, mislead, and even lie is precisely what the historian's craft is meant to confront."[124] Skepticism about our sources' reportage of emotions is thus warranted but differs little from any other historical argument. Furthermore, insincerity or duplicity in emotional expression reveals its own truth.[125] Even sources that only employ emotion language incidentally reveal what their audiences must have understood to be plausible and either desirable or undesirable expressions of emotions, individually and collectively, which can be compared to other emotional expressions in other communities. Emotions that can be considered mere *topoi* or clichés ossified in rhetorical tradition can tell us about emotional norms and emotional communities. "Artificial sentiments," in fact, "tell us about conventions and habits; these have everything to do with emotion. . . . [I]nsincerity tells us about how people are supposed to feel. . . . For the historian, this is precious enough."[126] Other emotion historians see such caveats as unnecessary, rejecting the search for "authenticity" as a historiographical goal.[127]

For emotion words and emotional utterances do not simply describe a state (real or imagined) or merely reveal or enforce rules for emotional display.[128] They create or construct reality.[129] As some utterances are not just descriptive but performative, bringing about a change in reality (e.g., *hoc est enim corpus meum* or "I now pronounce you husband and wife"), so emotional utterance can also be "emotive," "a form of speech act that is neither descriptive nor performative."[130] To say "I am angry at him," or "I am really happy to hear that,"

124. Rosenwein, *Emotional Communities*, 28; and see also Rosenwein, *Generations*, 9.

125. Rosenwein, *Emotional Communities*, 28.

126. Rosenwein, *Emotional Communities*, 29.

127. See Boddice and Smith, *Emotion, Sense, Experience*, 31, with further discussion.

128. Note that Rosenwein herself highlights the relevance of current constructed emotion neuroscience for the history of emotions (Rosenwein and Cristiani, *What Is the History of Emotions?*, 107), a confluence also suggested in Rosenwein, *Generations*, 5–6.

129. The power of emotional expression to construct reality has long been theorized by historian and anthropologist William Reddy, who drew on speech act theory and cognitive science to posit the functioning of "emotives." See Reddy, *Navigation*, 63–111; Rosenwein and Cristiani, *What Is the History of Emotions?*, 45–49; and Boddice, *History of Emotions*, 62–77.

130. Reddy, *Navigation*, 104.

actualizes the experience of those emotions or "blank[s] out" other possible emotional states (that is, closing off the alternative expressions "I pity him" or "I am envious").[131] Many can see emotions in action in their own experience in the phenomenon of self-talk, especially negative self-talk, which brings about the affective state it purports to describe.

While such a thesis of the "real" impact of emotion words through the application of speech act theory has been long debated among historians, the neuroscience of emotions confirms the role of emotions and emotion words for historical change.[132] In fact, the words or concepts we use to describe and classify affect as emotion—in a sense also the emotionology of earlier history of emotions—have a real impact on cognition and embodiment; they describe "authentic" emotions, in the sense that the words and concepts that cultures develop and promote change the perception of reality, change experience, and even change the body and brain physiologically.[133]

Emotion and Early Christianity

One of the things we can hope to approach through attention to emotion is the experience of being Christian, that is, what it felt like to be a Christian. With attention to emotions through the perspectives described above, we have a great deal of evidence of what some Christians encouraged and expected other Christians to feel. Following the reasoning of the theory of psychological construction along with the historical study of emotional utterances and communities, we can also have some confidence that we are approaching what it felt like to be a Christian, because they tell us. As sources as early as the Gospel of John, even as early as the first surviving Christian text, Christians understood or expected Christian emotions to be peculiar, to set Christians apart from those on the outside, and to constitute a component of their identity.

131. Rosenwein, *Emotional Communities*, 18.

132. See the varied critiques in Plamper, *History of Emotions*, 261–62.

133. For emotion's effect on perception and realism see Jolie Baumann Wormwood et al., "You Are What I Feel: A Test of the Affective Realism Hypothesis," *Emotion* 19 (2019): 788–98; Erika H. Siegel et al., "Seeing What You Feel: Affect Drives Visual Perception of Structurally Neutral Faces," *Psychological Science* 29 (2018): 495–503; and Jonathan R. Zadra and Gerard L. Clore, "Emotion and Perception: The Role of Affective Information," *WIREs Cognitive Science* 2 (2011): 676–85. Bodily practices also influence emotional and social experience, C. Nathan DeWall et al., "Acetaminophen Reduces Social Pain: Behavioral and Neural Evidence," *Psychological Science* 21 (2010): 931–37.

That emotions of the self, of the community, and of the other can solidify a sense of identity can be seen readily in the contemporary United States, which has led the world in centering emotion in public life and discourse in the past generation. An identity of self and group belonging can form around a constellation of emotion concepts, say sadness (and melancholy, depression, ennui, etc.), expressed through word, art, and self-presentation, as in goth culture. The very concept of a "hate group" speaks to the emotional identity of a group's insiders and the emotional identity of their others and critics ("In this house we believe love is love"). We are surrounded by a cultural politics of emotion that reflects and enforces a sense of who we are and who we are not. A woman of the professional managerial class posts an Instagram of herself drinking from a "Male Tears" mug. A red-hatted man at a protest wears a baggy "Fuck Your Feelings" t-shirt. A 12-step group announces in their welcome literature, "We are not a glum lot!" Whatever emotional practices may be at play at the individual psychological level, such phenomena point to the value of emotion in marking and enforcing identity, how *we* feel (or admit or talk about how we feel) and how *they* feel. Such ways of marking identity and belonging by one's feelings are rooted in North American cultural trends and thus quite different from ancient passions and emotional norms, whether encouraging happiness as a normative life goal or encouraging the professional recategorizing of ordinary painful emotions as pathological states.[134]

The literature on early Christian identity is enormous and has tracked the rise of identity and belonging as political and cultural concerns, especially in Anglo-American culture with its increasing global hegemony. Overwhelmingly, the scholarship on identity has wrestled with questions of the nascent "Christian" self-understanding as part of, against, complementing, or simply other than the "Judaism" from which it descended or which it appropriated; more recently the identities of the scholars who construct these sorts of divisions have come under interrogation.[135] This leads to all sorts of complicated

134. Happiness in ancient Jewish and Christian biblical discourse within the context of contemporary "happiness studies" is covered from diverse perspectives in Brent A. Strawn, ed., *The Bible and the Pursuit of Happiness: What the Old and New Testaments Teach Us About the Good Life* (New York: Oxford University Press, 2012). The rise of depression as a sort of master category for negative affect is analyzed from sociological and historical angles in Allan V. Horwitz and Jerome C. Wakefield, *The Loss of Sadness: How Psychiatry Transformed Normal Sorrow into Depressive Disorder* (New York: Oxford University Press, 2007); and Ashley Frawley, *Significant Emotions: Rhetoric and Social Problems in a Vulnerable Age* (London: Bloomsbury Academic, 2023).

135. Judith M. Lieu, *Christian Identity in the Jewish and Graeco-Roman World* (Oxford:

questions, not only about whether and when one should refer to Christians, given that the term itself only appears in the second or third generation of believers in the messiahship of Jesus of Nazareth. The matters are no less complicated for Judaism, or is it Jews or Judeans or *Iudaioi*?[136] The elements of identity formation include various aspects of life in addition to the names Christians use for themselves and others: the texts they read, rituals, the explicit drawing of social boundaries, the cultivation of social memory, gender roles, and the multitudinous ways that Christians moved throughout the world (the "grammar of practice"), as well as the explicit claims of ethnic or racial identity.[137] Accordingly, early Christian identity studies have focused on the period of the New Testament extending into the second century and targets the tangled definitions of Jew and Christian and the so-called parting of the ways; more recent work has shifted the focus into late antiquity, which changes the nature of the question from Christians' relationship with Judaism to other aspects of identity.[138]

Such studies of early Christian identity, focused on the problem of Jewish and Christian (and Jewish-Christian) self-definition, have not seen emotion as an important component in constructing identity and community among the Christ followers. This is somewhat surprising. The Fourth Gospel is far from the only early text to highlight its community's practice of love (*agapē*) as forming a distinctive emotion that separates them from other groups. Paul and 1 Peter, for example, both independently discuss Christian love as constituting identity.[139] In recent studies of love and identity in early Christian letters, emo-

---

Oxford University Press, 2004); Judith M. Lieu, *Neither Jew nor Greek? Constructing Early Christian Identity* (London: T&T Clark, 2016); James D. G. Dunn, *Neither Jew nor Greek: A Contested Identity* (Grand Rapids: Eerdmans, 2015); and Terence L. Donaldson, *Gentile Christian Identity from Cornelius to Constantine* (Grand Rapids: Eerdmans, 2020). Recent work has merged historical issues of Christian identity with more presentist and intra-academic concerns, as in David G. Horrell, *Ethnicity and Inclusion: Religion, Race, and Whiteness in Constructions of Jewish and Christian Identities* (Grand Rapids: Eerdmans, 2020), who focuses on the identities and ethnicities of modern scholarly communities.

136. E.g., explored in various permutations in Kotrosits, *Rethinking*.

137. As in Lieu, *Christian Identity* and *Neither Jew nor Greek*.

138. E.g., Karin Hedner Zetterholm, Anders Runesson, Cecilia Wassén, and Magnus Zetterholm, eds., *Negotiating Identities: Conflict, Conversion, and Consolidation in Early Judaism and Christianity (200 BCE–600 CE)* (Lanham, MD: Lexington Books/Fortress Academic, 2022); Éric Rebillard, *Christians and Their Many Identities: North Africa, 200–450 CE* (Ithaca, NY: Cornell University Press, 2012); and Donaldson, *Gentile Christian Identity*.

139. See Troels Engberg-Pedersen, *Paul on Identity: Theology as Politics* (Minneapolis: Fortress, 2021), 51–77; and Runar Thorsteinsson, "The Role of Morality in the Rise of Ro-

tion (or passion or sentiment or even feeling) is absent. One study, for example, frames the early discussion of love entirely as "morality," while another speaks of "ethics" within Paul's conception of the pneuma and works.[140] Theologians and critics have addressed the widespread call to joy in similar ways, avoiding language of emotion and feeling and describing joy exclusively as a theological virtue and eschatological doctrine.[141] This is not wrong, of course, but there is historical value in recognizing the emotional foundation of such experiences as love and joy, feelings which as emotions also are practices in and of themselves, and thus open to historical study.[142]

Two strands of scholarship have begun to incorporate emotions into the study of early Christian and Jewish identity: social identity theory (SIT), and some recent work applying affect theory to ancient sources. The sociological approach of SIT recognizes the centrality of "emotional significance" to group identity and belonging both on a general level and as part of "group actions," the point of which "is the attempt to create or preserve 'psychological group distinctiveness' to differentiate ingroup from outgroups."[143] The social settings, rituals, relationships, morals, and narratives all function to create emotional bonds and shared norms within a community, with moral teachings and narratives modeling emotional "prototypes," which the group and its members emulate.[144] In the later Middle Ages, for example, Mary plays a prototypical role for emotional practice (especially around grief) as a form of identity construction and maintenance through several modes of emotional

man Christianity," in *Exploring Early Christian Identity*, ed. Bengt Holmberg, WUNT 226 (Tübingen: Mohr Siebeck, 2008), 139–57.

140. Thorsteinsson, "Role of Morality," 140–46; and Engberg-Pedersen, *Paul on Identity*, 52–58.

141. Discussed in Matthew Elliott, *Faithful Feelings: Rethinking Emotion in the New Testament* (Grand Rapids: Kregel Academic, 2006), 178–81.

142. Scheer, "Are Emotions a Kind of Practice."

143. See overview addressed to New Testament specialists by Philip F. Esler, "An Outline of Social Identity Theory," in *T&T Clark Handbook to Social Identity in the New Testament*, ed. J. Brian Tucker and Coleman A. Baker (London: Bloomsbury, 2014), 13–39; the quotation is from Esler, "Outline," 19–20, quoting Henri Tajfel. Esler and others have applied the basic insights of SIT to offer an alternative to the kind of ethical, doctrinal, or moral readings of early Christian emotional discourse, as for example in Matthew's Beatitudes, which "represent neither 'eschatological blessings' nor '(ethical) entrance-requirements' but . . . group norms." Philip F. Esler, "Group Norms and Prototypes in Matthew 5.3–12: A Social Identity Interpretation of the Matthaean Beatitudes," in Tucker and Baker, *T&T Clark Handbook*, 147–71, at 158. One of the three components of group norms is the emotional (the others are the cognitive and the evaluative). Esler, "Group Norms," 169–70.

144. Esler, "Outline," 32–33.

mimesis.[145] All areas of life and modes of emulation also carry an "emotional component [which] also emerges in the degree to which antipathy is directed toward members of various outgroupings."[146]

The other approach to the emotional contours of early Christian identity is through affect theory. Such studies tend not to privilege "emotion" as a category, but emotion lurks beneath their approaches that glide across currents of affect theory, excavating the queer pleasures of both suffering and scholarship within affects like shame, trauma, and diasporic grief, which so often speak only mutely from the prelinguistic affective archive.[147] Scholars adopting the affect theory approach have offered compelling approaches to early Christian emotions, beyond those focusing on identity.

The Outline of This Book

There are a number of ways to approach the emotions of the early Christians. One example would be to trace early Christian history through emotional communities, which encourage and discourage the expression of certain emotions. Sometimes such communities are sufficiently well defined for such analysis, such as the monasteries of northern Egypt or Augustine and his parishioners in Hippo. Other times, communities are more difficult to identify, and their contours and existence are thus the subject of generations of debate, such as the "community of the beloved disciple" or the "Q community." From another perspective, "Christianity" itself may be understood as a community, as Christians defined themselves as part of a universal faith or "race" or "nation" against others.[148] Another way that ancient emotions have been approached is to focus on emotions or emotional constellations, which could include a range of emotions within a textual corpus (Aristotle, John Chrysostom), or

145. Miri Rubin, *Emotion and Devotion: The Meaning of Mary in Medieval Religious Cultures* (Budapest: Central European University Press, 2009), 45–47.

146. Esler, "Group Norms," 159.

147. E.g., in analyzing the Valentinian *Gospel of Truth* as an archive of diasporic grief (grief over the loss of Judean self-determination, one presumes), Kotrosits claims that "it is the very absence of references to national belonging in the Gospel of Truth that become the imprint of diasporic trauma" (*Rethinking*, 177). That is, the absence of any emotional language of grief, loss, and dispossession speaks to the ancient author's great obsession with such issues, hidden, however, through his "affective redirections" but accessible to the symptomatic reading of modern scholars.

148. E.g., Horrell, *Ethnicity and Inclusion*; and Denise Buell, *Why This New Race: Ethnic Reasoning in Early Christianity* (New York: Columbia University Press, 2005).

monographs on individual emotions (anger, disgust, remorse, shame, envy, love, etc.).[149] The latter approach has been especially influential within ancient history and classical studies, as well as in biblical studies.

These approaches have their advantages and are not mutually exclusive. In this volume I have tried to remain cognizant of these approaches and to move between them by organizing my discussion around emotions or emotional constellations. I use the term emotional constellations because each "emotion" incorporates more than a single term, which may differ in their nuances and indeed differ in their conceptions over the course of antiquity. Feelings, furthermore, may also be expressed in the absence of their conceptual names.[150] When I say "joy," for example, I include a range of related emotions of a positive valence that indicate satisfaction and pleasure as a moral good, including also concepts like cheerfulness and elation, *chara*, *euphrosynē*, and *hilarotēs*, which may be usefully contrasted with a concept like happiness (*eudaimonia*). I also recognize that "joy," as in the modern usage of English, or specifically in my early twenty-first-century American dialect of English, cannot be quite the same as the Greek *chara*, or other related terms, any more than "emotion" is identical to the Greek *pathos* or the Latin *perturbatio*. Fortunately, there is more than enough common ground between our worlds to make sense of the similarities and differences. The history of emotion is a process of dialectic and translation, not diagnosis.[151]

I have focused on five emotional complexes that figure especially prominently in the development of early Christianity, in the ways Christians think about themselves as communities and individuals, in ritual and theology, and in their cooperation and conflict with others: Joy, Sadness, Anger, Disgust, and Envy, followed by a brief conclusion (with a few comments on Love). It is not a comprehensive catalog, and they are not the only emotions that deserve

149. So, e.g., Blake Leyerle, *The Narrative Shape of Emotion in the Preaching of John Chrysostom*, Christianity in Late Antiquity 10 (Oakland: University of California Press, 2020); Hockey, *Role of Emotion*; and Konstan, *Emotions of the Ancient Greeks*. For select individual emotions, see Virginia Burrus, *Saving Shame: Martyrs, Saints, and Other Abject Subjects* (Philadelphia: University of Pennsylvania Press, 2011); Fulkerson, *No Regrets*; and Sanders, *Envy*.

150. Noted in the context of looking for "emotion" in ancient Christian and Hebrew texts by N. T. Wright, "Joy: Some New Testament Perspectives and Questions," in *Joy and Human Flourishing: Essays on Theology, Culture, and the Good Life*, ed. Miroslav Volf and Justin E. Crisp (Minneapolis: Fortress, 2015), 39–61; and Nathan MacDonald, "Is There Happiness in the Talmud?," in Strawn, *Bible and the Pursuit of Happiness*, 58, at 57–73.

151. As noted by Ute Frevert, *Emotions in History: Lost and Found* (Budapest: Central European University Press, 2011).

extended treatment. These emotions, however, played significant parts in early Christian debates about theology, ethics, and identity. I have selected in each chapter what I see as important touchstones or telling exempla in the history of early Christianity from the first to the fifth centuries. In each chapter I have tried to pay attention to change over time, as well as to the coexistence of competing or alternative emotional communities within Christianity. I also engage with recent work on early Christian emotions, especially when such studies clarify the varying perspectives to emotions history discussed in this chapter. Throughout, it will be clear that Christians understood themselves from the start as an intentionally emotional community, set off and distinguishable from other communities by the emotions they evince and the emotions they repress. In real life emotions do not exist as discrete entities, and communities do not form themselves around individual emotions. Emotions, rather, are chained or linked in groupings or scripts. Communities coalesce, furthermore, with shared emotional vocabularies and practices, not around a single emotion or emotional constellation. Nonetheless, an approach like this, focusing on the individual emotions or emotional clusters or scripts, as many studies in various aspects of emotions research have done, has numerous advantages, not least of which is to provide an accessible foundation for other studies, which is the aim of this book as an introduction and invitation to the study of early Christian emotions.

2
Joy

One of the earliest Christian homilies is preserved in two late antique manuscripts found in 1945 in Upper Egypt.[1] While it comes to us in two Coptic versions, in the early Lycopolitan dialect and very fragmentarily in the Sahidic dialect, it is a translation of a second-century Greek original, perhaps delivered by the Roman teacher and poet Valentinus.[2] Since its recovery, scholars have hailed this sermon as of great importance for the early history of Christianity both for its literary merits and its witness to early Valentinian thought. Indeed, "it must have had a rhetorical power that ranked with the great masterpieces of Christian prose," a power that still arrests the reader even in an imperfect translation into a minor dialect of Coptic.[3] Even beyond the literary and theological significance of this text, the *Gospel of Truth* "affords a rare glimpse of the actual human atmosphere of a church meeting, in which a magisterial gnostic

1. *The Gospel of Truth* is preserved in full as NHC I 3, and fragmentarily as NHC XII 2. On the *Gospel of Truth* as homily, see Harold W. Attridge and George W. MacRae, SJ, "The Gospel of Truth," in *Nag Hammadi Codex I (The Jung Codex)*, ed. Harold W. Attridge, NHS 22 (Leiden: Brill, 1985), 66–67. Earlier homiletic material arguably includes short speeches in Acts (3:12–26; 20:18–35) and perhaps Hebrews, according to *Apostolic Fathers* 1:154.2 (Ehrman, LCL); Clement (below) is a rough contemporary to the *Gospel of Truth*.

2. On the potential authorship by Valentinus, see Bentley Layton with David Brakke, *The Gnostic Scriptures*, 2nd ed. (New Haven: Yale University Press, 2021), 309–10; and discussion by Einar Thomassen and Marvin Meyer, "The Gospel of Truth," in *The Nag Hammadi Scriptures*, ed. Marvin Meyer (New York: Harper One, 2007), 34. Others approach the question with extreme levels of skepticism, as in Philip L. Tite, *Valentinian Ethics and Paraenetic Discourse: Determining the Social Function of Moral Exhortation in Valentinian Christianity*, NHMS 67 (Leiden: Brill, 2009), 218–21. Here, as is typical of early Christian literature, issues of dating are contested and revised serially.

3. Layton with Brakke, *Gnostic Scriptures*, 308.

preacher addresses a congregation, speaking from personal authority."[4] The sermon gives a picture of a real Christian gathering in the second century, of embodied people—women, men, free, slave—participating in the collective effervescence of teaching, communion, and ritual. It is a situation in which one might expect to find, not unlike the homilies of early or late modernity, an appeal to emotions and a focus on the shared emotional lives and transformations of the assembled community.[5] "Valentinus" does not disappoint.

The preacher begins and closes his sermon by evoking the emotional power of Christian proclamation. It is an emotional outlook that his hearers should share, not just with each other but with God. "The gospel of truth," he begins, "is joy (*telēl*)."[6] In this rendering, the opening statement is propositional, something like the "God is love" of 1 John 4:8. A slightly different translation brings out the performative function of emotion: "The proclamation of the truth is a joy."[7] In this rendering, the "joy" of the gospel is not just theological virtue; it is an action, an experience of gaining knowledge (*souōnf*, *gnōsis*) of the Father, an acquaintance grounded in the very embodied and cognitive experience of delivering and receiving the homily in community, all of which instantiates joy as a shared experience. The centrality of communal joy, as a theological proposition and embodied emotional practice, is the preacher's thesis statement.

The experiential and emotional aspect of the *Gospel of Truth* is reflected at the close of the long opening sentence: "The term 'proclamation' refers to the manifestation of hope, a discovery for those who are searching for him."[8] Joy is part of a process of searching and finding—which travels with Christian hope—a feeling that the listening audience should come to experience themselves, collectively and individually, to be developed as part of Christian knowledge (*gnōsis*) and ritual.

4. Layton with Brakke, *Gnostic Scriptures*, 308.

5. Stephanie L. Cobb provides a rich picture of the emotional transformation and emotional contagion that likely occurred in early Christian worship, focusing on the collective reading of martyrologies, but the subject is just as relevant to homiletic performance; *Divine Deliverance: Pain and Painlessness in Early Christian Martyr Texts* (Oakland: University of California Press, 2016), 6–10. The cultivation of collective emotional sensibility in worship is covered for the early modern period by Susan C. Karant-Nunn, *The Reformation of Feeling: Shaping the Religious Emotions in Early Modern Germany* (Oxford: Oxford University Press, 2010). Emotional contagion and the collective experience of emotion is well studied across disciplines, so Christian von Scheve and Mikko Salmela, eds., *Collective Emotions: Perspectives from Psychology, Philosophy, and Sociology* (Oxford: Oxford University Press, 2014).

6. *Gos. Truth* (NHC I 16.31, Thomassen).

7. *Gos. Truth* (NHC I 16.31, Layton).

8. *Gos. Truth* (NHC I 17.1–3, Layton).

The sermon concludes with a description of the heavenly fullness, about which "all will speak individually,"[9] where all is pleasant, without anger or bitterness, envy or groaning, free from all evil and ill feeling.[10] This is a place the preacher, slipping into first person for the only time in the sermon, claims that he has himself been, a place suffused with the Father's love and the Spirit's joy (*telēl*).[11] The preacher returns to emotions throughout the *Gospel of Truth*; they are tied to his understanding of the emotional nature and origin of the material world, an idea elaborated further by later Valentinians. But for now, it suffices to observe the role of emotion, here joy and love (*agapē*), in framing this important witness to second-century Christianity. The preacher claims to have experienced a certain quality of emotion, which he has shared with the Father and the Spirit, and contends that this is something that his audience may be able to speak of individually (*poueei poueei*, NHC I 41.3), and through the collective proclamation of the truth.[12]

The *Gospel of Truth* is not alone in promoting a conversion of the emotions in response to a sermon.[13] Like the *Gospel of Truth*, the homily now known as 2 Clement exhorts its audience toward emotional transformation, as part of reflecting on the relationship of Jesus Christ to God and understanding the way that Christ suffered (*pathein*) for our sake.[14] Much as the *Gospel of Truth* characterizes the Christian's prior existence as a "fog" or "mist" (*hlastn*) driven by the force of "error" (*planē*), 2 Clement describes a former life under the thrall of images and idols as "nothing other than death . . . beset by darkening gloom, our vision blurred by such mist."[15] Second Clement's metaphors of

9. *Gos. Truth* (NHC I 41.3, Thomassen).

10. *Gos. Truth* (NHC I 42.4–16).

11. *Gos. Truth* (NHC I 43.16–22). The significance of the preacher's shift into first person is discussed by Attridge and MacRae, *Nag Hammadi Codex I, Notes* (NHC 23), 134.

12. A recent affect theory perspective reads emotion out of the text but reads into it a dialectic between pleasure and trauma, including the trauma of diasporic displacement, none of which appears in the surface of the texts but rather haunts the writer like the transgenerational ghosts of abuse or deeply repressed affects visible only symptomatically in their absence. Maia Kotrosits, *Rethinking Early Christian Identity: Affect, Violence, and Belonging* (Minneapolis: Fortress, 2015), 173–99.

13. Second Clement is perhaps the earliest surviving Christian homily outside the New Testament, possibly dating to the 140s. It is certainly not by Clement of Rome, the bishop to whom it has been traditionally attributed as his second letter to the Corinthians. The author and his location are unknown, with Rome, Alexandria, and Corinth among the hypotheses (*Apostolic Fathers* 1:158–60 [Ehrman, LCL]).

14. 2 Clem. 1.2.

15. *Gos. Truth* (NHC I 17.11, 33, Layton); 2 Clem. 1.6 (Ehrman).

gloom (*amaurōsin*) and mist (*achlyos*) resonate with the emotional states of confusion and sadness.[16] Clement's audience, he proclaims, have been rescued by Christ's compassion (*splangchnistheis*, literally, his visceral gut feeling), whereby they are saved from the forces of error (*planē*) and destruction, a process that the preacher describes as "com[ing] into being from nonbeing."[17]

Second Clement foregrounds this newly transformed emotional state, calling on his community to rejoice (*euphranthēti*, quoting Isa 54:1).[18] He urges collective feelings, to love one another, to feel and eschew the same emotions as one another (*sympaschein*, to feel passion together), not to envy or fear other creatures but to fear only God.[19] At the end of the sermon, 2 Clement returns to the theme of joy and happiness that it began with: "The pious should not be sad (*lypeisthai*), even if he should suffer hardship in the present times. A happy (*makarios*) time awaits him. When this one is brought back to life with the ancestors, he will rejoice (*euphranthēsetai*) in the age without sadness (*alypēton*)."[20] Like the *Gospel of Truth*, 2 Clement gives a vivid picture of an early Christian community at prayer. Woven through the preacher's exhortation is a sense that becoming a Christian is a process of emotional conversion, from an experience dominated by fear, gloom, confusion, envy, anger, and doubt to a new emotional state, which Christians share in communion as bodies and souls at worship—an experience of joy and love.

From the time of Paul, Christian writers, leaders, teachers, moralists, and visionaries emphasized the distinctiveness of Christian joy (*chara*). Joy is by no means a uniquely Christian concept, as Christians worked within the traditions of Greek philosophy, with which many were familiar whether through formal education or cultural osmosis.[21] Christians also drew on Jewish traditions about joy, transmitted most directly through the Christian appropriation of the Jewish Scriptures in their Greek translation and perhaps also through the continuing interactions between Jews, Christians, and "Jewish-Christians."

16. LSJ s.v., referring to Aeschylus in both cases.

17. 2 Clem. 1.8 (Ehrman). On the bodily semantics of *splanchnon* and related words see David E. Fredrickson, *Eros and the Christ: Longing and Envy in Paul's Christology* (Minneapolis: Fortress, 2013), 15, 35–36; and F. Scott Spencer, *Passions of the Christ: The Emotional Life of Jesus in the Gospels* (Grand Rapids: Baker Academic, 2021), 171–205.

18. 2 Clem. 2.1; Ehrman translates "jubilant."

19. 2 Clem. 4.3; 4.4; 5.1; 5.4. The emotional and embodied semantics of sympathy and compassion are discussed by Françoise Mirguet, *An Early History of Compassion: Emotion and Imagination in Hellenistic Judaism* (Cambridge: Cambridge University Press, 2017), 31–37.

20. 2 Clem. 19.4.

21. See Ilaria L. E. Ramelli and David Konstan, "The Use of XAPA [*chara*] in the New Testament and Its Background in Hellenistic Moral Philosophy," *Exemplaria Classica: Journal of Classical Philology* 14 (2010): 185–204.

Christians put a special mark on the emotion. From the beginning, followers of Jesus presented their way as one of joyful suffering, a life suffused by a transcendent feeling of connection (*koinōnia*) with God, his Son, his Spirit, and the other members of the assembled body (the *ekklēsia*, what will become "the Church"). This joy is felt presently but focused eschatologically, pained with the suffering of the cross but anticipating the inevitable triumph of the gospel. In this chapter, I hope to give a sense of the ways that early Christians envisioned this emotion as a part of the life of individuals and community, an emotional practice and a marker of community and identity.

"Rejoice in the Lord Always": Paul and Peter as Apostles of Joy

Christians of late antiquity surrounded themselves with images of their moral exemplars and predecessors in the faith, among the most popular being the apostle to the gentiles and the first bishop of Rome. From a basic emotions perspective, such expressions might be able tell us something about the emotional lives of the apostles as imagined by their late antique followers.[22] Ancients devoted a great deal of thought to reading the face, though such physiognomic analysts were more interested in discovering personality traits, virtues and vices, and the true nature of a soul than identifying emotional states.[23] The *Life of Antony*, for example, observes rather obviously that the monk's joyful soul shone forth in a cheerful face, just as a sorrowful soul is revealed in a sad face.[24] Such banalities are hardly helpful for portraits of the apostles. When Paul and Peter gaze out from the images from their earliest surviving portraits, in fourth-century catacomb paintings from the Vatican, I am at a loss to identify their inner state, as they gaze neutrally, intently, even blankly

22. Though the reliability of reading the face (even among modern people) has come under sustained critique from other psychologists, such as Lisa Feldman Barrett, *How Emotions Are Made: The Secret Life of the Brain* (Boston: Houghton Mifflin Harcourt, 2017), 42–55.

23. See Georgia Frank, *The Memory of the Eyes: Pilgrims to Living Saints in Late Antiquity*, Transformation of the Classical Heritage 30 (Berkeley: University of California Press, 2000), 134–70. See also Susan Matt, "Recovering Emotion from Visual Culture," in *Reading Roman Emotions: Visual and Textual Interpretations*, ed. Hedvig von Ehrenheim and Marina Prusac-Lindhagen, Acta Instituti Romani Regni Sueciae 4.64 (Stockholm: Svenska Institutet I Rom, 2020), 19–28.

24. Frank, *Memory*, 144.

at the viewer.[25] A constructed emotions perspective would point out the great unreliability of even trying.[26]

Fortunately, the letters of the historical Paul reveal a great deal about how he felt and how he expected his correspondents to feel in return. We see an effusively emotional apostle in his letters. He rages; he feels jealousy and zeal; he evinces his pain and sorrow, and he expresses his love and joy throughout his letters. These emotions define his experience as a believer in Christ Jesus and the modes by which his followers and communities should know and relate to one another and God. To a large extent it is emotion that sets Christians apart from others and by which they conceived and created the world they experienced.[27]

The most prominent emotion that Paul (and the roughly contemporaneous author of 1 Peter) promote for themselves and others is joy, a good emotion (as the Stoics would call it, a *eupatheia*) that unites them as a community, locally and across the sea, in communion or community (*koinōnia*) with Christ.[28] Joy fills these letters and is part of the vision of identity as being "in Christ" or "Christian."

Paul does not preach the gospel as a way to happiness. Ancient philosophers thought a great deal about happiness and still influence the robust field of happiness studies among philosophers and psychologists. They define happiness as overall well-being and fulfillment in life, something like "prosperity combined with virtue," as Aristotle defines it in his *Rhetoric*, the mix of good fortune and intentionality that fosters a life of autonomy, virtue, and moderate pleasure.[29]

25. E.g., the early portraits of the saints in Robin Margaret Jensen, *Face to Face: Early Portraits of the Divine in Early Christianity* (Minneapolis: Fortress, 2005), 186–89.

26. As showed quite dramatically in Barrett, *How Emotions Are Made*, 42–43.

27. See Katherine M. Hockey, *The Role of Emotion in 1 Peter*, SNTSMS 173 (Cambridge: Cambridge University Press, 2019), 36–39, on the world- and reality-constructing power of emotions.

28. Foundational to my discussion of Paul is Stephen C. Barton, "Spirituality and the Emotions in Early Christianity: The Case of Joy," in *The Bible and Spirituality: Exploratory Essays in Reading Scripture Spiritually*, ed. Andrew T. Lincoln, J. Gordon McConville, and Lloyd F. Pietersen (Eugene, OR: Cascade, 2013), 171–93; and Ryan S. Schellenberg, *Abject Joy: Paul, Prison, and the Art of Making Do* (Oxford: Oxford University Press, 2021), whose work models the thoughtful and creative integration of history of emotions perspectives into the study of Paul's letters; also cf. the helpful studies by Ian Y. S. Jew, *Paul's Emotional Regime: The Social Function of Emotion in 1 Thessalonians and Philippians*, LNTS 629 (New York: T&T Clark, 2021); and Matthew Elliott, *Faithful Feelings: Rethinking Emotion in the New Testament* (Grand Rapids: Kregel Academic, 2006).

29. *Rhet.* 1.5, in Darrin M. McMahon, *Happiness: A History* (New York: Grove, 2006), 46. The psychology of happiness is much more diverse and robust than I can capture

Happiness has become the positive emotion par excellence in contemporary culture. Academics, technocrats, and entrepreneurs have developed whole industries and public initiatives to foster happiness (and the related states of well-being and human flourishing). My home university developed a popular "science of happiness" course for undergraduates. A "science of well-being" course was for some years the most popular course at Yale; more than four million have enrolled in the course online. Despite the dissenters from our regime of feeling good, happiness is big money.[30] Religious self-help writers have caught on, as one popular book confidently proclaims, *God Wants You Happy*.[31]

This would have been news to Paul and indeed to Jesus. As widely as discussion of happiness (*eudaimonia*) pervades Greco-Roman philosophy, the authors of the New Testament show no interest in the concept: The word "happiness" never even occurs, either in its Aristotelian version or the *ataraxia* of the Epicureans.[32] Even where "happy" shows up in English translations, the Greek term in question (*makarios*) points to a more basic English sense of happy, meaning fortunate. English "happy" is etymologically connected to "happen," "happenstance," and "hapless"; thus the American "pursuit of happiness" historically refers not to emotional well-being but the pursuit of success, good fortune, and property.[33]

Instead of Greco-Roman or late capitalist happiness, Paul preaches a gospel of joy: *chara*.[34] As an emotional concept developed by Christians against the

here, and is covered widely, as in Daniel M. Haybron, *Happiness: A Short Introduction* (Oxford: Oxford University Press, 2013); and Samuel S. Franklin, *The Psychology of Happiness: A Good Human Life* (Cambridge: Cambridge University Press, 2010).

30. William Davies, *The Happiness Industry: How the Government and Big Business Sold Us Well-Being* (London: Verso, 2015); Eric G. Wilson, *Against Happiness: In Praise of Melancholy* (New York: FSG, 2008).

31. Father Jonathan Morris, *God Wants You Happy: From Self-Help to God's Help* (New York: Harper One, 2011), blurbed by the progressive Jesuit James Martin and a number of conservative celebrities.

32. An absence that fits poorly with contemporary psychological emphases on happiness, a contradiction negotiated by Colleen Shantz, "'I Have Learned to Be Content': Happiness According to St. Paul," in *The Bible and the Pursuit of Happiness: What the Old and New Testaments Teach Us About the Good Life*, ed. Brent Strawn (New York: Oxford University Press, 2012), 187–201. McMahon (*Happiness*, 20–59) surveys philosophical conceptions of happiness in classical Greece.

33. The influences and valences of early American and Jeffersonian happiness are explored in McMahon, *Happiness*, 314–31.

34. The vocabulary of joy and related emotion words in the various authors of the New Testament is tabulated by Felix Just, SJ, at https://catholic-resources.org/Bible/Joy-Rejoice.htm; Morrice's word-study approach covers the main range of positive emotion words with

backdrop of Greek philosophers and Hebrew prophets and poets, joy differs from the well-being or life satisfaction of *eudaimonia*: It is an exuberant passion you can feel in your guts, a materiality that ancient Stoics recognized.[35] Theorists of joy emphasize the difficulty, even impossibility of capturing the experience of joy in language, even as they continue to try, much like the romantic poets.[36] Joy expresses an expansive delight in the presence of a good; "joy is excess," an exuberance and outflowing that points to its shared experience.[37] Unlike happiness, joy is available to conscious knowing and reflection. To be joyful is to recognize one's own joy, unlike happiness, which is experienced more as a flow state and slips away once you focus on it or try to be happy.[38] Joy captures the most basic of human experiences, the bonding of mother and baby, of care, warmth, and sustenance.[39] Aristotle saw joy as the expression of erotic longing and union, felt perhaps at its most biting in orgasm.[40] Still, we should not take joy as frivolous. Rather, "joy is a language and experience of profound religious and existential seriousness. It is an individual and social manifestation of, and response to, things that matter most."[41] So when it is in the language of joy (*chairein*) that Greek speakers greet one another and close their letters, we should take seriously their emotional effusiveness as expressing something important about norms and experience.[42] Unlike happiness, joy is not "solipsistic." It is always in recognition of (or predicting) something good.[43]

Paul's joy evokes such observations of modern psychologists and theologians, as well as some ancient philosophers. This excessive and exuberant joy

---

comparison to the Septuagint and select classical literature. William Morrice, *Joy in the New Testament* (Grand Rapids: Eerdmans, 1985).

35. Margaret Graver, *Stoicism and Emotion* (Chicago: University of Chicago Press, 2007), 18–21, 28–30, on the materiality of the soul and the feeling of affect.

36. Adam Potkay, *The Story of Joy: From the Bible to Late Romanticism* (Cambridge: Cambridge University Press, 2007), 16–20; Charles Mathewes, "Toward a Theology of Joy," in *Joy and Human Flourishing: Essays on Theology, Culture, and the Good Life*, ed. Miroslav Volf and Justin E. Crisp (Minneapolis: Fortress, 2015), 65.

37. Mathewes, "Toward a Theology of Joy," 65.

38. Mathewes, "Toward a Theology of Joy," 65–66. Happiness as a flow state is most famously promoted by Mihalyi Csikszentimihalyi, *Finding Flow: The Psychology of Engagement with Everyday Life* (New York: Basic, 1997).

39. Potkay, *Story of Joy*, 14–15.

40. Schellenberg, *Abject Joy*, 160.

41. Barton, "Spirituality and the Emotions," 187 (italics removed). The complementarity of joy and seriousness in pedagogy is explored by Zena Hitz, *Lost in Thought: The Hidden Pleasures of the Intellectual Life* (Princeton: Princeton University Press, 2020).

42. Schellenberg, *Abject Joy*, 156–59; Morrice, *Joy*, 68–69.

43. Mathewes, "Toward a Theology of Joy," 66. On this aspect in Stoic philosophy of joy, see Hockey, *Role of Emotion*, 108.

differs from the rather individualist nature of ancient *eudaimonia* in its "overflowing" (e.g., 2 Cor 8:2) among Paul and his coreligionists. In short, *chara* is a collective experience, in a single mind, soul, and body, all of which Christians share with Christ. Paul conceives of his joy as something that distinguishes his community from outsiders. It is eschatological—the cognition that something very good is imminent, the triumphant return of Christ and the end of the current age. But it is no less fully present and experienced in the life of the community and its members.[44] And his joy explicitly does not depend on anything "happening" to him but is an emotional, mental, and predictive outlook expected of the community even in the face of misfortune, suffering, and pain.

Joy runs through most of Paul's authentic letters, to a greater or lesser degree, but the letter that embodies Paul's joy most fully is his letter to the Philippian Christians, written while Paul was apparently imprisoned and facing a very uncertain future, even death.[45] Near the end of this letter Paul commands his followers, "Rejoice (*chairete*) in the Lord always; again I will say, Rejoice" (Phil 4:4). We should not take it as mere commonplace. It is in fact one of Paul's signature teachings also in 1 Thessalonians and the Corinthian correspondence (2 Cor 6:10, *lypoumenoi aei de chairontes*). His letter to the Thessalonians underscores that this is no mere suggestion or teaching of his own. God commands that they always feel joy: "Rejoice always, pray without ceasing, give thanks in all circumstances; for this is the will of God in Christ Jesus for you" (1 Thess 5:16). The second command, to pray without ceasing, would have a long history in Christian spirituality, but the first command—rejoice always—is no less important and no less enigmatic. How should one always be joyful, even in the face of suffering? In his short public letters, Paul does not give a detailed account of his psychagogy, how he leads his followers in transforming their emotions. But throughout these letters, Paul points to dual roles of his letters, "both a display of joy and pedagogy in joy."[46] He expects such a transformation into a state of unceasing joy from his coreligionists. In this sense, emotion shapes Christian practice as distinctively as prayer, an embodied, conscious act and orientation that shapes the connection between members of the group and puts them in relation with God.[47]

44. Barton, "Spirituality and the Emotions," 189.

45. Philippians has received attention in recent studies drawing on emotions history methodologies, including Schellenberg, *Abject Joy*; Jew, *Paul's Emotional Regime*; and Barton, "Spirituality and the Emotions," 184–89.

46. Barton, "Spirituality and the Emotions," 187.

47. That emotions are acts or practices is integral to the approach of psychological construction, so in Lisa Feldman Barrett, "The Conceptual Act Theory: A Precis," *Emotion Review* 6 (2014): 292–97. Also cf. Monique Scheer, "Are Emotions a Kind of Practice (and

Paul presents himself as an emotional exemplar and his own joy as constant (Phil 1:4, cf. 1:25), to which he returns across his letters.[48] It cannot be a mere commonplace but appears as a distinctive feature of his literary personality. While Paul's joy suffuses his authentic letters and his self-presentation as a leader and writer, it largely disappears in the letters written falsely in his name.[49] Yet New Testament scholarship has traditionally played down the emotional exuberance of Paul and his letters, arguing "that joy is not emotional in these passages but rather theological and eschatological."[50] A denial of the emotional content of a concept like *chara* is rooted in a widespread belief that emotions are irrational and thus beneath the dignity of serious theological or philosophical thought. Generations of cognitive science and the philosophical, anthropological, and historical studies that developed alongside it have shown such prejudices to be groundless.[51] Paul does not (merely) preach joy as a propositional claim or theological virtue but feels it and models it so as to be learned and imitated by others in his communities.

This shared emotion of joy shapes Paul's identity in Christ and his communities' identity. An important part of any group's social identity is their emotions, their feelings toward themselves and toward outsiders. In joy, Paul suggests himself as their emotional exemplar and that they imitate him (3:17) in their emotional lives, no less than their ethical lives. They are to match his own joy in themselves, even in the face of distress and toil and pain.[52] Such joy is distinctive in "its intersubjectivity: each of the remaining eleven occurrences [after 1:18, 3:1, and 4:4] pertain to emotions that arise within a web of mutual care, concern, and affection comprising Paul, Timothy, Epaphroditus, and his Philippian addressees."[53] This communal, mimetic joy is more command than eschatological hope: "But even if I am being poured out as the libation over the sacrifice and the offering of your faith, I am glad and rejoice with all of you—and in the same way you also must be glad and rejoice with me" (2:17–18).

Is That What Makes Them Have a History)? A Bordieuian Approach to Understanding Emotion," *History and Theory* 51 (2012): 193–220.

48. E.g., Phil 1:18; 2:17–19, 29; 3:1, 17; 4:1, 10; Gal 4:27; 5:22; 1 Thess 1:6; 2:19; 2 Cor 1:24; 7:13, 15; 9:1; Rom 12:12; 15; 15:10, 13; 16:19.

49. Noted by Just, https://catholic-resources.org/Bible/Joy-Rejoice.htm, specifically observing that the language of joy is absent from the letter to the Ephesians. Colossians is an exception.

50. Elliott, *Faithful Feelings*, 179; Schellenberg also notes the tendency of New Testament scholars to claim that "Paul's joy was not really an emotion at all" (*Abject Joy*, 154).

51. Elliott exposes some of these negative attitudes toward emotion in New Testament studies, in *Faithful Feelings*, 178–81.

52. Elliott, *Faithful Feelings*, 172–74.

53. Schellenberg, *Abject Joy*, 155; also Jew, *Paul's Emotional Regime*, 95–97.

Paul underscores this unity on a psychological level as well, as "he urges his addressees to amplify his joy by nourishing a shared orientation (τὸ αὐτὸ φρωνῆτε [*to auto phrōnēte*])—intersubjectivity encompassing heart, soul, and mind (τὴν αὐτὴν ἀγάπην ἔχοντες, σύμψυχοι, τὸ ἓν φρονοῦντες [*tēn autēn agapēn echontes, sympsychoi, to hen phronountes*])."[54] It is not an expectation like virginity (which may be preferable but not necessary 1 Cor 7:25–39.) or dietary rules (1 Cor 8:1–13). To rejoice and be glad—always—is a clear command, of a "shared joy" and a "shared possession, a product of reciprocal goodwill."[55] We should therefore not minimize Paul's radical call to emotional transformation. It "is real joy—a felt emotion, not a theological corollary."[56] But it is further not the joy of a self-help manual, that God wants the Philippians to be happy. Paul's exuberant language of joy, though in the affliction of imprisonment, expresses an embodied and psychic experience, which he models for his companions through his own bodily feelings and sufferings, sent through letters across the waves, encouraging them to be affected by his joy, as he himself is affected by the joy that he predicts they might also feel.[57] Joy is a nonnegotiable feature of belonging to Christ, an emotional identity—and necessarily a embodied experience—that takes on further significance given Paul's general conceit that the church is a very real body shared communally and with Christ.[58]

The value—and command—of feeling joy as a distinctively Christian emotion is shared by the first letter attributed to Peter, probably written in the generation after Paul, which significantly preserves the first use of the word "Christian" as a self-designation (4:16).[59] First Peter also first reflects the influential concept that Christians form the true chosen people or "race" (*genos*, 2:9) described in the Jewish Scriptures.[60] Much like Paul, Peter connects

54. Schellenberg, *Abject Joy*, 165.

55. Quotations from Schellenberg, *Abject Joy*, 156. The connection of suffering with the command to joy is drawn by L. Gregory Bloomquist, "Subverted by Joy: Suffering and Joy in Paul's Letter to the Philippians," *Interpretation* 61 (2007): 270–82.

56. Schellenberg, *Abject Joy*, 171.

57. Schellenberg, *Abject Joy*, 171; also Jew, *Paul's Emotional Regime*, 88–89.

58. A point underscored for both Luke and Paul in Barton, "Spirituality and the Emotions," 189. Emotional language should be considered no less embodied than Paul's concerns about *porneia* or food; cf. Dale Martin, *The Corinthian Body* (New Haven: Yale University Press, 1995).

59. See the collected studies of David G. Horrell, *Becoming Christian: Essays on 1 Peter and the Making of Christian Identity*, LNTS 394 (London: Bloomsbury T&T Clark, 2013). Also cf. Kotrosits, *Rethinking*, who is unimpressed by 1 Peter's use of *christianos* as a useful datum for early "Christian" identity, "since the only time the word 'Christian' is used it is a tiny and circumstantial notation" (64).

60. E.g., Denise Buell, *Why This New Race: Ethnic Reasoning in Early Christianity* (New York: Columbia University Press, 2005); Horrell, *Becoming Christian*.

the identity of the *christianos* with collective and individual emotional experience of suffering (or being affected or influenced by passion, *paschetō*, 4:15) and managing emotion, here not to feel shame but more broadly to feel joy in the face of suffering.[61]

The community's expectation of suffering is at the heart of this short letter. It is commonly surmised that the letter was written to the communities of Asia Minor, which (the likely pseudonymous) Peter mentions at the letter's opening, so these Christians possibly face similar sorts of persecutions and pressures to those that inspired John's Apocalypse.[62] As mentioned already, these sufferings are among the experiences that lend the audience some of their sense of identity as Christians: They suffer in a particular way, and this way of suffering binds them together and differentiates them from others. Perhaps foremost, Peter assures his audience that their sufferings are analogous to sufferings of Christ, which themselves are at the core of the prophecies about him and about salvation (1:10–11). Christ suffered for them, as they are now to suffer in imitating him (2:21), suffering for the benefit of others (3:17–18), and by doing so to share in Christ's sufferings (4:13). The mimetic quality and function of suffering encourages Christians to identify themselves with Christ. The terms behind the common English translations of "sufferings" give us some sense how. Peter's language of *paschō*, *pathēmata*, and *lypēthentes* just as well addresses emotional pains and passions as it does bodily afflictions, although there is no need to draw a strict division between bodily and emotional experience of pains or pleasures, whether in the context either of contemporary neuroscience or of ancient psychology.[63] The sufferings of this community participate as much in Jesus's grief and desolation as the scourge on his back or the nails in his limbs.

Christ's *pathēmata* form the foundation for the audience's identity both with Christ and community and, counterintuitively, their joy. In all such sufferings, they suffer like Christ (2:19–21; 3:17–18), a model for communal norms and prototypical attitudes and behaviors.[64] To follow the model of this exemplar,

61. First Peter's understanding of joy is most fully analyzed in Hockey, *Role of Emotion*, 105–75.

62. Discussed by Paul J. Achtemeier, "The First Letter of Peter," in *Harper Collins Study Bible* (San Francisco: HarperSanFrancisco, 2006), 2060–61.

63. E.g., 1 Pet 2:21; 1:11; 4:13; 1:6. The overlap between emotional and bodily pain is discussed in Andrew Crislip, "Pain, Emotion, and Identity in Early Christianity," *Journal of Early Christian History* 12 (2022): 27–51.

64. Philip F. Esler, "An Outline of Social Identity Theory," in *T&T Clark Handbook to Social Identity in the New Testament*, ed. J. Brian Tucker and Coleman A. Baker (London: Bloomsbury, 2014), 32–34.

Christians must prepare mentally, gird the loins of their minds (*dianoias*, 1:13), transform their emotions, in which *chara* forms the center of the emotional constellation. They should not fear like outsiders (literally, "Do not fear their fear," 3:14). Rather, in words that recall the beatitudes, they are fortunate (or blessed, *makarioi*) should they suffer righteously (3:14; 4:14). They should rejoice in sharing Christ's sufferings (4:13) and exult (*agalliōmenoi*) while being distressed or grieving (*lypēthentes*). Peter's admonitions share with the Pauline tradition the call to transform their mutually experienced sufferings into joy, identifying mentally and bodily with Christ's sufferings, as the Paul of Colossians proclaims, "I am now rejoicing in my sufferings (*tois pathēmasin*) for your sake, and in my flesh I am completing what is lacking in Christ's afflictions for the sake of his body, that is, the church" (Col 1:24). Their experience of sufferings or passions, and the deliberate transformation of them into joy and exultation does not just conform them in identity with Christ. It also forms the foundation for a transformation of shared emotional experience.[65] For Peter, much as Paul claims, followers of Christ share a unified mind or mental outlook; they are of a single, humble mind, tender-hearted and loving; they feel or suffer together (*sympatheis*) even at a distance (3:8). Across the world, the same sorts of sufferings and passions (*ta auta tōn pathēmatōn*) are visited upon the brethren (5:9). They do not just suffer together. They feel the same emotion together, a single joyous mind, in the face of suffering and distress.[66]

Christian Joy and Philosophical Joy: Some Observations

Paul's insistence that his flock "rejoice always" recalls the divergent ways that contemporary moral philosophers conceived of the passions, especially the positive or pleasurable emotions. Paul, like those who followed him in the Christian tradition, would find the terminology used by Peripatetic and Epicurean philosophy uncongenial; Aristotle's emphasis on *eudaimonia* as the goal of existence clashed with Christian understanding of demons (*daimōn*/*daimonion*) as unremittingly evil, while the Epicurean conception of joy as maximized pleasure (*hēdonē*) would have struck Christians as, well, hedonistic. Christians further did not adopt the Epicurean language of *ataraxia* ("being undisturbed") when describing ideal Christian emotions, although calmness, rest, and freedom from anxiety were all emotional states that Christians found desirable.

65. Hockey, *Role of Emotion*, 142–76.

66. More fully elaborated in Hockey, *Role of Emotion*, 105–75.

Several general features of the Stoic approach to emotions provide helpful comparisons with both modern approaches to emotion and some early Christian approaches. The materialist Stoics understood emotions as embodied and physiological processes. Passions had two parts, comparable to (though not the same as) modern cognitive and constructive approaches to emotion. The first is a bodily reaction, a feeling, pre-passion (*propatheia*), or movement, in response to some perception.[67] This nonrational pre-passion, such as the sudden startle at a surprising snake-like form, is similar to the contemporary concept of affect, that universal matrix of valence (attraction or aversion) and intensity.

The passions proper, for Stoics, are a second movement of the psyche by which one appraises, as cognition, the stimulus and the embodied first movement and the external stimulus that provoked it.[68] Thus, emotions have the potential to be practical or rational, though are quite often irrational and nonpractical. This understanding of emotions as meaning-making concepts has commonalities with the theory of psychological construction discussed in the introduction. An important distinction is that in emotional construction emotions are not strictly cognitive but also predictive; they do not merely interpret external reality but create it, along with all other activities of our predictive brains.

The cognitive and appraisal aspects lead to a third characteristic of Stoicism and emotion—the elaboration of emotional classification. While other philosophers, such as Aristotle, also identified and defined the emotions, Stoics developed a distinctive taxonomy of the passions, with four cardinal passions or emotions: fear, distress, desire, and pleasure. Fear and distress apprehend something harmful or negative in the future or present, respectively; desire and pleasure apprehend something beneficial or positive, again either in the future or present.[69] Each of these generic passions included varied lists of more granular passions.[70] Fear, for example, comprises reluctance, shame, superstition, and panic, to mention a few passions.[71] All are vices and can be eliminated from the properly trained person through a sort of cognitive therapy, as the individual comes to recognize that their fear or anxiety, envy or anger are irrational, based on faulty presumptions of harm or value. In the end, for the Stoic, the only thing of value is to live virtuously. Thus, to feel fear of death, hope for a

67. Graver, *Stoicism and Emotion*, 85–99; Ramelli and Konstan, "Use of XAPA," 190.

68. A useful summary aimed at New Testament study is in Hockey, *Role of Emotion*, 55–85, which covers Stoic ethics with far more detail and nuance than I can here.

69. Graver, *Stoicism and Emotion*, 53–55.

70. Graver, *Stoicism and Emotion*, 55–59.

71. Graver, *Stoicism and Emotion*, 56.

promotion, jealousy over one's beloved, or anger or shame at a public slight are all irrational, since none of these externalities truly delivers harm or benefit. They are indifferent to the virtuous life of the philosopher. But the Stoic is not without emotion, at least not entirely. The Stoics posited three "good emotions" (*eupatheiai*) as counterparts to the four *pathē* that should be eliminated. Caution replaces fear, will replaces desire, and joy (*chara*) replaces pleasure. At the end of one's cognitive training, the Stoic sage could hope to attain a state of *apatheia*, not apathy but a freedom from the irrational emotions, though still with access to the good emotions of joy, will, and caution.[72]

Amid all the complications and trajectories of Stoic philosophy, often reconstructed from fragments and later testimonies into a consensus account by modern interpreters, the apostle does not advocate a clear Stoic approach to emotions.[73] Paul does not use the technical terminology of Stoics or reflect their emphasis on the bipartite structure of feeling and cognition or their exacting emotional taxonomy. Paul, furthermore, does not advocate a freedom from negative emotion (*apatheia*) as a goal for his community, especially clear in Paul's treatment of the passion of *lypē* (sadness, grief, distress, pain), which will be covered in the next chapter.

But for all their differences, Paul still swims in the same waters as the Stoics, especially in his admonition to feel joy. To many in the ancient world the general desirability of joy rather than emotional pain would seem intuitive and uncontroversial. Paul's insistence that Christians feel joy even in the midst of suffering might easily evoke Stoic parallels. Seneca, the eclectic Stoic contemporary to Paul, conceives of joy (*gaudium*) "as a steady state" rather than an event, available for the sage to experience continually.[74] Joy was crucial for Stoics, and more broadly Stoics asserted that the Stoic sage should normally and consistently feel joy.[75]

Paul advocates a similar unceasing joy. He feels it, even in the midst of suffering imprisonment, along with its certain discomfort and lack, and probably also physical pain and anticipation of death.[76] And he expects and repeatedly

72. E.g., Graver, *Stoicism and Emotion*, 210–11, reflecting on the discussions throughout the book.

73. Margaret Graver, "Anatomies of Joy: Seneca and the *Gaudium* Tradition," in *Hope, Joy, and Affection in the Classical Tradition*, ed. Ruth R. Caston and Robert A. Kaster (Oxford: Oxford University Press, 2016), 123–24.

74. Graver, "Anatomies of Joy," 131.

75. Graver, *Stoicism and Emotion*, 51.

76. The emotional pains of imprisonment, ancient and modern, are discussed in Schellenberg, *Abject Joy*; also Barton, "Spirituality and the Emotions," 184.

urges his community that they too should feel joy without ceasing. Ancient Stoics were not necessarily the cold individualists reflected in contemporary popularizations. They recognized the goods of sociality, friendship, and love in their ethic, surely as part of their belief that they participated in a benign and providential nature.[77] Yet, Paul more explicitly underscores the necessity of a collective experience of the good emotions, an experience which is distinctively their own. In his letter to the Philippians, most clearly, joy is felt by the individual but is mutually transmitted within the community, and even across distances, bodily by emissaries and virtually through letters, between Ephesus and Philippi. Paul rejoices in them, they rejoice in him and in each other, and, significantly, they share in the joy of Christ. In joining this new movement, they have moved from their old social location and emotional reality to a new shared sociality and emotionality, feeling together and with the Christ who unites them. Paul's insistence that they share a soul and mind, and share that with Christ, is a motif that his letter shares with the Greco-Roman genre of friendship letters, which also shares much with common Stoicism, though Paul's assertions of shared mind and body and frequent repetitions of joy language go beyond the bounds of most letters of the time.[78]

Johannine Joy

Christians at the turn of the second century through the rise of Constantine privileged joy as a Christian emotion, achievable as both an ideal and steady state, even in the face of the harshest of afflictions. Alongside Paul's call to unceasing joy, John's Gospel provided an early model or emotional script for a community bound by unceasing joy.[79]

77. Graver, *Stoicism and Emotion*, 173–90.

78. See Stanley K. Stowers, *Letter Writing in Greco-Roman Antiquity* (Louisville: Westminster John Knox, 1986). I have compared Stowers's collection of letters, and Paul's use of joy and *homonoia* language far outstrips the contemporary pagan letters. The one letter that seems at least broadly comparable to Paul's is a late fourth-century letter of the emperor Julian (ruled 360–363), a former Christian, turned apostate and persecutor. It seems likely that Julian is drawing on what he would see as excessive Christian emotionality in his letter, which is a parody of the genre.

79. Petra von Gemünden, *Affekt und Glaube: Studien zur Historischen Psychologie des Frühjudentums und Urchristentums*, NTOA/SUNT 73 (Göttingen: Vandenhoeck & Ruprecht, 2009), 279–308, which focuses on identity and hostile emotions in John; Potkay, *Story of Joy*, 38–42; George L. Parsenios, *Departure and Consolation: The Johannine Farewell Discourses in the Light of Greco-Roman Literature*, NovTSup 117 (Leiden: Brill, 2005); Gert J. C. Jordaan, "The Joy of Seeing Christ: A Thematic Study of Joy in the Gospel of John," *In die*

Jesus's farewell discourse begins with a command to avoid emotional disturbance: Let your heart not be troubled (*mē tarassesthō*, 14:1), which he later repeats, adding that his disciples should not let their hearts feel afraid (14:27). Jesus's consoling words in these three chapters reflect themes in Greek and Roman consolation literature, in which the movement from sadness to a reasonable emotion of joy commonly features.[80] The troubling issue at hand is Jesus's imminent departure, a journey on which the disciples can neither accompany him nor, as Thomas complains, know where he is going (14:5). After Jesus consoles them, he insists that their love for him will enable them to keep his commandments and words, while he and his Father will dwell with them. Most immediately, love leads to the disciples' joy (*chara*): "If you loved me, you would rejoice that I am going to the Father" (14:28), which functions performatively as a command. Anyone who truly loves Jesus (and what reader of John would not?) will feel joy. Here the reason for joy is limited: They should rejoice because they know Jesus is headed for a better place. But as Jesus's farewell consolation continues the scope and meaning of his followers' joy expands and is interwoven with the mutual love of the Father for Jesus and of Jesus for the disciples, a binding love that culminates in the disciples' emotional practice (by keeping the commandments) and emotional unity in a renewed and fulfilled experience of joy: "I have said these things to you so that my joy may be in you, and that your joy may be complete" (15:11).

The emotional unity of the disciples with Jesus and the Father sets them off against outsiders ("the world," 15:18), who hate them. This hate forms a sharp boundary between their enemies and the friends and disciples of Jesus, as the former expel them from the synagogues because they lack the knowledge of the Father and Jesus that his followers have (16:2–3).[81]

Jesus then predicts the disciples' imminent joy. Now, because he has said that he is going away, "sorrow has filled your hearts." But soon the Paraclete will clarify all things, and their mourning and weeping—most proximally at Jesus's crucifixion—will prove temporary, to be replaced by a joy that is anything but.[82] While the world rejoices, they will weep, "but your sadness will turn into joy" (16:20). John draws on imagery of Eve, cursed with sadness and pain (*lypē*) in childbearing (Gen 3:16 LXX), a sadness and affliction turned into joy (*chara*) and forgotten with the birth of a child (John 16:21). The disciples' temporary

Skriflig 49(2), Art. 1968; Michaelsami Arockiam, *The Concept of Joy in the Johannine Literature* (Delhi: ISPCK, 2002).

80. Parsenios, *Departure and Consolation*, 95–97.

81. See discussion in Arockiam, *Concept of Joy*, 178–215.

82. The language of mourning here typifies that of funereal grieving, pointing to the imminent death of Jesus, as suggested by Jordaan, "Joy of Seeing Christ," 6.

sadness will turn into joy in the new world to come with resurrection and spiritual rebirth, and this joy will be everlasting: "So you have sadness now, but I will see you again, and your hearts will rejoice, and no one will take your joy from you," a joy which, again, will "be complete" if they only ask (16:22, 24).[83] This joy, inextricable from a mutually interpenetrating love, transcends ordinary joy—it is "made complete" in John's distinctive language—and draws the disciples, Jesus, the Father, and the Paraclete together as community, set against "the world" and its emotions (e.g., 17:13–14, 21–22).[84]

While Paul uses the language of unceasing joy and John of a joy made complete, they presume that joy is not merely a feeling that the individual should experience, as Seneca might advise a correspondent, but that joy will be shared by the community as whole.[85] Furthermore, like Paul, John's Jesus preaches joy as a lasting feeling, reconceptualizing or incorporating suffering and loss. It marks a boundary crossing, from old to new, from outsider to insider. To abandon the joy of the Christian is something akin to becoming unbaptized for Paul or unborn again in the case of John. No less than naming, ritual, clothing, and shared stories and myth, emotion forms a type of practice that is no less important for establishing identity and maintaining boundaries for a group.[86]

Joy in the Second Century and Beyond

By the mid- to late second century, homilists and moralists were building on these models for emotional community and expression. The *Gospel of Truth*

83. Arockiam, *Concept of Joy*, 178–93.

84. Potkay, *Story of Joy*, 42, describes this as "a nexus between love, joy, and exclusivity." Arockiam, *Concept of Joy*, 194–235, theorizes different types of joy (joy and joy made complete), which coexist in some tension in John in various parts of its redaction.

85. Parsenios, *Departure and Consolation*, 90–94, cites relevant Roman consolation literature.

86. How this Johannine emotionality compares to philosophical schools is a larger question. Cf. the contrasting perspectives of Gitte Buch-Hansen, "The Emotional Jesus: Anti-Stoicism in the Fourth Gospel?," in *Stoicism in Early Christianity*, ed. Tuomas Rasimus, Troels Engberg-Pedersen, and Ismo Dunderberg (Grand Rapids: Baker Academic, 2010), 93–114; and Harold W. Attridge, "An 'Emotional' Jesus and Stoic Tradition," in Rasimus et al., *Stoicism in Early Christianity*, 77–92. Attridge finds any Stoic connection ambiguous; at most "the resemblance remains formal" (89). Similarly the Jewish biblical context for John is too great a subject to address here. See, for example, Potkay, *Story of Joy*, 34–36; and Marianne Meye Thompson, "Reflections on Joy in the Bible," in *Joy and Human Flourishing: Essays on Theology, Culture, and the Good Life*, ed. Miroslav Volf and Justin E. Crisp (Minneapolis: Fortress, 2015), 17–39.

and 2 Clement, for example, vividly show communities at worship, encouraged by skilled preachers to reflect on and narrate their individual and collective journeys from states of confusion, gloom, and despair to a state of joy and love they share with one another and with all of heaven. They show how seriously and normatively later generations of Christians took the communal emotional experiences modeled through Paul, John, and 1 Peter.

This emphasis on joy as a normative and communal feeling is seen beyond the homilies. *The Shepherd of Hermas*, for example, has a lot to say about how his fellow Christians are to live the good life, through enacting an emotional regimen of constant joy (*chara*) and cheerfulness (*hilarotēs*), while wholly extirpating sadness or grief (*lypē*) as toxic to the Christian and the community. Although little read today, it would be among the most popular early Christian texts through late antiquity and was included in a couple of the early deluxe biblical manuscripts. Scholars have long tried to determine the historical identity of the author or authors and its redaction history, if any.[87] Here I work with the single-author hypothesis or something close to it, given that the "thematic unity of the book in spite of some divergences indicates a guiding hand throughout."[88] The author may have lived in Rome in the 140s–160s (a date, like most, still debated) and describes himself in terms characteristic of a freed slave; according to some traditions, he may have been the brother of a bishop of Rome, Pius.[89] But beyond his lengthy collection of visions (the *Shepherd* is by far the longest of the so-called Apostolic Fathers), much else is hard to pin down.

His relationship to other early Christian literature is also hard to pin down. Though writing in Rome a solid century after Paul and a couple generations after the evangelists, he does not cite any New Testament literature, nor does he cite anything from the Old Testament. The only source he explicitly cites is the now lost Book of Eldad and Modad.[90] But he shares themes with other first- and second-century sources, including Hellenistic Jewish and Greco-Roman moral teachings, as well as with James and the Didache, such as Hermas's discussion of the "two ways" tradition of ethical instruction and a special interest in condemning doubt.[91] But all in all, while there are echoes and allusions to

87. Manuscripts, issues of authorship, and reception are covered in Carolyn Osiek, *The Shepherd of Hermas*, Hermeneia (Minneapolis: Fortress, 1999), 1–28, esp. 8–10 on the issues of authorship.

88. Osiek, *Shepherd of Hermas*, 10.

89. Osiek, *Shepherd of Hermas*, 18–23, who is open to the possibility of an earlier date as well.

90. Osiek, *Shepherd of Hermas*, 24, 30–31.

91. Osiek, *Shepherd of Hermas*, 24–25.

sources familiar from the early empire (including Paul), Hermas's visions are a world unto themselves.

Hermas addresses passions and aberrant thoughts in various ways throughout this sprawling collection. Through his, at times contentious, interactions with a cast of heavenly figures, who frequently chide him for his failures and ignorance, he reflects on the doubt, hesitancy, or "doubled-souledness" (*dipsychia*) that afflicts members of his community, an understandable difficulty for newly converted people to a marginalized faith.[92] He also centers repentance or conversion (*metanoia*) as what some have seen as the major theme of the work. For Hermas *metanoia* does not entail an event—and certainly not a rite—but a lifelong process of self-fashioning.[93] The underlying meaning of the word points to its cognitive foundation, a change of mind, and Hermas writes of the Christian way as a conversion of the emotions, as others before him had. The Stoics understood conversion or repentance as emotional; *metanoia* was counted among the passions, located under the generic heading of *lypē* or distress, pain felt at the recognition of one's own fault. For a more traditional Stoic this would, like all species of distress, ill befit the sage. But later philosophers, such as Philo, influentially for Christians, recognized the positive effects of *metanoia* in moral reformation. This is the case for Hermas, who, though he will hold no regard for the passion of *lypē* itself, sees *metanoia* as an ongoing cognitive or emotional orientation for the Christian.[94]

Hermas offers guidance on the emotional expectations for Christians in his community, with special attention to the desirable feeling of cheerfulness (*hilarotēs*)—and occasionally to joy (*chara*)—and the spirits or desires of quickness to anger (*oxycholia*) and sadness (*lypē*).[95] Hermas does not use the language of passions but envisions the Christian surrounded by spirits (*pneumata*) both good and evil, which anticipates later Christian reflection on emotions as human psychic responses to the external goading of demons, evil thoughts, or spirits.

Fortunately for Hermas, through the moral and sentimental education provided by his heavenly interlocutors he has the potential to rid himself of these evil spirits through the process of lifelong change of mind (*metanoia*) and to inhabit a more ideal Christian subjectivity, which itself mani-

92. Osiek, *Shepherd of Hermas*, 30–31; Andrew Crislip, "*The Shepherd of Hermas* and Early Christian Emotional Formation," StPatr 83 (2017): 238–39.

93. Crislip, "Shepherd of Hermas," 235; Osiek, *Shepherd of Hermas*, 28–30.

94. Crislip, "Shepherd of Hermas," 236–37, with further bibliography.

95. For *oxycholia*, see Herm. Mand. 5.2 (34), which connects it with subsequent feelings of bitterness, anger, and wrath.

fests the indwelling of another spirit, the Holy Spirit. To have the Holy Spirit within links the Christian experientially with God through good feelings.[96] The *Shepherd* codes this model Christian self as youthful, beautiful, cheerful, and masculine, as the lady church urges a weepy and forlorn Hermas, "Be a man, Hermas."[97] Whatever Hermas calls these motions in the soul—spirits, passions, emotions, thoughts—his collection of visions and commandments is an important witness to early Christian emotions in that it represents an attempt to identify and transform the emotional lives of its readers, to the formation of an emotional community. Though not exactly the sort of self-help guide useful for historians of late modern emotions, this kind of handbook of emotional behavior provides evidence for changes in the way people spoke about emotion and the rules individuals were encouraged or expected to follow in displaying emotions. From the cognitive perspective of psychological construction, such naming and regulating of feelings would necessarily have affected the embodied experience of emotion, as shared and modeled within a community of believers.

Much like the *Gospel of Truth* and 2 Clement, the *Shepherd* presents the Christian way—the life of *metanoia*—as a journey from painful to pleasant emotion, from sadness and confusion to joy and hope. Hermas's interactions with his heavenly companions expand on this duality of sadness and joy and ground them further in the contexts of bodily experience and social frisson, the latter including conflicts between richer and poorer members and the tensions of making a living versus Christian quietism.[98] While it occasionally addresses the emotion of joy (*chara*), the *Shepherd* overwhelmingly privileges cheerfulness (*hilarotēs*) as a distinctive feature of Hermas's emotional lexicon. The word is rare in the New Testament (only in 2 Cor 9:7 and Rom 12:8),

96. Jonathan E. Soyars, *The Shepherd of Hermas and the Pauline Legacy*, NovTSup 176 (Leiden: Brill, 2019), 115–27; Osiek, *Shepherd of Hermas*, 33.

97. Herm. Vis. 1.4 (4). The intersection of the process of conversion and standards of manliness is discussed by B. Diane Lipsett, *Desiring Conversion: Hermas, Thecla, Asenath* (New York: Oxford University Press, 2011), 19–53; and Steve Young, "Being a Man: The Pursuit of Manliness in The Shepherd of Hermas," *JECS* 2 (1994): 237–55. Second-century and later Christian sources offered masculine models for women as well, as seen in Gos. Thom. 114, the Acts of Paul and Thecla, and the *Life of Syncletica*, to take a few examples.

98. Recently anatomized by Angela Kim Harkins, *An Embodied Reading of the Shepherd of Hermas: The Book of Visions and Its Role in Moral Formation* (Sheffield: Equinox, 2023); Mark Grundeken, *Community Building in the Shepherd of Hermas: A Critical Study of Some Key Aspects*, VCSup 131 (Leiden: Brill, 2015); Carol Osiek, *Rich and Poor in the Shepherd of Hermas: An Exegetical-Social Investigation*, CBQMS 15 (Washington, DC: Catholic University of America Press, 1983).

and unique to Hermas among the Apostolic Fathers.[99] Perhaps as the Greek Bible refers frequently to God's face (*prosōpon*) as cheerful, Hermas describes God's heavenly intermediaries as cheerful—the heavenly Rhoda, the elderly woman, the angel, and the shepherd.[100] The emissaries model this good cheer for Hermas and his fellow Christians to imitate, and he is on occasion able to feel it in his soul.[101]

Hermas's commendations of Christians as members of a community bound by shared joy or cheerfulness are reflected in other Christian sources from the second and third centuries. Martyr literature shows a similar call to express and feel joy. The martyr texts do not likely preserve eyewitness accounts of the deaths of Christian witnesses nor reliably represent the emotions experienced by the martyrs themselves. Rather, like the homilies, they reflect the communal life of the church, in worship, reading, and reflection. The martyrologies were pedagogical; they taught their readers how to be Christians, how to prepare for martyrdom, and how to feel. As such, the martyr texts offer emotional guidance in narrating the sufferings and deaths of moral exemplars.

In the influential *Martyrdom of Polycarp*, the second-century bishop of Smyrna goes to his execution steeled by a heavenly voice, who advises him, as Hermas was told, "Be strong . . . and be a man."[102] He displays his manliness in his speech, daring the proconsul to burn him alive, as far better than the fires coming for the impious: "As he was saying these things and much else, he was filled with courage and joy."[103] The *Martyrdom* makes clear the imitative role of the hero, modeling emotions for those who read aloud his exploits and could imagine themselves in his place, including for Polycarp's own followers, who speak in the first person. After gathering Polycarp's burned bones and burying them, they say, "The Lord will allow us to gather in that place with as much exultation and joy as possible and to celebrate the birthday of his martyrdom,

99. Rudolf Bultmann, s.v., *TDNT* 3:299.

100. E.g., Herm. Vis. 1.1 (1); 1.4 (4); 3.10 (18); Herm. Sim. 8.1 (67); 9.9 (86). The Lord, rather, feels joy (*echarē*), Herm. Vis. 3.13 (21).

101. E.g., Herm. Vis. 4.2 (23); Herm. Sim. 9.10 (87). For more details, see Crislip, "Shepherd of Hermas."

102. *Mart. Pol.* 9.1, as translated in Éric Rebillard, *Greek and Latin Narratives About the Ancient Martyrs* (Oxford: Oxford University Press, 2017).

103. *Mart. Pol.* 12.1 (Rebillard). He was further not "troubled" (*tarachthenta*); discussed by Stephanie L. Cobb, *Dying to Be Men: Gender and Language in Early Christian Martyr Texts* (New York: Columbia University Press, 2008), 82–84. The Stoic Chrysippus identified the paired emotions of *chara* and *tharsos* (courage) as evidence "that the mind was located in the chest." Ramelli and Konstan, "Use of XAPA," 189. One can feel and observe it in one's bodily affect and comportment.

both for the memory of the those who have contended and for the training and preparation of those to come."[104] They share this joy and prepare themselves mentally and emotionally through ritual celebration and reading, which they share with the martyr himself, who now wears the "crown of immortality, rejoicing (*agalliōmenos*) with the apostles and all the just."[105]

Polycarp has good company in modeling joy for early Christian readers. A *Martyrdom of Pionius the Presbyter and His Companions* shows the practices and embodiment of joy in several martyrs, whose deaths in the persecution of Decius (250–251) are narrated in a late antique martyrology.[106] The exemplar of Polycarp looms over the narrative, set on the martyr's "birthday" on which his followers are expected to show special joy. After celebrating the martyr's feast, the Christians are harangued by the city temple warden, who demands they go to the agora to make a sacrifice as required by the emperor's decree. In the agora, Pionius speaks "with a radiant face," embodying joy, as he launches into Christian apologia.[107] Later his face is "fiery," while it was once pale.[108] This emotion can be read on the face and in the body. When Pionius tells the crowd that he wishes he could convert them, they laugh at him, which is then countered by his companion Sabina, who laughs back. While they laughed from contempt, she laughs from joy: "And as Sabina was smiling, the *neokoros* (warden) and the men with him said: 'You laugh?' And she said: 'If God wills it, yes. For we are Christians, and whosoever trusts in Christ unreservedly will laugh in joy forever.'"[109] Pionius is not without sadness and pain. He grieves in shared emotion with Christians who visit him in prison; they weep for him and for their own lapses, having succumbed to force and sacrificed to the emperor. But Pionius frames this pain (*ōdinō*) as of childbirth, for they had not yet been born as Christians.[110] Perhaps here is a memory of Jesus's farewell discourse, as he describes his disciples' pain (*lypē*) as labor pangs, soon to be replaced by joy (John 16:20). Pionius's pain soon would be. When he goes to his victory in the arena, "He observed that his own body was sound and in good shape" and "he was filled with a great joy."[111] This joy and well-being—despite being

104. *Mart. Pol.* 18.3 (Rebillard).

105. *Mart. Pol.* 18.3 (Rebillard, slightly altered).

106. Rebillard, *Greek and Latin Narratives*, 47–49, on the dating of the person and the text.

107. *Mart. Pion.* 4.1 (Rebillard).

108. *Mart. Pion.* 10.1 (Rebillard).

109. *Mart. Pion.* 7.5 (Rebillard).

110. *Mart. Pion.* 12.1–4.

111. *Mart. Pion.* 21.2 (Rebillard). The nails do not lessen his bodily integrity. When his torturers offer to remove them for his confession, he says, "Indeed, I felt that they are in place" (21.4).

pierced and burned—culminates in a good death: "As if sighing he breathed his last peacefully and without toil."[112]

The martyrdoms of Polycarp and Pionius are just two among many such examples, which narrate the martyrs' end in emotional terms, with the mastery (or even absence) of emotional and somatic pain and a holistic experience of joy. Such literature entertained and edified through liturgical practice, offering preparation for Christian spiritual advancement and for enduring persecution. It also had didactic or psychagogic effects similar to the homilies or Hermas's visions, encouraging shared emotional response through their collective reading and performance.[113] The message is clear: A Christian is to express and feel joy and to eschew sadness or distress, to enact the hope promised by the Gospels in the here and now.

Hewing more closely to the philosophical correction of the passions, Valentinian literature shows another way of conceiving Christian well-being as found in a cure (*iasis*) or conversion (*epistrophē*) of the emotions. Working in the tradition of the more homiletic *Gospel of Truth*, such Valentinian thinkers were among the earliest Christian commentators on the Gospels and among the earliest to attempt a systematic theology, a holistic Christian theory of God, creation, incarnation, salvation, eschatology, and so on.[114] Their heresiological critics describe a Valentinian myth of origins in explicitly emotional terms, as Christ cures the fallen aeon Sophia's passions (distress, fear, perplexity, and ignorance, which then are transformed into the basic matter or our world). "Freed from passion, Wisdom (Sophia) now experiences joy (*chara*)," while the heavenly fullness is reestablished at rest and joyful.[115] Other Valentinian literature preserves similar teaching.[116] Significantly, these Valentinian thinkers center the emotions, and more specifically the "therapy of emotions," a process of curing or transforming emotions, which parallels aspects of Hellenistic

112. *Mart. Pion.* 21.9 (Rebillard).

113. See a fuller discussion in Cobb, *Dying to Be Men.*

114. Surveyed in Layton with Brakke, *Gnostic Scriptures*, 331–39; and Ismo Dunderberg, "The School of Valentinus," in *A Companion to Second-Century Christian 'Heretics,'* ed. Antti Marjanen and Petri Luomanen, VCSup 76 (Leiden: Brill, 2005), 64–99.

115. Quote from Ismo Dunderberg, *Beyond Gnosticism: Myth, Lifestyle, and Society in the School of Valentinus* (New York: Columbia University Press, 2008), 102, the full narrative at 98–102. Reported in Irenaeus of Lyon, *Haer.* 1.2.1–1.2.6; Layton with Brakke, *Gnostic Scriptures*, 350–52. I return to this myth in more detail in chapter 3.

116. Dunderberg, *Beyond Gnosticism*, 101–7; see Einar Thomassen, *The Spiritual Seed: The Church of the 'Valentinians,'* NHMS 60 (Leiden: Brill, 2006). Not unexpectedly, the formation and interaction of the trajectories of Valentinian thought are complex and disputed.

philosophy along with earlier Christian voices from Paul on.[117] Distinctively the Valentinians approach the healing of emotions through myth and ritual. Through the intercession of "Christ as healer of the soul," Christians participate in the primordial healing of Wisdom's emotions through the rituals of baptism, the bridal chamber, and redemption (*apolytrōsis*), rites still obscure from our ancient sources.[118]

The Christian philosopher Clement of Alexandria (ca. 150–ca. 215) preserved extensive quotations from a Valentinian teacher named Theodotus, of whom he was quite critical, although Clement also understood Christianity as guiding its members from gloom to joy.[119] Theodotus's fragments reflect this Valentinian cure of the emotions played out in myth and ritual, reflecting on the passionate fall and healing of Wisdom. Theodotus himself, Clement claims, taught that the Father and the Word suffered along with the aeons (in the heavenly realm), a suffering that Clement understands in the language of passions—having compassion (*sympatheia*) is to experience the passion (*pathos*) of another.[120] This co-suffering of the Godhead and the entirety had a pedagogical goal, "for the correction (*diorthōsis*) of the one who experienced passion" (that is, Sophia), and "even through the passion of the twelfth aeon the entireties were educated (*paideuthenta*)."[121] This correction and education leads to a purification of passions, and later emissions of angelic elements and seeds "were not produced as passions," and the "human being . . . of the superior seed," too, "separated from himself the passions."[122] Ultimately the fallen aeon herself, upon seeing the savior, rejoiced (*ēgalliasato*), was granted acquaintance and healing of her passions (*iasis tōn pathōn*), which led to the crafting of the material world from them.[123]

117. See Dunderberg, *Beyond Gnosticism*, 195–218, for the "therapy of emotions."

118. Dunderberg, *Beyond Gnosticism*, 111–17.

119. In an introductory treatise on Christian theology, Clement contrasts the joy-bearing, grief-curing song of the Word with the morose and sorrowful tales of pagan antiquity, Clement of Alexandria, *Exhortation to the Greeks* 1, LCL (Cambridge, MA: Harvard University Press, 1919), following the emendation of Reinkins and Staehlin (*penthos* for *peithos*). Selections from the *Excerpts from Theodotus* are introduced and translated by David Brakke in Layton with Brakke, *Gnostic Scriptures*, 501–29. A full edition and translation is in R. P. Casey, *The Excerpta ex Theodoto of Clement of Alexandria: Edited with Translation, Introduction, and Notes*, SD 1 (London: Christophers, 1934).

120. *Exc.* 30.1–2; see Layton with Brakke, *Gnostic Scriptures*, 511, and the note to 30.1.

121. *Exc.* 30.2–31.2 (Brakke).

122. *Exc.* 41.1, 41.4 (Brakke).

123. *Exc.* 45.1, 45.2–49.2; a teaching also familiar from the heresiologists Irenaeus and Hippolytus.

As is typical of Valentinian thought, the creation myth played out in the heavenly realm is recapitulated in human history. While the human being of the superior seed was separated also from passions (that is, a model for the human beings of our created order), the material and ensouled Adam, in whom the divine soul is hidden, was at first "susceptible to passion," an anthropological truth that Genesis 2:23 points to: "Now this is the bone of my bone and flesh of my flesh."[124] The savior's incarnation, however, points to the way out from emotion; by the water and blood that flowed from his side on the cross, "he makes it clear that, by the flow of the passions from those who experience passion, the essences are saved, because they have become without passions."[125]

One way that such Christians could correct the passions was through ritual. The selections in Clement describe both the Valentinian rituals of bridal chamber and baptism as emotionally transformative. The bridal chamber ritual is the "fullness of joy" promised in John 3:29. Additionally, when approaching baptism, it was fitting to rejoice (*chairontas*). Not a passive but an intentional state, this joy tempered with caution protects the Christian by fasting, prayer, and imposition of hands, to prevent unclean spirits—the very passions or thoughts that the Christian has worked so hard to be rid of—from accompanying the one being baptized into the water.[126] In the Valentinian conception of a world knit together by passions, this was a reasonable threat, and it was thus all the more important to focus on rectifying one's passions, especially with a joyful mind, a feeling exemplified by the heavenly fullness.[127] This joy is not a state of happy contentedness but an intently action-oriented emotion.

Political Emotions

We see such a high valuation, and even expectation, of joy as inextricable from the gospel even through the early Constantinian period. Eusebius's *Life of Constantine* depicts Constantine's Christianizing revolution as deploying radiant joy, gladness, and happiness, in contrast to the misery and gloom of past sufferings. Eusebius does not hide his bias as imperial partisan, but the

124. *Exc.* 51.1–2 (Brakke).

125. *Exc.* 61.3 (Brakke).

126. *Exc.* 83.

127. Other Valentinian literature, the *Tripartite Tractate* especially, also speaks to the centrality of joy in the life of the Christian, an emotion that points to belonging in the church and communion with the heavenly aeons, Layton with Brakke, *Gnostic Scriptures*, 379–435.

Life is still the best account of the career of Constantine for all its excessive praise and motivated interpretations and is widely considered reliable in its historical detail, preserving the words of the emperor himself in letters and speeches.[128] The text is also highly literary.[129] As in any good literary work, emotions play a significant role in the narrative and should be taken as important data for assessing the history of the Constantinian era and its memory, which Eusebius presents as the unfolding of joy across the empire, a victory over gloom, misery, and envy, very much in line with the previous centuries' embrace of joy as central to practice, theology, and Christian identity.

Its opening lines foreshadow the emotional arc of the *Life*, praising the celebrations of all humankind in festivities marking important anniversaries of Constantine's reign (1.1).[130] And they had good reason to celebrate, who like all humankind "had no well-grounded hope of happiness after the termination of this mortal life."[131] As will be seen in the following chapter, this is a common trope in Christian literature, and here Eusebius points not just to the gospel as a cure for grief but to God's historical providence in the lives of Constantius and his son Constantine. Even the reign of Constantine's father was marked by good cheer and joy, and Constantius lived his life like any Christian would hope for, "in remarkable repose and tranquility, in the enjoyment of what is counted blessedness."[132] When Constantius passes away happy and old, Constantine is acclaimed Caesar with "joyful shouts," and "all the nations also under his dominion were filled with good cheer (*euphrosynēs*) and unspeakable joy (*chara*)."[133]

It is not only his own troops and supporters who are filled with joy at his rise. When Constantine defeated Maxentius and entered Rome, the (liberated

128. See introduction by Averil Cameron and Stuart G. Hall, *Eusebius: Life of Constantine* (Oxford: Clarendon, 1999), 1–53; and discussion by Timothy Barnes, *Constantine: Dynasty, Religion and Power in the Later Roman Empire* (Chichester: Wiley-Blackwell, 2014), 9–13.

129. Its literary features have only more recently been addressed more systematically. See Peter Van Nuffelen, "The *Life of Constantine*: The Image of an Image," in *Eusebius of Caesarea: Tradition and Innovations*, ed. Aaron Johnson and Jeremy Schott (Washington, DC: Center for Hellenic Studies, 2013), 133–49, who draws on Averil Cameron's 1991 observation of the lack of attention to the literary qualities of the *Life* to note that little had changed (Averil Cameron, *Christianity and the Rhetoric of Empire*, Sather Classical Lectures 55 [Berkeley: University of California Press, 1991], 53).

130. I follow, depending on the text, the translations of Ernest Cushing Richardson (*NPNF*), or Cameron and Hall, *Eusebius*.

131. *Vit. Const.* 1.3 (*NPNF*).

132. *Vit. Const.* 1.17 (*NPNF*).

133. *Vit. Const.* 1.22 (*NPNF*, altered).

or conquered?) Romans greeted him as if freed from prison, "their countenances expressive of the gladness of their hearts, [and] received him with acclamations and abounding joy (*chara*)."[134] As Constantine moves step by step east, eliminating enemies, finally to install himself as the Christian emperor and defender of Christian orthodoxy, the empire matches his march with a transformation of emotion. When Constantine releases Christians from their exile at the hands of his persecuting rivals, the mood changes understandably from mourning, grief, and gloom to joy and gladness, not just felt individually but produced collectively in festivities.[135] Such an emotional conversion cannot be simply due to Eusebius's literary imagination. Constantine himself, in the letters and speeches included in the *Life*, such as to the inhabitants of Palestine just mentioned, uses this language of emotional transformation. Such inverted emotions travel with his authority, which, Constantine himself claims in a letter, "spreads unstintingly to all lands the newly recovered cheerfulness (*tēn euphrosynēn*) of good men."[136] Constantine's address to the council of Nicaea draws on the same kind of emotional appeal, the reclamation of shared joy.[137] According to Eusebius, everyone left the council full of joy.[138] It might seem presumptuous to think the kind of emotional conversion proclaimed by John, Valentinus, 2 Clement, Hermas, and others should be made manifest through imperial fiat, but Eusebius does not shrink from going there: "One might have thought that a picture of Christ's kingdom was thus shadowed forth, and a dream rather than reality."[139] In the context of the emotional language of the *Life*, such a claim pertains not only to justice and right teaching but public feelings. This is not (or is not merely) a rhetorical invention of Euse-

134. *Vit. Const.* 1.39 (*NPNF*).

135. *Vit. Const.* 2.30–32, 42 (*chairontes*, 30; *euphrosynēs*, 32) freedom from miseries, grief, and gloom (2.30, *skythros* 31, 42). "The personal tone, and avowal of commitment to religious duty, are characteristic of Constantine's utterances," Cameron and Hall, *Eusebius*, 240.

136. As in *Vit. Const.* 2.24–42, which draws on the contrast of miseries and gloom with the current joy spread over the east. Quotation from *Vit. Const.* 2.42 (Cameron and Hall, altered); Friedhelm Winkelmann, ed., *Eusebius Werke* 1/1, GCS 55 (Berlin: Akademie 1975), 66. On this see also Guy Stroumsa, "Les martyrs chrétiens et l'inversion des emotions," in *Violentes émotions: Approches comparatistes*, ed. Philippe Borgeaud and Anne-Caroline Rendu Loisel (Geneva: Librairie Droz, 2009), 167–81.

137. *Vit. Const.* 3.12 (*synchairein*). While the speech may be a paraphrase rather than a translation, "The speech itself echoes the sentiments already attributed to Constantine when he heard of the division within the church." Cameron and Hall, *Eusebius*, 266.

138. *Vit. Const.* 3.21 (*euphrosynē*).

139. *Vit. Const.* 3.15 (*NPNF*).

bius. It reflects Constantine's own presentation of himself as a bringer of joy, of pleasant feelings.

Eusebius, of course, presents a very different type of evidence compared to the homilies and treatises, a propagandistic *bios*, along with public addresses of the emperor. But it reflects the distinctively Christian emotional norms and practices transmitted in communities from the first century on, and not merely clichés or commonplaces. Even if it were pure propaganda, it still tells us something important about the mentalities, values, and experiences of the fourth century, just as such shifts in emotional discourse contrast with or reflect changes in later historical periods.

In the summer of 2024, for example, the political landscape of the United States witnessed a comparable (if perhaps brief) emotional conversion, or as some today would call it, a "vibe shift," which is really another way of expressing the transmission of intensities spoken of by affect theorists.[140] After the aged and senescent President Joe Biden was unceremoniously pushed out of the Democratic primary that he had won, the popularly acclaimed usurper Vice President Kamala Harris marked the change of regime with a vibe shift in emotional discourse. Gone was Biden's campaign of fear, warning of the apocalyptic stakes of a Trump reelection, replaced with joy, an intentionally emotional campaign: "It is no accident that joy—a battle-tested version of it—has become the backbone of Ms. Harris's campaign," the *New York Times* reported.[141] The "battle-tested" joy is not "about fun and games." It is martial: "Adopting joy as a political shield has also allowed Ms. Harris and Mr. Walz to throw some bare-knuckled punches at Mr. Trump and his running mate."[142] This joy directly rebuked the emotional tenor and "gloomy vision of former President Donald J. Trump and other Republicans." While Trump committed all sorts of alleged criminal offenses against the nation, according to the vice presidential candidate Tim Walz, the worst offense of all was emotional: "The one thing I will not forgive them for is they try to steal the joy from this country. . . . But you know what? Our next president brings the joy. She emanates joy." Their opponents, rather, "seemed to scoff at the idea that happiness could

140. Lavanya Ramanathan and Christian Paz, "Democrats' Vibes Are Excellent. Can They Turn That into Votes? The Vibe Shift Explained," *Vox*, September 1, 2024.

141. Katie Rogers, "Harris Used to Worry About Laughing. Now Joy Is Fueling Her Campaign," *New York Times*, August 9, 2024, updated August 19, 2024. Also see Jeremy Siegel, "Why the Harris-Walz Campaign Is Talking About Joy, According to a Political Science Professor," *GBH*, August 7, 2024.

142. Rogers, "Harris Used to Worry About Laughing."

be enough to win a presidential election," and instead focused on retribution and hate.[143]

Whether all this talk of joy was authentic (and whose joy is it anyway?) is hard to say, though the campaign's joy did not win the day.[144] The rapid proliferation of "Kamala is brat" and "Brat summer" memes suggests that many people were feeling the vibes. Regardless, the very fact that a campaign embraced an emotional politics of joy says something significant about the mentalities, values, and experiences of a late-century empire at a precarious time of cultural and political instability, in some ways comparable to the political emotions promoted by Constantine and Eusebius, authentic or not. Historians Rob Boddice and Mark Smith even argue that "the whole notion of [emotional] authenticity, as something untouched by culture, something fundamentally human, something *basic*, should be cast aside," that is, the intuitive aim of "disentangling sincere feelings from conventional formulae."[145] I am fully on board with their call. Eusebius may or may not be reliable on the facts, but he along with the other sources I have touched on offer "historical testimony" of what it felt like to be a Christian in the Roman world and how that might be different from how it felt to be something else and how it felt to be a Christian in later periods.[146] This is because emotions as concepts do not work only at the level of discourse or norms of expression (again which posits a knowable distinction between authentic feeling and discursive convention). Rather, emotions and sensation are constructed in a permeable brain-body, permeable to themselves and to the world. Emotion words and concepts affect our plastic brain and our bodies, and the way humans sense, predict, and experience reality, a process that is inherently social, through the shared construction and propagation of emotion concepts. As Lisa Feldman Barrett writes, "Emotion words are not about emotional facts in the world that are stored like static files in your brain. They reflect the varied emotional meanings you construct from mere physical signals in the world using your emotion knowledge. . . . Emotions are not reactions *to* the world; they are your constructions of the world."[147] Or as Boddice and Smith write, drawing

143. Rogers, "Harris Used to Worry About Laughing.

144. Patrick Healy, "Joy Is Not a Strategy," *New York Times*, August 23, 2024.

145. Rob Boddice and Mark Smith, *Emotion, Sense, Experience*, Cambridge Elements: Histories of Emotions and the Senses (Cambridge: Cambridge University Press, 2020), 31, the latter quoting Hannah Newton, *Misery to Mirth: Recovery from Illness in Early Modern England* (Oxford: Oxford University Press, 2018), 28.

146. Boddice and Smith, *Emotion, Sense, Experience*, 33.

147. Barrett, *How Emotions Are Made*, 104.

on Barrett's work, "The creation of conceptual categories of what it means to be human [like joy, cheerfulness, grief, conversion], must in turn be formative of what it is like to experience being human."[148] By observing the creation of emotional concepts as constituting what it means to be a Christian, to live the good life, to flourish as a human, in light of the dialogue between social science, neuroscience, and the historiography of emotions and the senses, we can hopefully get a feeling for what it felt like to be a Christian in antiquity and how potentially very different it was from contemporary expectations about emotion and human flourishing.

148. Boddice and Smith, *Emotion, Sense, Experience*, 36.

3
Sadness

Sadness lacks a bit in gravitas. A few years ago, I was at a party talking to an acquaintance. He asked what I was working on, and when I said I was writing a piece about the history of emotions he scrunched up his face and said in a mock whine, "Are you writing about sadness?" Yes, I said, with some chagrin, I was writing about sadness. Perhaps he'd intuited my love for depressing music (we'd both grown up on The Smiths and The Cure), or maybe it was something else.[1] But he clearly found something absurd or pathetic or just funny in the idea of studying the history of sadness. At any rate, his reaction planted a seed—maybe I didn't want to be the sadness guy in early Christian studies.

And there is something pathetic about sadness. The Twitter (X) account @sosadtoday wouldn't be so darkly humorous if it were @sodepressedtoday or @somuchgrieftoday. To speak of sadness is not to recall the sensitive existentialist overtaken by ennui or the Ivy-educated *New Yorker* staff writer cut down by the "noonday demon" of depression. Rather, if Pixar's *Inside Out* is any guide to the popular imaginary, the archetype of sadness is Phyllis from *The Office*.

Narratives of grief, however, have special poignance and prestige, and depression calls forth profoundly from the depths, gesturing toward a spiritual subtlety, a modern recurrence of the old connection between religion and melancholy that Robert Burton had plumbed in the 1600s.[2] Compare, for example, a current podcast, "Depresh Mode," hosted with perhaps unintentional irony

1. It's not a difficult intuition. Around that same time my wife gifted me a history of depressing music, Adam Brent Houghtaling, *This Will End in Tears: The Miserabilist Guide to Music* (New York: It Books, 2012).

2. For example, Joan Didion, *The Year of Magical Thinking* (New York: Knopf, 2005); William Styron, *Darkness Visible: A Memoir of Madness* (New York: Random House, 1990); Nell Casey, ed., *Unholy Ghost: Writers on Depression* (New York: William Morrow, 2001);

on the Maximum Fun podcast network, which targets a progressive college-educated audience with weekly discussions about mental illness. The title's pun, intentionally or not, points to the great prevalence, cultural currency, and even "fashion" of depression.

Critics are divided on why depression has become such a common phenomenon (whether emotion or illness) and how it connects with the constellation of other bad feelings, sadness, grief, melancholy, and so on. A growing collection of voices has traced the rise in depression to political and systemic injustice, a "political depression," emotional traumas stemming from the most globalized violence to the most personal microaggressions, less individual than collective, a "public feeling."[3] This approach to depression as a political emotion has influenced the changing topography of counseling, which increasingly has moved away from localizing the "problem" in the thoughts and emotions of the client toward the systems of oppression keeping the client down.[4] The system is sick, and if you're not depressed you're not paying attention. This approach is especially indicative of contemporary affect theory, which tends to frame feelings and emotions as inseparable from the struggle over power.[5] Specialists have begun exploring how such phenomenologies of contemporary affect—centering on intersectional identity and discrimination amid globalized neoliberalism—might help to understand the experience of emotion among early Christians.

On the other hand, from an evolutionary perspective, depression can be seen as intense sadness by another name, a reaction to loss, albeit with a self-preservation streak. The defeated animal shrinks (physically and socially) from conflict; the humiliation of defeat—literally being made small or of low status—can be an important part of the experience of depression, which is not recognized in psychology's *Diagnostic and Statistical Manual* (DSM) but ties into the recent trend of understanding depression as a political emotion. Those of low status, either chronically or cast down suddenly, withdraw from conflict, lick their wounds, and ruminate on next steps, potentially signaling submis-

Robert Burton, *The Anatomy of Melancholy* (New York: New York Review Books, 2001), 3.311–432.

3. Cf. the influential interventions from an affect theory perspective in Ann Cvetkovich, *Depression: A Public Feeling* (Durham, NC: Duke University Press, 2012), 1–26, 115–53; and Sarah Ahmed, *The Promise of Happiness* (Durham, NC: Duke University Press, 2010).

4. Elsie Jones-Smith, *Theories of Counseling and Psychotherapy: An Integrative Approach*, 3rd ed. (Thousand Oaks, CA: SAGE, 2021), 334–89.

5. Donovan O. Schaefer, *Religious Affects: Animality, Evolution, and Power* (Durham, NC: Duke University Press, 2015).

sion to a more powerful foe, thus preserving the chance for later success.[6] In this perspective, sadness, grief, and DSM-style major depressive disorder are kinds of deep animal affect, preconscious and prelinguistic, kicking in to preserve the organism to fight another day.

Still, the intersecting modern concepts of sadness, depression, dysthymia, melancholia, "nerves," and so on, are just that, concepts, and thus are projects with historical contexts and subject to historical analysis.[7] Their historical contingency, however, renders them no less real and no less painful, as so many can attest today. But a diagnosis of depression, or grief, or sadness, or melancholia depends not so much on the internal workings of the brain but on the position of sufferer and healer within the specific constraints of a society. The label we give to an emotion depends very much on context, on cause, timing, class, gender, race, and power, among other factors.

With all the complicated ways of feeling bad as modern historical and political subjects, "sadness" has the advantage of neutrality, a certain remove, though it may lack the visceral pull and cultural currency of depression or grief.[8] Sadness is the more expansive and general term, and includes many ways of feeling bad: grief, distress, and pain, all of which fall under the Greek concept of *lypē*. In some sense, sadness is far stranger, now co-opted in different professional, medical, and social contexts into a proliferating taxonomy of emotional pain. In fact, whether in popular ways of speaking or in the professional jargon of the psychiatric and counseling professions, sadness has been pathologized as an emotion and recast as a mental disorder in the much more recent concept of depression.[9] Like pain, sadness in the early twenty-first

6. Christian A. Webb and Diego A. Pizzagalli, "Sadness and Depression," in *Handbook of Emotions*, 4th ed., ed. Lisa Feldman Barrett, Michael Lewis, and Jeannette M. Haviland-Jones (New York: Guilford, 2016), 859–60.

7. A growing library of studies trace the history of feeling bad, focusing on later modernity. See Clark Lawlor, *From Melancholia to Prozac: A History of Depression* (Oxford: Oxford University Press, 2012); Allan V. Horwitz and Jerome C. Wakefield, *The Loss of Sadness: How Psychiatry Transformed Normal Sorrow into Depressive Disorder* (New York: Oxford University Press, 2007); Jonathan Sadowsky, *The Empire of Depression: A New History* (Cambridge: Polity, 2023); Edward Shorter, *How Everyone Became Depressed: The Rise and Fall of the Nervous Breakdown* (New York: Oxford University Press, 2013).

8. Thus, the sociologist David A. Karp titled his foundational study of the contemporary epidemic of depression *Speaking of Sadness: Depression, Disconnection, and the Meanings of Illness*, 2nd ed. (New York: Oxford University Press, 2016).

9. Horwitz and Wakefield, *Loss of Sadness*; Shorter, *How Everyone Became Depressed*; also Allan V. Horwitz, *DSM: A History of Psychiatry's Bible* (Baltimore: Johns Hopkins University Press, 2021).

century came to be a feeling that we shouldn't have to feel, a problem to be solved, rather than something that tells us something crucial about ourselves and our bodies and our world.

The very recent history of emotions exemplifies the kinds of changes to be aware of when attempting to understand the emotional experiences of the early Christians. In just the past century, generation, and even decade, the way people speak about sadness, the metaphors they use, how they perceive the emotion to inhabit and pass between people, and the value and desirability of these feelings as sources of identity and meaning have changed enormously and have real effects, in health, the body, the economy, the family, and culture. And though we lack the kinds of testimonies made possible by our contemporary culture of emotional self-disclosure, early Christian attitudes toward sadness changed as well, more radically than any of the other emotional constellations discussed in this book.

Paul and Grief

Significantly, the earliest surviving Christian text is a letter about grief, about how Christians were distinctively and intentionally to manage their emotional reactions to loss. Paul wrote his letter, now 1 Thessalonians, from Corinth to the church in Thessalonike around 51 CE. Paul's letter foreshadows his approach to emotions seen in the previous chapter, describing his church as a community bound by emotion horizontally and vertically, to one another and to God. These emotions are not simply thrust on them by happenstance. They cultivate them and in turn model them (*hōste genesthai hymas typon*) for believers in other cities (1 Thess 1:7).[10] His congregation "became imitators (*mimētai*) of us and the Lord, for in spite of persecution you received the word with joy (*chara*) inspired by the Holy Spirit" (1:6). Paul goes so far as to describe believers as the embodiment of this shared emotion: "For what is our hope or joy or crown of boasting before our Lord Jesus at his coming? Is it not you? Yes, you are our glory and joy!" (2:19–20). Today this sounds more abstract and theological than I think Paul meant it. It points to a community modeled by a mutually reflecting image and as the instantiation of shared

10. Ronald A. Ward insists on the opposite: "The imitation cannot have been deliberate," instead it is "unconscious imitation." *Commentary on 1 & 2 Thessalonians* (Waco: Word, 1973), 36. I see no reason to insist on the unconscious nature of this emotional modeling.

emotion.[11] The church manifests God's emotions in the world much as it forms Christ's body. Whatever the specific practices of this joy, Paul's congregants live in sharp contrast to outsiders, *ta ethnē*. Paul's glory and joy, for example, forswear fornication and take wives without desirous emotion (*mē en pathei epithymias*, 4:5).

So far we are close to the kind of joyful community encouraged in Philippi. Paul insists on feeling joy in very difficult times, afflictions (*thlipseis*), widely interpreted as "persecutions" (e.g., 1 Thess 3:3). Unlike the community in Philippi, however, the believers in Thessalonike are racked with grief (*lypē*). Fellow believers had died, they reported, and they did not understand what would happen to them. It seems that Paul had left them with instructions to await the coming of the Lord, such that we can imagine that they had altered their lifestyles to anticipate it, including a very intentional emotional orientation of joy. But Jesus did not return.[12]

Paul advises that they should not be sad at the death of their fellow believers. To do so would show their ignorance. "But we do not want you to be uninformed (*agnoein*), brothers and sisters, about those who have died, so that you may not grieve (*mē lypēsthe*) as others who have no hope" (4:13). Interpreters have long debated the true depth of this command. The gentler interpretation holds that believers should not grieve in the same way (or to the same extent) as nonbelievers. Yet Paul appears to point to a stricter rule. The most grammatically straightforward reading, and most in keeping with the overall sense of Paul's argument, is that his followers are not to feel sadness at all at the deaths of their loved ones and fellow believers.[13] This is not to say that believers are never to feel sadness; by the time of his letters to Corinth Paul will clarify a proper practice of *lypē* in this new community. But here his command is absolute and in keeping with his uncompromising emotional standards described in the previous chapter. Believers are to feel no grief but

11. "Glory" (*doxa*) also carries the sense of reflection or image; cf. 1 Cor 11 (BDAG, 3rd ed., s.v. *doxa*, 1.d).

12. See the discussion of various interpretations in Ian Y. S. Jew, *Paul's Emotional Regime: The Social Function of Emotion in 1 Thessalonians and Philippians*, LNTS 629 (New York: T&T Clark, 2021), 115–16.

13. John M. G. Barclay, *Pauline Churches and Diaspora Jews*, WUNT 275 (Tübingen: Mohr Siebeck, 2011), 217–35. Barclay draws on James Frame's (1912) statement that "Paul speaks absolutely, for death has a religious value to him. . . . In view of this glorious consummation, present grief, however natural, is excluded," and he sees a parallel to the emotional divide between the *ethnē* and the believers in 4:5 (224). See also Jew, *Paul's Emotional Regime*, 117.

are to rejoice at all times (*pantote chairete*, 5:16). Paul sets the emotions of the believers apart from "the rest" of humanity, without distinction of Jew and gentile.[14] The time of destruction is indeed coming, sneaking up on the world, but the "sudden destruction will come upon them" (not *us*) like labor pains (5:3). But this is not the lot of the believers, who are not in the dark, and thus no thief will sneak up on them. The emotional telos differs as well, as the rest are bound for anger (*orgē*), but the believers are not, all bound together in a mutually affective community (5:9, 11).[15]

Paul's uncompromising emotional instruction would recall some Stoic voices from the early empire, who placed *lypē* among the four basic passions (desire, distress [*lypē*], fear, and pleasure), of which *lypē* alone had no corresponding "good emotion" (*eupatheia*).[16] Stoics were not averse to advising the wise to refrain from grieving the deaths of even their loved ones.[17] But Paul does not explicitly call on believers to abandon grief because it is irrational, in conflict with nature's providence, or indicative of a lack of self-control. Rather, for the believer another emotion, hope (*elpis*), displaces the grief felt by "the rest."

Paul discusses sadness most personally in letters to the church in Corinth. Here Paul advises a more nuanced approach to sadness among the believers, again with an eye toward forming a community bound by mutually felt and expressed emotion. I compare in some detail two approaches to grief in the Corinthian church, which demonstrate how early Christian emotions can be studied from the perspective of affect theory and from a more history of emotions perspective focusing on emotional discourse and rhetoric. The two approaches show different strategies of reading, the affective approach engaging with the texts more symptomatically (searching for the deeper currents of emotion and feeling hidden under the plain meaning of the text), and the more historical-critical or rhetorical approach engaging the text through

14. As Barclay observes, "Paul's rhetoric here refuses to acknowledge the ethnic or cultural distinctions between Jews and Gentiles which he recognizes elsewhere (1 Cor 1.22–24; Rom 1.14); rather, he agglomerates all non-Christian humanity into a single, nameless lump . . . It seems his rhetoric here is deliberately blunt: there can be only two categories in this discourse, not (even implicitly) three. Thus *all*, Jews and Gentiles (whatever their actual, and highly variegated, beliefs about the afterlife) are draped in the all-enveloping shroud of hopelessness: there are no exceptions to 'the rest who have no hope'" (Barclay, *Pauline Churches and Diaspora Jews*, 223).

15. As Barclay puts it, "the 'brothers' . . . who live in a community of mutual encouragement and support." *Pauline Churches and Diaspora Jews*, 226.

16. Margaret Graver, *Stoicism and Emotion* (Chicago: University of Chicago Press, 2007), 54.

17. Graver, *Stoicism and Emotion*, 177–78.

a more "surface reading," which need not be any less nuanced or insightful than a symptomatic reading.[18] Comparing these two approaches to sadness in Corinth provides a useful case study of the divergent and complementary results from different modes of emotions history.

Drawing on the insights of affect theory, Laura Nasrallah moves from Paul's Thessalonian community toward his next church established in Corinth, focusing on his first letter, where one may "find a similar theme [identity formed by grief]" in Paul's eschatological predictions (1 Cor 1:8; 3:13; 5:5; cf. 1 Thess 5:2).[19] First Corinthians seems at first glance a less than promising quarry for excavating grief and sadness, certainly compared to his later letters to the community compiled in 2 Corinthians. The word *lypē* (and any variation of it) never occurs in this long and wide-ranging letter.[20] From the perspective of the history of emotions, or the psychological construction of emotion, this is a significant lacuna. On a thematic level, Paul hardly addresses loss or pain. But from the perspective of affect theory, this does not pose a problem, since the modern critic can intuit the affective shimmers and hidden *pathē* apart, around, and beneath linguistic expression.

This literary excavation of grief in Corinth unsettles generalizations that have long suffused New Testament scholarship, which configures Corinth as a bustling, young port city in the time of Paul, attracting immigrants from afar and having the kinds of amenities that would satisfy the desires of merchants and sailors passing through.[21] It was also well suited to the sort of status-conscious mercantile class, which was such a prime target for Paul's message. After the city's destruction in 146 BCE, it was refounded (a full century before Paul's stay) "as a Roman colony in 44 BCE . . . not primarily repopulated by military veterans but by ex-slaves."[22] These freedmen were granted unusual

18. These two ways of reading are compared by Stephen Best and Sharon Marcus, "Surface Reading: An Introduction," *Representations* 108 (2009): 1–21. They write (in favor of surface reading), "Surface reading broadens the scope of critique to include the kinds of interpretive activity that seek to understand the complexity of literary surfaces—surfaces that have been rendered invisible by symptomatic reading" (1).

19. There are two slightly different versions of this paper: Laura Salah Nasrallah, "Grief in Corinth: The Roman City and Paul's Corinthian Correspondence," in *Constested Spaces: Houses and Temples in Roman Antiquity*, ed. David Balch and Annette Weissenrieder, WUNT 285 (Tübingen: Mohr Siebeck, 2012), 109–39; and Laura Salah Nasrallah, *Archaeology and the Letters of Paul* (Oxford: Oxford University Press, 2019), 141–78. Quotation from Nasrallah, "Grief in Corinth," 110.

20. Another word for grieving (*penthein*) occurs once (5:2) but in a very different context with nothing to do with lost loved ones.

21. Nasrallah, *Archaeology*, 146.

22. Nasrallah, *Archaeology*, 151.

privileges even apart from the general upward mobility of freedmen and their descendants, such as the ability to hold offices.[23] Such a city does not immediately call to mind a community bound by intergenerational trauma and collective grief, a kind of affective existence evoked by the essay's quotations of the philosopher of rhetoric Judith Butler and the poet and critic Claudine Rankin, whose reflections bookend the historical investigation.[24] Indeed, ancient writers such as the Augustan geographer Strabo and the second sophistic orator Aelius Aristides characterize Corinth as a significant and profitable port city, sited on a strategic isthmus and eyed by many as a prime target for canal construction.[25] From imperial sources one might well get the impression of Corinth as a fortunate, even happy, city.

But under this facade of cosmopolitan migration and trade, of mercantile vitality and vice, we may be sensitive to the shimmers of a persistent and endemic grief, an affective topography that does not usually register in standard New Testament introductions.[26] The study explores several avenues for excavating the grief of Corinth's Christians and others. For example, Cicero, writing a full century before Paul, recalled a visit to the Peloponnese where he saw Corinthian slaves working. He claims that the locals showed (and felt) no grief themselves. In fact, they looked like anybody else ("they might have been born in Argos or Sicyon"), and their dull, lower-class minds seemed unbothered by Corinth's ruins. He conjectures that "they had thought about the event for so long that their minds had become hardened with wear."[27] Ironically, in the minds of elites, with their higher emotional sophistication, the ruins of Corinth (just like those of Aegina, Megara, and Piraeus) are not as much "an emblem of grief" as of consolation, a useful reminder "that you were born a human being," as Cicero's friend Servius Sulpicius Rufus writes. He continues, "Take my word for it, I was not a little fortified by that reflection."[28] Cicero

23. Nasrallah, *Archaeology*, 151. But, she notes, there were still poor people in Corinth, as of course there were everywhere (cf. Matt 26:11). On the social class of the first urban Christ followers, see the summary of Rodney Stark, *The Rise of Christianity* (New York: Princeton University Press, 1996; repr., New York: Harper One, 1997), 29–47; and the foundational study of Wayne A. Meeks, *The First Urban Christians: The Social World of the Apostle Paul*, 2nd ed. (New Haven: Yale University Press, 2003).

24. Nasrallah, *Archaeology*, 143–44, 176–77, drawing on Judith Butler, *Precarious Life: The Powers of Mourning and Violence* (London: Verso, 2004), esp. 101–27.

25. Nasrallah, *Archaeology*, 147–48.

26. Indeed, "for some ancient writers, Corinth's history made it an emblem of grief." Nasrallah, "Grief in Corinth," 113.

27. Cicero, *Tusc.* 3.45 (Nasrallah, "Grief in Corinth," 113).

28. Cicero, *Fam.* 4.5.4 (Williams, LCL), in Nasrallah, "Grief in Corinth," 113–14.

and Rufus show a cultured appreciation of the affective topography of decay and destruction, which offered hard-won lessons for living well amid pain, a lesson (from their perspective) far beyond the ken of simple-minded plebes and enslaved Corinthians.[29] I am confident, however, that those dispossessed by the destruction of these cities and their descendants would have a very different report, if only we could hear them.

While Roman tourists to the east do not get us very far in excavating the feelings of actual Corinthians, perhaps we can glimpse them through the echoes or specters of affect that inhabited and moved among the worlds in which the now voiceless Corinthians lived. Perhaps the Corinthians of Paul's day still felt the pangs of grief of "slavery and former enslavement, migration, and poverty."[30] It is not clear why migration is necessarily a source of grief, rather than hope, excitement, disgust, envy, and so on. Nor is it explained what the grief of former enslavement would entail for people whose ancestors were freed and granted unusual civic privileges several generations prior, since the "Corinthian population (and its leadership) . . . newly freed from slavery" would have been a distant memory by Paul's day, if remembered at all.[31] Such was the lot most anywhere in the ancient world and hardly tells us anything about Corinth. But there may be other routes to pin down the shifting intensities of affect beneath and around the words of Paul, such as demographic trends, urban topography, and myth.

Perhaps, for example, Corinthians suffered from unusually high infant mortality. According to a study of several cities in the eastern Mediterranean, mortality rates were similar in Corinth and other cities, but "more children were dying in Corinth."[32] While this study (of ninety-four bodies from the Roman and Hellenistic periods) shows a significantly higher child mortality in Corinth compared to Paphos in Cyprus (30.9 to 20.4 percent), it has little relevance to Paul's church; the likely culprit was the destruction of Corinth two

29. Cicero's assumption that different classes of people felt differently and had access to different emotions speaks to a significant observation in the history of emotions, e.g., in the rhetorical approach of Daniel L. Gross, *The Secret History of Emotion: From Aristotle's "Rhetoric" to Modern Brain Science* (Chicago: University of Chicago Press, 2006).

30. Nasrallah, *Archaeology*, 153.

31. Nasrallah, *Archaeology*, 157. I suspect, given the prominent inclusion of contemporary voices like Butler and Rankin, the parallel must implicitly be with current discourse on the legacy of American slavery and the very tenuous research on intergenerational trauma, along with the current conflicts in the Levant, the tragic aftermath of civil wars in Syria and Libya, and the subsequent humanitarian crisis of migrants and refugees in Europe.

32. Nasrallah, *Archaeology*, 154.

centuries before Paul.[33] Such samples are furthermore small and not representative but randomly discovered and thus give little evidence of larger trends.[34] While the deaths of children undoubtedly grieved the residents of Corinth, there is little to show a special emotional connection between Corinth and their dead children.

What about the emotional topography of Corinth itself? While the city had been razed and repopulated as a Roman *colonia* long before Paul set foot there, it is worth imagining what legacies the many centuries of suffering might have inscribed in the lived environment of Roman Corinth, which could have shaped the emotional experience of Paul's believers deep beneath their conscious knowing, "a topography of grief."[35] The idea that a city, or any other place, could evoke a shared emotional baseline among its inhabitants makes intuitive sense. I certainly have entered into spaces—a city, a neighborhood, a room—that gave off a certain "feeling."

The Corinthians, from this perspective, were surrounded by grief, "which flowed and pooled in certain regions of the city and beyond," expressed in myth, monuments, iconography, and magic.[36] For example, Corinthians minted coins commemorating the myth of Melikertes, a drowning boy saved by a dolphin, though it is unclear why this would evoke grief and not wonder or joy or hope; as in so much affective scholarship, the emotions of others are simply asserted by intuition or empathy.[37] Other myths were situated in ancient Corinth, the memory of which might have structured the affects of the city's latter-day residents. Medea's descent into rage and murder of her children was set in Corinth. Demeter, too, lost (and found) her daughter Kore in the area of Corinth, though more closely connected to Eleusis in Attica. Again, that grief should be associated with these myths rather than other emotions is never proven, just asserted. Instead, it appears that in monumental representations the Corinthians were more interested in the divinely personified Terror (*deima*) as a public feeling in response to the mythic past.[38] While Demeter's loss is an important part of Greek myth, the story of Demeter and Kore much more affectively evokes joy and hope, given that it was the basis for the

33. Sherry C. Fox, "Health in Hellenistic and Roman Times: The Case Studies of Paphos, Cyprus and Corinth, Greece," in *Health in Antiquity*, ed. Helen King (New York: Routledge, 2005), 78, 80.

34. As acknowledged by Nasrallah, *Archaeology*, 154.

35. Nasrallah, *Archaeology*, 158.

36. Nasrallah, *Archaeology*, 144.

37. Nasrallah, *Archaeology*, 159.

38. Nasrallah, *Archaeology*, 161.

most popular and longest lived mystery cult in the ancient world, promising a continuing and blissful existence after death for the initiate.[39] Might curse tablets (*defixiones*) give a sense of the affective topography of Corinth? Of the seventeen tablets found under one of the temples of Demeter, none addresses sadness or grief directly but rather the usual magical desire for vengeance and destruction.[40] In line with the general emotional contours of magic and intracommunal cursing in antiquity, the emotional valence of such invocations speaks of hatred and envy, not grief.[41]

In this affect theory–inspired reading, these various signifiers—coins of the boy saved by a dolphin, public commemorations of myth, and a cache of rather ordinary curse tablets—point to a distinctive Corinthian obsession with the deaths of children, a grief that miasmically haunts the city even in the time of Paul.[42] Yet the excavation of these dried rivulets of grief in the end doesn't fill the emotional hole left in 1 Corinthians, which shows little interest in sadness. The emotional aporia, however, is important evidence on its own. It is worth sitting with Paul's silence to hear what it can tell us. The only place that grief is explicitly evoked is in the context of the believer who is sleeping with his stepmother, and here Paul points to the community's lack of mourning. They are puffed up or arrogant (*pephysiōmenoi*), when they really should have been mourning (*epenthēsate*) (1 Cor 5:2). The dominant emotion of 1 Corinthians is not grief but love (*agapē*), which comes to the fore in Paul's discussion of marriage and virginity, problems with the love-ritual itself, and the ecstatic excess of charismatic gifts in worship (1 Cor 12).

Instead, it is in the letters edited together as 2 Corinthians that we see a community bound by grief. In contrast to more phenomenological attention to the affective topography of this both ancient and young city, Paul's emotional rhetoric in 2 Corinthians reveals the intentionality and transformational power of emotion in Paul's community. Here Paul lays out a model for a transformative power of sadness (*lypē*), which complements his attempts at emotional formation in other letters.

Paul's "therapeutic epistle" offers a remarkable example of the intentional formation of an emotional community.[43] Paul begins the letter by emphasizing

39. Nasrallah, *Archaeology*, 167.

40. Nasrallah, *Archaeology*, 169.

41. Esther Eidinow, *Envy, Poison, and Death: Women on Trial in Classical Athens* (Oxford: Oxford University Press, 2016).

42. Euripides, *Med.* 1090–1115; Nasrallah, *Archaeology*, 170.

43. I follow and have benefited from L. L. Welborn's study of "pain" in 2 Corinthians, which accepts these sections of 2 Corinthians as from one of several letters edited together

the healing of sadness, consolation (*paraklēsis*), which occurs seven times in the first seven verses. Paul claims that the consolation he brings is mutual and connects him and his community with God, a consolation that moves back and forth among them: "The God of all consolation, who consoles us in all our affliction, so that we may be able to console those who are in any affliction with the consolation with which we ourselves are consoled by God" (1:3–4). It is not only God's consolation that moves among believers and God; emotions, too, pass between the community and its members. These passions are not what is cured through consolation but work in consort with consolation, or even as the means of consolation, because the passions of the believers meld with the passions of Christ, much as believers carry his spirit in their hearts (1:22), no less than they are his body (1 Cor 12:12–31). "For just as these passions (*pathēmata*) of Christ overflow (*perisseuei*) into us, our consolation abounds through Christ" (2 Cor 1:5).[44] Paul's correspondents experience "patiently the same passions which we feel" (1:6, my translation), which all adds up to hope (*elpis*), as they share in common their passions (*koinōnoi este tōn pathēmatōn*) and consolation (1:7).

Paul does not promote sadness as permanently desirable but temporary and with known cause and potential cure. Unlike his condemnation of grief at death, it is not to be wholly avoided. It even brings with it a salvific transformation through repentance or conversion (*metanoia*).[45] The proximate cause of the community's sadness is Paul himself, though the other believers bear their own guilt as well. Paul had made a sorrowful (*en lypē*) visit, to address the conflict over rival apostles who had criticized him, and in 2 Corinthians he vows not to do that again (2:1). His goal is rather to turn this sadness into joy, a joy shared between him and all the believers, "that my joy would be the joy of all of you" (2:4). He downplays his own sadness at the accusations made against him by a Corinthian critic, claiming that really the *lypē* was caused "to some extent—not to exaggerate it—to all of you," perhaps most painfully to Paul's own accuser, for whom he counsels forgiveness, "so that he may not be overwhelmed by excessive sorrow [*tē perissotera lypē*]" (2:5, 7).

Paul's letter continues by addressing his community's repentance, which he learned about in Macedonia, where he had his own problems with disputes

into the current epistle, "Paul and Pain: Paul's Emotional Therapy in 2 Corinthian 1.1–2.13; 7.5–16 in the Context of Ancient Psychagogic Literature," *NTS* 57 (2011): 547–70.

44. Translated following Welborn, who translates *pathēmata* as passion; it can also mean, and is usually translated more generically as, "suffering." Welborn, "Paul and Pain," 556.

45. Welborn, "Paul and Pain," 551.

and fears (*phoboi*), and which came as a consolation to him as to the downcast (*tapeinos*). Paul describes an emotional conversion, which in 2 Corinthians moves through their "longing" (*epipothēsin*), "mourning" (*odurmon*), and "zeal" (*zēlon*). All this Paul sums up as so much sadness or pain (*lypē*), which Paul inflicted upon them with his previous letter (*elypēsa hymas en tē epistolē*) (7:8). But now this grief has caused Paul joy, not pleasure in their suffering but joy because their sadness led to a change of mind; while usually this *metanoia* is rendered as "repentance," the "change of mind" points to Paul's insistence that a shift in emotions constitutes this conversion.

Paul draws a crucial distinction, which Christians would puzzle over for centuries, between a "worldly" sadness that leads to "death" (*thanatos*) and a "godly" sadness that leads to salvation (*sōtēria*) and earnestness (*spoudē*) (7:10–11). Paul's advice clarifies the less compromising rule of 1 Thessalonians. Paul is no Stoic, who advise the complete elimination of emotional distress (*lypē*).[46] Rather, sadness is twofold. The grief that the Christians in Thessalonike felt for their dead friends and relatives was worldly, based on a misapprehension of God's providential plan. But sadness can be transformative and turn the believer away from the things of the world to follow more closely the ways of God, which leads to salvation or health. Pain, dumb and brutal, can simply accompany the body to its death; we all know the nihilistic and world-destroying power of pain, bodily and emotional. Still, it is a commonplace among ancient doctors that the pain of medical treatment is salutary, and on the other side of the surgeon's knife or cautery is joy for the patient and healer alike. This is paralleled in the confluence of philosophy and medicine, such as in Plutarch and Epictetus, and Christian moralists would find this an extremely useful way to speak of healing the soul.[47]

Such commonplaces aside, Paul's insistence on the saving power of sadness is unusual in the ancient world and very much out of line with some streams of philosophical and moral exhortation, especially Stoicism.[48] While the Cynic orator Dio Chrysostom (ca. 40–ca. 115) asks, "What more abject creature (*tapeinoteron*) is there than a man who is held in thrall to pain (or sadness, *lypoumenoi*)?" Paul embraces abjection (*tapeinos*) as a model emotional state, as he describes himself in this very letter (2 Cor 7:6).[49] While Aristotle does not

46. Stoic views on the passions and pain are covered by Welborn, "Paul and Pain," 559–64.

47. Welborn, "Paul and Pain," 566. On late antique Christian medical metaphors, see Andrew Crislip, "Shenoute of Atripe on Christ the Physician and the Cure of Souls," *Le Muséon* 122 (2009): 265–95.

48. Welborn, "Paul and Pain," 563–65, 567.

49. Dio Chrysostom, *Or.* 16.1 (Welborn, "Paul and Pain," 563); as discussed by Ryan S.

address grief in his *Rhetoric*, other rhetorical authorities describe a "grieving style," positioning oneself as if grieving in order to rebuke one's audience.[50] Grieving letters can be seen in late antiquity, by Emperor Julian and Gregory of Nazianzus, for example, and earlier as well. But Paul goes well beyond the commonplaces of any rhetorical manual, which indeed he likely had no recourse to.[51] Not just to be sad but to advocate for the positive and saving value of the individual and communal experience of sadness/distress/grief will be a lasting impact of Paul's teaching. "Paul has few, if any, predecessors in the constructive role that he attributes to 'pain' (λύπη [*lypē*]). Paul emerges from [a] comparative study as the harbinger of an upheaval in the ancient therapy of the emotions, indeed, as the architect of a new concept of the 'self as sufferer,' which by the end of the second century, had achieved significant cultural currency."[52] Attention to the emotion words that Paul employs gives a rich picture of the emotional lives of his church and himself, and in fact shows them not to suffer passively the affects pooling and spreading stickily through the emotional topography of a notional city. Paul radically advocates a new way of feeling in his community, a change of mind crucial to their community, sharing in the spirit and mind of Christ and sharing in his passions, overflowing among and through them.

Paul's letter also reveals something quite unusual in antiquity, a lack approached in a different way through affect theory: the emotions of people outside the elite. As in most areas of life in antiquity, when it comes to emotions, elite voices dominate. These elites may well have felt different emotions than the non-elites. This makes sense from what we know about emotions as constructed and dependent on socialization and language. In fact, philosophers of emotion have long argued that different classes of people within a given society should feel different emotions. In his *Rhetoric*, Aristotle argues that certain emotions are available only to certain groups of people, anger for example. To feel anger, one must feel that one has been treated in a way incommensurable with one's rank, especially by someone without the standing to do it. For someone of low status, a slave for example, it would be inconceivable to feel anger,

Schellenberg, *Abject Joy: Paul, Prison, and the Art of Making Do* (Oxford: Oxford University Press, 2021).

50. David E. Fredrickson, "'Through Many Tears' (2 Cor 2:4): Paul's Grieving Letter and the Occasion of 2 Corinthians 1–7," in *Paul and Pathos*, ed. Thomas H. Olbricht and Jerry L. Sumney, SymS 16 (Atlanta: Society of Biblical Literature, 2001), 163.

51. See a critique of the traditional rhetorical analysis of Paul's letters as fitting into the various handbook categories of argumentation by Steven J. Kraftchick, "Πάθη [*Pathē*] in Paul: The Emotional Logic of 'Original Argument,'" in Olbricht and Sumney, *Paul and Pathos*, 39–42.

52. Welborn, "Paul and Pain," 548.

since there is no treatment that could be so poor as to be incommensurable.[53] To feel anger is an emotion of the elite.

This differential in emotion, of relative scarcity and excess, is corroborated in the literature of the Roman Empire, as elites focus much of their emotional advice on anger and its management.[54] The elite focus on anger may be related to the fact "that depression was largely absent. . . . [Rather,] the frustrations of life, commonly recognized as a major source of modern depression, tended in antiquity to produce emotions akin to anger."[55] As incongruent and radical as the idea of different emotions and emotional communities among different classes may be given the general assumption that emotions are universal mental faculties, Cicero seems to have assumed as much in his visit to Corinth. Those others, the enslaved and the poor, simply lacked the ability to feel in the way he did.

Paul's letter, however, reveals the emotional lives of people left out of elite philosophical discourse. Appropriately, in a letter about conflict and humiliation, it is notably not in anger that Paul writes and not in anger that his congregants respond. Many today would respond in anger to the sort of provocations he endured, as would any elite Roman. But Paul does not. Sadness, grief, and pain bind this community together, but they also offer a way toward healing and reconciliation. Here we have a witness to a very different type of emotional community, of a different class than the usual suspects. It gives a sense of the diversity of emotional experience and community and will have an enormous impact on later generations of Christian emotion.

Sadness and Its Critics

For all Paul's influence, Christians remained divided on how they should react to loss, disappointment, and death. The Fourth Gospel, even more strongly than Paul, brooks no exception in forbidding grief. Jesus predicts that all *lypē* will pass away from his believers, to be replaced by joy, just as the pains of childbirth (*lypēn*) fade into oblivion with the joy of a new child (John 16:16–24). Such calls for radical emotional transformation, one can imagine, made

53. Discussed in Gross, *Secret History of Emotion*, 1–6.

54. A list of the many treatises on anger is in William V. Harris, *Restraining Rage: The Ideology of Anger Control in Classical Antiquity* (Cambridge, MA: Harvard University Press, 2001), 127–28.

55. Harris, *Restraining Rage*, 16; further discussion in Welborn, "Paul and Pain," 564.

sense in a context of still current eschatological expectation or crisis. In the context of a less eschatological church, a church of household rules, business, and the messiness of city life, it is tempting to read such emotional language as less than authentically passionate and more the expression of theological virtues. It can be hard to accept the idea that Paul or John really expected believers not to feel sadness (or only to feel it in severely limited circumstances).

In the generations to follow, Christians took both approaches, some finding Paul's teachings inspiring and practicable, others finding them distasteful or extreme. An example of this focus on sadness is in the second-century Roman author Hermas discussed in the previous chapter, who composed a collection of narratives of his encounters with a heavenly shepherd, the lady church, and other visionary characters. While Hermas's visionary company devotes a good deal of time to encouraging Hermas, and all Christians, to express constant cheerfulness (*hilarotēs*), this guide to Christian life acknowledges the difficulty of emotional conversion. Far more often it is sadness that Hermas feels and to which he returns in spite of his heavenly interlocutors' exhortations.[56] He grieves over his sins, over perceived slights, and at his own ignorance.[57] Worldly affairs persistently tear apart Hermas's soul, which must have been a common tension for Christians across the empire, and still is today among converts to any new religious movement. This tension between the Christian community and the world drives the experience of doubt, hesitation, or double-souledness (*dipsychia*) that the *Shepherd* addresses.

The *Shepherd* also reflects on sadness in the Pauline tradition, including Paul's teachings on *lypē* in 2 Corinthians and in Ephesians, both of which help to center the problem of sadness for the Christian. Since Hermas is so concerned with *metanoia* as a lifelong process, it might seem natural for him to embrace Paul's distinction between the two types of sadness, that which is worldly and leads to death and that which is of God and leads to repentance. Hermas knows the passage, but his treatment reveals how uncomfortable with sadness some Christians had become a century after Paul's death.[58] He takes very seriously the command in Ephesians 4:30 that the believer not cause sadness or grief (*mē lypeite*) to the Holy Spirit, which for Hermas ties into his

56. E.g., Herm. Vis. 1.2 (2); Herm. Mand. 3 (28); Herm. Sim. 6.3 (63), 9.2 (79).

57. Andrew Crislip, "*The Shepherd of Hermas* and Early Christian Emotional Formation," StPatr 83 (2017): 242.

58. The influence of Paul has been of longstanding debate, but the Pauline legacy has been recently demonstrated, including in Hermas's teachings about sadness, Jonathan E. Soyars, *The Shepherd of Hermas and the Pauline Legacy*, NovTSup 176 (Leiden: Brill, 2019), 115–27. See also Crislip, "Shepherd of Hermas," 242–45.

belief in the influence of spirits on humanity. The Holy Spirit is one of these, and should—if the Christian is properly oriented—"reside in this flesh" as a "deposit."[59] To feel sadness (*lypē*) grieves (*lypeite*) the Holy Spirit, following the same participatory logic Paul himself introduced to the Corinthians in condemning *porneia*.[60] Given Ephesians' condemnation of grieving the Holy Spirit, it is understandable that the Shepherd picks out sadness as the worst of the spirits, chastising (again) Hermas: "You are senseless. . . . Do you not understand that sadness is the worst spirit of all and most to be dreaded by the slaves of God? That it corrupts a person more than any other spirit?"[61] Paul's description of a worldly grief (*hē tou kosmou lypē*) resonates with Hermas, who struggles with the tensions between Christian community and the demands of life in Rome.[62] This kind of sadness afflicts those who "merely believe" without truly immersing themselves in the difficult "inquiry into the truth" and "divine matters."[63] These believers (who are described later as two-minded) "become mixed up with business affairs and wealth and friendships with outsiders and many other matters that pertain to this age . . . they are overshadowed by these other matters and are corrupted and become barren in spirit."[64] The cure is in coming to "make careful inquiry into divine matters and the truth, and have their hearts directed towards the Lord," which will replace their worldly grief with a fear (*phobos*) of the Lord.[65]

Yet what to do about Paul's commendation of a godly grief? Hermas knows it but betrays his discomfort. The Shepherd explains "how grief wears out the holy spirit and then again saves it."[66] When a *dipsychos* attempts some matter, such as the business affairs Hermas mentions, and fails at it, "this grief enters into him, and it grieves the holy spirit and wears it out."[67] A similar process happens with irascibility, which like double-mindedness leads to *lypē*. But in response, "grief again enters into the irritated person's heart; he grieves for

59. Herm. Mand. 3.1–2 (28) (Soyars).

60. See the explication by Dale Martin, *The Corinthian Body* (New Haven: Yale University Press, 1995).

61. Herm. Mand. 10.1.1–2 (40) (Ehrman, altered). Irascibility is also called the worst spirit elsewhere, but the treatise's focus on and invective against *lypē* definitely gives it the feel of the greatest threat to the Christian, so Carolyn Osiek, *The Shepherd of Hermas*, Hermeneia (Minneapolis: Fortress, 1999), 33; and Crislip, "Shepherd of Hermas," 243.

62. See careful synoptic discussion of Soyars, *Shepherd of Hermas*, 116–19.

63. Herm. Mand. 10.1.4 (40) (Ehrman).

64. Herm. Mand. 10.1.4, 5 (40) (Ehrman).

65. Herm. Mand. 10.1.5–6 (40) (Ehrman).

66. Herm. Mand. 10.2.1 (41) (Ehrman).

67. Herm. Mand. 10.2.3 (41) (Ehrman).

what he has done, and he repents (*metanoēsēi*) because he has done evil."[68] This sadness that leads to *metanoia* builds on Paul's teachings in 2 Corinthians 7:8–10, as it leads to a salvation or wholeness (*sōtēria*), at least of a sort. The *Shepherd* backpedals in praising the saving power of sadness, following the previous passage with, "Therefore, this grief is reputed (or appears, *dokei*) to bring salvation, because having done what was evil, he repented."[69] He is unwilling to say that the grief is truly salutary; it only appears to save. He continues by moving quite starkly away from Paul, even so far as undermining the message of 2 Corinthians. "Both double-mindedness and irascibility, therefore, grieve the holy spirit. And so, remove grief from yourself and do not crush the holy spirit that dwells in you; otherwise, it may petition God against you and leave you. For the holy spirit of God that has been given in this flesh cannot stand either grief or distress."[70] This is the closest Hermas gets to a positive use of sadness for the believer, and it is at best confusing, leaving the impression of the wholesale negative valence of grief, especially in comparison with other teachings in the work.

Believers should cleanse themselves of all grief and cast it away, clothing themselves with all cheerfulness, thus to live unto God.[71] While Hermas will fall into grief later in his visionary encounters, it is always the cheerfulness of God's messengers that shines through, to be imitated by the believers who are always cheerful.[72] Why Hermas even included his confusing reference to the grief that leads to repentance and salvation is unclear, but likely "the idea of two kinds of sadness was so well-known from 2 Cor 7:10 that the author feels he cannot *not* include it."[73] It is clear, at any rate, that he preferred to model a Christian life that wholly expunged sadness from the soul, which was to be filled instead with the Holy Spirit and display cheerfulness at all times.

As extreme as this might sound in later Christian centuries and today's post-Christian world, for contemporaries of Hermas this could have seemed wise and practicable advice. A generation after Hermas had lived and written in Rome, the physician and public intellectual Galen suffered a loss that would make most scholars break down in tears—his storerooms of books, custom and valuable medicines, and medical devices (some of his own invention) went up in flames along with many other buildings along the Sacred Way. He

68. Herm. Mand. 10.2.4 (41) (Ehrman).
69. Herm. Mand. 10.2.4 (41) (Soyars).
70. Herm. Mand. 10.1.4–5 (41) (Ehrman).
71. Herm. Mand. 10.3 (42).
72. Herm. Sim. 6.1 (61); 6.3 (63); 8.1 (67); 9.2 (79); 9.10 (87); 9.15 (92); 9.24 (101); 10.4 (114).
73. Osiek, *Shepherd of Hermas*, 137.

describes the magnitude of his losses in rich detail, down to the very *paragraphos* marks of his specially annotated manuscripts, clearly intending to pluck the heartstrings of his literary and elite audience.[74]

After this enormous loss to his professional and intellectual life, he claims, his friends regularly questioned why he did not suffer any distress or sadness (*lypē*) over it. In response he composed the short treatise *Peri alypias*, "On the Avoidance of Distress" (or "On the Avoidance of Grief").[75] His answer to the question and his explanation for why he never feels *lypē* differs from Hermas. No good and evil spirits for the doctor, and certainly no heavenly visions. But as for the underlying cause of sadness, they would have had much to agree on. For it is the world of business, possessions, and their loss, potential and actual, that drives the man to distress, a sadness (*lypē*) even to death. Galen tells of the grammarian Philides, who, upon learning that his books had gone up in the same flames, died from dejection (*dysthymia*) and sadness (*lypē*).[76] Paul's century-old description of a worldly sadness that leads to death would have sounded quite current among the second-century Roman elite, even if Galen would have little patience with his metaphysics.[77]

Galen's advice, however, differs starkly from the *Shepherd*, and depends on both a sort of Stoic cognitive *koinē* and his own great wealth. For him to be without distress was no great accomplishment compared to those who had nothing. His losses had merely moved him down a level in possessions, which he could hope to regain. At least he had not lost everything.[78] Far worse are those who, whatever their wealth, are always comparing themselves with others, for "they will always be poor, their desire (*epithymia*) being unfulfilled."[79] For Galen, thwarted desire and its persistent insatiability are the seeds of *lypē*, distress, pain, sadness.[80]

74. Galen, *De indolentia* 12–37.

75. A translation with critical essays is provided by Claire K. Rothschild and Trevor W. Thompson, eds., *Galen's "De indolentia,"* STAC 88 (Tübingen: Mohr Siebeck, 2014); with earlier translation in Claire K. Rothschild and Trevor W. Thompson, "Galen: 'On the Avoidance of Grief,'" *Early Christianity* 2 (2011): 110–29. Greek edition with French translation by Véronique Boudon-Millot and Jacques Jouanna with Antoine Pietrobelli, *Galien: Ne pas se chagriner* (Paris: Les Belles Lettres, 2010).

76. Galen, *De indolentia* 1–7.

77. For a full comparison of Paul within the Galenic and medico-philosophical context of the early empire, see L. Michael White, "The Pathology and Cure of Grief (λύπη [*lypē*]): Galen's *De indolentia* in Context," in Rothschild and Thompson, *Galen's "De indolentia,"* 221–49.

78. Galen, *De indolentia* 44–49.

79. Galen, *De indolentia* 43 (Rothschild and Thompson).

80. On later Christian reflection on sadness as "thwarted desire," cf. J. Warren Smith,

While the *Shepherd of Hermas* and other second-century writers (Christian and pagan) commended a path toward a freedom from sadness, Christians continued to debate the proper attitude toward it, how and whether to distinguish between different types of grief (worldly and godly, salvific and deadly), and to elaborate on the specific risks of sadness and its potential value as a religious practice to be cultivated among community members and between the Christian and God.[81] I wish to highlight three later examples of Christian authors who elaborate on sadness (or its repression) as a distinctive practice, each of which represents a trajectory of emotional formation that would persist long after late antiquity: the Clementine *Homilies*, Evagrius of Pontus, and Augustine of Hippo (with his mentor Ambrose).

The Clementine *Homilies*

The Clementine literature includes two narrative collections which center the journeys and teachings of Peter and feature Clement—future bishop of Rome—as narrator and amanuensis for the apostle. These two lengthy "novels" (the *Recognitions* and the *Homilies*) appear to be fourth-century creations, each independently adapting an earlier base document, likely the *Preaching of Peter* (*Kērygmata Petrou*), which preserves "Jewish-Christian" traditions reflecting non- or anti-Pauline traditions and maintaining closer doctrinal and ritual connections with the Hellenistic Jewish origins of the Christian movement.[82]

The *Clementina* take issue with Paul's approach to the problem of sadness, in this case his instruction in 1 Thessalonians. At the opening of the *Homilies*, the character of Clement frames his autobiographical journey to Christian faith

Passion and Paradise: Human and Divine Emotion in the Thought of Gregory of Nyssa (New York: Crossway, 2004), 97. This was common among Stoics as well, Simo Knuuttila, *Emotions in Ancient and Medieval Philosophy* (Oxford: Clarendon, 2004), 53.

81. Other second-century Christian texts are discussed in the previous chapter, on joy, such as 2 Clement, the *Gospel of Truth*, and martyr texts.

82. For background see Donald H. Carlson, *Jewish-Christian Interpretation of the Pentateuch in the Pseudo-Clementine Homilies* (Minneapolis: Fortress, 2013), 1–11; Jan Bremmer, "Pseudo-Clementines: Texts, Dates, Places, Authors, and Magic," in *The Pseudo-Clementines*, ed. Jan Bremmer, SECA 10 (Leuven: Peeters, 2010), 1–23; and Nicole Kelley, *Knowledge and Religious Authority in the Pseudo-Clementines: Situating the "Recognitions" in Fourth Century Syria*, WUNT 2/213 (Tübingen: Mohr Siebeck, 2006), 1–17. On anti-Pauline elements, see Simon Légasse, *L'Antipaulinisme sectaire au temp des pères de l'église*, CRB 47 (Paris: Gabalda, 2000), 29–39.

as from a pervasive sadness and despair toward joy, in ways which readers of 2 Clement and the *Gospel of Truth* would have found familiar. Clement describes himself among Rome's fortunate, a citizen, yet tormented by existential concerns about mortality and the lack of any hope for posthumous existence. Like all others, he will be forgotten. He will pass away into nothingness, as the world itself will dissolve.[83] For Clement this is a chronic state of "depression and pains" (*athymias kai ponous*). The young philosopher has such "painful sadness" (*odynēran lypēn*) that he was nearly wasting away with emotion (or passion, suffering, or disease, *pathos*).[84] In search of an answer and in hope for immortality, he sought out philosophers. When one taught the immortality of the soul, he was overjoyed (*echairon*), but when another taught the death of the soul, he was sad (*elypoumēn*) and further depressed (*ēthymoun*) that he could find nothing but disagreement.[85] Continuing to doubt (*aporoumenos*) he toyed with Epicurean consolation for a time: why bother being sad now (*to lypeisthai*)? Why not procrastinate his grief till death, knowing that he'll not exist anyway, and thus have no pain at all? He abandons this for the safer bet of righteousness and self-control.[86] But where to find the correct teaching?

In Rome, he hears a man preaching a new hope from Judea, promising eternal life for those who change their ways, and seeks out Barnabas and then Peter, whom he attends for the rest of the twenty books of the *Homilies*, traveling, teaching, and battling enemies, the greatest of whom is Simon Magus.[87] The *Homilies* return to the problem of sadness and grief within a long debate between Peter and Simon over the origin and power of sin, with each figure representing aspects of Paul's teachings. Pain and death may have entered the world with evil, with sin, but Peter rejects any sense of death, evil, and pain as ontological forces in the world: "Evil, then," he starts,

> does not exist always, yea, it cannot even exist at all substantially; for pain (*to algein*) and death belong to the class of accidents (*symbainontōn*), neither of which can co-exist with abiding strength. For what is pain but the interruption of harmony? And what is death but the separation of soul from body? There is therefore no pain when there is harmony.[88]

83. *Hom.* 1.1. Here the *Recognitions* has a similar opening. Bernhard Rehm, ed., *Die Pseudoklementinen, I: Homilien*, GCS 42 (Berlin: Akademie, 1969).

84. *Hom.* 1.2.1.

85. *Hom.* 1.3.

86. *Hom.* 1.4.

87. *Hom.* 1.7.

88. *Hom.* 19.20 (*NPNF*). I have discussed these passages previously with a focus on the

This disharmony will be remedied in Christ's kingdom, and man "will suffer no pain, so that he will not be mortal."[89]

Simon continues to press Peter about that other class of pains in this present world, emotions (*pathē*): "I am speaking about desire (*epithymia*), anger (*orgē*), sadness (*lypē*) and the like." For Peter, these sufferings are no different from the pains of disease and injury; they will not "always exist," but "belong to the things that are accidental."[90] Peter's approach reads as a sharp rebuke to Christians like Hermas and Paul before him, taking a more Aristotelian approach to the passions, aiming for moderation or *metriopatheia* of emotion, a utilitarian balance rather than extinguishing potentially harmful passions. Desire, Peter says, has its purpose, created for us by God so that we might carry out his most fundamental command, to be fruitful and multiply (within marriage of course). Anger, too, has its role, to help protect us from harm, presumably in self-defense. And in a pointed rebuke of Paul's unsparing command in 1 Thessalonians, sadness was also instilled in humanity by God, here for grief at the death of loved ones:

> Moreover, we are capable of grief (*lypē*), that we may be moved with sympathy at the death of relatives, of a wife, or children, or brothers, or parents, or friends, or some others, since, if we were not capable of sympathy, we should be inhuman (*ananthrōpoi*). In like manner, all the other affections (*ta panta*) will be found to be adapted for us, if at least the reason for their existence be considered.[91]

Compared to the emotional teaching of Paul or Hermas, the Peter of the Clementine *Homilies* offers an utterly reasonable and moderate model for Christian emotional practice. This is not to say it is easy to maintain *metriopatheia* in a world full of temptation, threat, and loss, any more in the ancient world than the modern. Still, the Clementine view of Christian emotional practice falls in line with common Aristotelian and later Platonic views of the passions: Passions complement a positive understanding of the Jewish law as foundational to Christian piety in late antiquity.[92]

problem of pain in discussion of early Christian identity. Andrew Crislip, "Pain, Emotion, and Identity in Early Christianity," *Journal of Early Christian History* 12 (2022): 27–51.

89. *Hom.* 19.20 (*NPNF*).

90. *Hom.* 19.21 (*NPNF*).

91. *Hom.* 19.21 (*NPNF*).

92. For which see also Carlson, *Jewish-Christian Interpretation.*

Evagrius of Pontus

Christians continued to debate the proper feeling and expression of sadness and grief throughout late antiquity. Among the most insightful and influential students of sadness was Evagrius of Pontus (345–399). Evagrius rose quickly through the ecclesiastical ranks in the intellectual and political circle that emerged around the Cappadocian fathers, Gregory of Nazianzus, Gregory of Nyssa, and Basil of Caesarea. He followed Nazianzen to Constantinople when he took up the bishop's throne there. Evagrius was ordained as a reader and surely partook in all the excitement the capital had to offer the young and ambitious. According to versions of his biography, this included an affair with a woman married to a court official.[93] After a frightening dream, he got out of town quick and headed to Jerusalem with a vow to devote himself to the ascetic life. There he fell into further dissolute behaviors and spent six months sick and bedridden, incurable by any doctors. In the end it was spiritual direction that healed him, under the expert therapy of the Roman transplant Melania the Elder, who recognized God's hand in the disease, a punishment for his broken vow of piety. This was his final erring, and he set out to the monastery of Kellia ("the Cells") of northern Egypt, where he would spend the last two decades of his life praying, teaching, and writing on topics ranging from the practical methods of asceticism to the most abstract and speculative of theology, an enormous and influential literary output only partially preserved today due to posthumous controversies over aspects of his theology and his inspiration from Origen.[94]

Evagrius's most well-known influence lies in his approach to identifying the evil thoughts that afflicted his fellow ascetics, which he addresses in many of his practical works on the ascetic life.[95] In its most well-known formulation, Eva-

93. The following is related in the Coptic version of Evagrius's biography in the *Lausiac History* of Palladius in Tim Vivian, trans., *Four Desert Fathers: Pambo, Evagrius, Macarius of Egypt, and Macarius of Alexandria* (Crestwood, NY: St. Vladimir's Seminary Press, 2004), 69–92.

94. See Elizabeth A. Clark, *The Origenist Controversy: The Cultural Construction of an Early Christian Debate* (Princeton: Princeton University Press, 1992). Controversies especially came to a head in the reign of Justinian in 553.

95. Evagrius's ascetic works, with a full introduction, are translated by Robert E. Sinkewicz, *Evagrius of Pontus: The Greek Ascetic Corpus* (Oxford: Oxford University Press, 2003), on whose translations I normally depend. The major handbook on thoughts, preserved in Syriac, is translated, also with important introduction, by David Brakke (Evagrius of Pontus, *Talking Back: Antirrhētikos*, trans. David Brakke, CS 220 [Collegeville, MN: Liturgical, 2009]).

grius developed a taxonomy of eight such thoughts (*logismoi*)—gluttony, lust, avarice, sadness, anger, acedia, vainglory, and pride—a list that looks familiar to the seven deadly (or cardinal) sins of the Roman Catholic tradition and indeed is the source of the western European list, transmitted through his follower John Cassian and Irish and Roman interpreters, through whom the revised version of "sins" entered the medieval confessional.[96] The most conspicuous among these is sadness, which does not show up in the medieval cardinal sins tradition. From a medieval or modern perspective, its absence is not surprising—how could it be a *sin* to be sad? But from as early as Paul, not to mention Stoic tradition, sadness had a clear negative influence on the Christian, which should be avoided in most or all circumstances.[97] Evagrius set the stage for how sadness would change from a vice to a virtue in the Middle Ages and beyond.

Significantly, Evagrius targets thoughts rather than sins. He points to the external origin of negative and unwanted strands of thinking and rumination. In this way, Evagrius works in a tradition of thinking about cognition seen earlier in the *Shepherd*, which prefers "spirits," as do Evagrius's student Cassian, Hellenistic Jewish tradition, and others.[98] The unpredictable and external origin of thoughts makes intuitive sense to nearly anyone. Who hasn't found themselves suddenly deep in rumination on some past trauma or future fear and wondered, How did I get here? Thoughts themselves are not sins but demons, casting themselves at monks to distract them from pure prayer with worries about the future, thoughts of home, memories of past joys and failures, concerns about health and sickness, and annoyance at one's peers.

The passions or emotions themselves, in contrast, occur in the monk's reactions to these thoughts in his soul. This is where the ascetic's self-control

96. Surveys of this process abound; see, for example, Columba Stewart, OSB, "Evagrius Ponticus and the 'Eight Generic *Logismoi*,'" in *In the Garden of Evil: The Vices and Culture in the Middle Ages*, ed. Richard Newhauser, PIMS 18 (Toronto: Pontifical Institute of Medieval Studies, 2005), 3–34; and Carole Straw, "Gregory, Cassian, and the Cardinal Vices," in Newhauser, *Garden of Evil*, 35–58.

97. See discussion in Douglas Burton-Christie, "Evagrius on Sadness," *Cistercian Studies Quarterly* 44 (2009): 395–409; and Andrew Crislip, "The Ascetic Construction of Emotions: *Lupe* and *Akedia* in the Works of Evagrios of Pontos," in *Managing Emotion in Byzantium: Passions, Affects and Imaginings*, ed. Margaret Mullett and Susan Ashbrook Harvey (London: Routledge, 2023), 240–65.

98. As addressed by John Cassian, *The Institutes*, trans. Boniface Ramsay, OP, ACW 58 (New York: Newman, 2000); and the Hellenistic *Testament of the Twelve Patriarchs*. On the emotions in his larger collection of *Conferences*, which addresses despair, see Niki Kasumi Clements, "Emotions and Ascetic Formation in John Cassian's *Collationes*," StPatr 83 (2017): 251–69.

comes into play, not in the absence of thoughts but in managing the psychological reaction to them. Drawing on Stoic theory of the emotions, along with Aristotelian and Platonic conceptions of the soul, Evagrius teaches a method for achieving freedom from negative emotions, or *apatheia*.[99]

While some of these demonic goads were not what we or the ancients would consider passions and/or emotions—gluttony, fornication, and avarice, for example—his description of the contours of these thoughts often carried with them complex emotional valence. Gluttony, for example, was not merely the desire to eat excessively. It could also manifest in worry about one's health.[100] Avarice was not generally a love of wealth as we might think of it today but could merely be the monk's anxiety that when he got old there would be no one to care for him.[101] What would be prudent financial planning today was a demonic distraction in the spiritual life of the Egyptian desert. In his catalog of 498 such thoughts, which he called *Antirrhetikos*, or *Talking Back*, Evagrius offers a rich phenomenology of the experience of being a monk in the late-fourth century, based on his own contemplation and the confessions of his many disciples and fellow ascetics. It is no accident that Evagrius placed sadness (*lypē*) in the middle of his list of eight thoughts. Other thoughts, Evagrius thought, provoked desire within the Christian, for physical pleasure, comfort, revenge, entertainment, and recognition. But sadness pricks no pleasure on its own, a libidinal lack familiar to many who have suffered from an extended bout of depression.[102] Rather, sadness the fellow traveler follows along with any and all of the other thoughts, a pitfall for any who suffer loss or failure in their various desires. It "has no strength unless the other passions are present, as a fetter is without strength unless there is someone to attach it."[103] Loss, whether from the object relations school or affect theory, is recognized as the catalyst for sadness and grief.[104] The monk feels this loss most poignantly in his voluntary exile away from family and friends, his abandonment of worldly success and secular honor.[105] The monk's

99. For a fuller discussion, see Brakke, introduction to *Talking Back*, 1–40; and Sinkewicz, *Evagrius of Pontus*, xxi–xxxvii.

100. E.g., *Antirrhetikos* 1.3.

101. E.g., *Antirrhetikos* 3.2.

102. *Eight Thoughts* 5.12 (PG 79:1156).

103. *Eight Thoughts* 5.9 (PG 79:1156, Sinkewicz).

104. For example, from the perspective of psychology, John Bowlby, *Loss: Sadness and Depression* (New York: Basic, 1980); or from affect theory and cultural studies, David Eng and David L. Kazanjian, eds., *Loss: The Politics of Mourning* (Berkeley: University of California Press, 2002).

105. *Foundations* 5 (PG 40.1256).

sadness shares much with the worldly sadness of the *Shepherd of Hermas*, also channeling Paul's bifurcation of the emotion in 2 Corinthians.

Sadness posed a grave threat to the Christian monk, preventing the core goal of ascetic practice: contemplative prayer. Evagrius writes that "the monk afflicted by sadness cannot move the mind towards contemplation or offer up pure prayer," here again recalling the *Shepherd*'s claim that sadness weighs down the Christian's prayer from ascending to God.[106] Sadness further bore a uniquely self-destructive potential, "the maw of a lion [that] readily devours one afflicted by it," and "a worm in the heart, [which] consumes the mother who gave it birth."[107] Far more than any of the other thoughts, sadness afflicts the monk with a violent physicality that demonstrates the blurred lines between physical and psychological pain inherent in the concept of *lypē*. Sadness burns, stings like a scorpion, strikes the face, and blooms into "incurable illness."[108] These injuries should not be taken metaphorically. Ancient *lypē* hurts, just as grief and depression are experienced through embodied pain in a variety of cultures, including our own.[109] The violence of sadness further connects it with another passion, anger, to which I will turn in chapter 4. Perhaps surprisingly, Evagrius presents sadness as closely chained to anger, especially in the loss and disappointment that anger also reacts to. I suggested that the prominence of sadness in Paul's Corinthian correspondence is related to the relative inaccessibility or inappropriateness of anger for Romans of lower status. Anthropological and historical studies have shown that anger and sadness are frequently linked in diverse ways, which is also suggested by some neuroscientific studies.[110] It is no accident, then, that he places sadness and anger next to one another in his list of thoughts. The trio of sadness, anger, and listlessness [*akēdia*] are linked as the three thoughts associated with the "spirited" (*thumoeidēs*) part of the Platonic soul. As seen in the various

106. *Eight Thoughts* 5.6 (PG 79.1145D–64D), at 1156 (Sinkewicz). Also *Eight Thoughts* 5.20; 5.21. Herm. Mand. 10.3 (42).

107. *Eight Thoughts* 5.2; 5.3 (PG 79:1156, Sinkewicz); *Vices* 4 (PG 79:1144, Sinkewicz).

108. E.g., *Antirrhetikos* 4.33; 4.41; 4.53; 4.56; 4.65; 4.76 (Brakke).

109. See recent analysis by Helen Rhee, *Illness, Pain, and Health Care in Early Christianity* (Grand Rapids: Eerdmans, 2022); Crislip, "Pain"; Crislip, "Ascetic Construction," 248–49. A review of scientific research on the intersection of emotion and pain is in Mark A. Lumley et al., "Pain and Emotion: A Biopsychosocial Review of Recent Research," *Journal of Clinical Psychology* 67.9 (2011): 942–68.

110. Carol Barr-Zisowitz, "'Sadness': Is There Such a Thing?," in *Handbook of Emotions*, ed. Michael Lewis and Jeannette M. Haviland-Jones, 2nd ed. (New York: Guilford, 2000), 614–18, addressing the work of Sylvan Tomkins, a major influence on more humanistic affect theory.

responses to emotion in Corinth, anger and sadness both respond to loss, humiliation, and outrage, anger actively and sadness more passively (or with Paul, perhaps, passive-aggressively).[111]

Evagrius shares much in common with the *Shepherd of Hermas*'s great distrust of sadness as a threat to prayer and Christian life, though framed within a more philosophically sophisticated and systematic phenomenology of the passions and thoughts that ascetics experience. But Evagrius expands his discussion of sadness and grief beyond the pain of *lypē*. Like Paul, he sees in some forms of sorrow a salvific potential. But in contrast with Paul's obscure distinction between two types of *lypē*, Evagrius identifies the more positive side of sadness as a different emotional concept of "grief" or "mourning" (*penthos*).[112] While sadness evokes the passivity of *passion*, a feeling suffered, the soul drowned or crushed, this *penthos* is truly an emotional practice, as purposeful with positive drive as sadness is fettered by aimless and thwarted desire.[113] Evagrius sees *penthos* as action oriented, manifested in tears, preparing the monk's mind for prayer: "By sorrowing you may be able to calm the wildness that there is in your soul and obtain forgiveness from the Lord."[114] Far from the *Shepherd*'s warning that sadness weighs down the Christian so his prayers cannot reach God, tears for Evagrius assist in prayer and petitions, both pleasing God and focusing the aim of the monk's petitions.[115]

Tears are also useful in countering the thought of acedia. While acedia would in the Latin Middle Ages incorporate aspects of sadness and later turn into the "sin of sloth," in the time of Evagrius it was marked by a listlessness that distracts the monk from the norms of ascetic life, an anomic state in which monks drifted variously into laziness and distraction, bitterness, withdrawal, or excessive and misguided zeal in asceticism.[116] To counter this demon, Evagrius advises an emotional practice of self-therapy through dialectical weeping:

111. Crislip, "Ascetic Construction," 252.

112. The classic study of *penthos* is Irénée Hausherr, SJ, *Penthos: The Doctrine of Compunction in the Christian East*, trans. Anselm Hufstader, OSB, CS 53 (Kalamazoo, MI: Cistercian Publications, 1982), which collects thematically a rich variety of sources from the patristic through the Byzantine periods, though outdated methodologically. See, for the later Syrian context, Hannah Hunt, *Joy-Bearing Grief: Tears of Contrition in the Writings of the Early Syrian and Byzantine Fathers*, The Medieval Mediterranean 57 (Leiden: Brill, 2004). Here I follow the reading by Jeremy Driscoll, "Penthos and Tears in Evagrius Ponticus," *Studia Monastica* 36 (1994): 147–63.

113. Driscoll, "Penthos," 150, on tears as a gift. On the dangerous passivity of sadness in anthropological studies, see Barr-Zisowitz, "Sadness," 614.

114. *Prayer* 5 (PG 79:1169D, Driscoll).

115. Driscoll, "Penthos," 150–53.

116. See Andrew Crislip, "The Sin of Sloth or the Illness of the Demons? The Demon of

> When we are oppressed by the demon of listlessness, we should divide our soul in two with tears, making one part console the other, sowing good hopes in ourselves and singing David's words, "Why are you depressed my soul, why do you disturb me? Hope in God, because I will praise him, the Savior of my person, my God" (Ps 41:6[42:5])?[117]

It is against tears that the demon battles, and it is tears that can rid the monk of acedia. But this weeping does not lead to sadness per se, certainly not the passion of *lypē*, but to joy, as the monk's tearful self-consolation recalls the Sermon on the Mount, calling blessed (*makarios*) those who weep. Evagrius reads this gospel macarism as promising peace and joy for the monk at the withdrawal of the demons.[118]

Sociologists and philosophers have shown the power of crying for transforming the self and as a function of active thinking and introspection.[119] I see this in Evagrius, who offers an important innovation in Christian thinking about sadness, offering an emotional granularity (in the language of psychological construction) to this feeling and prescribing an emotional practice, defining and encouraging a different emotional concept. The very practice of labeling these feelings constructs new experiences at the intersections of society, physiology, and psychology, much as reclassifying fear as anxiety, pain as trauma, a weed as a flower, or a milkshake as a smoothie all have very real effects on experience. Evagrius divides grief, first into the emotion of sadness (*lypē*), which like others before should be entirely eliminated by the ascetic in the goal of eliminating the passions (*apatheia*). In contrast, he develops a positive function for tears in Christian emotional practice, but these are pointedly not of *lypē* but of *penthos*, a godly mourning for sins—one's own and the world's—that binds one in communion with God, focuses the mind on effective prayer, and repels the wiliest and most protean of the demons that attack the monk, the thought of acedia. Along with his contemporary ascetics with whom he was in constant dialogue, Evagrius would lay the foundation for a Christian emotional practice that would shape the monastic communities

---

Acedia in Early Christian Monasticism," *HTR* 98 (2005): 143–69. The history of the emotion and sin in the Middle Ages is surveyed by Siegfried Wenzel, *The Sin of Sloth: Acedia in Medieval Thought and Literature* (Chapel Hill: University of North Carolina Press, 1960).

117. *Praktikos* 27 (Tugwell), with slight alteration by Driscoll, "Penthos," 154.

118. Driscoll, "Penthos," 157–59.

119. As noted by Jack Barbalet, "Weeping and Transformations of Self," *Journal for the Theory of Social Behavior* 35 (2005): 125–41; and Jerome Neu, *A Tear Is an Intellectual Thing: The Meanings of Emotion* (New York: Oxford University Press, 2000), 14–46.

of the late antique and Byzantine eastern Mediterranean and Near East, the gift of joy-bearing grief.[120]

The Christian transformation of sadness continued beyond the Christian East, with its own complicated history in the monasteries and churches of western Europe, of which the intertwined histories of tears and devotion will be immediately visible in cathedrals and museums, with their spiritual centering of the crucified man of sorrows and his grieving mother.[121] Here I want to conclude with a snapshot of the kind of early Christian emotional change in the western Mediterranean that set a cornerstone for the affective lives of the later Middle Ages, in the writings of Ambrose and Augustine, focusing their reflections on the dangers and possible benefits of sadness.

Ambrose and Augustine

Ambrose (ca. 339–397), bishop of Milan, addressed the place of sadness within Christian life in his reflections on the story of the garden of Eden (*On Paradise, De paradiso*) and more specifically on God's curse against the snake and the human couple in Genesis 3:15–19. Ambrose takes up a theme often overlooked in modern studies of the Eden story but front of mind for ancient Jewish and Christian interpreters of the story of the so-called fall, and in fact very much present in the original Hebrew telling of the story.[122] While most contemporary translations render God's sentence on Eve and Adam in very bodily terms ("pangs," "pain," "toil"), the Greek text used by Jews and Christians centers the emotionality of the punishment in language that will be familiar from the first few centuries of Christian emotional discourse: "I shall increase your sorrows (*lypas*) and your sighing (*stenagmon*); in sorrows (*lypais*) you shall give birth

120. See, e.g., Hunt, *Joy-Bearing Grief*; and Kallistos Ware, "'An Obscure Matter': The Mystery of Tears in Orthodox Spirituality," in *Holy Tears: Weeping in the Religious Imagination*, ed. Kimberley Christine Patton and John Stratton Hawley (Princeton: Princeton University Press, 2005), 242–54.

121. The longer histories of which may be further explored in Rachel Fulton, *From Judgment to Passion: Devotion to Christ and the Virgin Mary, 800–1200* (New York: Columbia University Press, 2002); Miri Rubin, *Emotion and Devotion: The Meaning of Mary in Medieval Religious Cultures* (Budapest: Central European University Press, 2009); and Elina Gertsman, ed., *Crying in the Middle Ages: Tears of History* (London: Routledge, 2012).

122. See Andrew Crislip, "Emotions in Eden and After: Ancient Jewish and Christian Perspectives on Genesis 2–4," *JBRec* 6 (2019): 97–133; Hanneke Reuling, *After Eden: Church Fathers and Rabbis on Genesis 3:16–21*, Jewish and Christian Perspectives Series 10 (Leiden: Brill, 2006).

... in sorrows (*lypais*) you shall eat of it all the days of your life" (Gen 3:16–17 LXX, my translation). The emotionality of humanity's transition from paradise to the world outside was not lost on ancient interpreters of Genesis, who—from Philo to the late antique ascetics—reflected on the historical causality of human emotion.[123]

Drawing on Philo, Ambrose reads the trio of snake, woman, and man allegorically.[124] The snake is pleasure (*delectatio*), the woman is the feelings (or perceptions) of soul and mind (*sensus animi mentisque*, or *aisthēsis*), and the man the mind (*nous*).[125] The fall presents less a problem of interpersonal or interspecies relations than a psychological one: "If Eve, that is, the emotions (*sensus*) of the first woman, had kept her lamp lighted, she would not have enfolded us in the meshes of her sin. She would not have fallen from the height of immortality which is established as the reward of virtue," and would not have led the mind, that is Adam, into error.[126] In keeping with a long tradition of other ancient interpreters, God curses both the man and the woman with emotional pain due to their transgression. Ambrose translates the Septuagint's *lypē*—used for both Eve and Adam, in contrast with more gendered modern translations—as *tristitia*, a deep sadness and gloom that brings out the passionate nuances of the curse even more pointedly than *lypē*, which still carries the broader semantics of pain and distress of various sorts.[127]

Ambrose interprets this curse of the emotional pain of sadness in dialogue with Paul's advice to the Corinthians. While some sadness is worldly and leads to death, other sadness is godly and leads to salvation. It is the latter, fortunate sadness that catches Ambrose's theological imagination. Sadness distinguishes

123. The various ways Christians and Jews approached the emotional repercussions of the Eden story are surveyed in Crislip, "Emotions in Eden"; and Reuling, *After Eden*, both of which address the intersection of so-called physical and emotional pain in this terminology. See also the recent study of pain terminology, including *lypē*, by Han Baltussen, "Labelling Pain: Early Greek Concepts from Homer to the Hellenistic Era," in *Pain Narratives in Greco-Roman Writings: Studies in the Representation of Physical and Mental Suffering*, ed. Jaqueline R. Clark, Daniel King, and Han Baltussen, Studies in Ancient Medicine 58 (Leiden: Brill, 2023), 12–43.

124. On Philo's influence, see Reuling, *After Eden*, 81, 93.

125. *Parad.* 2.11 (PL 14.295); Ambrose of Milan, *Hexameron, Paradise, and Cain and Abel*, trans. John J. Savage, FC 42 (New York: Fathers of the Church, 1961).

126. *Parad.* 2.11 (Savage, PL 14.295).

127. See Rhee, *Illness, Pain, and Health Care*, 126–40; and Helen King, "The Early Anodynes: Pain in the Ancient World," in *The Management of Pain: The Historical Perspective*, ed. R. Mann (Carnforth, UK: Parthenon, 1988), 51–62. On the appropriateness of the translation, see Reuling, *After Eden*, 100.

the snake's curse from humanity's. While the snake will crawl on and eat of the earth for all time, which speaks allegorically of worldly entanglements, humanity will have a great "benefit" in their toil—sadness.

> For it is written: "Cursed is the earth in thy works; in sadness shall you eat thereof all the days of your life." The two sentences seem to have a certain similarity, yet in that similarity there is great difference. There is a difference in the way a person eats of the earth, as the serpent is related to have done and the manner in which this is recorded of the man: "In sadness you shall eat." That very phrase "in sadness" makes the precise difference. . . . It is for my benefit that I should eat the earth in sadness rather than with delight, that is to say, that I should appear to feel a certain sadness in my bodily acts and senses rather than experience pleasure in sin. Many, in fact, because of their manifold iniquities have no awareness of sin. But he (Paul) who says: "I chastise my body and bring it into subjection," feels sadness because of regret for the sins to which we are subject. He himself did not have such serious faults for which he ought to feel sorrow. Hence he teaches us that that kind of sorrow is of value which has, not this world, but God, as its end.[128]

The bishop then proceeds to cite 2 Corinthians 7:9–10. Ambrose significantly places Paul's conception of sadness at the very heart of the story of human nature. While any number of Jewish and Christian readers saw the story of the first transgression as the origin of passions, sadness, fear, and shame, Ambrose sidesteps any detailed discussion of the downside of being sad and raises up the great blessing of *tristitia*.[129] It is sadness that makes the difference between human and animal, between Adam and the snake, and bestows the gift of repentance (*poenitentia*). God's providence established sadness as the way for humans to recover their footing before God after their catastrophic fall.

While Ambrose traces the curse's origin to Eve, he focuses on Adam as its recipient and compares his toil of *tristesse* in the fields (beneficial for repentance) with the serpent's pointless eating of dust. Adam bears blessed sadness, and he is not alone. Ambrose gestures toward the patriarchs of the Old

128. Ambrose, *Parad.* 15.75 (Savage, PL 14.330–31).

129. For the history of this interpretation, see Crislip, "Emotions in Eden and After." See further the discussion, on different Ambrosian texts, in Susan Wessel, *On Compassion, Healing, Suffering, and the Purpose of the Emotional Life*, Reading Augustine (New York: Bloomsbury Academic, 2020), 37–38.

Testament who "were sorrowful in the midst of their bodily labors and who attained grace, while those who found delight in such pleasure continued to be punished."[130] This marks a change in gendered emotional norms from the second century, as the *Shepherd*, for instance, insists that any *lypē* is sinful and unbecoming of a Christian, and moreover unmanly. Here, Ambrose frames *tristitia* as a core part of the emotional constitution of men, a gift from God and the primary mode of religious transformation and salvation.

The history of tears as a tool of religious transformation and as emblematic of the performance of a kind of Christian masculinity will have a long and complex history in western Europe and in the Christian east. No one would have more influence than Augustine (354–430) on Christians of the West in their understanding of sadness as a part of spirituality, community, and conversion.[131] Augustine's reflections on sadness run throughout his literary works and triangulate him amid Paul, Evagrius, and Ambrose, drawing on a robust biblical tradition of weeping and sadness and setting himself against the tradition, Stoic and Christian, of aiming for a life free from painful emotion (*apatheia*).[132] Augustine, rather, centered the experience of sadness as a virtue and a distinctively Christian emotion; his "rehabilitation of grief marks his profoundest break not only from the cognitive therapy of Stoicism but from all the various forms of philosophical self-help associated with classical culture."[133]

Augustine treats the problem of sadness in some of his most famous and influential works, including his *Confessions*, *City of God*, and the *Expositions on the Psalms*. In *City of God* (ca. 413–26), Augustine takes Ambrose's insights on emotion in the garden of Eden and makes them more explicit, setting them apart from the kind of Stoic-influenced emotional thinking of Cicero (and implicitly that of some Christians of the east, like Evagrius) and the views

130. Ambrose, *Parad.* 15.75 (Savage, PL 14.331). Ambrose will take up women's sadness in some ascetic writings; women can now give birth in joy, rather than sorrow (cf. John 16) through asceticism, Reuling, *After Eden*, 96–103. Reuling writes, "Eve's ordeal has come to an end in Christian times, at least for more or less perfect women who bring forth spiritual offspring in exultation" (103).

131. See Wessel, *On Compassion*, 27–51, with a focus on the *Confessions* and *City of God*.

132. Catherine Oppel, "'Why, My Soul, Are You Sad?': Augustine's Opinion on Sadness in the *City of God* and an Interpretation of His Tears in the *Confessions*," *Augustinian Studies* 35 (2004): 199–204, who notes the Christian advocates of *apatheia* as among the targets of his criticism, although he only names the Stoics (200). I am indebted to Oppel's insightful exposition of the *City of God* and *Confessions*.

133. James Wetzel, *Augustine and the Limits of Virtue* (Cambridge: Cambridge University Press, 1992), 104, cited in Wessel, *On Compassion*, 35.

of sadness expressed by Hermas, who presents sadness as both unchristian and unmanly. For Augustine, sadness is a virtue, which flies in the face of a dominant Stoic tradition. He attacks this influential approach to sadness from a number of directions. Sadness, he claims, is not bodily but mental, playing down the semantic overlap of emotional and psychological pain so important to ancient sadness. Instead of Cicero's earlier translations of *lypē* as *aegritudo* (pain or sickness), Augustine makes a point of translating it as *tristitia*, like Ambrose before him, even preferring it to *dolor*, which speaks both of the pain of loss and the pain of the cross.[134] *Tristitia*, he claims, is mental, and furthermore has a virtuous side, for which he looks to Jesus's several expressions of sorrow and weeping in the Gospels (Mark 3:5; John 11:35; Matt 26:38), and of course Paul's teaching in 2 Corinthians.[135] Furthermore, not to feel sorrow would be inhuman—we are sad because we are vulnerable and weak, qualities that connect us to the incarnate Jesus, although his wounds and weakness are not the same as ours. When we cry unwillingly, at a funeral for example, "we entertain these emotions because of the weakness of our human condition, but this was not true of Lord Jesus, for even His weakness derived from his power."[136] According to Augustine, Paul encouraged the feeling of passions, in line with both scriptural and Latin philosophical literature, "for the total absence of feeling of affliction, as long as we dwell in this place of wretchedness, is assuredly, as a lettered individual of the secular world thought and remarked, 'not without cost in bestiality of mind and torpor of body.'"[137] To inhabit a state of Stoic or Evagrian *apatheia* (or *impassibilitas*) might be desirable all things considered "but is irrelevant to the present life. . . . Accordingly the ἀπάθεια [*apatheia*] which we mentioned will exist only when there is no sin in man."[138] Before that time, such freedom from painful emotion would only cause harm, whether without fear or without pain (*dolor*), not unlike the rare modern condition of congenital analgesia which causes immense harm

134. *Civ.* 14.7; Oppel, "Why My Soul," 202–3; Augustine also used *dolor* in certain contexts (Wessel, *On Compassion*, 39) as when he reflected on the death of his friend of his Manichaean days: "Augustine described the grief he felt—the *dolor*—as a profound sense of emptiness and emotional pain." This contrasts with his mature grieving of *tristitia* and *maestitudo* (46).

135. *Civ.* 14.8–9; Oppel, "Why My Soul," 203.

136. *Civ.* 14.9 (Walsh). Translations and Latin citations of the *City of God* follow Augustine of Hippo, *De Civitate Dei: Books XIII and XIV*, ed. and trans. P. G. Walsh (Liverpool: Liverpool Classical Texts, 2017).

137. *Civ.* 14.9 (Walsh). In this larger discussion Augustine brings together Rom 1:21; Ps 68:21; and Cicero, *Tusc.* 3.12.

138. *Civ.* 14.9 (Walsh).

to those who suffer it.[139] It is indicative of the other city (of man) to try to restrain such emotions:

> Moreover, the city, or in other words the community (*societas*), of the impious . . . are rattled by these debased emotions as by diseases and agitations. And if that community contains any citizens who appear to restrain such emotions and to tone them down, they are so arrogant and puffed up in their impiety that by this very attitude their conceit increases as their pain recedes. Then if a number of them through a vanity which is as monstrous as it is rare have come so to love this restraint in themselves that they are not roused or awakened, swayed or affected by any emotion at all, they suffer the total loss of their humanity rather than attain true tranquility.[140]

But the city of God is a community bound by painful emotions no less than joy and hope, which connects them together and with God. In such painful emotion, especially sadness, the Christian gains hope of salvation through a change of mind or conversion, enacting both the primal movements of the first man and the human—though perfect—emotions of Christ.

Augustine's own archetypal and wandering journey toward Christianity was itself punctuated by powerful experiences of sadness, related in his *Confessions* (written ca. 398). From his first reconstructed wails as an infant, to the loss of his friend as a youth, to his conversion in the Milan garden, to the loss of his mother Monica, his autobiographical *Confessions* is a story of sorrow and its transformations, from the recognition of humanity's fallen and sad state in book four to the Christian power of tears at the death of his mother in book nine.[141] *Confessions* anticipates in autobiographical form the transformative potential of tears that the bishop Augustine would later flesh out in the *City of God*. Unlike his earlier tears for the sufferings of tragic actors or for his lost friend, which constitute an idolatry of sorts, substituting a love for creatures instead of the creator, the sadness and weeping for his mother truly instantiate love, love toward his beloved and for God, and not a love of himself and of

139. *Civ.* 14.9.

140. *Civ.* 14.9 (Walsh).

141. See especially Oppel, "Why My Soul"; Kim Paffenroth, "The Young Augustine: Lover of Sorrow," *Downside Review* 118 (2000): 221–30; Kim Paffenroth, "Tears of Grief and Joy: *Confessions* Book 9: Chronological Sequence and Structure," *Augustinian Studies* 28 (1997): 141–54; Wessel, *On Compassion*; and Paul Helm, "Augustine's Griefs," in *Augustine's "Confessions": Critical Essays*, ed. William E. Mann (Lanham, MD: Rowman and Littlefield, 2006), 147–60.

his own sorrow, which characterized his previous sufferings.[142] This weeping offers genuine comfort: "I took comfort in weeping in your sight over her and for her . . . and I now beseech you in behalf of my mother's sins."[143] Augustine's attitude toward sadness here, expressed in the very specific context of grief at the death of loved ones, points to a shift in the Christian practice of emotions in late antiquity, in contrast with contemporary writers of the Greek east, such as John Chrysostom, who could be "strongly ambivalent" about tearful mourning in Christian ritual, as it could pose a general breach of decorum and more seriously "may foster the temptation to blaspheme."[144] Augustine, far away from the intellectual ferment of the east in the provincial backwaters of Hippo Regius in North Africa, was free to think freely and personally about emotions as experience and practice. For Augustine, "Grief and sorrow are wounds that are not experienced by the perfection and omnipotence of Divinity, but they are wounds that can heal us in our human imperfection and weakness."[145]

Conclusion

Although I have divided joy and sadness into separate chapters, it should be clear that Christians viewed them dialectically, as always in dialogue, as sometimes mutually exclusive, and ultimately by the end of antiquity as coexisting in a tensive complementarity. While Paul carved out a place for sadness in his community and spirituality, by the second century Christians of a variety of theological persuasions shifted to conceiving of their faith as promising a path out of emotional gloom and depression, through a pedagogical or ritual curriculum of joy, which for the Christian should become a constant state as they share in the emotional effusion of God, Christ, and the Holy Spirit. For Christians in the second century, this could have made a good deal of sense, if Edward Gibbon was not entirely wrong in his famous characterization of Antonine Rome as the age in which humanity was at its happiest. Stoics certainly thought it plausible for the properly trained to achieve lasting joy and freedom from emotional distress. Christian communities radically expanded this to

142. Paffenroth, "Young Augustine," 226; Wessel, *On Compassion*, 46–48.

143. *Conf.* 9.12.33; 9.13.55 (Ryan), cited by Paffenroth, "Young Augustine," 226.

144. Blake Leyerle, *The Narrative Shape of Emotion in the Preaching of John Chrysostom*, Christianity in Late Antiquity 10 (Oakland: University of California Press, 2020), 80–81, though of course Chrysostom's approach to grieving as a human phenomenon is nuanced, as in the fuller analysis (63–111).

145. Paffenroth, "Young Augustine," 228.

induct a diverse group of people into a community of joy, who likely would never have had the opportunity to learn at the feet of a proper philosopher. That Christianity was widely assumed to be a religion of joy is reflected into the fourth century, very literally written into the imperial history of the first Christian emperor and influencing Constantine's own understanding of his salvific role in the empire. Why wouldn't one expect that ascension of Christ and his apostles to the pantheon of Rome could transform the emotions of the empire as it would bring the saving medicine of immortality to all?

Such was not to be. Christians after Constantine's revolution continued to find inspiration in Paul's obscure bifurcation of sadness, the sadness that saves and the sadness that kills. Authors like Evagrius in the east and Augustine in the west show differing ways that bishops and ascetics rethought the spiritual risk and value of feeling bad. They hint toward an emotional revolution in the medieval Greek east and Latin west that would raise the status of sadness and tears as signifiers and practices of personal and communal sanctity, in ways that many ancient Christians would hardly recognize and would likely disapprove of.[146] But that later history of the intertwined emotions of sadness and joy moves far beyond the bounds of early Christianity.

146. See the diverse perspectives in Gertsman, *Crying in the Middle Ages*.

4

Anger

In May of 2024, *USA Today* reported on a new trend in health and wellness—the "rage ritual."[1] While screaming out one's trauma is not exactly new (as in primal scream therapy's brief heyday in the 1970s), the accompanying images of "wealthy white women" screaming to the heavens in a forest while pounding the earth with sticks spread the viral story around social media. This and other videos of rage rituals "resonated, particularly with women. In comments, women describe how moving it is to see other women embody their anger—an emotion experts say society often discourages women from expressing."[2] The videos also inspired ridicule. Judging by her website, however, her own self-presentation as a "witchy" guru of "wild wisdom," and her good-natured back and forth on Fox News of all places, retreat leader Mia Banducci seemed fine with some laughter, as long as it would bring more disciples to the ways of sacred rage.[3]

The ritual is but the most dramatically videogenic twenty minutes of longer retreats, which range from short Zoom sessions to five-day retreats and can cost upward of $4,000, and capitalize on anger's ambiguity as a social and moral emotion. Anger is both inherently dangerous and a necessary precursor to combating injustice (or combating an enemy force on a battlefield), an ambiguity to which ancient philosophers like Aristotle were well-attuned.[4] Ban-

1. Charles Trepany, "Women Are Paying Big Money to Scream, Smash Sticks in the Woods. It's Called a Rage Ritual," *USA Today*, May 8, 2024; updated May 28, 2024.

2. Trepany, "Women Are Paying Big Money to Scream"; and Mary Harrington, "Wealthy White Women Turn to 'Rage Rituals' in the Woods," *Unherd*, May 13, 2024.

3. Olivia Reingold, "I Went to Karen Summer Camp," *The Free Press*, May 27, 2024; retreat website accessed at miamagik.com/wildwisdom.

4. William V. Harris, *Restraining Rage: The Ideology of Anger Control in Classical Antiq-*

ducci's word choice—*rage*—points to the dangerous, unstable, and violent end of the anger spectrum. We do not call it road anger but road rage because it is both incredibly dangerous to court conflict behind the wheel of a 2,000-pound weapon and utterly irrational: Why get riled up and risk violent conflict with a stranger over what even the most un-Stoic among us would consider an indifferent triviality? Even when rage claims high moral ground, it is uncontrollable and even intentionally violent, such as the 1969 "Days of Rage" organized in Chicago by the Students for a Democratic Society and Weathermen. Yet, in the forest, ritual rage expresses a righteous critique of all that is wrong with the world—sexism, racism, the patriarchy—and gives voice to environmental anxiety and outrage at violent conflict in the USA and abroad. And while it is all expressed in the old hydraulic metaphor of Freudian analysis (we've got to let this anger out or else we're going to blow), there is nothing of the old-fashioned contempt toward emotion as irrational. These outbursts of rage are reasonable and just.[5] They only erupt in such dramatic display because the emotion is unjustly cooped up and repressed by society's sexist expectations. And they are "real," potentially powerful and transformative.[6] They are also ways of thinking and feeling among a community of people and dramatically show the transmissibility of affect, passing among and through bodies, beyond or beneath the consciousness of the individual.[7]

Some aspects of these displays are old, even ancient. Surely the legend of the wild Bacchae is not lost on practitioners of forest rage rituals, those women driven into *mania* and out of the polis by the god Dionysus to engage in primal rituals in the forest, which in the famous myth (told in Euripides's tragedy) culminates in their dismemberment of Pentheus, king of Thebes, whom they had caught spying on them. Yet the rage rituals tap into distinctively contemporary changes in emotional practice, following a string of culturally prominent think-pieces extolling the virtues of female rage and the anger of the marginalized, much of which entered the publishing pipeline just shortly after Donald Trump won the 2016 election and rose with the tide of the #MeToo movement in the late 2010s. Just a few examples from elite traditional publications: "I Used to Insist I Didn't Get Angry. Not Anymore," *Good and Mad: The Revolution-*

---

uity (Cambridge, MA: Harvard University Press, 2001), 88–127; anger's duality (or multiplicity) is explored more globally by Barbara H. Rosenwein, *Anger: The Conflicted History of an Emotion* (New Haven: Yale University Press, 2020).

5. Rosenwein, *Anger*, 175–95, covers the celebration of anger in the past two decades.

6. For usage, see Lisa Feldman Barrett, "Emotions Are Real," *Emotions* 12 (2012): 413–29.

7. This approach to emotional contagion is described by Teresa Brennan, *The Transmission of Affect* (Ithaca, NY: Cornell University Press, 2004).

ary Power of Women's Anger, "The Power of Enraged Women," *Burn It Down: Women Writing About Anger*.[8] The titles express well the liberating and transformative potential of women's anger for the individual subject and society. Anger is a great speaker of truth, one's personal truth and truth to power, and powerfully destructive, even indiscriminately so, but in a good, cleansing way. The forest rage rituals commodify and ritualize a recent shift in the way elite culture talks and thinks about emotions and surely the way many feel these emotions, packaging this new way of feeling among other recently developed and marketized emotional practices generally thought of as "self-care."

The same cultural zeitgeist that has lifted up the angry voices of women as prophetic and transformative has also come to recognize the transformative—but pathological—power of rage among another group: white rural people (especially men).[9] These rage-filled rednecks are "big trouble" for the country, an "existential threat" to our very way of life, fueled by resentment and anger, suspicion and fear, fed to them both by a conservative media through a process of affective transmission they can hardly hope to understand and by an elite coastal media that unwittingly and ironically builds up rural folks' self-esteem as real Americans of the "heartland."[10] This invisible integration of media, religion, and capitalism reflects what is described by more Deleuzian theorists "as a 'resonance machine,' an affectively glued-together contraption 'in which heretofore unconnected or loosely associated elements *fold, bend, blend, emulsify, and resolve incompletely into each other*, forging a qualitative assemblage resistant to classical models of explanation.'"[11] I can't help but envision such an

8. Leslie Jamison, "I Used to Insist I Didn't Get Angry. Not Anymore," *New York Times Magazine*, January 17, 2018; Rebecca Traister, *Good and Mad: The Revolutionary Power of Women's Anger* (New York: Simon & Schuster, 2018); Elaine Blair, "The Power of Enraged Women," *New York Times*, September 27, 2018; Lilly Dancyger, ed., *Burn It Down: Women Writing About Anger* (New York: Seal, 2019).

9. Tom Schaller and Paul Waldman, *White Rural Rage: The Threat to American Democracy* (New York: Random House, 2024). Specialists in rural politics, however, find the book lacking in substance, a "salacious title" with "selective use of sketchy data," much of which do not demographically reflect rural communities at all, let alone representatively; so see Nicholas F. Jacobs, "New Book on Rural America Started with a False Conclusion, Then Looked for Evidence," *The Daily Yonder*, April 6, 2024; and Nicholas F. Jacobs and Daniel M. Shea, "The Truth About 'White Rural Rage,'" *Unherd*, April 6, 2024, which takes apart some of the loaded and presumptive emotional language of Schaller and Waldman.

10. Schaller and Waldman, *White Rural Rage*, 3, 21, 13.

11. Donovan O. Schaefer, *Religious Affects: Animality, Evolution, and Power* (Durham, NC: Duke University Press, 2015), 27, drawing on William Connolly, *Capitalism and Christianity: American Style* (Durham, NC: Duke University Press, 2008).

emulsifying and incompletely resolving machine as something out of a David Cronenberg film. And while the authors of the recent expose of *White Rural Rage* do not engage with emotions and affect from the approaches discussed in this volume, they echo the vibrant interest among affect theorists over the past two decades in diagnosing the pathological affects of white conservatives at the individual and mass population levels.[12]

The very contemporary debates about the risks and benefits of anger—either as an intentional practice of the self or an unconscious affect triggered in a sort of cultural "resonance machine"—relates to early Christian emotions in a number of ways. First, they show how quickly and powerfully emotions can change in biological and social bodies, as personal feelings, as cultural controversies, as identity markers, and as strategies of social transformation. While modernity has privileged the individual's experience of emotion, affect theorists, sociologists, and historians have shown that *this is not normal.* Our private emotions and public feelings were not like this not very long ago. Furthermore, this new emotional economy of anger is not merely a new discursive style or privileging of certain emotional expressions over others. The new way of anger has measurable effects on our bodies, not just our blood pressure but our gastro-intestinal systems, our brains, and more.[13] Of course, we can't observe emotional change in as granular detail or with such speed in antiquity, and we certainly can't run an fMRI or blood panel on our ancient informants. But the point remains: The way we feel and communicate shifts over time, and emotions drive social change as well.[14] These emotions are also real physiological forces within human bodies and transmissible among bodies, whether in close contact or at a distance through media.

The very current modalities of emotion show how anger is not evenly or equally distributed across a society, or rather, *should* not be equally accessible

12. E.g., Ahmed on British white hate, who draws inspiration from Freudian psychoanalysis, Sarah Ahmed, *The Cultural Politics of Emotion*, 2nd ed. (Edinburgh: Edinburgh University Press, 2014), 42–61 (with discussion of Freud at 50–52); Schaefer on rural evangelicals, *Religious Affects*, 60–91, via a reading of the documentary *Jesus Camp*; Connolly, *Capitalism and Christianity*; and (on the Westboro Baptists) Ann Pellegrini, "'Signaling Through the Flames': Hell House Performance and Structures of Religious Feeling," *American Quarterly* 59 (2007): 911–35.

13. Sumathi Reddy, "Anger Does a Lot More Damage to Your Body Than You Realize," *Wall Street Journal*, May 24, 2024, surveys some of the recent research. Also Harris, *Restraining Rage*, 47.

14. As shown in William Reddy's study of the emotional catalysts of the French Revolution, William M. Reddy, *The Navigation of Feeling: A Framework for the History of Emotions* (Cambridge: Cambridge University Press, 2001).

as a matter of rhetoric. The anger of the forest rage ritual, the anger of the intersectionally diverse contributors to *Burn It Down*, the fury of the thousands of pussy-hatted protesters against Donald Trump—this is *righteous* anger, expressed for just purposes, by people with proper educational and moral positionality to make these judgments. Rural white rage is the opposite, not only racist and ignorant, rooted in misinformation and bizarre conspiracy theories, and held by people with nary an MFA or PhD among them but unjustified and faintly ridiculous. All this posturing for control of scarce emotional resources signals the power of emotions and the emotional claims to power, the "cultural politics of emotion," so central to contemporary affect theory.[15]

For ancients, Aristotle most notably, but also Christians, Jews, and others, this emotional economy of anger would be utterly uncontroversial, as suggested in the previous chapter.[16] Certain people, the wealthy, the educated, the wise, the powerful, and the gods, had natural right to anger and the ability to deploy it properly. But others, the enslaved, women, country folk, the various ranks of the poor, simply could not have access to the same stores of anger, could not justifiably feel it, and if they did show anger it would be ridiculous and certainly not proper and moral. In his influential but not "rigorous or exhaustive account of the nature of the *pathē*," Aristotle leads off his discussion with anger (*orgē*), not unexpectedly.[17] Of all the emotions, anger received the most attention from ancient philosophers and moralists, so great was the violent danger it posed to close-knit societies always on the precipice of strife and factionalism (*eris*, *stasis*).[18] We know of over two dozen philosophical or moral treatises about anger from Greco-Roman antiquity, most lost.[19] And, as others have noted, the first surviving word of Greek literature is *mēnis*, wrath.[20]

As with all the emotions covered here, ancient anger differs from today's in its contours, semantics, and practices, though not in ways that render it unintelligible.[21] Greeks developed a rich vocabulary for anger, the *mēnis* just

15. Notably, Ahmed, *Cultural Politics of Emotion*; Schaefer, *Religious Affects*.

16. Daniel L. Gross, *The Secret History of Emotion: From Aristotle's "Rhetoric" to Modern Brain Science* (Chicago: University of Chicago Press, 2006), 1–5.

17. David Konstan, "Aristotle on Anger and the Emotions: The Strategies of Status," in *Ancient Anger: Perspectives from Homer to Galen*, ed. Susanna Braund and Glenn W. Most (Cambridge: Cambridge University Press, 2004), 100.

18. Harris, *Restraining Rage*.

19. Harris, *Restraining Rage*, 127–28.

20. Discussed with usual acuity by Rosenwein, *Anger*, 1. For a rather anti-foundationalist unpacking of *mēnis*, see the lecture by Rob Boddice, "Anger," Video Lecture, George Mason University Library, September 2023, https://doi.org/10.13021/MARS/8690.

21. See the brief remarks on the historical comparison of modern and ancient anger

mentioned (along with other archaic concepts like *cholos* and *kotos*), and the more common terms (in the classical period and later) *orgē* and *thymos*.[22] These concepts themselves changed considerably in their usage between the classical and Hellenistic periods, and even contemporaries differed in how they understood them, which is always a limitation when making claims about the ancient definitions of emotions, often drawing on Aristotle, whose definition would be influential even for the Stoics but was not normative. At the start of his discussion of anger's rhetorical usage, he defines *orgē* like other passions as a type of pain (*lypē*) in reaction to a socially embedded event: "Let anger, then, be defined as a desire, accompanied by pain, for [an apparent] revenge, due to an apparent slight affecting a man himself or one of his friends, by persons who ought not to slight him."[23] Some aspects of Aristotle's definition illuminate the contours of the previous modern examples. Anger depends on a slight, which in a society which places a high value on honor would be a very important matter indeed. It is also variably available depending on one's status. In Aristotle's definition, one can only feel anger at a slight by someone below him in status. In many or most cases in ancient literature, the masculine pronoun would be appropriate, and due to their status women were understood to feel these sorts of feelings quite differently.[24] The same goes for people of lower economic status or the enslaved. In Aristotle's system, they could not truly feel *orgē* when mistreated by someone of a higher status than them. Perhaps, as suggested in the previous chapter, such a negative affect would more likely show up as *lypē* (sadness or distress) than *orgē* for those who cannot rightfully revenge their slights.[25] Anger for Aristotle, furthermore, is action-based and public, the desire for conspicuous revenge rather than the long-simmering private resentment (to which I will return in chapter 6).

---

by Barbara H. Rosenwein, "Angers Past and Present," *Emotions: History, Culture, Society* 4 (2020): 35–38.

22. Harris, *Restraining Rage*, 50–71.

23. Aristotle, *Rhet.* 2.2.1.1378a (Freese).

24. William V. Harris, "The Rage of Women," in *Ancient Anger: Perspectives from Homer to Galen*, ed. Susanna Braund and Glenn W. Most (Cambridge: Cambridge University Press, 2004), 121–43. "Aristotle did not intend this as a rigorous or exhaustive account of the nature of the *pathē*. Clearly, it is designed to serve his present purpose [of teaching rhetoric]." Konstan, "Aristotle on Anger," 100.

25. This is not Aristotle's view, as he rather unusually does not treat *lypē* as a *pathos* in its own right in his *Rhetoric*. There is other psychological and historical research that suggests that this is quite plausible, e.g., Carol Barr-Zisowitz, "'Sadness': Is There Such a Thing?," in *Handbook of Emotions*, 2nd ed., ed. Michael Lewis and Jeannette M. Haviland-Jones (New York: Guilford, 2000), 614–16.

Anger is furthermore not instinctive, not a triggered circuit but cognitive or evaluative and intentional. In this social context, anger also is not really a disease of the soul or a vice to be eliminated, as the Stoics would argue, but has a necessary and positive function for justice, for setting the record straight and for getting what's yours.[26] Anger is also a necessary component of war and proper aggression, "for it is impossible to fear and be angry at the same time."[27] All this makes sense especially considering that Aristotle wrote this discussion of anger in the context of how to win at court.[28]

Most Christian writers, however, were not rhetors at court, though Aristotle's influence on educated Christians will be evident, along with Stoic philosophy, often set against a common field of Platonic understanding of soul and body. Whether Christians approached anger with an aim more of moderating the passion (Aristotelian *metriopatheia*) or eliminating it (Stoic *apatheia*), they, like ancient authors more generally, conceived of anger as much more intense and explosive than modern understandings or manifestations of anger.[29] As Aristotle notes, ancient anger (*orgē* and *thymos*) would be understood as more public and conspicuous than we experience it today, as well as more object and action oriented—an angry rage against specific people, not against abstractions or structural inequities, with the aim to do something about it, a public requital.

There were other, milder forms of anger (e.g., annoyance [*chalepainein*], irritation [*aganaktein*]), and many of the grievances and resentments that we would call forms of anger today would have been considered in the constellation of envy, for example.[30] And while philosophers and theologians drew out nuances between the major anger concepts of *orgē* and *thymos* (*orgē* is more moderate, for example, and *thymos* more extreme), distinctions are not maintained consistently in ordinary usage over the Hellenistic and Roman periods, including among the translators of the Jewish Scriptures and Christian writers.[31] Given the excellent scholarly treatments of ancient anger, I draw

26. Konstan, "Aristotle on Anger," 114.

27. Aristotle, *Rhet.* 2.3 (1380a32–34); Harris, *Restraining Rage*, 58. The context here is not about war, but the point holds. Stoics too recognized the value of anger but transformed it in their ethics into the "good emotion" of courage.

28. Konstan, "Aristotle on Anger," 110.

29. Harris, *Restraining Rage*, 63.

30. The former point is made by Harris, *Restraining Rage*, 63. See further chapter 6.

31. Harris, *Restraining Rage*, 54; the distinction is of Philodemus. As for Jewish and Christian writers, "The LXX uses [*thymos* and *orgē*] interchangeably to represent a large variety of Hebrew expressions for 'anger'. The NT reflects this usage, though when the subject

out such terminological distinctions only as necessary in addressing Christian writers, who were indeed extremely interested in anger as a Christian emotion, especially in later antiquity. I start, naturally, with Paul, followed by the reframing of anger's complexity in the gnostic *Gospel of Judas*, the ascetic writings of Evagrius of Pontus, and the monastic community of Pachomius.

Paul on Christian Anger

Compared to joy and sadness, the first generations of Christ followers were less interested in radically rethinking the contours and practices of the spirited passions, *thymos* and *orgē*. Still, anger does come up in the writings now included in the New Testament, in Paul's letters and in the Gospels. Much New Testament scholarship on emotions has focused on the latter, especially on those passages in which Jesus shows some form of anger himself (e.g., Mark 1:41 and John 11:33).[32] Here I am more interested in how early Christians conceived of anger as a practice to be cultivated or suppressed depending on context, and how anger was seen alternatively to threaten and to strengthen community. The Pauline letters give nuanced testimony for changing expectations about the practice of Christian anger over the first couple generations of Christian community.

Christians, like others, understood anger as an inherently volatile passion that needed control, a control which could be applied on several levels of psyche and behavior. These options have helpfully been distinguished in modern study as "(1) reining in angry actions and speech, (2) eliminating angry actions and speech, (3) reining in angry feelings, (4) eliminating angry feelings."[33] When Paul addresses anger as a human passion, he includes it in a list of vices, for example, "quarreling, jealousy, anger, selfishness, slander, gossip, conceit,

---

is divine anger Paul shows a marked preference for *orgē*. . . . The author of Revelation, on the other hand shows a preference for *thymos* . . . or for both words together." Stephen H. Travis, "Wrath of God (NT)," *ABD* 6:996.

32. E.g., F. Scott Spencer, *Passions of the Christ: The Emotional Life of Jesus in the Gospels* (Grand Rapids: Baker Academic, 2021), 43–70; Matthew Goldstone, "Murder, Anger, and Altars: The First Matthean Antithesis in Light of Exodus 21:14 and Its Early Rabbinic Interpretation," *NovT* 59 (2017): 339–54; Peter J. Williams, "An Examination of Ehrman's Case for ὀργισθείς in Mark 1:41," *NovT* 54 (2012): 1–12.

33. James A. Kelhoffer, "Suppressing Anger in Early Christianity: Examples from the Pauline Tradition," *GRBS* 47 (2007): 309. For much of the following I draw from Kelhoffer's careful insights.

and disorder" (2 Cor 12:20; see also Gal 5:20 and Jas 1:19–20). Paul's term for anger is plural, *thymoi*, which points not to a categorical concern with "anger" writ large but with "outbursts of anger," a pattern of behavior among his congregants that they need to tamp down.[34] In these limited discussions, Paul addresses outward manifestations of anger and likely also is concerned with the context of these outbursts, that is, within the community and targeted at members of the community. He has no problem with anger per se and in his letters mostly reflects on wrath as positive, focusing on God's anger.[35] In keeping with his personality and kingly role in the Jewish Scriptures, God righteously vents his anger (*orgē*) on unbelievers and sinners and with it marks a dividing line between members of the godly community and the others or outsiders; his wrath will fall upon the unbelievers and sinners, but members of the Christ community will be spared it through Jesus.[36]

Later Pauline letters reveal a change in Christian attitudes toward anger, moving toward a total elimination of angry expression. Colossians addresses anger in the community as part of a vice list again but now without exception: "You must get rid of all such things—anger (*orgē*), wrath (*thymos*), malice, slander and abusive language from your mouth" (Col 3:8). Colossians includes both main concepts for anger, and in contrast with Paul speaks of *thymos* in the singular, pointing to a general concept or category of anger rather than discrete and time-limited outbursts.[37] Such emotional expressions call back to a few sentences prior, where the author calls on the community to put to death worldly things. This is no call to moderation, but to elimination. Such "earthly" matters are "fornication, impurity, passion (*pathos*), evil desire, and greed (which is idolatry)" (Col 3:5).

At the very least Colossians demands the complete elimination of angry speech and expression (levels 1 and 2 above). It is plausible—though not explicit—that he further expects his congregants to control or even eliminate feelings of anger (levels 3 and 4).[38] This emotional norm—the elimination of *pathos* (harmful emotion) as no less dangerous than fornication (*porneia*),

34. Kelhoffer, "Suppressing Anger," 311–12.

35. An interesting reflection on early Christian understandings of God's anger in the context of ancient theologies is Elaine Pagels, "The Rage of Angels," in *Rage, Power, and Aggression*, ed. Robert A. Glick and Steven P. Roose (New Haven: Yale University Press, 1993), 235–44.

36. Rom 1:18; 1 Thess 1:10. Kelhoffer, "Suppressing Anger," 313. See also Gary A. Herion, "Wrath of God (OT)," *ABD* 6:989–96.

37. Kelhoffer, "Suppressing Anger," 312.

38. Kelhoffer, "Suppressing Anger," 314.

especially the fiery feelings of anger and wrath—presents a "new way of life," distinguishing their community in explicitly emotional terms, possessors of "the new self" (*ton neon*), clothed with affective goodness (Col 3:10, 12).[39] Although the connection is left under the surface, it is plausible that Colossians "synthesiz[es] in a novel way two components of the apostle's theology—God's anger and believers' need to get rid of anger."[40] While God's anger is righteous (and thus not a potentially sinful passion), humans are not to imitate God's emotion. Rather, by ridding themselves of angry expressions and feelings, and thus ceding those emotions to the one to whom they rightfully belong (the king), the community of believers may escape God's anger in the time of judgment.

The most significant Pauline teaching on anger is still brief and enigmatic, in the letter to the Ephesians, which builds on the teachings in Colossians 3:5–8.[41] The passage on anger in Ephesians 4:25–32 preserves an "apparent contradiction between 4:26a and 4:31," which "raises the question whether this author has an overall coherent theology of anger."[42] That there may be an unsettling lack of resolution in first-century views on anger is entirely plausible; early Christians had every right to remain ambivalent and not to ascribe to any coherent and consistent philosophy of passions.[43] Most people surely did not, and most don't today. Still, the author's comments on anger reveal a first-century attempt to form a community bound by shared feelings.

Like Colossians, the author of Ephesians encourages his readers to understand themselves as entering into a new state of being, casting off the ways of the outsiders or nations (*ethnē*), putting off old desires (*epithymiai*) and the old person (*ton palaion anthrōpon*) while putting on the new, all the while living as one new body and spirit with one another and with the Lord, "bearing with one another in love," and living with humility, patience, and gentleness (*praytēs*), the virtuous opposite of excessive anger according to Aristotle.[44] For Aristotle at least, this "even temper" did not mean the complete suppression of anger but its moderate practice, "that one should be angry with the right

39. Former quote from Kelhoffer, "Suppressing Anger," 314: "The effect in Col 3:5–8 is that the faithful have assurance of being protected from God's wrath, provided that they demonstrate their new way of life by refraining from the vices, including anger and wrath, listed in Col 3:8."

40. Kelhoffer, "Suppressing Anger," 313.

41. Kelhoffer, "Suppressing Anger," 314.

42. Kelhoffer, "Suppressing Anger," 317.

43. See Harris, *Restraining Rage*, 399.

44. Eph 4:1–24.

people for the right reasons—with people who have truly done one some injury—and also in the right manner and at the right moment and for the right length of time."[45] This understanding of moderate anger as a manifestation of the virtue of "gentleness" helps to make sense of the apparent contradiction of the Ephesian letter.

But the author of Ephesians, like Paul himself, was not interested in Aristotelian consistency in preaching the passions. He was interested in community, as embodied and emotional, of which anger was just one outstanding passion intertwined with the others, outstanding because of its duality as human vice and divine prerogative. Fundamental to anger is its sheer destructiveness, a common ancient fear which the author of Ephesians shared, "potentially destructive of individuals, marriages, friendships, households and the city-state."[46] Ephesians, in a way that would have been intuitive to many, presents emotions as vices not because they countermand Stoic-influenced imperatives for living as a sagely individual, but because they threaten the unity of community—both among other humans and between humans and God. Ephesians goes to some length to characterize the social units threatened by anger, as the church is a new humanity (2:15), a community of fellow citizens (2:19), and a household of God (2:19).[47] The author underscores the novelty of this new emotional community, as "All of us lived among [the disobedient] in the passions (*tais epithymiais*) of our flesh . . . and we were by nature children of wrath (*orgēs*), like everyone else" (Eph 2:3). But they no longer face an angry God, whose wrath is still poured out on the disobedient and unbelieving outsiders.

Righteous anger is a quality of the ruler, a commonplace found from the cultures of the ancient Near East to the late Roman Mediterranean. This kingly anger, an anger that is slow to kindle and just, features prominently in Jewish Scripture, and can be shared with God's representatives on earth, his prophets and rulers, such as Moses's anger in Exodus 32.[48] It is in this biblical context that the author frames his curious and much discussed commendation of anger in 4:26a, "Be angry and do not sin."[49] Significantly, this is a quote from

45. Harris, *Restraining Rage*, 94, drawing on Aristotle, *Nic. Eth.* iv.5.1125b27–1126b10.

46. Stephen C. Barton, "'Be Angry but Do Not Sin' (Ephesians 4:26a): Sin and the Emotions in the New Testament with Special Reference to Anger," *Studies in Christian Ethics* 28 (2015): 28.

47. Barton, "Be Angry," 23, 31.

48. Barton, "Be Angry," 23–26.

49. Barton, "Be Angry"; Daniel B. Wallace, "ΟΡΓΙΖΕΣΘΕ in Ephesians 4:26a: Command or Condition?," *Criswell Theological Review* 3 (1989): 353–72; Thiago Bittencourt,

the Septuagint Psalm 4:4(5), a song of contrition and hope in the mouth of David (God's chosen king), oppressed by enemies. As such, for anyone familiar with the text (and since the author gives it no citation, it seems he presumed its familiarity), it clearly speaks in the voice of a king in a particular context, in which anger is just and justifiable. The quotation is followed by another commonplace, "Do not let the sun go down on your anger," familiar in Greco-Roman culture and in the Matthean Beatitudes.[50]

But the Ephesian teaching gives a different sense, focusing not on the subject's own emotion but the emotion provoked in others. The anger here is not *orgē* or *orgizomai* but the rarer term *parorgismos*, which despite its common translation does not mean "anger"; rather, it refers to things that provoke anger (generally not one's own but the anger of others, such as a king or God).[51] "Paul's" rendering of this common advice does not mean "never go to bed angry" but calls Christians to make amends for anything that might have provoked anger in others. In this sense, there is less of an apparent contradiction with the author's later, uncompromising position on anger.

Ephesians 4:28–5:2 gives the sense of a new community freed from the divine anger of their former lives. There is, notably, no mention of God's anger here.[52] Rather, the author "calls for sublimation: instead of becoming angry, one can experience the transcendent through noble acts of kindness, tenderheartedness, and forgiveness," practices which crucially occur "within the community."[53] In this new community, household, *politeia*, or *ethnos*, one can reasonably be expected to "put away . . . all bitterness (*pikria*) and wrath (*thymos*) and anger (*orgē*)" (4:31), and a father could be expected to avoid giving any cause for anger or resentment (*parorgizete*) among children (6:4), a radical change in emotional practice given the high value of parental discipline and the status of the Roman paterfamilias.[54] Unlike Colossians, Ephesians does not

---

"Righteous or Dangerous? An Investigation of Ὀργίζεσθε in Ephesians 4:26a," *Southeastern Theological Review* 13 (2022): 25–39. These articles give a sense of the large literature on this half-verse.

50. See *Harper Collins Study Bible* (San Francisco: Harper San Francisco, 2006), 1987–88: "a maxim found in non-Christian writings of this period." Cf. Matt 5:21–22.

51. Bittencourt, "Righteous or Dangerous," 36. The situation is similar in the Matthaean Beatitude: Before making an offering remember if anyone has a reason to be angry with you (has something against you), cf. Matt 5:23.

52. Kelhoffer, "Suppressing Anger," 316.

53. Kelhoffer, "Suppressing Anger," 316.

54. Kelhoffer, "Suppressing Anger," 316. The dangers of fathers causing anger and resentment in their children (at least metaphorically) will be the catalyst for the letter of 1 Clement, discussed in chapter 6. It is in this same context that the author commands his congregants

adduce fear of God's wrath as motivation for good behavior. Instead, it is "the greater good of the community" that calls for a transformation of emotional practice, more demanding than in Colossians.[55] The author of Ephesians goes farther than Paul and calls Christians to rein in and eliminate expressions of anger and behaviors that could provoke anger in others and even more radically to eliminate feelings of anger. This is not just rhetoric, or need not be just rhetoric. Anthropologists have engaged with numerous peoples who cultivate emotional practices to eliminate anger or produce non-anger and describe themselves as living without anger (although this does not mean they live without violence and war).[56] Such societies provide empirical evidence that "the Buddha's 'abandon anger' and Seneca's 'avoid anger' are on the whole possible, given certain community practices of trust and sharing."[57] The same can be said for the Pauline emotional communities.

The Anger of Judas

Christians in Paul's wake dedicated much effort to teasing out the proper role of anger in Christian community and ethics, aware of the tension between anger's extreme dangers and the seeming necessity for some sort of *thymos* or anger to rule properly, most clearly seen in the royal anger of the God of Israel and in the incarnate Son of God. For those remembering the life and teachings of Jesus, anger was thus a contentious issue. Should the perfect and divine human feel or express such a violent emotion as anger? Should the Son and Word of God incarnate rightly feel and express the anger appropriate to a king?[58] Or should he bear the affectless *apatheia* of a quasi-Stoic philosopher?[59] These differing expectations show up in the *Gospel of Judas*, which

to avoid causing grief to the Holy Spirit (4:30), the breath enlivening the communal body of the church with its varied members.

55. Kelhoffer, "Suppressing Anger," 316–17.

56. Rosenwein, *Anger*, 53–66.

57. Rosenwein, *Anger*, 59.

58. Manuscript variants describing Jesus's anger or the appropriateness of anger among his followers show part of the interpretive difficulties for early Christians. See Williams, "Examination"; David Alan Black, "Jesus on Anger: The Text of Matthean 5:22a Revisited," *NovT* 30 (1988): 1–8.

59. Cf. Harold W. Attridge, "An 'Emotional' Jesus," in *Stoicism in Early Christianity*, ed. Tuomas Rasimus, Troels Engberg-Pedersen, and Ismo Dunderberg (Grand Rapids: Baker Academic, 2010), 77–92; and Gitte Buch-Hansen, "The Emotional Jesus: Anti-Stoicism in the Fourth Gospel?," in Rasimus et al., *Stoicism in Early Christianity*, 93–114.

centers anger as human and divine emotion more than the canonical gospels which it subverts.

While Jesus expresses anger and annoyance in the New Testament Gospels, the *Gospel of Judas* depicts anger as an emotion alien to the divine personality of Jesus.[60] The difference here is not simply between human and divine emotions, but which class of human and which level of divinity. As a gnostic (or gnostic-ish) gospel, the *Gospel of Judas* depends on a duality between the perfect, heavenly realm of aeons (emanated from the true God) and a lower, material world, a dark and perverted reflection of the heavenly ideals (ruled by a pretender god). As such, there is a perfect human being and an earthly human, and the actual God (represented by Jesus) and the lower creator god, identified as the god of Israel.

As the *Gospel of Judas* presents it, the apostles misunderstand Jesus's message and role in the grand narrative of history. They continue to revere the creator god of Israel, which the *Gospel of Judas* associates with the cosmic bonds of stars and their fate along with the demands of cultic sacrifice. Among the twelve, Judas alone recognizes the unexpected subversive role that Jesus has against the god of Israel, about which he engages in a series of questions and answers about the nature of the world and history. The author takes a view of emotions closer to that of the Stoics than Aristotle; like the Sethian strain of gnostic speculation that influenced the *Gospel of Judas*, Judas privileges an emotional *apatheia* (freedom) rather than *metriopatheia* (moderation). In Sethian literature more generally this idea of an existence unmoved by the passions gets expressed as being "immovable" and in other Christian traditions overlaps with the idea of being at rest (*anapausis*).[61] Thus, while anger has a certain ambiguity in Judas—as in fact many basic aspects of this fragmentary text are still ambiguous—it seems safe in principle to expect the *Gospel of Judas* to hold a more wholly negative view of anger, in line with Sethian and with Stoic-influenced ethics more generally.[62]

60. The range of New Testament Gospel accounts of Jesus's anger is covered by Spencer, *Passions of the Christ*, 43–70.

61. On the immovable race, see Lance Jenott, *The Gospel of Judas*, STAC 64 (Tübingen: Mohr Siebeck, 2011), 51. Also, *Apocryphon of John*, NHC II 25.23–26.7. "Rest" is especially a Valentinian concept; see Jan Helderman, *Die Anapausis im Evangelium Veritatis: Eine vergleichende Untersuchung des valentinianisch-gnostischen Heilsgutes der Ruhe im Evangelium Veritatis und in anderen Schriften der Nag Hammadi-Bibliothek*, NHS 18 (Leiden: Brill, 1984).

62. Ismo Dunderberg, *Gnostic Morality Revisited*, WUNT 347 (Tübingen: Mohr Siebeck, 2015), 41–43. Hermas too held anger (*oxycholia*) as an emotion to be eliminated: Herm. Mand. 5.2 (34).

Jesus himself shows no anger in the *Gospel of Judas*. Instead, he laughs throughout his interactions with the disciples, which elicits their own confusion and indignation, as they think he is laughing at them (34). But Jesus is not laughing at them, he says, but at their god to whom they sacrifice. The *Gospel of Judas* shares this affective feature with other branches of gnostic or Sethian gospel retellings.[63] Jesus's laughter (34, 36, 44, 55), however, is not one of mirth and joy or gentle condescension but contempt and mockery. His role as the laughing lord draws on Jewish imagery, as in Psalm 2:2. To mock enemies is a royal feature, alongside righteous anger.[64] But here the divine quality of anger has been completely rejected, and Jesus's contempt echoes only with the sound of laughter.

The *Gospel of Judas* shares this idea of a true God without anger with other early Christian sources. The early letter of 1 Clement, which holds close to the Jewish Scriptures and is not in any way gnostic, also understands the true God—which in his case is the creator God—as "patient" (an opposite of anger), who "feels no anger (ἀόργητος [*aorgētos*]) toward his entire creation."[65] In the world of the *Gospel of Judas*, those who worship the true God imitate his freedom from anger. Those who worship the creator god will seethe along with him.[66] The disciples thus grow indignant (*aganaktei*) and angry (*orgē*) at Jesus's mocking laughter and rejection of their sacrifices (34:18–22). Not only is their anger not just; it is pathetic, rooted in their foolishness (*mntathēt*). Their psychic distress (*štortr*) provokes their anger (*cōnt*), which—significantly—likens them to their god, the creator god, and the malevolent stars that microcosmically manifest in their souls as an irritation (*auaganaktei*).[67] As with much of the codex, the text here is defective, so the precise reading is conjectural, but the overall sense is clear. The creator and the very structure of his creation (the stars) are filled with anger and other negative passions, which are reproduced in the psyches of his creatures who worship and imitate their god.[68]

63. Ingvild Sælid Gilhus, "Why Did Jesus Laugh? Laughter in Biblical-Demiurgical Texts," in *Humor and Religion: Challenges and Ambiguities*, ed. H. Geybels and H. W. Van (London: Bloomsbury, 2013), 123–40; Gedaliahu A. G. Stroumsa, "Christ's Laughter: Docetic Origins Revisited," *JECS* 12 (2004): 267–88.

64. David Brakke, *The Gospel of Judas*, AB 45 (New Haven: Yale University Press, 2022), 113.

65. Jenott, *Gospel of Judas*, 49; 1 Clem. 19:2–3; cf. 23:1.

66. Jenott, *Gospel of Judas*, 50, with reference to Elaine Pagels and Karen L. King, *Reading Judas: The Gospel of Judas and the Shaping of Christianity* (New York: Viking, 2007).

67. *Gos. Jud.* 34–35. Jenott, *Gospel of Judas*, 140; Brakke, *Gospel of Judas*, 81. See further discussion in chapter 6.

68. Brakke, *Gospel of Judas*, 113–14.

The anger of the world and the covenant forged between the creator and his foolish worshippers are not mere theological axioms. Their anger is an emotional practice, which the *Gospel of Judas* describes enacted in ritual, as the apostles relate to Jesus a disturbing dream vision. They see a large building with a large altar, surrounded by throngs who bring sacrifices before twelve priests, themselves murderers, lawbreakers, and homosexuals. Worse still, they bring their own family to slaughter on the altar, full of corpses.[69] Though the language of anger is not as rich as elsewhere, the whole scene reeks of it, and the disciples are quite agitated (*štortr*) at their vision of piles of human and animal corpses, throats slit, dismembered, and burned for their god.[70] The sacrifice reflects the god they are intended for, as Ialtabaoth is depicted as fiery, in line with the god of Israel's familiar fiery theophanies. The anger of the altar and its recipient will receive full recompense, as Jesus foretells: "The pillar of fire will fall suddenly." It will destroy the corruptible race, but "[the incorruptible] race will not move [by] the stars."[71] The angry world of Ialtabaoth and his foolish worshippers will be destroyed by the same emotional force that makes it turn.

The psychic disturbance characteristic of the "other" worshippers, the false Christians so vividly evoked in the altar dream, contrasts with that of the perfect human, characterized by a freedom from the passions, the strong or stable of mind, the immovable, those with *apatheia*.[72] The *Gospel of Judas* remains enigmatic, as its protagonist is condemned not to embody the perfect human himself, as Jesus did and as the true believers would. In keeping with other Sethian or gnostic literature, Judas as a would-be protagonist is left from full reunion with the aeonic fullness but still to be raised up to the peak of the middle dispensation. He does not overcome his anger in the *Gospel of Judas* at the end of the long, private question and answer session with Jesus, which concludes with Jesus telling him, "Already your horn has been exalted, and your anger has been kindled, and your star has passed by, and your heart has [. . .]" (with lacuna in the manuscript).[73] But Judas is not without some

69. *Gos. Jud.* 38.1–24.

70. The description of the altar is quite lacunose, so it is unclear what details the author wished to include.

71. *Gos. Jud.* 42.17–21 (Brakke). Cf. the fiery destruction of the angry cosmos and its gods in the gnosticizing treatise *On the Origin of the World.* Andrew Crislip, "Envy and Anger at the World's Creation and Destruction in the *Treatise Without Title 'On the Origin of the World'* (NHC II,5)," *VC* 65 (2011): 285–310.

72. *Gos. Jud.* 35.2–5.

73. *Gos. Jud.* 36.22–25 (Brakke).

hope. While still the thirteenth *daimon*, he will be raised up above the others of his human rank. Plausibly, along with other gnosticizing literature, Judas will take the place of the wrathful creator god Ialtaboath (the god of Israel) as a repentant betrayer, "promoted as high as is possible for those belonging to mortal humanity, and he will become the new ruler of the realm below the holy generation."[74] His anger holds him back from the blessed generation, but anger also drives him to commit that fateful deed. Ultimate salvation would lie for followers of the *Gospel of Judas* in freedom from the emotions of the creator god, emotions built into the very scaffolding of this world.

Evagrius of Pontus on Anger

Not far from where the *Gospel of Judas* was read, translated into Coptic, and ultimately laid to rest until it was raised up in the end times of the gray market antiquities trade, other Christians in other communities were also concerned with the dangers and uses of anger in the monastic life.[75] In the northern Egyptian monastery of Kellia, Evagrius of Pontus turned his psychologically astute gaze to the continuing presence of anger among those who had abandoned the world to seek solitude and prayer in the desert. As discussed in the previous chapter on sadness, Evagrius addresses several passions or emotions in his analysis of the demonically induced trains of thought that attacked ascetics. Like the Alexandrian Clement and those who wrote books like the *Gospel of Judas*, such ascetics aimed at working through a ladder of contemplation and self-perfection toward a state of knowing, to become a *gnostikos*.[76]

Anger (*orgē*), like sadness and listlessness, emerges out of the spirited part of the soul, and they influence one another, as they can interact to lesser degrees with the more appetitive thoughts of gluttony, lust, and greed, and the more rational thoughts of vainglory and pride. Anger was certainly among the most harmful of the demonic thoughts for the monk, as it could more than any other "[turn] one into a demon," a claim that many observers, both

74. Dunderberg, "Judas' Anger," 55–56.

75. We still do not know—and likely never will—the source and context of Codex Tchacos or the similar manuscripts from Nag Hammadi; the debate about origins is robust and now returns to possible connections with Pachomian monasteries, for which Hugo Lundhaug and Lance Jenott, *The Monastic Origins of the Nag Hammadi Codices*, STAC 97 (Tübingen: Mohr Siebeck, 2015).

76. The relevance of ancient ladders of perfection to the *Gospel of Judas* is developed by Dunderberg, "Judas' Anger." Evagrius's biography and thought are introduced in chapter 3.

pagan and Christian, would have agreed with, as they note—and describe with lurid detail—the twisted and ugly madness that possesses the angry.[77] Anger persisted in the monastic life as well, long after the temptations of lust and gluttony had been dispatched.[78] For the monk who had passed successfully through practical training in bodily and mental self-mastery to pass into the condition of "knowing"—the *gnostikos*—anger became an even more pressing concern. If desire for bodies is a young man's game, anger and resentment come to roost among the elders, in a sense filling the psychic void left by the conquered drives for sex, food, and wealth.[79] It is not hard to see how some thoughts like anger and vainglory (pleasure in others' praise) would become the "vices of monastic maturity."[80]

Anger has special risks. It is social, so its triggers never go away as long as one lives in the hell of other people. And there is no exit. In Evagrius's thinking the monk should not (or must not) withdraw from community or conflict to cure anger. To leave the community is spiritual death.[81] The temptation to withdraw from conflict is a demonic ruse, as isolation lets resentment fester. Much as the catalyst for anger is social interaction, as Jesus and Paul observe, its ultimate resolution also lies with other people, especially the people who have angered us or whom we have angered.[82] Anger is further "more susceptible to rationalization," certainly more than lust or gluttony and also more than depression or boredom.[83] There is always a good reason for one's anger, and it's inevitably someone else's fault. And as we have already seen, anger has a positive value in ancient philosophical thought, so rooting out the disordered thinking (and practices) of *orgē* requires a degree of subtleness that fornication and pride do not. For this reason anger is a principal concern in

77. Gabriel Bunge, *Dragon's Wine and Angel's Bread: The Teachings of Evagrius Ponticus on Anger and Meekness* (Crestwood, NY: St. Vladimir's Seminary Press, 2009), discussed in Andrew Louth, "Evagrios on Anger," StPatr 47 (2010): 179. Cf. Galen's influential descriptions of angry people (e.g., in his *On the Passions and Errors of the Soul*), character types reflected in Christian moralizing, as, e.g., Basil, *Homily* 10, *Against Those Who Are Prone to Anger*. Galen would not approve of the demonic comparison of course. Evagrius sees rage and resentment leading to insanity, *Prayer* 65.

78. Columba Stewart, OSB, "Evagrius Ponticus on Prayer and Anger," in *Religions of Late Antiquity in Practice*, ed. Richard Valantasis (Princeton: Princeton University Press, 2000), 65.

79. Stewart, "Evagrius Ponticus on Prayer and Anger," 67.

80. Stewart, "Evagrius Ponticus on Prayer and Anger," 68.

81. Stewart, "Evagrius Ponticus on Prayer and Anger," 68.

82. Louth, "Evagrios on Anger," 183. Stewart, "Evagrius Ponticus on Prayer and Anger," 67.

83. Stewart, "Evagrius Ponticus on Prayer and Anger," 67.

Evagrius's work for experts, the *Gnostikos*, more so than other thoughts, and "the supreme virtue of the 'Knower' [Gnostic] is freedom from anger (*aorgēsia*, *Gnost.* 5)," a conceit with which his contemporary readers of the *Gospel of Judas* would likely have agreed.[84]

Like the other afflictions of the spirited part of the soul, anger has a physicality to it, feelings of heat, the boiling over of the soul and all of the bodily agitation that ensues, along with bodily wasting and pallor at night.[85] The angry monk is further plagued by visions, sometimes of the demonic beasts that famously afflicted Antony but more ordinarily the faces and words of those humans who have done him wrong, infuriating and humiliating memories relived—and surely twisted and enhanced—over and over. Memory was a major threat to the monk prone to anger and resentment.[86] Such memories and visions impeded the monk from prayer and spiritual advancement, blinding the monk as if by smoke or mist and thickening his soul. This should not be seen as mere metaphor but likens the monk's soul to the thickened and dark bodies of the demons themselves who fell farther from God and afflict the monk out of resentment and envy.[87] The subtle physicality of demons manifests in the felt physiology of the emotions. In Evagrius's interpretation, the risky position of the monk in the night is why Paul advised not to go to bed with anger still simmering (Eph 4:26). That's when the demons use angry memories most effectively.[88]

Anger's ambiguity lies in its utility. Evagrius divides anger into two types, natural and unnatural. Anger in accordance with nature is directed against demons and against one's own libidinal desires for pleasure. Unnatural anger targets other human beings and the offenses of day-to-day life, slights, criticism, feelings of persecution, and the memories thereof.[89] Evagrius draws on Platonic and Stoic ideas of the soul to contrast the natural "resistant or repelling tendency (*thymos*)" with mere "desire (*epithymia*)."[90] The Scriptures,

84. Stewart, "Evagrius Ponticus on Prayer and Anger," 67–68.

85. Louth, "Evagrios on Anger," 181, citing *Praktikos* 11 and *Vices* 5. Stewart, "Evagrius Ponticus on Prayer and Anger," 67.

86. Louth, "Evagrios on Anger," 181–83, who notes the false etymology between resentment (*mēnis*) and memory (*mnēmē*) drawn by Maximus the Confessor. Stewart, "Evagrius Ponticus on Prayer and Anger," 67.

87. Cf. Louth, "Evagrios on Anger," 181–82.

88. Evagrius, *Praktikos* 22.

89. Louth, "Evagrios on Anger," 181; Stewart, "Evagrius Ponticus on Prayer and Anger," 67.

90. Stewart, "Evagrius Ponticus on Prayer and Anger," 67.

so central to Evagrius's method for countering the whispering temptations of demons, offered abundant resources for this healthy and natural anger, as the author of Ephesians recognized in the Davidic Psalm 4. To be angry against the demons is no sin. Exemplars like David, Aaron, Moses, and Joshua offered models of righteous anger against their enemies and God's enemies, who could be interpreted allegorically as demonic hosts themselves.[91] At the same time, Moses and David model anger's human and humane cure, gentleness.[92]

The duality of anger, however, can make even the proper use of Scriptures problematic. There is much matériel to be found there that could be very dangerous in the wrong mind. Evagrius mentions the case of the angry monk who reaches for the Psalms for a cure and finds himself drawn (demonically) to the Israelite prayer for righteous retribution in Psalm 137, biblical inspiration to dwell on the painful memory of loss and humiliation and to luxuriate in the anticipation of violent revenge—the image of one's persecutors' children smashed against the rock.[93] But Evagrius reframes this psalm as not about natural anger and the repulsion of demons. It points to the virtue of patience, of watchful waiting for God's justice to pour down in time. Much as he addresses the duality of sadness, Evagrius is much more concerned with the risks of anger than its utility. Evagrius's interpretation of this righteously angry psalm shows that whatever anger's very real uses against demonic temptation, the risks of unnatural anger against one's colleagues and community far outweigh them. It is thus the elimination of anger that Evagrius predominantly addresses, which is achievable.[94] As he writes, "It is impossible to love all of the brothers equally. But one can deal with all of them without passion (*apathōs*), free from resentment and hate."[95]

Pachomius, Anger, and Leadership

Around the time that Evagrius was growing up in Asia Minor and making his journey toward the Nile and the *Gospel of Judas* was being translated into Coptic, other ascetics were experimenting with ways of organizing their selves and communities to better live out the emotional norms of Christianity and actu-

91. E.g., Origen, *Homily 27 on Numbers*, in Origen, *An Exhortation to Martyrdom, Prayer and Selected Works*, trans. Rowan A. Greer (Mahwah, NJ: Paulist, 1979).

92. Louth, "Evagrios on Anger," 184.

93. *Antirrhetikos* 5.13.

94. Louth, "Evagrios on Anger," 184–85.

95. Evagrius, *Praktikos* 100 (Stewart).

alize the communal practices of the earliest Christians. In the Egyptian south, Pachomius founded a confederation of communities—the *Koinōnia*—which would become a model for monasteries in medieval Europe and elsewhere.[96] This collective of monasteries or coenobia was based on a well-defined hierarchy and written rules for groups of ascetics, who could number from the hundreds to the thousands, cloistered from the world by the built environment, generally living in walled compounds with strict controls of entry and exit. In Pachomius's communities, novices underwent testing and training before becoming members, memorizing portions of Scripture and the community rules, which would later be codified in various forms after the founder's death. After his death, further memories were put down in narratives of the institutional history of the community, whose versions survive in Coptic, Arabic, and Greek. These *Lives* show, among other things, the changing feelings about emotions and spirituality in early Christianity.[97]

The First Sahidic *Life of Pachomius* (S^1) provides a compelling counterpoint to the debates about anger as a Christian emotion in Egyptian tradition and the memory and use of earlier Christian (and biblical) teachings on emotion. The fragmentarily preserved *Life of Pachomius* is especially valuable among Egyptian sources and Christian hagiography more broadly, because it provides an institutional history of the early Pachomian movement that does not shy from conflict, failure, and change.[98] Compared to the idealized portraits of saints in the lives and encomia of late antiquity, this early Coptic *Life of Pachomius* stands apart in its narrative of conflicts over authority and the feeling of verisimilitude (if not historical reliability) in its memories of Pachomius's emotional life.

The fragmentary *Life of Pachomius* begins with the young anchorite Pachomius sitting alone and encountering a man of light who asks, "Why are you sad and troubled?"—a scenario found in other earlier texts such as the *Shepherd of Hermas* and the *Apocryphon of John*. While this encounter foretells an emotional change for the saint, it plays out quite differently for Pachomius, whose

96. Pachomius's death is traditionally dated to 346 but may be around a decade earlier.

97. English translations of much of the corpus are in Armand Veilleux, *Pachomian Koinonia*, 3 vols., CS 45–47 (Kalamazoo, MI: Cistercian, 1980–1982); historical studies include Philip Rousseau, *Pachomius: The Making of a Community in Fourth-Century Egypt* (Berkeley: University of California Press, 1985); and James E. Goehring, *Ascetics, Society, and the Desert: Studies in Early Egyptian Monasticism* (Harrisburg, PA: Trinity Press International, 1999).

98. James E. Goehring, "The First Sahidic *Life of Pachomius*," in *Religions of Late Antiquity in Practice*, ed. Richard Valantasis (Princeton: Princeton University Press, 2000), 19–33.

sadness turns not to Hermas's cheerfulness but to anger, which Pachomius feels in tension with grief throughout his life. He is at first "indignant" at the visionary man's call to serve other men but ultimately takes his advice, although without convincing his fellow ascetics, who apparently sense a change in his demeanor. When his brother "angrily" admonishes him for being conceited, Pachomius becomes "agitated."[99] For a fourth-century reader in Upper Egypt his emotional agitation or movement (*afkim*, semantically similar to *štortr* and *tarassō*) starkly contrasts with the emotional norms of other Coptic literature, such as the *Gospel of Judas*, which valorized being "immovable" (*atkim*) or "at rest" as an ascetic ideal, along with the elimination of anger.

Pachomius recognizes his feeling as anger, in line with Aristotle's definition, the pain of being slighted by one's inferior and the desire for retribution.[100] But instead of reacting with righteous anger at his brother, he reproaches himself, and "he grieved deeply," taking Jesus as his model, who according to 1 Peter did not revile or get angry (1 Pet 2:23), and is unmoved by the more positive descriptions of Jesus's anger in the Gospels.[101] Anger returns a few days later in reaction to another slight from his brother, and Pachomius spends the whole night standing and praying on a brick, weeping so much that the brick had eroded into mud by morning—a nice touch of hagiographical hyperbole. But rather unexpectedly, and similar to Evagrius's teaching, the *Life of Pachomius* does not present the saint as freeing himself from anger but rather bifurcates the emotion. He refines his anger like the biblical exemplar of David, "who says, 'Forsake wrath, renounce anger' [Ps 36:8]." Indeed, "from that day on he did not get angry (*cōnt*) again as men of the flesh do." The latter clause is an important caveat. Pachomius later gets "angry (*cōnt*) on occasion," but this is "after the manner of the saints."[102] He imitates not ordinary humans but saintly men who carry out God's royal anger.

It takes some time, however, for this saintly anger to build as his community grows. As in other versions of the *Life of Pachomius*, Pachomius aims to

99. *V. Pach.* S[1] Frag. 3 [6]; Goehring, "First Sahidic *Life*," 25

100. *Afkim hmpefhēt . . . nterefnau je afpefhēt noucs*, *V. Pach.* S[1] Frag. 3 [7–8]; Goehring, "First Sahidic *Life*," 26; *VS* 1 (in the edition of Veilleux, *Pachomian Koinonia*, vol. 1).

101. From his long self-reproach, e.g., "I am not yet [faithful]. . . . Why can't I suffer without anger (*ouešnoucs*)?" *V. Pach.* S[1] Frag. 3 [7–8]; Goehring, "First Sahidic *Life*," 26; *VS* 2. The typical word for grief is *mkah nhēt*, e.g., *afmkah nhēt emate*, *VS* 1. Dilley notes that literally this is "heart pain," Paul Dilley, *Monasteries and the Care of Souls in Late Antique Christianity: Cognition and Discipline* (Cambridge: Cambridge University Press, 2017), 230. On *lypē* as grief and pain, see chapter 3.

102. *V. Pach.* S[1] Frag. 3 [9]; Goehring, "First Sahidic *Life*," 26; *VS* 3.

form a *Koinōnia* based on the original ideals of the Jerusalem church (Acts 4) and the apostle Paul (1 Cor 9:22), in which all shared their belongings and all were cared for according to their weaknesses.[103] But in this version of the *Life of Pachomius*, Pachomius fails, an unusual feature in a monastic Life, which as a literary genre tends to idealize ascetic existence and the character of the saint. Unlike the weak Pachomius, his early fellow monks are "strong men," bullies who refuse to take Pachomius seriously as a leader.[104] He serves them and cooks for them, even nonascetic foods, all the while fasting himself.[105] This inspires only "contempt and great insolence" from the others.[106] Yet he shows not a whit of anger toward them, and bears it in "great patience" (anger's obverse) with a "troubled heart and sighing."[107] Pachomius even voices the tragic hope of one trapped in an abusive relationship, that his patience, humility, and emotional suffering will teach his errant monks a lesson, and they'll come around and love him back.[108]

Remarkably for a hagiographical portrait, Pachomius shifts his emotional stance after enduring some five years of contempt and humiliation. Realizing that his position of ostentatious humility is not teaching the monks the right lesson, he prays one night in a sorrowful (*efmokh nhēt*) plea.[109] What precisely God said is lost in a lacuna between fragments, but the heart of the message is clear. When the narrative resumes Pachomius lays down a new rule: Obey or leave.[110]

His brothers, however, are completely unimpressed by his change of heart: "They looked at one another, sneering and laughing."[111] Again, the similarity of these errant monks' contempt and laughter to the affective appearance of Jesus in gnostic texts would probably not be lost on a fourth-century Coptic reader. But now, inspired by whatever God had revealed to him, Pachomius lets loose

103. Rousseau, *Pachomius*, 66–71.

104. *V. Pach.* S[1] Frag. 4 [18]; Goehring, "First Sahidic *Life*," 30; *VS* 116: *nehenjōōre gar ne hmpeusōma.*

105. *V. Pach.* S[1] Frag. 4 [12]; Goehring, "First Sahidic *Life*," 27; *VS* 5.

106. *Mnoukataphronēsis mnounoc mmntathote, V. Pach.* S[1] Frag. 4 [13]; Goehring, "First Sahidic *Life*," 27; *VS* 5.

107. *Hnoumkah nhēt mnouašahom, V. Pach.* S[1] Frag. 3 [14]; Goehring, "First Sahidic *Life*," 28; *VS* 6.

108. *V. Pach.* S[1] Frag. 3 [13] citing Ps. 25(24):18; *thbbio, pahise*; cf. 24:17, *nethlipsis mpahēt*; Goehring, "First Sahidic *Life*," 27; *VS* 5.

109. *V. Pach.* S[1] Frag. 3 [15–16]; Goehring, "First Sahidic *Life*," 28–29; *VS* 6–7, 114–115, quoting from *VS* 6.21.

110. *V. Pach.* S[1] Frag. 4 [17]; Goehring, "First Sahidic *Life*," 29; *VS* 116.

111. *V. Pach.* S[1] Frag. 4 [18]; Goehring, "First Sahidic *Life*," 29–30; *VS* 116.

his anger in full Davidic righteousness. Lacking "a staff or weapon for fighting," Pachomius takes a door key in hand as a makeshift cudgel and chases them bodily from the monastery, never to return.[112] This new Pachomius appears in the fragments that follow in the First Sahidic *Life of Pachomius* as well as in the longer Copto-Arabic *Life of Pachomius*, harsh, angry, and fearsome, willing to purge his community of the morally weak and sinful.[113]

On occasion Pachomius's affective leadership appears to have provoked a threat of violence or violence itself. Having sensed through angelic clairvoyance that bakers were violating the strict rule of silence, Pachomius tasked his second-in-command Theodore with investigating misdemeanors in the bakery. An angel tells Pachomius to be strict, especially with Theodore. "So now," the angel asks, "if Theodore comes to you and raises his hand to you, will you hold him excused?"[114] When Theodore reported the bakers' transgression to Pachomius, "Pachomius saw [Theodore] raise his hand to him." The *Life of Pachomius* obscures the reason for Theodore's response, but it seems clear that he is "on the verge of hitting Pachomius."[115] At this threat Pachomius "laughed in his face with great anger (*efmeh njōnt emašō*)" and unforgivingly sends Theodore off to cry in penitence for his negligence.[116] Theodore would remain in a liminal state of authority for the rest of Pachomius's lifetime, both the clear heir apparent to the father of the *Koinōnia* (at least the clear favorite among the rank and file monks) and a possible upstart suspected (by Pachomius) of conspiring to take the leadership himself. Thus, he alternated between working at Pachomius's side and exile.

When Pachomius was dying of a pestilence sweeping through the monasteries, Theodore was back at his side, which again points to the tension between sadness and anger as privileged emotions in the community. His followers grieve his forthcoming death so excessively that Pachomius sends Theodore out to order them to stop. But the monks refuse to obey, and Theodore returned to his side "and continued to weep over him with profound

112. *V. Pach.* S[1] Frag. 4 [17]; Goehring, "First Sahidic *Life*," 30; *VS* 117.

113. In *V. Pach.* S[1] Frag. 6 [24] (Goehring, "First Sahidic *Life*," 31; *VS* 118), Pachomius ejects his own nephew for "some wicked affairs" and "continued to operate in this way all the days of his life" (Goehring).

114. *V. Pach.* SBo 77 (Veilleux); *VB*, 82.

115. This act has been interpreted as a threat of violence. Ewa Wipszycka, *The Second Gift of the Nile: Monks and Monasteries in Late Antique Egypt*, trans. Damian Jasińsky, Supplements to the Journal of Juristic Papyrology (Warsaw: University of Warsaw, 2018), 212. In the same *Life of Pachomius*, Theodore later beats other monks weeping at Pachomius's death.

116. *V. Pach.* SBo 77 (Veilleux); *VB*, 83.

sorrow (*hnounoc nouōšf nhēt*)."[117] To forestall such grief in the future (and as apologia for why the founder of the order curiously has no known tomb) Pachomius orders Theodore to move his body from his grave in secret. He punctuates his order by grabbing Theodore's beard and punching him in the chest: "Theodore, pay attention. Do not leave my body in the place where it will be buried."[118] Nothing like a bit of violence to sharpen the mind. To the end, Pachomius models a saintly anger in leading his sometimes-fractious monks, though later parts of his community's institutional histories suggest a change in emotional values in later generations, privileging the saintly mourning seen in other late antique monastic sources.[119]

Conclusion

Of all the emotions, anger attracted the most attention from ancient philosophers and moralists. Ancients recognized the threat of angry feelings to erupt suddenly into violence and retribution in a culture based on agonistic competition and driven by the love of public honor and the avoidance of shame. While envy, too, was seen as a particularly dangerous and pernicious passion (to which I will turn in chapter 6), anger's duality made it an even more fascinating topic for discussion, as many saw a positive role for anger in righteous living. For Christians, anger featured consistently in God's personality in the Old Testament and even in some passages in the Gospels.

Early Christians addressed anger in a number of ways. While Paul was not particularly vexed by anger, any more than other ill-tempered outbursts, some after him moved toward a more Stoic-sounding advocacy of eliminating angry expressions and feelings. This is especially well developed in the *Gospel of Judas*, which takes the angry feelings of the god of Israel seriously as influencing the very structure of the cosmos and the emotional lives of his worshippers. Jesus, as messenger of the true God, is free from anger, and Judas's inability to free himself from the passion prods him to hand Jesus over and at the same time prevents him from ascending past the lower realm to the heavenly fullness. Contemporaneous Egyptian Christians embraced more positive roles for anger in the life of the ascetic, though never escaping the intrinsic ambiguity of

117. *V. Pach.* SBo 121 (Veilleux); *VS*, 93.

118. *V. Pach.* SBo 122 (Veilleux); *VS*, 94.

119. Ingvild Sælid Gilhus, "'Tears Flowed from His Eyes Unceasingly': Weeping and Total Devotion in Egypt in Late Antiquity," *Religion* 53 (2023): 116–34.

the emotion. For Evagrius, anger had its time and place, channeling the kingly anger of God and his earthly representatives to repel demonic hosts, a natural anger. But still, anger more generally threatened the monk and his practice, remaining a thorn in the side when many of the other temptations of desire and comfort had been conquered. Anger was also threatening for Pachomius, who resisted it for years and embraced the kind of spirituality of sadness and abject humility seen in the previous chapter. But Pachomius, at last, discovered the challenges of running an organization on tears and eventually embraced his inner David, openly angry, demanding, and at times violent—in a saintly way, of course. All of these approaches to anger, control, elimination, bifurcation, and encouragement, would continue to be explored in Christian writers and communities throughout late antiquity.

5

Disgust

Many psychologists place disgust among the basic emotions, certainly in part due to its distinctively stereotyped facial expression of recoil: lip curled, nose wrinkled. And if one thinks of emotions as "triggered," disgust—like that other strange core emotion, surprise—fits the bill. Revulsion at rot or feces or creepy crawlies feels instinctual and primitive, compared to joy, sadness, or anger, which all call out for narrative and rumination.

Yet disgust—like all emotions—is a concept, constructed neurologically, psychologically, and socially through the intersection of bodily affect, mental interoception, and the world outside our bodies.[1] Disgust furthermore does not get triggered by external stimuli, at least not straightforwardly, but like all emotions is predicted by our brains in a learning process that continues throughout the life cycle.[2] Disgust can thus be provoked by substances (and behaviors) that are neither intrinsically threatening to the organism nor revolting, by adducing emotional concepts into the brain's normal process of simulation ("your brain's guesses of what's happening in the world").[3] Which is why disgust can be so powerful a social force and so relevant to the history of religious movements, as recent cognitive science "shows that what we see, hear, touch, taste, and smell are largely simulations of the world, not reactions to it."[4]

Still, humans tend to find a core set of elicitors disgusting, which gives an appearance of universality and makes ancient affects of revulsion and disgust

1. Reviewed in Lisa Feldman Barrett, *How Emotions Are Made: The Secret Life of the Brain* (Boston: Houghton Mifflin Harcourt, 2017), 84–111.

2. E.g., Barrett, *How Emotions Are Made*, 116–18.

3. Barrett, *How Emotions Are Made*, 27.

4. Barrett, *How Emotions Are Made*, 27.

viscerally recognizable, even when our informants do not use a lexicon of disgust words. Such elicitors will surprise no one: bodily fluids, decay, feces, open wounds, swarming insects, and so on. This kind of disgust—the instinctive retch when I, for example, accidentally take a bite of something spoiled—is commonly called core disgust. If this were all there was to disgust, it would not deserve a chapter here.

Disgust is also a moral emotion, a revulsion we feel at others' behaviors and beliefs.[5] Like anger, we use disgust to judge and discriminate between right and wrong—categories that obviously are historically and culturally contingent—and to mark social boundaries of identity and exclusion.[6] Paul Rozin, considered the founder of modern disgust psychology, has called disgust "the body and soul emotion."[7] This is perhaps the more common context for disgust language in day-to-day life: That behavior is disgusting, gross, creepy! Ewww, I can't believe he said that! This moral disgust works not just on an individual level. It is a primary way that groups distinguish themselves. We criticize or suspect others for their dietary practices, their sexual norms, or their supposed hygiene. At the same time, to advocate against feeling disgust is also a way of advocating and enforcing morality; to feel disgust at this or that practice, an unfamiliar food, for example, or homosexuality, or (today) polyamory, marks one as a bad person, an Other, perhaps of a lower or less sophisticated class.[8] It is no accident that the stereotyped facial expression of disgust shifts so easily into contempt.

Thus, for good or ill, disgust shapes the ways that humans think about morality and group identity, which psychologists and philosophers have doc-

5. Explored from various perspectives by William Ian Miller, *An Anatomy of Disgust* (Cambridge, MA: Harvard University Press, 1998), 179–205; Simone Schnall et al., "Disgust as Embodied Moral Judgment," *Personality and Social Psychology Bulletin* 34 (2008): 1096–1109; Jessica Tracy, "Find Something Morally Sickening? Take a Ginger Pill," *Aeon*, February 21, 2020.

6. On the complicated neurological relationship between disgust (moral and core) and anger, see Megan Oaten et al., "Moral Violations and the Experience of Disgust and Anger," *Frontiers in Behavioral Neuroscience* 12 (2018): art. 179.

7. Paul Rozin, Jonathan Haidt, and Clark McCauley, "Disgust: The Body and Soul Emotion," in *Handbook of Cognition and Emotion*, ed. Tim Dalgleish and Mick J. Powers (New York: Wiley, 1999), 429–51. Also see Paul Rozin et al., "Glad to Be Sad, and Other Examples of Benign Masochism," *Judgment and Decision Making* 8 (2013): 446; Rozin's influence on disgust psychology will be reflected in citations below, for which see the profile by Molly Young, "How Disgust Explains Everything," *New York Times*, June 15, 2023 (rev. from Dec. 27, 2021).

8. E.g., Martha C. Nussbaum, *Hiding from Humanity: Disgust, Shame, and the Law* (Princeton: Princeton University Press, 2004); also Jonathan Haidt, *The Righteous Mind: Why Good People Are Divided by Politics and Religion* (New York: Pantheon, 2012).

umented in exploring the cognitive and emotional contours of politics and religion.[9] Recent studies have focused on the mechanisms and depictions of disgust as a moral emotion in Mediterranean antiquity, including the Hebrew Bible and New Testament.[10] Early Christians approached disgust as a moral emotion in divergent ways. In the first centuries, two primary modes of disgust talk emerge in early Christian sources. One mode, found in a range of New Testament texts, including the Gospels and Paul, rarely evokes the emotion of disgust in moral exhortation and narrative. While purity was an important component of the emerging Christian sense of community and theology, such authors conspicuously refrain from the language of disgust or disgust-eliciting imagery, even in contexts where it would be expected. In a related way, an author may alternatively turn on its head the moral logic of disgust as indicative of sin, shame, and exclusion. Another mode of Christian disgust appears in other sources in the New Testament (Revelation, the Pastorals, Jude, and 2 Peter) and extrabiblical literature from the second century onward. Such Christian authors employ a rich vocabulary of disgust to draw theological and social boundaries between right-thinking Christians and other wrong-thinking or disturbing Christians. Right-thinking Christians are to view disturbers and heretics with disgust, as disgusting people, both for their teachings and their actions. Christians in late antiquity drew on earlier models in elaborating these two moral uses of disgust, sometimes encouraging feelings of disgust as a form

9. Paul Rozin, Jonathan Haidt, and Clark McCauley, "Disgust," in *Handbook of Emotions*, ed. Michael Lewis, Jeannette M. Haviland-Jones, and Lisa Feldman Barrett, 4th ed. (New York: Guilford, 2016), 815–34; Daniel Kelly, *Yuck! The Nature and Moral Significance of Disgust* (Cambridge: MIT Press, 2011), 101–36; Miller, *Anatomy of Disgust*; Zhaoliang Yu et al., "'Look Not at What Is Contrary to Propriety': A Meta-Analytic Exploration of the Association Between Religiosity and Sensitivity to Disgust," *British Journal of Social Psychology* 61 (2022): 279–99.

10. E.g., Donald Lateiner and Dimos Spatharos, eds., *The Ancient Emotion of Disgust* (Oxford: Oxford University Press, 2016); L. Juliana Claasens, "From Fear's Narcissism to Participatory Imagination: Disrupting Disgust and Overcoming the Fear of Israel's *Ḥērem* Laws," in *Mixed Feelings and Vexed Passions: Exploring Emotions in Biblical Literature*, ed. F. Scott Spencer, RBS 90 (Atlanta: SBL Press, 2017), 77–96; Thomas Kazen, "Disgust in Body, Mind, and Language: The Case of Impurity in the Hebrew Bible," in Spencer, *Mixed Feelings*, 97–116; Colleen Shantz, "Emotion, Cognition, and Social Change: A Consideration of Galatians 3:28," in *Mind, Morality, and Magic: Cognitive Science Approaches in Biblical Studies*, ed. István Czachesz and Risto Uro (London: Acumen, 2014), 251–69; Stephen D. Moore, "Retching on Rome: Vomitous Loathing and Visceral Disgust in Affect Theory and the Apocalypse of John," *BibInt* 22 (2014): 503–28.

of emotional practice to encourage other morals and to draw boundaries of identity and belief between Christians (or the right Christians) and others and sometimes modeling a practice of overcoming disgust either through aesthetic transformation or as a form of ascetic practice in itself.

Ancient Disgust and Its Identification

Disgust poses some challenges compared to other ancient emotions or passions.[11] It never received the sort of sustained philosophical or theological reflection that other human emotions did in antiquity, like anger, love, envy, or joy.[12] While the modern study of emotions since Darwin has classified disgust among the common or core emotions, it was not considered a *pathos* in the significant literature devoted to emotions among philosophers. A likely explanation lies in the common experience of disgust as an overwhelming and instinctive response, literally visceral. This fits poorly with ancient conceptualizations of emotion as cognitive and evaluative.[13] Nonetheless, ancient authors, especially non-philosophers, addressed and used the bodily and mental feelings of revulsion, distaste, and surfeit for a variety of purposes and with a variety of words: *aēdēs*, *bdelygma*, *miainō*, *molynō*, *sikchos*, and *stygeros* (and their verbal and nominative forms). Whatever the words, a modern reader can feel recognizable stirrings of revulsion, as well as fascination, in ancient descriptions of the stink of bodily fluids and open sores, whether for comedy or tragedy. Whatever words we use, we share the same bodies between today and the ancient Mediterranean, and similar projective metaphors from the same bodily processes speak to us today.

11. Nonetheless, ancient historians have found disgust an attractive topic for some time. Disgust in Greco-Roman, biblical, and early Christian sources is approached respectively from a range of perspectives in Lateiner and Spatharos, *Ancient Emotion of Disgust*; Thomas Kazen, *Emotions in Biblical Law: A Cognitive Science Approach* (Sheffield: Sheffield Phoenix, 2011); Blake Leyerle, "Refuse, Filth, and Excrement in the Homilies of John Chrysostom," *Journal of Late Antiquity* 2 (2009): 337–56; Susan Wessel, *Passion and Compassion in Early Christianity* (Cambridge: Cambridge University Press, 2016), 65–97; Susan Ashbrook Harvey, *Scenting Salvation: Ancient Christianity and the Olfactory Imagination*, Transformation of the Classical Tradition 42 (Berkeley: University of California Press, 2006).

12. Such as studied through an Aristotelian lens by David Konstan, *The Emotions of the Ancient Greeks: Studies in Aristotle and Classical Literature* (Toronto: University of Toronto Press, 2006).

13. Lateiner and Spatharas, *Ancient Emotion of Disgust*, 6–7.

In fact, disgust is identified with the most consistent global facial expression among the purported six basic emotions.[14] Yet, for such a gut feeling, disgust is the most specifically human of the core emotions; what we can identify as disgust is uniquely displayed by humans.[15] It develops relatively late, between the ages of three and seven, and furthermore depends entirely on socialization or "enculturation."[16] Without socialization, disgust never develops.[17] For those who approach emotions as concepts or "constructed," neurologically, psychologically, and socially, disgust provides a valuable example of how socially and culturally contingent emotions are, even as automatic and innate as they can feel.

As noted already, students of disgust traditionally divide disgust elicitors twofold: the materially disgusting and the morally disgusting.[18] Responses to such elicitors are sometimes distinguished as core disgust and projective disgust, core disgust being the reaction to the material elicitors typical across human societies, such as bodily fluids, feces, swarming organisms, and body-envelope violations.[19] Some biologists have reduced these elicitors even further to a primal avoidance of parasites (parasite avoidance theory), which expands to all manner of material substances and behaviors and people (projective disgust).[20] The "term projective disgust describes cases in which elicitors of core disgust are projected upon individuals as means of stigmatizing and mar-

14. The universal or basic emotions school is described by Jan Plamper, *The History of Emotions: An Introduction*, trans. Keith Tribe (Oxford: Oxford University Press, 2015), 147–63. See further in chapter 1, and also Ruth Leys, *The Ascent of Affect: Genealogy and Critique* (Chicago: University of Chicago Press, 2017), 76–128; and Barrett, *How Emotions Are Made*, 42–55.

15. Carolyn Korsmeyer, *Savoring Disgust: The Foul and the Fair in Aesthetics* (Oxford: Oxford University Press, 2018), 34; also Lateiner and Spatharos, *Ancient Emotion of Disgust*, 11, who compare it to laughter as a uniquely human response. Barrett critiques the research on animal emotions in *How Emotions Are Made*, 252–77.

16. Paul Rozin, Jonathan Haidt, and Clark R. McCauley, "Disgust," in *Handbook of Emotions*, ed. Michael Lewis, Jeannette M. Haviland-Jones, and Lisa Feldman Barrett, 3rd ed. (New York: Guilford, 2008), 765.

17. Rozin, Haidt, and McCauley, "Disgust," 3rd ed., 765.

18. Korsmeyer, *Savoring Disgust*, 36.

19. Common disgust elicitors are described in Rozin, Haidt, and McCauley, "Disgust," 4th ed., 816–22. For the Roman context, see Donald Lateiner, "Evoking Disgust in the Latin Novels of Petronius and Apuleius," in Lateiner and Spatharos, *Ancient Emotion of Disgust*, 203–34; and with reference to the Gospels, see F. Scott Spencer, *Passions of the Christ: The Emotional Life of Jesus in the Gospels* (Grand Rapids: Baker Academic, 2021), 118–19.

20. Valerie Curtis, *Don't Look, Don't Touch, Don't Eat: The Science Behind Revulsion* (Chicago: University of Chicago Press, 2013).

ginalizing them."[21] This "'moral' disgust revolves around immaterial elicitors, such as morally ambivalent behavior, ideologies, or criminal actions."[22] While many see core disgust as primary and moral disgust its metaphorical application, some have argued provocatively that disgust has a social origin—for example, the rejection of socially parasitic people—which became expanded to bodily processes of revulsion and expulsion.[23] Such cross-culturally common disgust elicitors—material and moral—are useful in identifying possible disgust when the disgust terms are not explicitly used.

It furthermore remains significant that ancient theorists did not categorize such feelings into an abstract concept of disgust the way Stoics did for *lypē*, *phobos*, and so on. This points to an important challenge—always present in the cross-cultural study of emotion but more acute for disgust—that we not presume ancient ways of feeling are the same as our own. While there are passages from ancient authors like Plato and Plutarch that have been taken as intentionally disgusting by modern interpreters, one should be wary of conflating ancient feelings or emotions with modern assumptions about disgust as emotion, when they might more accurately be understood in context as expressions of desire, fascination, or awe, for example.[24] Such disgust elicitors may alert us to historical difference, to discover something else where we might today expect disgust, or disgust as it is currently felt.[25]

As intuitive as such categories of core and projective or moral disgust may be, cognitive science warns against a hard distinction between core and projective. In fact, "no clear line separates the literal from the metaphorical use of the word *disgust*."[26] The permeability of physiological and metaphorical

21. Lateiner and Spatharas, *Ancient Emotion of Disgust*, 23.

22. Lateiner and Spatharas, *Ancient Emotion of Disgust*, 23; Miller, *Anatomy of Disgust*, 179–205.

23. Joshua Rotman, Jasmine M. Dejesus, and Emily Gerdin, "The Social Origins of Disgust," in *The Moral Psychology of Disgust*, ed. Nina Strohminger and Victor Kumar (London: Rowman & Littlefield International, 2018), 27–52.

24. Rob Boddice, *A History of Feelings* (London: Reaktion, 2019), 62–72. Affect theory also emphasizes disgust's power to repel and attract, as in Sarah Ahmed, *The Cultural Politics of Emotion*, 2nd ed. (Edinburgh: Edinburgh University Press, 2014), 85, presented in its more typical language of bodies, objects, and surfaces.

25. Boddice, *History of Feelings*, 62–72.

26. James A. Russell, "The Greater Constructionist Project for Emotion," in *The Psychological Construction of Emotion*, ed. Lisa Feldman Barrett and James A. Russell (New York: Guilford, 2014), 429. Rozin, Haidt, and McCauley ("Disgust," 4th ed., 822) also conclude, "In sum, there is continuing controversy, but emerging evidence indicates that moral disgust is not just a metaphor." Cf. Kazen ("Disgust in Body, Mind, and Language," 105) on a related

disgust points to a crucial feature of disgust as an early Christian emotion. Disgust is a concept implicated in morality, sanctity, and purity, and thus also in establishing and maintaining social boundaries and hierarchies: "Disgust is precisely the emotion that guards the sanctity of the soul as well as the purity of the body."[27] The following sections identify some divergent and competing ways that early Christians approached disgust, its use, and its suppression in the intersection of embodied feeling, metaphor, intergroup boundary setting, and purity.

Disgust and Its Transformations: Paul

It is striking how rarely disgust language occurs in the literature of the earliest Christ followers, especially the letters of Paul and the New Testament Gospels.[28] When disgust words are used, they tend to fall within the semantic domain of purity concerns in Jewish tradition (*bdelygma* [and related forms]: disgusting or loathsome; *miainō* [and related forms]: to be stained with bodily fluids or filth; *molynō*: to be stained or defiled; and *stygeros* [and related forms]: to be hated, abominated, or loathed).[29] Yet this language of disgust rarely occurs in the first generations of Christian literature. Paul uses disgust words

debate in Hebrew Bible studies: "When this linguistic data is taken seriously, we see that much of the literal-metaphorical debate [about purity] is misguided."

27. Paul Rozin, "Food for Thought: Paul Rozin's Research and Teaching at Penn," *Penn Arts and Sciences*, Fall 1997, cited in Korsmeyer, *Savoring Disgust*, 34; and further in Rozin, Haidt, and McCauley, "Disgust," 4th ed., 820–22, while disgust in social conflict and boundary-setting is described at 826–27. Disgust's activation as part of marking social hierarchy in Roman society is discussed by Lateiner and Spatharos, *Ancient Emotion of Disgust*, 13.

28. In two books on emotions in the New Testament, disgust plays no role. See Matthew Elliott, *Faithful Feelings: Rethinking Emotion in the New Testament* (Grand Rapids: Kregel Academic, 2006); and Voorwinde, *Jesus' Emotions*, thankfully augmented now by Spencer, *Passions of the Christ*. The following is adapted from Andrew Crislip, "Disgust in Early Christianity: The New Testament and Its Early Reception," *Biblica* 102 (2021): 593–617, with permission from Peeters Press.

29. I draw this list of terms partly from Lateiner and Spatharos, *Ancient Emotion of Disgust*, 5, compared with Edwin Hatch and Henry A. Redpath, *A Concordance to the Septuagint*, 2 vols. (Oxford: Clarendon, 1897). *Aēdēs*, *sikchos*, and related words do not occur in the New Testament, nor does *sikchos* appear in the Septuagint. Kazen, *Emotions in Biblical Law*, 71–94, discusses disgust as an emotional component of biblical purity laws. *Stugeō* terminology appears only in 3 Maccabees, but the other terms are common.

sparingly, and even then in a projective or metaphorical sense.[30] He refers to consciences as potentially defiled (1 Cor 8:7) and calls on his Corinthian beloved to cleanse themselves from bodily and spiritual defilement (2 Cor 7:1). He once refers to fellow Jews who "loathe" idols, a positive disgust at impurity that they evince hypocritically (Rom 2:22). Paul also uses language of moral purity and impurity in a number of contexts.[31] While impurity and purity can be connected to feelings of disgust, Paul draws on neither the lexicon of revulsion and distaste nor disgust-eliciting imagery—foul fluids, insects, wounds, and so on—in these passages.

Disgust words are furthermore almost entirely lacking from the Synoptic Gospels, and what terms occur are projective, even as purity remains a theme in Jesus's eschatological career.[32] The Synoptics mention the coming desecration of the temple (Matt 24:15 // Mark 13:14), and in Luke Jesus calls what is prized by human hearts an abomination to God (Luke 16:15). Yet, the emotional terminology of disgust, visceral or metaphorical, core or projective, plays little into the theological or narrative concerns of these first-century texts.

Of course, one need not use disgust words (abomination, staining, corruption, and so on) to indicate the feeling. In this light, more interesting than the use of simple disgust terms is how the Gospels and Paul address narrative situations where the elicitors of core or projective disgust are present (bodily fluids, feces, animals, body-envelope violations, sexual matters, and disease). For example, in 1 Corinthians 5 Paul addresses the situation of a member of the Corinthian congregation cohabiting with his stepmother, apparently without being roundly condemned by the others. This (perhaps borderline) incest is exactly where one would expect disgust language; incest is a prime elicitor of projective disgust cross-culturally and certainly was in Greco-Roman antiquity.[33] While Paul embraces a rhetoric of purity in calling for the wrongdoer to be expelled, as from the social body, he neither betrays any disgust on the

30. The importance of metaphor in ancient Israelite and Jewish purity discourse is emphasized by Jonathan Klawans, *Purity, Sacrifice, and the Temple: Symbolism and Supersessionism in the Study of Ancient Judaism* (New York: Oxford University Press, 2006).

31. E.g., Rom 1:24; 6:19; 14:20; 1 Cor 7:14; 2 Cor 6:17; 7:1; 12:21; Gal 5:19; 1 Thess 2:3; 4:7.

32. See Jodi Magness, "'They Shall See the Glory of the Lord' (Isa 35:2): Eschatological Perfection and Purity at Qumran and in Jesus' Movement," *Journal for the Study of the Historical Jesus* 14 (2016): 99–119; and Thomas Kazen, *Jesus and Purity Halakhah: Was Jesus Indifferent to Purity?* (Stockholm: Almqvist & Wiskell, 2002).

33. Ancients took sex with a stepparent as incest, and it was explicitly banned in Roman and Jewish law, Joseph A. Fitzmyer, SJ, *First Corinthians*, AB 32 (New Haven: Yale University Press, 2008), 233–34.

level of emotion words nor encourages his correspondents to feel it. Instead, he encourages sorrow; his congregation should "have mourned (*epenthēsate*)" so that the wrongdoer would have been cast out (1 Cor 5:2). The absence of disgust in the narrative context of incest is quite conspicuous.

One may also sense the absence of disgust in Paul's decree that "there is neither Jew nor Greek."[34] This is such a theological commonplace, it is easy to overlook how radical a shift in feeling and emotional practice this was. Ancient authors testify to feelings of revulsion toward both Jews and Greeks as outsiders and others, disgust at diet, smells, alleged animality, and sexual norms.[35] Yet Paul does not evoke any disgust at this merging of Jewish and Greek identity. Rather, the experience that Paul points to better fits the emotion of awe.[36] While Paul does not use explicit emotion words, Colleen Shantz adduces other "religious experiences" in Paul's letters as parallels indicative of the desired emotional experience.[37] These parallels, along with the insights of cross-cultural and cognitive psychology, echo ancient writers who frame ostensibly disgusting narratives as inspiring awe (*phobos*). While Paul's claim to the Galatians might not sound immediately emotional, it models a practice of shifting feelings of disgust into awe as a cognitive and emotional experience that was a significant transformation in the early Christian movement.[38]

Ancient Greek and Roman authors also used sights and smells to evoke disgust in their readers: rotting teeth, filthy bodies and body parts, excreta, and animals. Ancients were disgusted with many of the same things that we are. From the perspective of affect theory, embodied intensities beneath or outside of language drive our cognition and sociality without our ever knowing it, and an affect theory approach might help excavate this emotional world.[39] Jamie Gunderson draws on the phenomenology of affect to draw out hidden emotional experiences by attention to images and smells, drawing on the concept of the "imagetext": "an interface of sensory representations (including textual and visual elements, and possibly aural, tactile, olfactory, or gustatory discourses) bound up in an affective engagement between a writer/speaker and

34. Shantz, "Emotion, Cognition, and Social Change."

35. Shantz, "Emotion, Cognition, and Social Change," 258–63.

36. Shantz, "Emotion, Cognition, and Social Change," 263–68.

37. Shantz, "Emotion, Cognition, and Social Change," 264–65.

38. Shantz, "Emotion, Cognition, and Social Change," 269.

39. See also Joseph A. Marchal, "The Disgusting Apostle and a Queer Affect Between Epistles and Audiences," in *Reading with Feeling: Affect Theory and the Bible*, ed. Fiona C. Black and Jennifer L. Koosed (Atlanta: SBL Press, 2019), 113–40.

their audience in the transmission of (embodied) knowledge."[40] Scholars who draw out the hidden currents of disgust flowing beneath Paul's letters insist that they work not out of prurience and transgressive delight in contaminating an ostensibly holy topic.[41] Rather, they show Paul in his full humanity as an outwardly and deeply emotional evangelist, far from the "unfeeling" and "rational" Paul of "scholarly anaesthetizing," an embodied man whose emotions—with those of his peers—pass from person to person and are hard to clean off; they are "sticky."[42]

The text under examination as "imagetext" here is 2 Corinthians 11:2–4, as Paul warns his wayward congregants about the temptations of rival apostles. The passage is instructive for how affect theory can draw out a very unexpected emotionality from Paul, especially since there is nothing disgusting in the passage, at least on the level of ordinary language or imagery.

In fact, Paul is explicit in his emotional tone and the affective response he encourages in his audience. He is jealous with a godly jealousy, and he recalls and reclaims his spiritual children's love for him, that they not consort with any other Christ or apostles (11:2). He compares the Corinthians to Eve, tempted by the serpent, an image which evokes the love triangles between Eve, Adam, and the serpent, and Eve, the serpent, and God, as well as the diabolical emotion of envy (*phthonos*), which overlaps semantically in Hellenistic Greek with Paul's godly *zēlos*.[43] On a surface reading, the emotionality of Paul's exhortation speaks straightforwardly of jealousy and the travails of love.

Gunderson transforms a discourse of jealousy into one of disgust, first, by simply cutting the jealousy out, omitting the first clause of 11:2 without explanation (*zēlō gar hymas theou zēlō*) when 2 Corinthians 11:2–4 is quoted at the beginning of the discussion. Instead her quotation begins with "I promised . . ." She notes that she cites the NRSV translation "with slight modification," but

40. Jamie Gunderson, "The Super Foul Apostles: Sexual Impropriety, Disgust, and Stinky Affective Histories in 2 Cor. 11:2–4," *BibInt* 30 (2022): 581. On the surface, this differs little from the way historians of emotions have approached emotions in general. Texts and visual materials will not always employ the lexicon of passions themselves but draw on embodied associations with affective states, an oozing sore for disgust, the sweetness of a flower for love.

41. Marchal ("Disgusting Apostle," 113) foregrounds the disjunction between the disgusting and perverted with "such sacred texts" as Paul's letters.

42. E.g., Gunderson, "Super Foul Apostles," 598, 585–86; Marchal, "Disgusting Apostle," 116. Stickiness, under the influence of Sarah Ahmed, is a leitmotif of both essays.

43. See chapter 6 of this volume.

for a reader without the actual text front of mind, this gives a misleading sense of the passage. It is on this foundation that Paul's house of disgust is built.[44]

In this reading, the core of Paul's disgust is the snake of 11:3, which evokes the story of Eden. Affectively, snakes are associated most prominently with fear (*phobos*), certainly in classic psychological studies of emotion. At the same time, they undoubtedly evoke awe (also *phobos*), with their unique physiology, strange beauty, and marvelous ability to shed their skin. In fact, fear (*phoboumai*) is the precise emotion that Paul evokes in 11:3. But in this affective reading, the snake primarily functions as a phallic symbol, whose imagery might evoke Apuleius's tale of Cupid and Psyche (written over a century after Paul), in which an oracle predicts that Psyche will be ravished by a fearsome divine serpent (who actually turns out to be the incomparably beautiful Cupid himself).[45]

From this alleged phallic imagery, the snake of 11:3 now "evokes a dramatically disgusting picture that both capitalizes on the assembly's apparent pleasure in promiscuity and slanders the sexual transgressors with phallic imagery."[46] This "imagetext" allegedly then calls to mind ithyphallic sculpture (moving from snakes to fish for some reason), all of which coated Paul's Corinthian readers with the characteristic stickiness of ancient disgust, "presented through a metaphor of stinky sexual impropriety," "imagery not only disgustingly dramatic but also disgustingly comical."[47] Thus, within a few paragraphs Paul's emotions of jealousy (*zēlō*) and fear (*phoboumai*) are completely erased and replaced with a chain of deeply submerged allusions to sexual impropriety and phallic imagery to create an allegedly disgusting passage, so disgusting (and somehow comical) that it conceivably "induced his Corinthian audience to retch along with [Paul]."[48]

Underlying all this is the tendency to simply assume the unspoken affects beneath the surface of the text. Why, for example, would Paul or his audience find the Genesis snake disgusting? Snakes are not necessarily or normally disgusting, neither slimy nor sticky (like a slug), nor parasitic. And snakes don't smell particularly bad. That's why they make good house pets. They furthermore have always been fascinating and attractive to humans. The sense of awe they evoked surely was a reason why snakes featured so prominently in

44. Gunderson, "Super Foul Apostles," 591.
45. Gunderson ("Super Foul Apostles," 592) draws on Lateiner, "Evoking Disgust," 220.
46. Gunderson, "Super Foul Apostles," 593.
47. Gunderson, "Super Foul Apostles," 598, 593.
48. Gunderson, "Super Foul Apostles," 598–99.

religious iconography, as in the cult of Asclepius (who appeared as a snake in his healing dreams) and Zeus Meilichios (who appeared as a snake in various myths).[49] So why assume the snake evokes disgust?

And what is disgusting about a phallus? Inhabitants of the ancient Mediterranean were surrounded by phallic images in public and private, in sacred ritual and communal festivities.[50] There is no accounting for taste, but given the sheer ubiquity of non-snakelike *phalloi* in Greco-Roman culture it seems a stretch to presume that ancient people were typically walking around retching in disgust, or that Paul's clear allusion to the serpent of Genesis would call to mind this mundane feature of ancient urban life. Furthermore, while ancient people, like everyone else, found stinky things disgusting, there are no bad smells in 2 Corinthians (though there are good smells in 2:15).[51] For all the affective rhetoric of stickiness and stinkiness, of sexual deviance and retching, there is precious little of it in the actual letters of Paul.

Disgust and Its Transformations: The Gospels

The Synoptic Gospels also place readers in situations where their expectations of disgust might be reversed. Three times Jesus is faced with sufferers from *lepra*, a dermatological condition distinct from what is generally described as leprosy today (Hansen's disease).[52] Leprosy has played a cultural role as disgusting and stigmatizing from antiquity until modernity and thus in thinking about moral and social boundaries.[53] It is thus striking that there is nothing disgust eliciting in the leprosy episodes. In two of them (Matt 8:1, 4 // Mark 1:10 // Luke 5:12, and Matt 11:5 // Luke 7:22) Jesus touches the afflicted to heal them.

49. The Greek fascination with snakes as divine, sacred, fearful, and awesome is discussed by Roberto Calasso, *The Marriage of Cadmus and Harmony* (New York: Knopf, 1993), 297–301.

50. See, e.g., Eva C. Keuls, *The Reign of the Phallus: Sexual Politics in Ancient Athens* (Berkeley: University of California Press, 1985). Gunderson ("Super Foul Apostles," 592) notes the commonality of the phallus but characterizes it as "a familiar form of slander." Marchal ("Disgusting Apostle") too finds disgust throughout Romans, "this disgusting letter," again without any real support from Paul's own words or the phenomenology of disgust as explored by psychologists, and also discovers phallic imagery ("dick jokes" [132]), e.g., reading Paul's *prosopopoeia* of Rom 7 as particularly disgusting (127–29).

51. Gunderson, "Super Foul Apostles," 594–96, on bad smells.

52. David P. Wright and Richard N. Jones, "Leprosy," *ABD* 4:281; Myrick C. Shinall Jr., "The Social Condition of Lepers in the Gospels," *JBL* 137 (2018): 916.

53. Shinall, "Social Condition."

In the third (Luke 7:11–19) Jesus heals from afar. In none does any character evince disgust and in none does the author include descriptive details that would evoke a disgust response in the reader. In fact, quite the opposite: Like Paul, the evangelists model a transformation of disgust.

We see this in the sole passage in the Synoptics to employ disgust-eliciting language: Luke's parable of the rich man and the pauper Lazarus, who lies at the city gate "covered with sores" (Luke 16:20). This is undoubtedly meant to evoke disgust or revulsion, compounded by the description of dogs (considered filthy and disgusting in antiquity) licking his open wounds (Luke 16:1). The brief description of Lazarus's state incorporates most of the cross-culturally typical elicitors of disgust: unclean animals, the close contact or interpenetration of human and animal, body-envelope violations, and consumption of bodily fluids. Yet, Lazarus is the hero, transformed from object of disgust and pity into one of desire and emulation. The pauper ascends to paradise at Abraham's side, while the rich man goes to Hades, where he wants nothing more than Lazarus to touch his tongue with a drop of water (an unrequited desire that the rich man would have previously considered revolting). Luke uses this imagery of sores, pus, and dogs as emblematic of the apocalyptic reversal of fortune. Just as one should not trust in one's wealth, one should not trust one's feelings of disgust, feelings which, in Rome as today, were commonly connected to a sense of superiority.[54] Some contemporary jurists and philosophers have posited a kind of wisdom of disgust. To feel disgust at some action or phenomenon reliably indicates that it is indeed morally wrong.[55] The Lukan parable vividly turns such moral logic on its head, as the rich man's instinctive response to Lazarus's abjection is proven utterly unreliable.

Disgust elicitors occur in several stories in the Fourth Gospel, and apart from one mention of Jesus's captors' refusal to enter Pilate's headquarters in order to avoid ritual defilement (John 18:28), disgust elicitors function along the same lines as we have seen in Paul and Luke, more subverting normal expectations about revulsion than intensifying them.[56] We can observe this

54. For which, in the Roman context, see Robert A. Kaster, *Emotion, Restraint, and Community in Ancient Rome* (Oxford: Oxford University Press, 2005), 108–33; and Lateiner and Spatharos, *Ancient Emotion of Disgust*, 13.

55. Critiqued in Martha C. Nussbaum, *From Disgust to Humanity: Sexual Orientation and Constitutional Law* (Oxford: Oxford University Press, 2010), 8–13; also Kelly, *Yuck!*, 138–40.

56. In contrast to the claim that the "Fourth Gospel . . . is structured by disgust, by its convulsive, heaving movements of revulsion, expulsion, and exclusion," Stephen D. Moore, "Why the Johannine Jesus Weeps at the Tomb of Lazarus," in Spencer, *Mixed Feelings*, 303.

in the raising of Lazarus, about which recent scholarship helpfully shows how affect theory can reveal the sticky transmission of disgust beneath the surface of the text. It has even been claimed that Jesus weeps not out of grief but out of disgust: "What makes Jesus's eyes water in 11:35 is a certain smell, indeed a certain unmistakable stench, as yet only wafted on the breeze, for he is still some distance from Lazarus' tomb."[57] This reading of the Lazarus episode poses several challenges, such as whether it is possible for humans to cry from exposure to foul odor. The literature on crying is enormous and encompasses evolutionary biology, psychology, history, and beyond.[58] Yet there is no culture to my knowledge that communicates disgust through tears, and none that understands crying as a marker of disgust.[59] Further, in the narrative context set up by John, Jesus cannot weep from the smell of Lazarus's corpse because he hasn't smelled it yet; he is not even in sight of it (11:34), let alone close enough to catch the scent of decay from a sealed tomb.[60]

While the foul odor of Lazarus's corpse is inescapable once the tomb is opened, disgust terms are conspicuously absent, despite Lazarus's decaying corpse (11:39). True, the sisters warn Jesus that "already he smells," but this need not be read as a sign of disgust; the phrasing *ēdē ozei* emphasizes time as much as scent. The point is not to warn Jesus that it would be unpleasant to open the tomb but that it would be pointless and that it is, moreover, his fault for delaying (11:5–6, 21). Jesus had a chance to help, and declined. Despite the smell, neither the women nor Jesus avoid or shrink from the corpse, nor does the author include any further disgust elicitors for narrative color, in contrast with later apocryphal adaptations of the story, which revel in disgusting details.[61]

Thus, despite the smell of their brother and friend's body, John does not say or even imply that the women or Jesus feel disgust. Nor should they. Hu-

57. Moore, "Why the Johannine Jesus Weeps," 303.

58. See the comprehensive survey of Ad Vingerhoets, *Why Only Humans Weep: Unravelling the Mysteries of Tears* (Oxford: Oxford University Press, 2013).

59. Vingerhoets, *Why Only Humans Weep*, 81, includes two taxonomies of crying based on eliciting events and social function (of ten and five basic categories of tears). Disgust is not among them.

60. In his review of Moore's essay, F. Scott Spencer notes that any mention of Jesus actually smelling Lazarus or feeling disgust "is undetectable in the text and beside the point," beside the point because, for Moore, disgust is just so "sticky" that words or expressions are not necessary for analysis (Spencer, *Passions of the Christ*, 126).

61. Andrew Crislip, "Resurrection, Emotion, and Embodiment in Egyptian Monastic Literature," in *Unity of Body and Soul in Patristic and Byzantine Thought*, ed. Anna Usacheva, Jörg Ulrich, and Siam Bhayro, Contexts of Ancient and Medieval Anthropology 1 (Leiden: Brill, 2021), 144–69.

mans engage in behaviors with loved ones that put them into contact with disgust-eliciting substances and smells, in sex, in child-rearing, in caring for the sick, the elderly, and the disabled, and in death.[62] The challenges of caring for such bodily needs (before and after death) are profound, but feelings of disgust (like any emotion) can be significantly mitigated by professional training and by simple affection, love (*agapē*), which the Gospel insists Jesus felt for Lazarus, and which we may presume his sisters felt as well. Therefore, there is no disgust at the tomb. The Fourth Gospel elsewhere insists on the Christian transformation of joy, sadness, and love. Disgust is no less prime for a conversion of emotion.

Jesus's resurrection offers another opportunity for the evangelists to meditate on the moral power of disgust. Here again, even where Luke and John include graphic details of bodily suffering, the evangelists evoke very different emotional responses in the narrative. In Luke's telling, Jesus presents his hands and feet as proof of his resurrection to quell his disciples' understandable fear (*tetaragmenoi*) and doubt (*dialogismoi*) (Luke 24:38). The apostles' response is not disgust but joy and wonder (Luke 24:41, *apo tēs charas kai thaumazontōn*). Nowhere does any concern with disgust enter the narrative.

The case is the same for John's even more graphic telling. When the risen Jesus shows Thomas his wounds, he does so without any language of disgust (20:27).[63] While Thomas had previously claimed he would not believe unless he could put his fingers and hand in Jesus's wounds (20:25), he does not do so when given the opportunity, not out of disgust but as a sign of his faith and projecting awe and wonder (20:28). The Fourth Gospel does not identify explicitly what emotions it imagines the disciples feeling, but the Lukan evocation of joy and wonder seems more apposite to Thomas's statement of belief (20:27–28). The evangelist expects his readers to be "happy" (*makarioi*) in understanding Jesus's resurrection, even if they have not witnessed the Messiah's wounds themselves (20:29). While a corpse or a wounded body might indeed be objects of disgust, they need not be, any more than Plutarch's abattoir imagery or Leontius's unstoppable desire to gaze at executed criminals, to which I return later.[64] The gruesome sights described in the Gospels are not meant as objects of disgust but as cause for wonder, fascination, joy, and happiness.

62. Rozin, Haidt, and McCauley ("Disgust," 4th ed., 828) focus on the neutralized (or even positive transformation) of disgust elicitors in sexual intimacy, but the phenomenon applies to other areas of intimacy and love.

63. Cf. Moore, "Why the Johannine Jesus Weeps," 305–8; and Crislip, "Disgust in Early Christianity," 603–4.

64. Boddice, *History of Feelings*, 62–72.

Christian Disgust and Anti-Heretical Polemic

This revaluation of disgust coexists with another emotional trajectory that encourages disgust as a virtuous marker of morality and in-group cohesion. This practice embraces a wisdom of disgust, core and projective, to guide the embodied Christian through a world filled with threats to one's spiritual health.

Perhaps the earliest Christian text to employ the moral power of disgust is the Revelation of John, in which several instances of disgust language occur, although less explicitly than the most "disgusting" passage in the Gospels (Luke's description of Lazarus). Revelation has also been characterized from an affect theory perspective as singularly concerned with disgust and vomit: "The movement [vomiting] is also the predominant (e)motion that Revelation seeks to induce in its audience, a heaving of the stomach, obtained by rhetorically thrusting its fingers down the audience's throat. Revelation is a work of disgust. It wants its audience to retch on Rome."[65]

Yet disgust remains at best a leitmotif in John's visions. Apart from two passages referencing the abominations and impurities of the whore of Babylon and her cup and the pollutions of those excluded from the New Jerusalem (Rev 17:4–5; 21:8, the former of which could be disgusting with sufficient imagination), the only elicitor of disgust in Revelation is single mention of spitting water: "So, because you are lukewarm, and neither cold nor hot, I am about to spit you out of my mouth" (3:16). This expulsive act is performed (rhetorically) by God and is furthermore—and significantly—not directed at Rome but at Christians. Even this expulsion is not, to be fair, "retching," which in English refers to expelling matter from the stomach or esophagus.[66] God will indeed spit them out (*emesai*), but he expels the lukewarm water from his mouth (*stomatos*), far lower on any register of disgust.

Rather than disgust at Rome, God's expulsion of lukewarm Christians points to the actual density of disgust language in the earliest strata of Christian textuality. It is in the short, second-century letters now included in the New Testament that we find visceral language of disgust as a felt emotion. And like God's spit-take in Revelation, the focus of disgust is other Christians.

65. Moore, "Retching on Rome," 524.

66. *Oxford English Dictionary*, s.v. "retching." It is unclear why contemporary affect studies resolve so effortlessly into intertwined discussions of sexual transgression and vomit. In Marchal's affective reading of Romans, vomit terms occur nine times and retch terms three; in Gunderson's reading of 2 Corinthians, retching occurs five times and vomit once, all in spite of the fact that Paul never so much as alludes to vomiting, let alone an "embarrassingly erect member" or "dick jokes" (Marchal, "Disgusting Apostle," 132).

Here, in these marginal corners of the canon and beyond, one can find the sticky affective substances so sought after in postmodern biblical studies.

The Epistle of Jude conflates disgusting behavior with the theology and ecclesiology of other Christians. Jude signals his interest in disgust by condemning Sodom and Gomorrah and their "sexual immorality (*ekporneusasai*) and . . . unnatural lust," a marker of disgust-based virtue signaling familiar in many periods of history (Jude 7).[67] The Sodomites and Gomorrans parallel the proximate target of his condemnation—"certain intruders" intent to "pervert the grace of God into licentiousness" (4), whom he calls "dreamers" (8). They, like the foul residents of the cities on the plain, "defile (or stain) the flesh" (*sarka men miainousin*, 8; cf. 23). They are themselves "stains" or "blemishes" (*spilades*) on the love-feasts (*en tais agapais*, 12). Outsiders thus defile and spoil the emotion and emotional practices of the community.[68]

Textually dependent on Jude, 2 Peter also draws on the common disgust elicitor of homosexuality and compares false prophets to the Sodomites and Gomorrans.[69] He condemns their "defiled" or "stained desire" (*en epithymia miasmou*), which, like Jude before him, he connects with their contempt for authority (2 Pet 2:10). He compares them to animals, "born to be caught and killed" (2:12), and calls them "blots and blemishes" (*spiloi kai mōmoi*), citing Jude 12 and incorporating Levitical language of leprosy (in contrast to the instances of actual leprosy in the Gospels). The same false prophets are trapped in the "defilements" or "stains" of the world (*ta miasmata*). They are like pigs and dogs; they delight in vomit and filth (2:22).[70]

The short letters to Timothy and Titus proceed in the same manner. Like Jude and Pseudo-Peter, Pseudo-Paul takes aim at other would-be Christians, chattering and spreading impiety; their teachings are disgusting, which "spread like gangrene" (2 Tim 2:17). The "rebellious people, idle talkers and deceivers" are "impure" and "defiled" (*memiantai*) in their minds (Titus 1:10–15). They are "loathsome" (*bdelykoi*, Titus 1:16). Others among Titus's imagined congregation are abominable (*stygētoi*, Titus 3:3). In Titus, much like 2 Timothy, Jude, and 2 Peter (and to a lesser extent Revelation), we see the primary Greek

67. See Nussbaum's exploration of the intersection of disgust and Christian debates about (predominantly male) homosexuality, *Hiding from Humanity*, 1–25.

68. The "stain" of v. 12 is a textual problem, recognized as such since antiquity. "Stain" is a reading that goes back to 2 Pet 2:13. Cf. Jude 23 for the (moral) staining of clothing. See Jerome H. Neyrey, *2 Peter, Jude*, AB 37C (New Haven: Yale University Press, 1993), 74–75.

69. See Neyrey, *2 Peter, Jude*, 120–22, for overview of the state of the question and bibliography.

70. 2 Peter cites Prov 26:11.

terms of disgust used (*miasma*, *stygētos*, *bdelyktos*, and *spilos*), an embrace of the moral power of disgust so sublimated in the Gospels and Paul.

These texts, apocalyptic and epistolary alike, model and encourage feelings of revulsion as reliable markers of morality and virtue. Christians should recognize certain behaviors and beliefs as revolting or disgusting, stained, rotted, corrupted, and loathsome (like gangrene or dogs eating vomit and feces). Like God they should be prepared to spit the offending substances out. Christian disgust as a moral emotion targets neither Rome nor outsiders (e.g., "Jews" or "heathens") but other Christians, who teach the wrong things (perhaps the Jewish law and circumcision, perhaps fanciful philosophical myths), claim prophetic or charismatic power, and contemn or disrespect proper Christian authority.[71]

The language of Christian disgust as virtuous recurs in second-century theological polemics, which elaborate on the motifs of disgust in the New Testament texts, focusing revulsion at other Christians, including heretics and apostates. We may see this in Papias's narration of Judas's death. Already by the turn of the first Christian century, storytellers had begun to flesh out the death of the first apostate with or without disgusting imagery. More disgusting is Luke's version (Acts 1:18), in which Judas falls to his death disemboweled. Papias elaborates on this body-envelope violation; after betraying Jesus and setting out to enjoy his new riches, Judas's body swells with interstitial water. Papias does not skimp on the details or the explicit language of disgust (*aēdēs*).[72] Just one example: "His genitals became more disgusting (*aēdestēron*) and larger than anyone's; simply by relieving himself, to his wanton shame, he emitted pus and worms that flowed through his entire body."[73] As in Luke's version, Judas died on his land, and Papias claims that it still stinks so much that passersby must hold their nose. "This was how great an outpouring he made from his flesh on the ground," he writes.[74]

Much as apostates prompt core and projective disgust, so do those so-called Christians who disturb and teach the wrong things: heretics, as second-

71. Note the theme of purity in 2 Peter and Jude (and in other books) discussed in Neyrey, *2 Peter, Jude*, 10–14.

72. See Anna Rebecca Solevåg, *Negotiating the Disabled Body: Representations of Disability in Early Christian Texts*, ECL 23 (Atlanta: SBL Press, 2018), 117–31. Solevåg observes that Papias's description of Judas is intended to establish boundaries of Christian propriety and belonging (130–31) but insists that implicit in the passage are traces of ancient physiognomy and standards of masculinity.

73. Papias frag. 4 (Ehrman, LCL).

74. Papias frag. 4 (Ehrman).

century Christians would label them. The earliest surviving anti-heretical treatise evokes readers' disgust to reinforce theological right teachings. Irenaeus of Lyon's (ca. 180) primary target is the school of Valentinus. Early in the first of his five volumes against the heresies, Irenaeus presents the foundational creation myth taught by the Valentinian teacher Ptolemy, who posited that the phenomenal world of perception and embodiment was formed out of an ancient cosmic error, which Ptolemy traces to one of the divine aeons in the heavenly fullness named Wisdom (Sophia).[75] Wisdom had strained to achieve the impossible—to gain acquaintance (or *gnōsis*) of God the father—and in her failure she produced passions of sadness (*lypē*), fear (*phobos*), disturbance (*ekplēxis*), and ignorance (*agnoia*), and was expelled with her passions from the fullness.[76] This process is recapitulated outside the heavenly fullness by another "Wisdom," Lower Wisdom or Achamoth.[77] Ptolemy envisions a world of matter bound up with and created through the primal passions of Wisdom and Achamoth. The seas and rivers, for example, are remnants of her tears at recognizing her error and ultimately of her repentant reacceptance into the fullness, a model for the gnosis and repentance that Christians can experience.[78]

The myth was probably quite poetic in Ptolemy's (now lost) telling, but Irenaeus turns to disgust to render the myth offensive. It is well known that the one bodily fluid that does not generally trigger disgust is tears. Irenaeus wonders, surely in her distress Wisdom perspired as well. If the tears produce saline waters, then fresh water and fountains, he claims, are her sweat.[79] Imagine drinking a cup of Sophia's sweat! That's just the kind of practice that heretics like. And what of "hot and pungent" waters? Irenaeus refrains from naming the substance, but the implication is clear: "You ought to know what she did and from what member these were emitted! Indeed, such products fit

75. Sometimes called the "Grande notice" of Irenaeus, whose sources and import are reassessed by Giuliano Chiapparini, "Irenaeus and the Gnostic Valentinus: Orthodoxy and Heresy in the Church of Rome Around the Middle of the Second Century," *ZAC* 18 (2013): 95–119. The Greek text is preserved in a lengthy quotation in Epiphanius of Salamis; see François M.-M. Sagnard, *La Gnose valentinienne et le témoignage de Saint Irénée* (Paris: Librarie philosophique J. Vrin, 1957), 31–50.

76. Irenaeus, *Haer.* 1.2.1–4; Adelin Rousseau and Louis Doutreleau, ed. and trans., *Irénée de Lyon, Contre les hérésies, Livre I*, vol. 2, SC 264 (Paris: Cerf, 1979), 42.

77. Irenaeus, *Haer.* 1.4.

78. Irenaeus, *Haer.* 1.4.1–2.

79. Irenaeus, *Haer.* 1.4.4.

in well with their hypothesis."[80] Disgust guides the Christian better than any theological argument to stay away from the ridiculous and foul heretics.[81]

Later polemicists embraced disgust as a marker of social boundaries and purity, making visceral the line between insider and outsider. As an apostate like Judas might die in a wormy exsanguination, so might the high and mighty pagan elites, perhaps no one more than the persecuting emperor Galerius, whose death the former imperial rhetor Lactantius (ca. 240–ca. 320) details with gusto.[82] Lactantius draws on a legacy of disgusting deaths in addition to Judas, such as the death of Antiochus IV Epiphanes (2 Macc 9:9) and possibly also the mythological sufferings of Laocoön and others.[83] Lactantius's account reads as if he had read deeply in contemporary disgust psychology, as he hits so effortlessly the primary cross-cultural elicitors of disgust. Galerius's disease of course hits hardest on his genitals, targeting the intuitive disgust at sexual deviance, and violates his body envelope in manifold ways—the wound splits open and resists any suture, spreading across his body. His "whole seat dissolved in decay" and worms infested his body. His members "had lost their form," with some parts desiccated, thinned, and shrunken, others distended and shapeless, or "spread out like leather bags." Due to his "dissolving buttocks," "the route for faeces and that for urine were confused" and "he was consumed by worms and his body dissolved into putrefaction amidst intolerable pains." The great emperor had literally become a sack of shit.[84] His stench had spread throughout the palace and the city itself, as Lactantius extends his narrative excess to obvious metaphor on the Roman body politic.

Heretics too could meet their end in disgust. Most famously, the condemned priest Arius is remembered as having died in history's worst case of explosive diarrhea, graphically described by the historian Socrates.[85] As with Galerius, God's judgment is loosed upon the arch-heretic's bowels as he rushed toward a latrine, with a tragic end for the Alexandrian presbyter. His "bottom

80. Irenaeus, *Haer.* 1.4.4; St. Irenaeus of Lyons, *Against the Heresies*, trans. Dominic J. Unger, ACW 55 (New York: Paulist, 1992), 32; modified with Rousseau and Doutreleau, *Contre les hérésies*, 71.

81. Cf. Nussbaum, *Hiding from Humanity*, 8–13.

82. Lactantius, *Mort.* 33. Other deaths of the persecutors are not disgusting.

83. Patrick Cook, "Lactantius on the Death of Galerius: A Re-Reading of *De Mortibus Persecutorum* 33," *VC* 73 (2019): 385–403.

84. Lactantius, *Mort.* 33 (Cook, "Lactantius on the Death").

85. See Ellen Muehlenberg, "The Legend of Arius' Death: Imagination, Space and Filth in Late Ancient Historiography," *Past and Present* 227 (2015): 6–10.

fell through along with his excrement. The thing which doctors call the rectum immediately fell out through his bottom, with a lot of blood following, and the rest of his intestines flowed out together with his spleen and his liver, and he died immediately."[86] The moral is clear; the disgust one feels in imagining Arius's wretched end should be projected morally at the teachings he espoused, as well as toward those who espouse them, a moral disgust that encourages theological and disciplinary purity. The contrast is immediate and visceral between this late antique delight in disgust's moral force and the far fainter traces of disgust in the first centuries of Christian literature.[87] Ancients were well attuned to the power and rhetoric of foulness and revulsion. Amid such an imaginary of filth and bodily violation, it is difficult to imagine an ancient reader considering Paul to be a "disgusting apostle" or the Fourth Gospel "structured by disgust."[88]

Heretics are not just disgusting. They delight in the foul, especially bodily fluids, which late antique Christians extrapolate beyond biblical metaphors of dogs and pigs returning to their own vomit and feces. In the most extravagant example of this trend, Epiphanius of Salamis (ca. 315–403) wrote a theological "medicine chest" to combat the poison of heresy. His account of the Gnostics, whom he insists are his contemporaries, employs core and moral disgust seen in Irenaeus and other earlier sources, now taken to an extreme. The Gnostics are defined by their pollution and the disgust they elicit, as the devil led them on "so as to pollute (*mianai*) the minds, hearts, hands, mouths, bodies and souls of the persons he has trapped in such deep darkness."[89] His account brings together all of the aspects of the moral and core disgust that we have seen so far and more: body-envelope violations, illicit sexual behavior, contact and consumption of bodily fluids, cannibalism, disease, animals, and swarming insects. It is no accident that Epiphanius draws on Revelation, 2 Peter, and Jude,[90] whose metaphorical disgust elicitors Epiphanius literalizes in the ritual activities of the heretical Gnostics.

These Gnostics go by the nickname Borborites, or "filthies," an epithet which points to Jude's characterization of intruders as pigs who wallow in

86. Socrates, *Church History* 1.38.7 (Muehlenberg).

87. John Chrysostom also draws on excrement imagery in his public sermons, for which see Leyerle, "Refuse, Filth, and Excrement."

88. See Marchal and Moore above.

89. *Pan.* 26.3.4; Frank Williams, trans., *The "Panarion" of Epiphanius of Salamis*, 2nd ed., NHMS 63 (Leiden: Brill, 2009); Karl Holl, ed., *Epiphanius. Ancoratus und Panarion (Haereses 1–33)*, GCS 25 (Leipzig: Hinrichs, 1915).

90. In *Pan.* 25.3.1, he traces the Gnostics to the Nicolaitans of Revelation. He cites Jude in *Pan.* 26.11.3–4 and 26.13.7–8.

filth, *borboros*.[91] These heretics are disgusting, and they revel in it. They are like a disease, "a malignant itch, or leprosy."[92] They are "like a swarm of insects, infecting us with diseases, smelly eruptions, and sores through their error with its mythology."[93] They are like dogs and pigs, "for they dispose of their corruption like dogs and pigs," who "are polluted in this way and eat their bodies' discharge."[94]

Unlike Irenaeus, Epiphanius's disgust is not merely projective but aimed at alleged ritual elements integral to their gnostic view of the universe and their scriptural interpretation. Their myth, Epiphanius claims, places the heavenly aeon Barbelo in a role that evokes Wisdom in Ptolemy's myth. Like Wisdom, Barbelo weeps, but, unique to Epiphanius's version, she brings about her return to the heavenly fullness by collecting the ejaculate of the rulers of the material world. She "keeps appearing in some beautiful form to the archons and stealing the seed which is generated by their climax and ejaculation—supposedly to recover her power which has been sown in various of them."[95] The ritual consumption of semen, participating in the mythological actions of Barbelo and the Last Supper, forms the core of their eucharistic rituals, which include orgies, followed by eucharists celebrated with semen ("the body of Christ") and menstrual blood ("the blood of Christ"), which Epiphanius describes in detail.[96] The Gnostics violate all sexual and bodily boundaries; they share wives in common, men have sex with one another, and other men masturbate and consume their own semen (in a bizarre interpretation of Eph 4:28).[97] Should any Borborite get pregnant, they "extract the fetus at the stage which is appropriate for their enterprise, take this aborted infant, and cut it up in a trough with a pestle. And they mix honey, pepper, and certain other perfumes and spices with it to keep from getting sick, and then all the revelers

91. This pejorative is perhaps derived satirically from the Barbeloites, as the Barbelo was one of the primary aspects of God that Gnostics worshipped. Bentley Layton with David Brakke, *The Gnostic Scriptures*, 2nd ed. (New Haven: Yale University Press, 2021), 254.

92. *Pan.* 25.7.2 (Williams).

93. *Pan.* 26.1.2 (Williams).

94. *Pan.* 26.11.4 (Williams), citing Jude 8–10.

95. *Pan.* 25.2.2 (Williams). Layton with Brakke (*Gnostic Scriptures*, 254) suggests this, and other aspects of Epiphanius's account may be indebted to Manichaean influence.

96. *Pan.* 26.4.5–26.5.7; 26.9.3.

97. *Pan.* 26.4.1 (sharing spouses); 26.11.7 (homosexuality); 26.5.7; 26.11.1–2 (masturbation and semen consumption). The Borborite theology invented by Epiphanius shares much in common with the disgust Christology discovered by Stephen Moore in John, in which Jesus is disgusted by the very nature of embodiment and creation, and then instantiates that disgust in flamboyantly revolting ritual (Moore, "Why the Johannine Jesus Weeps," 303, 307).

in this <herd> of swine and dogs assemble, and each eats a piece of the child with his fingers."[98] This, he claims, is what they call "the 'perfect Passover.'"[99] Epiphanius claims great discomfort at detailing such disgusting acts, but feels "compelled to [do so] from the excess of the feeling of grief (*algousēs*)."[100] Epiphanius pushes the boundaries of disgust and prurience here, as does Socrates's narrative of Arius's death, but the point is clear. Virtuous Christians, pure Christians, feel disgust at heresy. Not to feel disgust is to be a heretic, to be disgusting. At the same time, it is hard not to suspect that Epiphanius and his readers—for all his puritanical moralism—must have experienced a mix of push and pull, of revulsion and attraction, disgust and fascination, in these disgusting rituals, not so different from readers today.[101]

Disgust and Self-Fashioning

Ascetically inclined Christians in late antiquity took a different approach to disgust. Rather than encouraging disgust as a moral emotion to draw boundaries between groups, such writers—all from Egypt in the following discussion—saw disgust much more in line with the attitude I have highlighted in Paul and some Gospel passages, as an emotion to manage and overcome, and which might through cognition, ritual, and practice transform the self and the community.

The philosopher and biblical scholar Origen (ca. 185–ca. 254) placed a kind of disgust at a critical juncture in his theory of the origin of the world and the descent of humanity into its present embodied and fallen state. In *On First Principles* and in other works, Origen posits an original existence of humanity as pure minds (*nous*), who existed in perfect bliss and contemplation of God. He likely drew on earlier Platonic speculations of the descent of souls into mortal bodies, an idea Plato developed in the *Phaedrus* and was taken up by the Alexandrian Jewish philosopher Philo. Philo, for example, allegorically interpreted the birds of Genesis 15:11 (LXX) as souls, "which, although they were raised in the air and the most pure ether, could not bear the satiety (κόρος [*koros*]) of the divine good things, and migrated to the earth, the region

98. *Pan.* 26.5.5 (Williams).

99. *Pan.* 26.5.6 (Williams).

100. *Pan.* 26.3.3 (Williams).

101. This dialectic is emphasized among affect theorists, as in Ahmed, *Cultural Politics*, 82–100; and Sianne Ngai, *Ugly Feelings* (Cambridge, MA: Harvard University Press, 2007), 332–54.

of the things mortal and evil."[102] This *koros* lacks an equivalent in English, but the feeling is clear enough: satiety (*satietas* in Rufinus's translation of Origen), carelessness, lassitude, boredom (*taedium*, also Rufinus), and disgust.[103] The disgust here is not a revulsion at something spoiled but a feeling of excess, consuming so much of a good thing that it loses its appeal, and its good taste turns bad (disgust, *dégoût*). In Origen's theology there is nothing wrong with the feast offered by God for our rational natures, "feeding on the food which is the understanding and love of God."[104] God plays no role in the origin of evil. It was simply the rational natures' "negligence and disgust," their *koros* or *satietas*.[105]

As a consequence of the rational minds' disgust—their pushing away from the table, overfull and bloated at the sheer excess of the banquet—they fell into the cold void, clad first in souls (which Origen surmised from a false etymology of *psychē* from *psychrein*, to be cold), and then later in flesh, perhaps from a reading of the tunics of skin of Genesis.[106] Parts of this are still contested because some of Origen's cosmological and anthropological speculations are lost following his anathematization during the reign of Justinian (ca. 553). One anathema condemns anyone who "says or holds that the souls of human beings were preexistent in that they used to be minds (νόες [*noes*]) and holy powers, but were struck by satiety (κόρος [*koros*]) of the divine contemplation and were changed for the worse and therefore cooled down from God's love, and hence were called 'souls' and for punishment were sent down to bodies."[107] But in light of other passages, whether in the Greek or in Rufinus's

102. Philo, *Her.* 239–240 (Roukema), in Riemer Roukema, "Origen on the Origin of Sin," in *The Evil Inclination in Early Judaism and Christianity*, ed. James Aitken, Hector M. Patmore, and Ishay Rosen-Zvi (Cambridge: Cambridge University Press, 2021), 201–11. Cf. Plato, *Phaedr.* 247–248; Roukema, "Origen," 209; and Marguerite Harl, "Recherches sur l'origénisme d'Origène: La 'satiété' (κὸρος) de la contemplation comme motif de la chute des âmes," StPatr 8 (1966): 378–83.

103. "Κόρος nomme alors le seuil de saturation, le dégoût" (Harl, "Recherches," 378); Roukema, "Origen," 204–5; Douglas Cairns, "*koros* (κόρος)," in *The Encyclopedia of Greek Tragedy*, ed. Hanna M. Roisman (Oxford: Wiley-Blackwell, 2014), 751–52.

104. Origen, *Princ.* 2.1.7, cited in N. Joseph Torchia, "Satiety and the Fall of Souls in Origen's *De principiis*," StPatr 18.3 (1989): 455.

105. Roukema, "Origen," 205–6, drawing on the discussion of theodicy in Harl, "Recherches," 390–95.

106. Roukema, "Origen," 209–10.

107. Roukema, "Origen," 205, citing Herwig Görgemanns and Heinrich Karpp, *Origenes vier Bücher von den Prinzipien*, Texte zur Forschung 24 (Darmstadt: Wissenschaftliche Buchgesellschaft, 1976), 822.

Latin translation, there is little doubt that this primal disgust played a catalytic role in Origen's theories about the origin of the created world and humanity in our present condition.

His view of disgust contrasts with Irenaeus. While Irenaeus mocked the Valentinians by drawing disgusting implications from their theories, Origen offered a different emotional catalyst as a solution to the same problem: How did humans end up in a world of suffering and painful emotions (*pathē*) with God himself not bearing moral responsibility for the error? Instead of an aeon's emotional distress at her failure to comprehend the divine father, the fault lies in all rational minds who would become humanity, who had carelessly stuffed themselves with the goodness of God's love to the point of disgust, a satiety and lassitude which set the whole drama of creation and redemption in action.

Christians in this theological and ascetic tradition encouraged a practice of disgust that did not foster it as a moral good for dividing insiders and outsiders but rather as an opportunity for moral growth and learning. By overcoming disgust, we thick, stinking, and sticky humans might overcome our embodiment on a journey back to God. Such a transformation of disgust as an emotional practice is already observed in some of the early strata of Christian reflection on the norms and powers of emotion, which modeled practices—ritual and cognitive—that reversed culturally and even evolutionarily powerful responses to disgusting elicitors. Paul broke down social barriers, quite controversially in eating (e.g., Gal 2), a site where disgust between groups plays a primary role.[108] Luke's Jesus placed disgust in his parables of the coming reversal of fortunes, with the sick and oozing body of Lazarus. When John's Jesus veers into ancient commonplaces about cannibalism in disputing with his critics, no language of disgust intrudes, either from Jesus or his Jewish critics, who fight not with him but "among themselves," and not with accusations launched from disgust but from wonder: "How can this man give us his flesh to eat?"[109] All this points to an incipient Christian manipulation of disgust as an emotional practice.

Disgust's malleability as a social and moral emotion has long been observed. Affect theories tend to present this as a paradox, an enigma at the heart of revulsion that resists reduction, "deeply ambivalent, involving desire

108. E.g., Rottman, DeJesus, and Gerdin, "Social Origins of Disgust," 36–38.

109. See discussion by J. Albert Harrill, "Cannibalistic Language in the Fourth Gospel and the Greco-Roman Polemics of Factionalism," *JBL* 127 (2008): 133–58, who emphasizes disgust more than wonder.

for, or an attraction toward, the very objects that are felt to be repellent."[110] It's just that slippery and sticky. A history of emotions perspective might resolve this apparent ambivalence or paradox by close attention to the lexicon and rhetoric of disgust in a given source, as in a passage from Plato's *Republic* (439e–440a) in which a certain Leontius describes his urge to observe a dead body.[111] While some see this as showing the paradoxical attraction of the disgusting, another perspective reads this within the overall rhetoric of this section of the *Republic*, which addresses mastery of the soul and turns the story pedagogically to the readers themselves. By consuming Plato's dialogue as a guide to emotional asceticism, they can practice the mastery of their own emotions, including disgust: "As such, the dialogue itself becomes the rhetorical vehicle of control—the platform for the mastery of reason in the soul—that is at the heart of the *Republic*. In diminishing affect to the point of undetectability, it is an affective practice par excellence."[112]

The emotional practice woven throughout Plato's rhetoric in the *Republic* offers a helpful model for disgust in late ancient Christianity. I highlight two sources from the early fifth century among the theological inheritors of Origen, which reflect the transformation of disgust seen in Paul and some Gospel passages. Contemporary psychology of disgust describes the self-transformative power of intentionally manipulating disgust, or "'benign masochism': enjoyment of a normally negative experience when it is not threatening and is at some distance from the self, perhaps as an exercise of mind over body."[113] This concept gets to much the same place as historians and others have in conceptualizing emotional practices as techniques of self-fashioning and mastery, a cognitive and emotional practice no less ascetically transformative than fasting or prayer.[114]

Palladius, later bishop of Helenopolis in Bithynia, wrote an entertaining and edifying memoir in the 420s of his days traveling among the monks of

110. Ahmed, *Cultural Politics*, 84. See also Miller, *Anatomy of Disgust*, 110; Ngai, *Ugly Feelings*, 333.

111. Boddice, *History of Feelings*, 70–71. The story of Leontius appears in major works on disgust, such as Korsmeyer, *Savoring Disgust*, 42; and Lateiner and Spatharos, *Ancient Emotion of Disgust*, 8.

112. Boddice, *History of Feelings*, 72.

113. Rozin, Haidt, and McCauley, "Disgust," 4th ed., 828; Rozin et al., "Glad to Be Sad"; and Karolina Dyduch-Hazar and Vanessa Mitschke, "Affective Preferences in Benign Masochism," *Journal of Research in Personality* 107 (2023): 104429.

114. An important study of the cognitive aspects of Christian asceticism is by Inbar Graiver, *Asceticism of the Mind*, PIMS Texts and Studies 213 (Toronto: PIMS, 2018).

Egypt in the later decades of the fourth century. The *Lausiac History* (named for its dedicatee) is full of wonders, some disgusting, as in two stories of monks gifted with the charism of healing.[115] Palladius says that he and the great ascetic teacher Evagrius (discussed in chapters 3 and 4) were summoned by the bishop to visit a certain Apa Benjamin in his residence. The tone is one of wonder: "Come here, see a new Job who possesses boundless gratitude while in a state of great bodily swelling and incurable sickness."[116] They find a saint with the body of a sinner, so swollen with dropsy "that another person's fingers could not reach around one of his," and "when he died, the door and jambs were pulled down so that his body could be carried out of the house, so great was the swelling."[117] There are no swarming worms or exsanguinating or excretory explosions, but the deformity of Benjamin's body provokes disgust in Palladius and Evagrius: "Unable to look any longer at the terrible suffering, we turned our eyes aside."[118] Though the gesture can show shame, in the ancient world as in the modern, "Hiding one's face from despised persons is a hallmark of disgust."[119] Palladius includes this story, he says, not to revel in disgust but to guide an emotional transformation, so that "we might not be too surprised (*xenizōmetha*) when some accident befalls just men."[120] This surprise is not shock so much as wonder at the incongruity of something that doesn't fit, something strange (*xenos*) and out of place. In light of the ancient philosophical tradition of retraining one's passions or affects and the modern psychology of benign masochism, of exposing oneself to unpleasant stimuli so as to gain emotional mastery over them, Palladius's graphic story serves to prepare his readers so that they, unlike Evagrius and the author himself, might not feel disgust at the sight of just people suffering from body-envelope violations.[121]

115. *Hist. Laus.* 12.1; Cuthbert Butler, ed., *The Lausiac History of Palladius*, 2 vols., TS 6 (Cambridge: Cambridge University Press, 1898).

116. *Hist. Laus.* 12.1–2 (Meyer); Robert T. Meyer, *Palladius: The Lausiac History*, ACW 34 (New York: Paulist, 1965).

117. *Hist. Laus.* 12.2–3 (Meyer).

118. *Hist. Laus.* 12.2 (Meyer).

119. Spencer, *Passions of the Christ*, 114–15. He draws on philosopher Martha Nussbaum, *Hiding from Humanity*.

120. *Hist. Laus.* 12.3 (Meyer); see discussion in Andrew Crislip, *Thorns in the Flesh: Illness and Sanctity in Late Ancient Christianity* (Philadelphia: University of Pennsylvania, 2013), 16–19.

121. One could also read this in the context of post-Freudian theories of abjection and horror and against affective theories of the paradoxical push and pull of disgust, or in the matrix of practices of self-humiliation as a tool against pride, for which see Virginia Bur-

Palladius tells of another gifted healer who suffers disfiguring disease. Stephen was afflicted with an ulcerous cancer of his testicles and penis (*tous topous tōn didymōn kai tēs balanou*).[122] As Benjamin's swollen body recalls Judas's dropsy, Stephen's urological cancer recalls Judas as well as any number of other sinners, such as Galerius. Whatever literary shimmers might be seen behind the story, venereal ailments are almost by definition a source of disgust and shame. And this is what Palladius's narrator (the monk Evagrius) feels, watching Stephen under the knife, as "his members were being cut away like locks of hair."[123] The visitors were "deeply grieved (*hypolypoumenōn*) at this and were disgusted (*siainomenōn*) that a person who lived a life like his should suffer disease and such surgical remedies."[124] Stephen responds to their disgust by offering some edifying words: It was only his body suffering (surely deservedly), and it would prepare him to obtain a pain-free eternity.[125] Here again, Palladius says that his goal in telling the story is that his readers not find a strangeness here (*xenithōmetha*), and might thus master their disgust. Stephen's own ascetic practice points to such a self-mastery. When undergoing surgery, his flesh cut away like hair, "he was completely without pain (*anaisthētos*), thanks to the superiority of his spiritual preparation."[126] If Stephen could, through ascetic self-mastery, control his pain (itself an emotion) while having his penis and testicles cut away, surely Evagrius and the others could apply a similar self-mastery over their emotions and not feel disgust.[127]

Self-mastery through disgust appears also in the *Life of Syncletica*, who taught and guided disciples in the late fourth and fifth centuries. Her teachings are preserved in versions of the *Sayings of the Desert Fathers and Mothers* and in a *Life and Teachings of the Holy and Blessed Teacher Syncletica*, which bookends a lengthy compendium of her teachings with biographical narratives.[128] Surely the most notable aspect of her biography is her death from an

rus, *Saving Shame: Martyrs, Saints, and Other Abject Subjects* (Philadelphia: University of Pennsylvania Press, 2011), 84–86.

122. *Hist. Laus.* 24.2; Meyer leaves these details out in his translation.

123. *Hist. Laus.* 24.2 (Meyer).

124. *Hist. Laus.* 24.3 (Meyer), with first clause altered to clarify the emotions.

125. *Hist. Laus.* 24.3.

126. *Hist. Laus.* 24.2 (Meyer, altered).

127. On pain as emotion, see chapter 3 in this volume, and Andrew Crislip, "Pain, Emotion, and Identity in Early Christianity," *Journal of Early Christian History* 12 (2022): 27–51.

128. Elizabeth Bryson Bongie, trans., *The Life and Regimen of the Blessed and Holy Teacher, Syncletica* (Toronto: Peregrina, 1995), 5–8; Andrew Crislip, "Syncletica," *Brill Encyclopedia of Early Christianity* (Leiden: Brill, 2024).

aggressive cancer of the lungs and later her jaw, a three-year battle against the devil and disease described in graphic detail and which caused some conflict among her followers.[129]

Readers have taken the disgusting imagery of the *Life* in a number of directions. Her hagiographer certainly found it significant to detail the corruption of her lungs, which she violently hacked up, and the spread of rot and gangrene through her jaw and mouth, which produced a stench so foul that the hagiographer claims—with hyperbole or ironic disdain—that her followers suffered more than she did.[130] The *Life*, along with other contemporary ascetic sources, develops the suffering of illness—normally seen as passive (*pathein*, *passio*)—as even the highest form of ascetic self-mastery.[131]

For recent interpreters working within the affectively laden matrixes of queer theory and disability studies, Syncletica's life story offers grounds for radically reconceiving the concept of disgust and the binaries of beauty and revulsion, fragrance and stink. A study, for example, sets Syncletica's *Life* in dialogue with contemporary Chicana lesbian feminist poetry and memoir, a reading which reconfigures the affective response of Syncletica's followers. In the ancient *Life*, her followers act much like Palladius and Evagrius in the *Lausiac History*, at least before they learned emotional mastery; the disciples are disgusted and turn away from the suffering Amma, avoiding the stinking saint "for quite long periods of time," approaching "when need called," and even then only by "burning a lot of incense."[132] Such behavior could not have been much comfort for the sick woman, and the gratuitous excess of incense would have compounded any sense of stigma and burden that might have lurked in her mind.

But in Peter Mena's reading, her "pungent stench" marks her holiness and, with her ailing body, will "become the uniting element between the saint, her community, the hagiographer, and the reader."[133] But this misreads the *Life*.[134]

129. See Harvey, *Scenting Salvation*, 217; Crislip, *Thorns in the Flesh*, 100–108; Elizabeth Castelli, "Mortifying the Body, Curing the Soul: Beyond Ascetic Dualism in the Life of Saint Syncletica," *Differences* 4 (1992): 134–53; Peter Anthony Mena, "Scenting Saintliness: The Ailing Body, Chicana Feminism, and Communal Identity in Ancient Christianity," *Journal of Feminist Studies in Religion* 33 (2017): 5–20; Virginia Burrus, *Early Christian Ecopoetics: Cosmologies, Saints, Things* (Philadelphia: University of Pennsylvania Press, 2019), 118–23.

130. *Vit. Syn.* 111–112.

131. Crislip, *Thorns in the Flesh*, 100–108.

132. *Vit. Syn.* 111 (Bongie).

133. Mena, "Scenting," 10.

134. As he conflates the *Life*'s mention of "the sweet fragrance of her most glorious suf-

For example, Mena claims that "as Syncletica becomes more ill and the putrid odor of her body becomes stronger, her fellow ascetics seek to help her find a cure."[135] The *Life*, in contrast, presents her followers as behaving only in their own self-interest: "Her companions urged her to anoint the offensive places with unguents for sake of their own weakness."[136] Yet he reads this passage to the contrary:

> Followers' care for the ailing Syncletica, coupled with the porosity of her body, allows them to scent both her sweet sufferings and her decaying stench. This connectivity diminishes the gulf between her and them—again, reconfiguring health and community is the point. As her body decays further, her community receives the foul scent. We know they are repulsed by it. We know they withdraw and are unable to withstand the funk of her body without the aid of incense. We also know they take with them the stench of death and decay as they come and leave. Still they come, continuing to be present throughout her entire ordeal.[137]

I am not sure how one reads "They used to withdraw for quite long periods of time" (*Vit. Syn.* 111) to mean that they were "present throughout her entire ordeal," or what it means to "scent . . . sweet sufferings" or how "they take with them the stench" (or how "we know" it).[138] In this rereading, her followers do not suppress or overcome their disgust, but come to hold up the disgusting as an aesthetic and moral good for their community. They come to see the beauty in rot and stench and hold onto the memory and experience of smelling the saint's disfigured and gangrenous body as a marker of communal identity.[139] This might offer an edifying lesson for us, but it is not what the *Life* says. The companions do not revel and delight in her stench as a marker of communal identity—they avoid it and avoid her; and against her protests they bully her

ferings" (21) with her later illness (111) into a sort of virtual text, though they are separated in the *Life* by ninety chapters and set in obvious contrast to one another (Mena, "Scenting," 14).

135. Mena, "Scenting," 18.

136. *Vit. Syn.* 111 (Bongie).

137. Mena, "Scenting," 15.

138. As Steve Pile ("Emotions and Affect in Recent Human Geography," *Transactions of the Institute of British Geographers* n.s. 35 [2010]: 17) notes in his critique of affective geography, affect theory relies on a powerful array of metaphors, to sometimes strange effect. In Mena's essay, e.g., "The body is permeable to traumas and 'difficult lessons'" ("Scenting," 13). How is a body permeable to a trauma or a lesson? Or, "Her students hear her teachings and literally [*sic*] inhale her knowledge through her saintly scent" (17).

139. Mena, "Scenting," 15–20.

into accepting medical treatment, which she eventually accedes to, and "from this the excessive stench was destroyed."[140] The followers get what they wanted: no more stench.

Virginia Burrus also returns to Syncletica's disgusting end in exploring the possibilities of an early Christian "ecopoetics," which makes sense as many ancient people saw the human body as a microcosm, made up of the same stuff and interacting with nature (*physis*) through the ebb and flow of the seasons and movements of the cosmos. Part of Syncletica's ascetic journey is a rejection of "female self-adornment or self-fashioning (κόσμησις)," and her subsequent refashioning of disgust constitutes "a new aesthetics."[141] As part of this aesthetic refashioning of disgust, Burrus centers Syncletica's ascetic practice of imagining (in graphic detail) a beloved person as a decomposing corpse, which resembles the Buddhist practice of corpse meditation.[142] But unlike the practice of *aśubhabhāvanā*, Burrus reads this as an aesthetic transformation of disgust into beauty, which she expands into the claim that "all bodies are queer and unstable, terrifyingly vulnerable and wondrously resilient at once."[143] The *Life*'s narration of the gruesome and painful decline of one such "sick, frail, and smelly" person "[invites] us to discover their strength and beauty," "to discover beauty where it is often obscured or denied."[144] Like Mena's refiguring of disgust, Burrus's reading of Syncletica's *Life* offers an edifying intervention into the common

140. *Vit. Syn.* 111 (Castelli); Elizabeth A. Castelli, trans., "Pseudo-Athanasius, *The Life and Activity of the Holy and Blessed Teacher Syncletica*," in *Ascetic Behavior in Greco-Roman Antiquity: A Sourcebook*, ed. Vincent L. Wimbush (Minneapolis: Fortress, 1990), 265–311. Mena never cites or discusses this important passage, which undercuts his reading.

141. Burrus, *Ancient Christian Ecopoetics*, 120, 122, quoting Lynda L. Coon, *Sacred Fictions: Holy Women and Hagiography in Late Antiquity* (Philadelphia: University of Pennsylvania Press, 1997), 40. Burrus's approach to hagiography has been influenced by affect theory, including its main inspiration, Silvan Tomkins, and his popularizer among humanists, Eve Kosofsky Sedgwick; see Burrus, *Saving Shame*, 1–13.

142. Burrus, *Ancient Christian Ecopoetics*, 121.

143. Burrus, *Ancient Christian Ecopoetics*, 122. The Buddhist practice of *aśubhabhāvanā* shares much with Syncletica's teaching as a practice to destroy lustful desire and to accept the transience of the body, but I see no move toward the aesthetic transformation of the "foul" or "impure" as a source of beauty. E.g., "*aśubhabhāvanā*," in *The Princeton Dictionary of Buddhism*, ed. Robert E. Buswell Jr. and Donald S. Lopez Jr. (Princeton: Princeton University Press, 2014); and Edward Conze, *Buddhist Meditation* (London: Routledge, 2008), 103–7.

144. Burrus, *Ancient Christian Ecopoetics*, 122–23.

stigmatization of old age and disability and embraces the transmutability of concepts and categories so typical at the intersections of disability and queer theory. Why can't "disability" (what is often considered as "other" or stigmatized) be "the essential characteristic of being human"?[145] Why can't every body be queer? Why can't we craft a new aesthetics, in which the disgusting and ugly (pus, rotting flesh, open wounds, foul stench) are reconfigured as sources of beauty and strength?

Both of these affectively rich treatments of the *Life of Syncletica* function as postmodern hagiographies, repurposing ancient holy lives for the sacred spaces of post-Christian late capitalism. But the ancient *Life of Syncletica* proposes a different form of self-transformation. Much like the contemporaneous stories of the *Lausiac History*, and I think in the wake of Origen's centering of disgust (and whose influence on Syncletica and Palladius is observable), disgust as an emotion has great pedagogical power for the Christian, not because it is paradoxically a source of beauty or communal identity but because by recognizing and mastering it one can come closer to God, to the freedom from passions (*apatheia*) we fallen beings were designed for. Syncletica's technique of corpse meditation, indeed, is the key to making sense of Syncletica's sickness unto death. By reading this disgusting passage, we engage in what psychologists call benign masochism, embracing unpleasant experiences so that we might on the other side emerge with a mastery over those emotions. Syncletica's wayward disciples stand in for the reader, in our initial reticence to consume such stomach-turning material. Yet her disciples are unlike Palladius and Evagrius, who learn their lesson about disgust in the text. Syncletica's disciples more closely resemble Jesus's disciples in Mark; they don't "get it" in the story itself; but we know, since the text survives, they eventually learned how to master their disgust in writing and reading the *Life*. As the writing of hagiography could function as a form of asceticism, disgust in the *Life of Syncletica* (as in the *Lausiac History*) is a benignly masochistic ascetic practice, a technology of the self recognizable in ancient philosophy and in modern psychology.[146]

145. As the influential professor of English Rosemarie Garland-Thomson puts it (Burrus, *Ancient Christian Ecopoetics*, 122).

146. On the ascetic practice of writing, see Derek Krueger, *Writing and Holiness: The Practice of Authorship in the Early Christian East* (Philadelphia: University of Pennsylvania Press, 2004).

CHAPTER 5

Conclusion

Early Christians through late antiquity describe common and intuitive disgust elicitors in a variety of contexts, including both "core" and "projective": incest, skin disease, body-envelope violations, unclean animals, and dead bodies. Yet the absence of disgust words and reactions in Paul, Luke, and John is conspicuous. When emotion words are used in the context of such disgust elicitors, Paul and the evangelists describe—and thereby model for their audiences—very different passions. They instead express grief (1 Cor 5; John 11), surprise (Luke 24:41), joy (Luke 24:41), and happiness (John 20:29). Such instances of "disgust" are useful examples of the challenges of addressing emotions across historical divides, so comfortable is it to conflate ancient experience to modern common sense. It is also helpful to remember that in the perspective of psychological construction and emotions history, disgust—as emotion—is not a psychological faculty or physiological reflex but a concept; it is a way of making sense of internal and external sensations within a certain embodied context. While an image like a dead body or an open sore might incite a similar preconscious affective response across time and cultures (as generally intense and unpleasant), the emotional sense (and emotional category) one makes out of that experience is not universal but differs among cultures and contexts. When we do not see the emotional language we expect, it is good to be aware that something interesting is at work.

I recall attending a panel in the SBL Bible and Emotion section some years ago about some of the texts I have addressed here. I asked a speaker whether there was any evidence (biological, psychological, anthropological) of humans crying in response to disgust elicitors, an issue which had come up in the paper. After the session a woman came up to me and asked if she could talk with me about my question. I was delighted, of course, expecting her to tell me how brilliant my intervention was. Not so. She asked, genuinely puzzled, "Don't you find dead bodies disgusting?" I answered (something to the effect of), it doesn't matter what I feel as much as what the text says, which I still think is an important principle of historical reading. But, as affect theory suggests, it is still useful to reflect on what we as scholars feel when engaging with the archive. Upon reflection, no, I don't find dead bodies disgusting, not necessarily. I'm of an age to have encountered a few, a corpse in the woods while on a trail run, a deceased man rolled out of my apartment complex on a stretcher, open-casketed bodies at funerals, and I've held the arm of a loved one as she breathed her last in a hospital. In no case have I ever felt disgust. Who would?

Still, disgust is an immensely powerful social and moral emotion as well as a core bodily response. Significantly, it can be consciously and unconsciously altered, through socialization, persuasion, and mimesis. A recent study in cognitive neuroscience shows just how malleable allegedly basic or universal emotions like disgust are. This study showed test subjects a mix of images to elicit responses of fear and disgust, along with "neutral" images. Subjects were then led to classify their responses to the emotions as "fear," "disgust," or a new emotional concept, "morbid fascination."[147] The subjects were told (incorrectly) that the experiment would identify which emotion they were feeling from an fMRI scan.[148] What the fMRIs actually revealed to the scientists was a biological marker for changing emotion *concepts*, not emotions themselves. When subjects classified their reactions to disturbing images, such as victims of auto accidents, as "fascination" rather than disgust or fear (usually through experimental prompting or manipulation), their brains became more active. This is not because the scan identified a locus or circuit in the brain for "morbid fascination," but because the brain has to work harder in learning and applying a new emotion concept, just as the brain and body have to work harder at any new or unfamiliar activity.

We cannot study ancient texts in the same way as modern experimental subjects, and it is precarious to intuit how a hypothetical ancient reader would have responded to a text. My point here is that when Paul reframes the proper emotional response to incest as grief, when Luke and John reframe the proper emotional response to open wounds as joy and wonder, or when ascetics teach and model cognitive exercises to manage, suppress, or redirect disgust impulses, it not only reflects the difference and diversity of ancient emotional experience, though that it is itself important. It also encourages among their readers a process of emotional learning and transformation, taking place not just on the plane of discourse (which we can observe) but through physical changes in the body and brain (which we cannot). The trend toward minimizing disgust language and imagery in moral exhortation and narrative in favor of emotional experiences of grief, happiness, joy, and awe should be considered

147. Suzanne Oosterwijk et al., "The Neural Representation of Typical and Atypical Experiences of Negative Images: Comparing Fear, Disgust and Morbid Fascination," *Social Cognitive and Affective Neuroscience* 11 (2016): 11–22.

148. This is not currently possible; in the perspective of the psychological construction theory of mind and emotion, it is inherently impossible, since emotions do not exist as circuits or programs in the brain or body but are concepts and thus immeasurable.

an important component of the early Christian movement, inseparable from its ritual, morality, and narratives.[149]

Yet this shift in emotion, however widespread it may be in Paul's letters and the Gospels and in some ascetic trajectories in late antiquity, did not become normative among early Christian writers. More influential I suspect was the disgust encouraged by anti-heretical writers from the New Testament into late antiquity, who embraced a moral language of disgust, identifying others as disgusting in their teachings and rituals and evoking a righteous disgust in their readers as theological guide—we will know they are not Christians by our disgust.

149. Cf. Shantz, "Emotion, Cognition, and Social Change," 269, who hypothesizes that the "emotional-cognitive competition" reflected in Gal 3:28 "raises another means that was available for this remarkable, if partial, attempt at sociocultural change in Christian origins. . . . Certainly it seems a remarkable resource for social transformation."

6

Envy

If you were to administer a standard analogies test and asked for an antonym for happiness or joy, almost certainly the most popular answers would be sadness or grief. The pairing of happiness with sadness, grief with joy, sits as intuitively in contemporary English as the tragic and comic masks. Ask an ancient Greek the same, and you might get a very different response: The opposite of happiness is envy. From the earliest writers of prose and poetry, Greeks saw happiness bound in hostile tension with envy: "That happiness is an early symptom of misfortune, that 'inherent' within happiness is the power to bring on misfortune, above all through the agency of resentment [or envy] (*phthonos*), whether of men or gods, is a vision that was to persist among the Greeks when almost all others had faded."[1] The great contrast between Athens and Sparta was in some sense symptomatic of different strategies to control the destructive power of envy. The Athenian "[discovery of] the excellence of the individual" was counterbalanced by "a fierce resentment against that excellence," an envy (*phthonos*) finding its most visible outlet in the practice

1. Roberto Calasso, *The Marriage of Cadmus and Harmony* (New York: Knopf, 1993), 262. Envy is a special interest as early as Hesiod and reflected in many later authors, such as Pindar and Herodotus; see Patricia Bulman, *Phthonos in Pindar* (Berkeley: University of California Press, 1992); Thomas Harrison, "The Cause of Things: Envy and the Emotions in Herodotus' *Histories*," in *Envy, Spite and Jealousy: The Rivalrous Emotions in Ancient Greece*, ed. David Konstan and N. Keith Rutter, Edinburgh Leventis Studies 2 (Edinburgh: Edinburgh University Press, 2003), 143–63; and a survey in Stuart Lasine, *Divine Envy, Jealousy, and Vengefulness in Ancient Israel and Greece* (London: Routledge, 2023); the Greek dialectic of happiness and envy was described long ago by Ulrich von Wilamowitz-Moellendorf, quoted in Helmut Schoeck, *Envy: A Theory of Social Behaviour*, trans. Michael Glenny and Betty Ross (New York: Harcourt, Brace & World, 1966), 119.

of ostracism, which could target the best in the polis as easily as the worst.[2] Sparta saw these internal threats, and "chose to put into practice what would later earn them Aristotle's most damning criticism: 'they have lost the happiness of living.'"[3] The method of this pure unhappiness was twofold, first by structuring a society of equals (*homoioi*), a structure not of nature but custom, which "only comes into being through initiation."[4] Second, since envy thrives in aspirations of equality, the Spartans controlled it rigorously, externalizing their hate as the basis of their society, a terror inflicted on the masses of helots.[5] While the intense bonds between happiness and envy, joy and resentment, are not commonly discussed today, ancient Christians reflected on emotions as inheritors of this long tradition of worry about envy as a malevolent and primal, even diabolical, force, a social and psychological problem that captured the concerns of the most urbane philosopher and most common peasant alike.

Envy for Greeks resonated in discussions of the nature of god or the gods and the psychological traits humans should foster (or not) in imitating them, ever aware of the gods' inherent nemesis toward humanity's success—reaching down to punish anyone with enough *hybris* to declare himself happy.[6] In a bold rejection of this common posing of human happiness against divine envy, Plato identified envy as a trait definitionally incommensurate with god, who must be *aphthonos*, unbegrudging in generosity, a personality trait to be emulated by the philosopher.[7] Envy as a personality trait contrary to godliness also appears in the Bible in the important claim of the Wisdom of Solomon that the devil's envy (*phthonos*) was the source of death and the defining emotion of those who belong to his part, which may show the influence of Plato's critique of traditional Greek attributions of punishing envy to the gods.[8] The curious relationship of envy and divinity further occurs in extrabiblical literature, for example in the *Life of Adam and Eve*, as the snake in Eden tempts

2. Calasso, *Marriage*, 255–56, drawing on the story of Aristides the Just, from Plutarch, *Life of Aristides* 7.7; Schoeck, *Envy*, 205–7, who notes that the arbitrariness of ostracism in ancient Athens posed no moral problem, as they acted in imitation of the gods, who in envy punished capriciously and arbitrarily. Schoeck cites the work on Athenian envy by Svend Ranulf.

3. Calasso, *Marriage*, 263.

4. Calasso, *Marriage*, 250–51.

5. Calasso, *Marriage*, 254–55.

6. Peter Walcot, *Envy and the Greeks: A Study of Human Behaviour* (Warminster: Aris & Phillips, 1978), 22–51.

7. F. G. Hermann, "φθόνος in the World of Plato's Timaeus," in Konstan and Rutter, *Envy, Spite and Jealousy*, 53–83.

8. M. W. Dickie, "Envy," *ABD* 2:530.

Eve by claiming his own emotion to be grief (*lypē*) but accuses God of feeling envy (*phthonos*).[9] Throughout antiquity, Christians wrestled with the ubiquity and danger of these feelings.

Yet, the psychosocial role of envy in early Christian literature has been overlooked in modern scholarship, an omission which I think would strike ancient readers as odd,[10] as it might also psychoanalytic theorists, who would influence contemporary affect theory. The post-Freudian psychoanalyst Melanie Klein placed envy's genesis at the breast and the formative problem of the infant's "lost prenatal unity with the mother and the feeling of security that goes with it."[11] Since the happy feeling at the breast can never match up to the lost transcendent unity of mother and child in the womb, conflict within the infant's psyche and between infant and mother is inescapable. It is in fact necessary for human development and the "enrichment of . . . personality," for example, as "a fundamental element in creativeness."[12] A "complete enjoyment" at the breast flourishes with the proper development of love and gratitude and strengthens "this early bond as the basis for all later relations with one loved person."[13] But the obverse of this loving and gracious joy is envy. Envy is not the insatiable desire to consume but the resentment that "another person possesses and enjoys something desirable—the envious impulse to take it away or to spoil it."[14] It is the latter element, to spoil the good, that comes to the fore in ancient envy and distinguishes it from both greed and emulation—the envious does not covet another's good; he wants it destroyed.[15]

While Klein was primarily interested in envy as a feature of early childhood, the dynamics of anxiety, envy, and hate recur throughout the life cycle

9. *Greek Life of Adam and Eve* 18 (*OTP* 2:279); Lasine, *Divine Envy*, 45–46.

10. This was noted a generation ago by Anselm C. Hagedorn and Jerome H. Neyrey, "'It Was Out of Envy That They Handed Jesus Over' (Mark 15.10): The Anatomy of Envy and the Gospel of Mark," *JSNT* 69 (1998): 15; cf. Dickie, "Envy," who according to Hagedorn and Neyrey "is no worse off than the commentators on Mark 15.10 who simply ignore the mention of envy there." The situation seems little changed in the past quarter century.

11. Melanie Klein, *Envy and Gratitude and Other Works 1946–1963* (New York: Free Press, 1975), 179.

12. Klein, *Envy and Gratitude*, 186. See the clear overview by Bénédicte Vidaillet, "Psychoanalytic Contributions to Understanding Envy: Classic and Contemporary Perspectives," in *Envy: Theory and Research*, ed. Richard H. Smith (Oxford: Oxford University Press, 2008), 270–76.

13. Klein, *Envy and Gratitude*, 187.

14. Klein, *Envy and Gratitude*, 181.

15. See Joseph Epstein, *Envy* (New York: Oxford University Press, 2003), 22; Vidaillet, "Psychoanalytic Contributions," 273.

and may be recognized in the familiar concept of the "inferiority complex" and more generally in the context of social comparison.[16] Envy and jealousy can result from the sense of inferiority and impotence and function "as dynamic motive forces," which are as relevant to ancient struggles over status and honor as they are to today's meritocracy.[17] In this perspective, envy is a primal drive, which "distorts [one's] whole perception of the world," a perversion of human cognition and motivation, "the mark of Cain."[18]

While the influence of psychoanalysis has waned in many areas, Melanie Klein's thinking has influenced affect theory, and through it biblical studies. Eve Kosofsky Sedgwick, at the cutting edge of affect theory, draws on Klein's infant psychology for basic concepts of affective reading, such as the paranoid/schizoid and depressive positions (concepts which have little to do with common usage of paranoia and depression).[19] Sedgwick's influence on biblical studies is considerable. In dialogue with Sedgwick and Klein, for example, Jennifer Knust embraces an affectively "paranoid" reading of Genesis 9 and questions whether a reparative (or depressive in Klein's terms) reading of the text is really possible. The text is just too harmful.[20] This critical paranoia is "marked by hatred, envy, and anxiety" but is also "an essential survival strategy."[21] The primal emotionality of this reading comes out in the affective framing of the study, which, as is common among adopters of affect theory, brings the emotional experience of the author to the surface: "Upset and unhappy, I have adopted the stance of a historical-critical killjoy, making it my duty throughout this essay to spoil the happiness of others." To spoil others'

16. Mark D. Alicke and Ethan Zell, "Social Comparison and Envy," in Smith, *Envy*, 73–93.

17. Robert E. Anderson, "Envy and Jealousy," *American Journal of Psychotherapy* 56 (2002): 477–78; Colin Wayne Leach, "Envy, Inferiority, and Injustice: Three Bases of Anger About Inequality," in Smith, *Envy*, 101–3; Richard H. Smith, David J. Y. Combs, and Stephen M. Thielke, "Envy and the Challenges to Good Health," in Smith, *Envy*, 290–314; Vidaillet, "Psychoanalytic Contributions," 268.

18. Marguerite Beecher and Willard Beecher, *The Mark of Cain: An Anatomy of Jealousy* (New York: Harper & Row, 1971), 1. Though primal, it is not innate but a function of socialization through family and society.

19. Eve Kosofsky Sedgwick, "Paranoid Reading and Reparative Reading, or, You're So Paranoid, You Probably Think This Essay Is About You," in *Touching Feeling: Affect, Pedagogy, Performativity*, ed. Sedgwick (Durham, NC: Duke University Press, 2003), 123–52.

20. Jennifer Knust, "Who's Afraid of Canaan's Curse? Genesis 9:18–29 and the Challenge of Reparative Reading," *BibInt* 22 (2014): 391–92. Again, these technical terms of psychoanalysis and affect theory differ from popular usage.

21. Knust, "Canaan's Curse," 410, 412, the former passage quoting Sedgwick, "Paranoid Reading."

happiness is a source of pleasure: "Yes, there can be joy in killing joy," Knust writes, which brings into sharp focus the ancient dialectic of happiness and envy.[22] Germans might consider it something close to Schadenfreude, "malicious joy."[23] While a contemporary affect theorist might disagree, as the Greeks would define it, to take pleasure in destroying the joy of another is nothing other than envy, *phthonos*.

And define it they did. Aristotle was especially influential in his taxonomy of envy and jealousy, as he carved emotional experience at the joints in the *Art of Rhetoric* and his ethical treatises. He identified three emotional concepts within the general constellation of rivalrous emotions, each of which is a species of pain or distress (*lypē*) occurring in specific socially embedded situations: *phthonos*, *zēlos*, and *to nemesan* (related to *nemesis*).

Indignation (*to nemesan*) is the opposite of pity, the pain felt at another's undeserved *mis*fortune. Indignation, rather, is "being pained at undeserved *good* fortune."[24] Like pity, indignation is a moral emotion, not a vice, and thus appropriately felt by the gods (hence the familiar concept of *nemesis*). Of course, determining who is deserving or undeserving depends on a variety of factors. One might be deserving of some good (beautiful armor) but undeserving of another (a beautiful spouse), and it is much more likely to feel indignation at the nouveaux riches or the suddenly successful than old money.[25] The term itself is not used widely by Christians (or others in the Roman period), although the language and concept of indignation remains. Still, even Aristotle concedes that it can be difficult to distinguish between righteous indignation and the more malicious passion of envy, which modern scholars of envy have also observed.[26]

Phthonos, or envy, differs in its morality and the relative status of the person feeling it. Envy is

> a certain kind of distress at apparent success on the part of one's peers in attaining the good things that have been mentioned [in the preceding section on indignation], not that a person may get anything for himself but because of those who have it. The kind of people who feel envy are those

22. Knust, "Canaan's Curse," 410, here drawing on Sarah Ahmed, *The Promise of Happiness* (Durham, NC: Duke University Press, 2010).

23. Schoeck, *Envy*, 178.

24. Aristotle, *Rhet.* 2.9.1; Aristotle, *On Rhetoric*, trans. George A. Kennedy (New York: Oxford University Press, 1991).

25. Aristotle, *Rhet.* 2.9.10.

26. Aristotle, *Rhet.* 2.9.3; Schoeck, *Envy*, 162, 176; Leach, "Envy, Inferiority, and Injustice."

> who have, or seem to themselves to have [more fortunate acquaintances among] those like themselves.[27]

It is important for Aristotle that the envious and the envied be similar in status, goals, or identity, unlike indignation, which moves across status and is appropriate for a god to feel toward an uppity mortal. We humans only envy people like us, or whom we consider like us, and are especially envious about honor:

> But since people seek honor in comparison with antagonists and rivals in love and in general those wanting the same things, necessarily they are most envious of these. . . . And people have envy of those who have acquired something or been successful. These, too, are near and like; for clearly, they do not attain this good because of themselves, so distress at this causes envy. And [they envy] those who have or have acquired whatever naturally belongs to themselves or what they once had.[28]

For Aristotle and countless moralists and philosophers after him, envy is a wholly malicious emotion, devoted neither to justice nor to self-improvement but simply to hate, to destroy the goods of another.[29] When we say that comparison is the thief of joy, that comparison is an act of envy.[30]

But not all rivalrous emotion was harmful, especially given how central competition was to ancient Mediterranean society. Aristotle uses another concept, *zēlos*, to refer to the emotional drive toward emulation and competition. *Zēlos* is "a distress at the apparent presence among others like him by nature, of things honored and possible for a person to acquire." *Zēlos* resembles envy in the necessity that it is among relative equals.[31] A difference lies in the availability of the desired good. Were I to feel distress at a peer's height or perceived beauty, this would be envy, as there is little I can do to gain height or fundamentally change my appearance. But were I to feel distress at a peer's better tennis skills or success as a teacher, this could be *zēlos*, as this distress could reasonably drive me to improve my backhand or learn techniques to

27. Aristotle, *Rhet.* 2.10.1 (Kennedy).

28. Aristotle, *Rhet.* 2.10.7–8 (Kennedy).

29. Aristotle, *Rhet.* 2.11.8 See Schoeck, *Envy*, 13–17; Solomon Schimmel, "Envy in Jewish Thought and Literature," in Smith, *Envy*, 18–19.

30. See broader discussion in Alicke and Zell, "Social Comparison and Envy."

31. Aristotle, *Rhet.* 2.11.1 (Kennedy); Alicke and Zell, "Social Comparison and Envy," 78–83.

improve class discussions and would not necessitate any loss from the honor and goods of my rival. Thus, says Aristotle, "emulation is a good thing and characteristic of good people, while envy is bad and characteristic of the bad; for the former [person], through emulation, is making an effort to attain good things for himself, while the latter, through envy, tries to prevent his neighbor from having them."[32]

Quite a different emotion is jealousy, which could be expressed in Greek as *zēlotypia*, or even *zēlos* or *zēlōtēs*.[33] While *phthonos* is driven by a sense of lack, jealousy is driven by possession and one's unwillingness to share (a lover, wealth, honor, and so on). So, when God declares himself to be *zēlōtēs* (Exod 20:5; 34:14 LXX), he communicates his special relationship with Israel that he will not share them with other gods, while also showing his zeal and rivalry, not afraid to compete with rivals to put them in their place.

Aristotle's taxonomy of the rivalrous emotions is rigorous and logical, and centuries of philosophers have followed in his path by carefully defining, redefining, and differentiating harmful varieties of envy from more socially and psychologically positive forms of emulation.[34] But as even philosophers will note, ordinary language does not follow rigorous rules, and terms for envy, emulation, indignation, and jealousy can be used interchangeably. This is the case in the early Christian centuries, in which *phthonos* and *zēlos* are used indiscriminately, and often as a pair (*phthonos kai zēlos*), while *zēlos* can also retain its positive sense of emulation, as it does in Paul.[35] The situation gets further complicated when moving beyond Greek, for example in Coptic, which has its own vocabulary of envy in addition to Greek loanwords.

For envy was not merely a rhetorical trope but was part of "a cultural system of values," and a pernicious human and divine force in society.[36] This cultural value system tended to see "the good" (whatever that might be) as "limited."[37] Modern capitalist ideals—of progress, trickle-down economics, or "the rising tide that lifts all boats"—simply did not exist. One's gain means another's loss, or as John the Baptist puts it, "He must increase, I must decrease" (John 3:30).

32. Aristotle, *Rhet.* 2.11.1 (Kennedy).

33. David Konstan, *The Emotions of the Ancient Greeks: Studies in Aristotle and Classical Literature* (Toronto: University of Toronto Press, 2006), 219–43.

34. See the recent study by Sara Protasi, *The Philosophy of Envy* (Cambridge: Cambridge University Press, 2021).

35. E.g., see Luke Timothy Johnson, "James 3:13–4:10 and the *Topos* ΠΕΡΙ ΦΘΟΝΟΥ," *NovT* 25 (1983): 327–47.

36. Hagedorn and Neyrey, "Anatomy of Envy," 17.

37. Hagedorn and Neyrey, "Anatomy of Envy," 20.

This expectation of limited good can result in a societal reluctance to advance or stand out among peers, as the successful or (literally) outstanding will attract the evil eye and envious attacks of others (human or divine). Ancient society, like many, was structured through conflict and rivalry, "agonistic," experienced as a contest for limited goods, in the family, sex, political power, and athletic achievement.[38] Ancient students of the soul saw the love of honor (*philotimia*) as a primary site for envy to manifest, as honor was "one's social credit rating or social entitlement to respect and interaction."[39] Such honor could be ascribed (such as through kinship and inheritance, including matters like birth order) and achieved as fame through success in agonistic contests.[40]

Contemporary perspectives on envy hardly convey the immense fear that envy provoked in the ancient world. Today, brands use envy as a positive attribute (Massage Envy, Envy apples, HP Envy laptops, Nvidia), or as an old shampoo commercial went: "Don't hate me because I'm beautiful." While ancients would agree that it is better to be envied than pitied, envy carried grave risks for the envied and the envier alike.[41] It was a sickness of the soul, a cancer which devours its host, like rust, poison, or a snake curled in the guts.[42] We should not take too metaphorically envy's threat to health, either today or in the ancient world.[43]

Envy was a product of social tension and conflict, especially prevalent in the closely bound communities of the Mediterranean, urban and rural, of intense competition for limited resources and little way to escape from prying eyes.[44] It traveled with hate, strife, and war, and a poet noted how easily envy (*phthonos*) leads to murder (*phonos*).[45] Just cross out a single Greek letter. To be seen by others was a threat in antiquity and not unique to our social media cultures of emulation, oversharing, and ostracism. Significantly, the Latin for envy (*invidia*) comes from "to look askance at." Ancient envy was further bound up in the culture of reciprocity and gift giving, the "sense and system

38. Hagedorn and Neyrey, "Anatomy of Envy," 22–23.

39. Hagedorn and Neyrey, "Anatomy of Envy," 24.

40. Hagedorn and Neyrey, "Anatomy of Envy," 24; and on birth order in the Jewish scriptures, 26.

41. See W. Gerrod Parrott and Patricia M. Rodriguez Mosquera, "On the Pleasures and Displeasures of Being Envied," in Smith, *Envy*, 117–32.

42. Esther Eidinow, *Envy, Poison, and Death: Women on Trial in Classical Athens* (Oxford: Oxford University Press, 2016), 71–72.

43. Smith, Combs, and Thielke, "Envy and the Challenges to Good Health."

44. Eidinow, *Envy*, 102.

45. Eidinow, *Envy*, 72.

of mutual obligation [which] oiled the wheels of ancient Greek life."[46] But the gift was full of risk, including the ingratitude and resentment of the person receiving the gift. I suspect few would intuitively contrast envy with gratitude today, but Melanie Klein saw them as a dialectic foundational to human psychology and social relations, incubated within the fraught relationship of infant and mother.[47]

Ancient envy was as much a practice as a feeling and could be deployed in various ways, from ostracism and lawsuits, to witchcraft, to feuding and murder.[48] It is not surprising that envy could be felt as an almost physical, and certainly a demonic force, even causing disease, such as eye disease, appropriately enough.[49] Envy manifested most commonly through social practices related to slander, malign speech, or gossip, especially as a way to cut the exceptional down to size.[50] The ideas of hate speech and violent/harmful words are now ubiquitous, as is "misinformation," the lies which travel halfway round the world before the truth gets its boots on. Ancients saw hate speech and violent words not in angry shouts but in quieter, secretive gossip and slander, which could spread through a community like pestilence and consume it like rust.[51]

Envy and the Earliest Christians

It is a bit strange how little attention has been given to envy in formative Christianity, as in the Gospel of Mark, for example, in which envy plays a rather central role in the motivations of some of the characters for the main point of the story, the passion. Specialists, of course, note the appearance of "envy" in Mark's Gospel, often finding it a plausible explanation for the action, sometimes not.[52] But envy has not reached the popular imagination about the last

46. Eidinow, *Envy*, 140.

47. Klein, *Envy and Gratitude*.

48. Hagedorn and Neyrey, "Anatomy of Envy," 32.

49. Eidinow, *Envy*, 157–58. It is fitting that Dante envisions purgatory's envious serving their time with their eyes sewn shut.

50. Eidinow, *Envy*, 109–13, 147.

51. Eidinow, *Envy*, 120–21.

52. E.g., Craig A. Evans, *Mark 8:27–16:20*, WBC 34B (Nashville: Thomas Nelson, 2000), 481–82, who incorporates the anthropological approach of Hagedorn and Neyrey; M. Eugene Boring, *Mark: A Commentary* (Louisville: Westminster John Knox, 2006), 421, with attention to the language of envy and the word choice of *phthonos*; also see Joel Marcus, *Mark 8–16*, AB 27 (New Haven: Yale University Press, 2009), 1036; a skeptical view is from

days of Jesus, I think. Out of curiosity I asked Google why Jesus was crucified. The AI helpfully wrote out a short paragraph and a list of eight reasons, and none of them was the reason that Mark and Matthew after him give: envy. "For [Pilate] recognized that it was out of envy (*dia phthonon*) that the chief priests had handed him over" (15:10). To be fair, this is the only use of the word "envy" in the Gospel. But this single instance of the word *phthonos* points to a wider presence of envy as the driver of conflict between Jesus and his rivals, which can be clarified by looking at the conflict through the cross-cultural anthropology of envy.[53]

As a primal emotional drive which ancients recognized and personified as a demonic and magical force in society, envy's role as motivation for the betrayal and arrest of Jesus makes a great deal of sense within Mark's narrative. While the political threat of the apocalyptic prophet from Nazareth surely evoked the political ire of his rivals and the Roman authorities, when one considers ancient emotional experience, Mark's claim of envy offers an entirely plausible motivation for the actions of his rivals. Jesus challenges the honor of his rivals in public contests, showing them up through miracle working and debate, even moving physically into their territory in the temple, not just threatening the tenuous political status quo but humiliating them. In the zero-sum game of ancient honor, Jesus's rising acclaim of the crowds and shouted Hosannas could only result in their loss.[54] That his fame would attract the evil eye and envy of others plausibly accounts for a variety of the distinctive narrative features of Mark's Gospel, such as Jesus's insistence that his healings be kept secret. Mark's "messianic secret" is of course a rich hermeneutic problem, but Jesus's attempt to retain secrecy or social invisibility, in spite of the unstoppable spread of his fame, speaks not just to a developing Christology but to a familiar strategy for managing reputation in a society consumed by envy.[55] Jesus's call to humility for his followers, and even his curious rejection of a compliment ("Why do you call me 'good'? No one is good but God alone" [10:18]) reflect strategies for avoiding and deflecting envy, strategies not only ancient but familiar if

---

Adela Yarbro Collins, *Mark: A Commentary*, Hermeneia (Minneapolis: Fortress, 2007), 720. A reasonable consensus view claims that Jesus "angered some of the chief priests" who, "fearing a possible uprising," set in motion the plan to arrest Jesus (Bart D. Ehrman, *Jesus: Apocalyptic Prophet of the New Millennium* [New York: Oxford University Press, 1999], 209). Envy is simply supplanted by intuition of the priests' real emotions.

53. Hagedorn and Neyrey, "Anatomy of Envy," 38.

54. Hagedorn and Neyrey, "Anatomy of Envy," 39–40.

55. Hagedorn and Neyrey, "Anatomy of Envy," 52–53; sometimes radical openness can also be practiced as a way "to obviate envy," effective or not (Schoeck, *Envy*, 29).

largely unacknowledged features of contemporary interpersonal relations.[56] From the perspective of a psychological and anthropological interpretation of envy, Mark's attribution (through Pilate) of envy as the motivation for the Jerusalem elite to hand over Jesus makes a great deal of internal sense within the gospel narrative. The question of envy as it pertains to the historical Jesus is another matter, of course.

But what of Judas, whose motivations and personality have also been such a rich quarry for interpretation? The dispute at Bethany seems a precipitating event for his decision to speak to the chief priests. While the identity of those who objected to the expense of the nard is not specified, Mark tells us their motivation: They were *aganaktountes pros heautous*, indignant, displeased, irritated, all facets of the constellation of rivalrous emotions as they were conceived in antiquity, falling close to the semantic range of indignation (*to nemesan*) though sometimes taken as anger (*orgē*).[57] In the world of peripatetic rhetoric, the emotion of the complainers at Bethany does not seem like anger, which is pain felt, along with a desire for revenge, at "a conspicuous slight . . . directed, without justification, against oneself or those near to one."[58] A better fit is an annoyance closer to ancient indignation (or resentment), or the Latin *invidia*, a painful response to the good fortune of others, alongside envy (*phthonos*) and emulation (*zēlos*).[59] Indignation is properly felt at seeing someone get what is not appropriate to them, which is not to say that the person is not good and not deserving at all. It is the excess—of honor, adulation, and expense, for example—that causes the pain of indignation.[60] Aristotle's definitions are ideal types and especially targeted to the use of the passions in a rhetorical or forensic setting, and Christians did not embrace his preferred term of *to nemesan*.[61] At any rate, Mark reflects a layman's use of emotional language. Still, from the perspective of ancient emotions, and quite recog-

56. Hagedorn and Neyrey, "Anatomy of Envy," 51–54; Parrott and Rodriguez Mosquera, "Pleasures and Displeasures," 122–24; on modesty as defense against envy, see Schoeck, *Envy*, 186.

57. William V. Harris, *Restraining Rage: The Ideology of Anger Control in Classical Antiquity* (Cambridge, MA: Harvard University Press, 2001), 53.

58. Aristotle, *Rhet.* 2.2.1 (Kennedy).

59. Aaron Ben-Ze'ev, "Aristotle on the Fortune of Others," in Konstan and Rutter, *Envy, Spite, and Jealousy*, 105–6; Robert A. Kaster, *Emotion, Restraint, and Community in Ancient Rome* (Oxford: Oxford University Press, 2005), 84–103.

60. Aristotle, *Rhet.* 2.9.6.

61. This might be a phenomenon parallel to the early Christian avoidance of the term *eudaimonia*, in spite of their great interest in positive affect, which possibly is due to its inherent association with Greek polytheism. *Nemesis* also appears to have become "fossilized"

nizable from a modern psychological perspective, the disciples react out of envy and resentment, "complaining indignantly to one another" (14:4) at the wrongful distribution of goods, rather than out of anger (as the NRSV renders it). The disciples' complaint resounds in Friedrich Nietzsche's characterization of the "man of resentment," who laments, "It's a shame to be happy! There is too much misery!"[62]

In Roman antiquity, as today, the "sharing of food and hospitality was . . . the chief mechanism for alleviating the envy occasioned by status distinctions."[63] A communal meal would be the logical way to help smooth over any indignant conflicts in the group that came to a head at Bethany, and (marvelously!) that is what happens. As Roman authors note, however, the communal meal is not always successful in resolving interpersonal envy.[64] It was certainly not on that night.

We see another example of this in 1 Corinthians. For all Paul's assertions of the church as a place where distinctions in status would be leveled, the inequality of wealth came to the fore in the Corinthian church in communal meals, erupting in factions (*schismata*), with some feeling contempt (*kataphroneite*) and shaming (*kataischynete*) those of lesser status (11:17–22). We are not told the emotional reaction of those dishonored and contemned by their fellow Christ followers. I suspect it was envy and resentment.

Indeed, Paul identifies envy as the driver of opposition to him in Philippi, opposition not from outsiders but from other preachers of Christ. Some are proclaiming Christ out of "envy and rivalry (*dia phthonon kai erin*), but others from goodwill" (Phil 1:15). While this is the only occasion of *phthonos* in the letter, as in Mark, envy travels in a number of guises in Philippians and in fact thematically ties the letter together.[65] David Frederickson argues persuasively

after the archaic period, used to describe divine motivations in a mythological context, as discussed by Lasine, *Divine Envy*, 28–29.

62. Cited in Schoeck, *Envy*, 179.

63. Carlin A. Barton, *The Sorrows of the Ancient Romans: The Gladiator and the Monster* (Princeton: Princeton University Press, 1993), 109.

64. Discussion of Roman meals gone wrong in Barton, *Sorrows of the Ancient Romans*, 109–12. See also from a social science perspective, Walter F. Taylor Jr., "The Family That Eats Together . . . : 1 Corinthians 11:17–34 from a Mediterranean Perspective," in *Exploring Biblical Kinship: Festschrift in Honor of John J. Pilch*, ed. Joan C. Campbell and Patrick J. Hartin, CBQMS 55 (Washington, DC: Catholic Biblical Association, 2016), 101–30.

65. I depend on the astute emotional analysis of David E. Fredrickson, "Envious Enemies of the Cross of Christ (Philippians 3:18)," *Word & World* 28 (2008): 22–28; David E. Fredrickson, *Eros and the Christ: Longing and Envy in Paul's Christology* (Minneapolis: Fortress, 2013).

that the envious proclaimers of 1:15 are the same as the "enemies (*echthrous*) of the cross of Christ" (3:18), as hatred or enmity (*echthra*) and envy are so tightly bound in antiquity. The envious do not covet the good of another, here Paul's honor. They want to destroy it out of hate, which in practice shows itself in gossip, slander, and malicious talk.[66] Paul's envious opponents speak out of "false motives" (*prophasei*) and insincerely (*ouch hagnōs*), out of "selfish ambition" (*ex eritheias*), simply to afflict their rival Paul (1:16–18).[67] Paul speaks of the problem of "muttering and arguing," again pointing to malicious talk and slander (2:14), as does his condemnation of his opponents as dogs (3:2), whose bites recall the sniping and backbiting of the envious.[68] In an ancient topos about the envious, the bites are likely to be turned upon themselves, as "their end is destruction; their god is the belly; and their glory is in their shame; their minds are set on earthly things" (3:19; also 1:28).[69] The enemies of the cross are other Christians, who envy Paul as someone fundamentally like them. It is perhaps not coincidental that Paul's Christ-proclaiming opponents slander him *dia phthonon*, just as Jesus's Jerusalem coreligionists and rivals bore false witness against him *dia phthonon*. For those inclined to see a Pauline influence on Mark, envy's role as motivation for the malicious talk of the protagonists' rivals and the potential or actual cause of their death may be added to the list of distinctive thematic similarities between the two.[70]

Envy, Community, and History

While the historical importance of envy has attracted the attention of few scholars of the New Testament (but a notable few), ancient Christian writers focused on envy as a significant problem in their communities as well as a catalyzing force in their reading of sacred history. The letter of 1 Clement

66. Fredrickson, "Envious Enemies," 24.

67. Fredrickson, "Envious Enemies," 25.

68. Fredrickson, "Envious Enemies," 25. Basil of Caesarea refers to his rivals in a similar way, by whose bites of heresy he is afflicted. Andrew Crislip, "Shenoute's Illness," in *The Rediscovery of Shenoute*, ed. Anne Boud'hors et al., OLA 310 (Leuven: Peeters, 2022), 210.

69. Fredrickson, "Envious Enemies," 26; see also Andrew Crislip, "Envy and Anger at the World's Creation and Destruction in the *Treatise Without Title 'On the Origin of the World'* (NHC II,5)," *VC* 65 (2011): 285–310.

70. Joel Marcus, "Mark—Interpreter of Paul," *NTS* 46 (2000): 473–87; Heidi Wendt, "Secrecy as Pauline Influence on the Gospel of Mark," *JBL* 140 (2021): 579–600; Michael Kok, "Does Mark Narrate the Pauline *Kerygma* of 'Christ Crucified'? Challenging an Emerging Consensus on Mark as a Pauline Gospel," *JSNT* 37 (2014): 139–60.

became attributed to the third bishop of Rome by Dionysius of Corinth by the year 170, though no internal evidence points to a historical Clement as author.[71] The traditional dating puts the letter in the late first century, perhaps in the persecuting reign of Domitian, but as usual there are debates, and the letter could plausibly be placed anywhere between the late first century (e.g., 98) and the middle of the second century (e.g., 138).[72] While 1 Clement is little read today, after a significant decline in circulation and readership in the Middle Ages, ancient Christians of various communities found it an authoritative, even scriptural voice, and it was "included among the books of the New Testament in several of our surviving manuscripts."[73]

Clement's lengthy epistle touches widely on the problems of Christian community, but what drives his missive most prominently is the outburst of "strife and discord" in Corinth, apparently a revolt of younger members of the church against the old guard.[74] In line with ancient trends identifying the passions as causes of political rivalry and conflict, Clement claims that the revolt of the young Christians is rooted in nothing other than "jealousy and envy" (*zēlos kai phthonos*), terms which he uses colloquially (not like Aristotle) as a pair and without clear distinction.[75]

The most influential aspect of Clement's approach to envy and jealousy is his framing of Christian sacred history as driven by these wicked passions. He encourages his audience to recognize these universally loathed emotions as connecting Christians and their feelings to their self-understanding as part of God's people and as part of a long history of God's people in a fallen world. Clement begins his history of envy with the devil himself, through whose envy death entered the world, citing Wisdom of Solomon 2:24: "God created human beings for incorruption and made them the image of his own nature, but through the envy (*phthonos*) of the devil death entered the world."[76] Given

71. David G. Horrell, *The Social Ethos of the Corinthian Correspondence: Interests and Ideology from 1 Corinthians to 1 Clement* (Edinburgh: T&T Clark, 1996), 238, on the dating.

72. *Apostolic Fathers* 1:18–28 (Ehrman, LCL); revisionist dating is covered recently by L. L. Welborn, "Retrospect on the Challenge to a Consensus on the Date of 1 Clement," *BR* 65 (2020): 95–103; with response by Clare K. Rothschild, "*Horror Vacui*: Welborn's 'Retrospect on the Challenge to a Consensus on the Date of 1 Clement,'" *BR* 65 (2020): 104–13.

73. *Apostolic Fathers* 1:28, 29 (Ehrman, LCL).

74. L. L. Welborn, *The Young Against the Old: Generational Conflict in 1 Clement* (Lanham, MD: Lexington/Fortress Academic, 2018); L. L. Welborn, "Jealousy, Envy, Strife, and Discord in First Clement," *Journal of Beliefs and Values* 38 (2017): 173–79.

75. 1 Clem. 4.7.

76. Clementine discussion of envy may be seen in Basil the Great and Gregory of Nazianzus. Martin Hinterberger, "Basil of Caesarea and Gregory of Nazianzun Speaking About

Wisdom's expulsion from the Protestant Bible, it is easy to overlook how important this text was to ancient Christians and how compelling was Wisdom's identification of envy as the source of death and human suffering.

Clement then traces the intersection of envy and death at the major turning points of biblical history until his own time. Moving from the catastrophic expulsion from Eden, Clement points to the story of Cain and Abel as a prime example of envy as historical catalyst. The word "envy," *phthonos* or *zēlos*, does not appear in the Septuagint version of the story; Cain's emotion is identified as sadness or distress (*lypē*), which is confirmed by his fallen countenance.[77] But for Clement, and indeed for almost all biblical interpreters after him, envy (*zēlos kai phthonos*) is the motive for the first murder and the source of violence in the world. God has honored Abel over Cain, so Cain destroys the good that pains him: Abel. The same envy drives the conflicts and betrayals in the stories of Jacob and Esau, Joseph and his brothers, Moses and Pharaoh, Aaron and Miriam against Moses, and David and Saul.[78] Envy's malign influence continued on "in quite recent times" with the martyrdoms of Peter and Paul and unnamed female martyrs, and finally in Clement's own community.[79] The emotion threatening to rend asunder his church, thus, is not some new thing; it lies at the root of all the ills that have faced humanity, and God's people, since Eden. Christians must therefore do everything to avoid envy: What passion could be worse? Other second-century sources, such as the Didache, 2 Clement, and Ignatius also identify envy as an emotion for the Christian to avoid, and indeed as something from which they can reasonably free themselves; Ignatius writes to the Romans that they have never felt envy, to their great honor.[80]

Opposition to envy is of course not distinctive for Christians. Greco-Roman and Jewish traditions saw *phthonos* and *zēlos* as uniquely destructive to community and individual.[81] But distinctive is Clement's identification of envy

Anger and Envy," StPatr 83 (2017): 331–32, 339–40, with further secondary bibliography; he does not discuss the Clementine source, focused as he is on later Byzantine literature, but the similarity is undeniable.

77. On envy's lack of "clear bodily symptoms" in an ancient context see Hinterberger, "Basil of Caesarea," 319. In contrast, Cyprian lists a number of physical manifestations of envy and jealousy, *Zel. liv.* 8, for which see below. Also see discussion in Andrew Crislip, "Emotions in Eden and After: Ancient Jewish and Christian Perspectives on Genesis 2–4," *JBRec* 6 (2019): 112.

78. 1 Clem. 4.7.

79. 1 Clem. 5. Curiously, Clement does not cite Mark 15:10 or its Matthean parallel.

80. Did. 3, 5; 2 Clem. 4; Ign. *Rom.* 3, 5, 7.

81. Ed Sanders, *Envy and Jealousy in Classical Athens: A Socio-Psychological Approach*

as catalyst for the arc of a sacred history which continues to influence his own time. Death was introduced into the world by *phthonos*, a bitter emotion that continued to affect humanity. Further distinctive is the early Christian attempt to place this emotion at the heart of his community's identity as Christians, and as *not others*, drawing on Wisdom's claim that "those who belong to [the devil's] party experience [envy]" (Wis 2:24 NETS). For Clement, envy defines what others are and what Christians should not be.

Clement's centering of envy as both a threat to the Christian community and a passion that connects his contemporaries with a line of heroes and villains back to the very origin of humanity would influence Christian moralists throughout late antiquity, whether directly or indirectly. Cyprian of Carthage (died 258) wrote the earliest surviving Christian treatise devoted to envy. Cyprian, like Clement, treats envy and jealousy as a pair (*invidia*, *zelus*, and also *livor*), which has its source in the devil's own emotions.[82] Cyprian follows Clement's historical genealogy closely, from Eden to the first murder, Esau and Jacob, David and Saul, and finally "the Jews" and Christ, reflecting Mark's identification of envy as motive for opposition to Jesus.[83] He does not trace the lineage to the persecution of Peter and Paul and then others in his own time, but much as Clement diagnoses envy as the cause of conflict within the church, the revolt of the young against the elders, Cyprian identifies envy as the source of complaints against bishops and priests, of heresies (*haereses*) and schisms (*schismata*).[84] The emotion most prominently linked with jealousy and envy is hatred (*odium*).[85]

Two other features of Cyprian's rather straightforward counsel on envy and jealousy are worth noting, as they recur in later sources. First, he notes that envy works in secret, hidden because the devil works his evil in secret and

(Oxford: Oxford University Press, 2014); Konstan and Rutter, *Envy, Spite and Jealousy*. Jewish concerns with envy are apparent in several of the Testaments of the Twelve Patriarchs (*OTP* 1:779).

82. 1 Clement is a likely source for Cyprian, so Michel Poirier, *Cyprien de Carthage: La jalousie et l'envie*, SC 519 (Paris: Cerf, 2008), 28, and for overviews of the treatise as a whole (13–17); see also Paul Blowers, "Envy's Narrative Scripts: Cyprian, Basil, and the Monastic Sages on the Anatomy and Cure of the Invidious Emotions," *Modern Theology* 25 (2009): 21–43; and Edwina Murphy, "Imitating the Devil: Cyprian on Jealousy and Envy," *Scrinium* 14 (2018): 75–91.

83. Cyprian, *Zelo liv.* 4–5; with discussion in Blowers, "Envy's Narrative Scripts," 29–30. Murphy ("Imitating the Devil," 89) notes that Cyprian's discussion of Jews is historical; there is no current conflict between Jews and Christians in his circle.

84. Cyprian, *Zelo liv.* 6.

85. Cyprian, *Zelo liv.* 3, 5–9.

because it is a vice that people tend to hide. Cyprian does not claim that this is due to the great shame of expressing envy (a typical claim) but that we hide it not because we do not take it seriously enough as the destructive passion that it is.[86] Although Cyprian does not discuss this, secrecy works in both directions, including the increase of secrecy by those fearing envy, to avoid attracting the "evil eye" (*baskania*) of rivals by hiding one's goods, including intangible goods like beauty, status, or happiness.[87] Second, Cyprian compares envy to disease and its absence to health.[88] As many note, envy by its very nature does not stay "in one form, or restrained within brief limits in a narrow boundary."[89] He employs very ancient metaphors: It is a "worm in the soul," "rust of the heart," "a plague-spot [*tabes*] of our thoughts."[90] Like Clement before him, Cyprian centers his counsel for the church in Carthage around the hidden feelings of envy and jealousy, and the hate that these passions engender. He further identifies envy as "the root of all evils" (not the love of money as Paul claims [1 Tim 6:10]), whose protean nature shifts into countless forms and conflicts.[91] From the first stirrings of the devil's envy toward humanity through the travails of the biblical patriarchs to the heresies and schisms of his own church, envy provides Cyprian with an emotional explanation for the ills of the world and the church. The narrative of salvation history also offers some hope for his church to counter this emotional plague.[92]

Later bishops and theologians found envy's place as the chief or root of all sin a compelling *topos* in their moral exhortation. This was not to exclude other emotions from the top rank, as even within a single text an author could describe more than one vice as the worst. Gregory of Nyssa, in this way, "on one occasion speaks of gluttony as the root of sin," but in his *Life of Moses* expands on envy (*phthonos*) as "the chief sin, the father of death, the first opening of sin, the root of wickedness, the beginning of grief, the mother of misfortunes, the ground of disobedience, the root of shame," after which he

86. Cyprian, *Zelo liv.* 1, 3; on the shame of envy, Protasi, *Philosophy of Envy*, 14; Schimmel, "Envy in Jewish Thought," 19.

87. Schoeck, *Envy*, 49, 51.

88. Also observed in the modern health sciences, Smith, Combs, and Thielke, "Envy and the Challenges to Good Health."

89. Cyprian, *Zelo liv.* 6 (*ANF*).

90. Cyprian, *Zelo liv.* 7 (*ANF*).

91. Cyprian, *Zelo liv.* 6 (*ANF*), discussed in Murphy, "Imitating the Devil," 90–91.

92. Cyprian, *Zelo liv.* 6 (*ANF*). I pass over Cyprian's emotional counsel here, which Paul Blowers describes as "straightforward and uncomplicated" ("Envy's Narrative Scripts," 31–32).

heads into the now familiar litany of biblical envy and the bodily metaphors of envy: sickness, bile, self-destruction, burning.[93] Athanasius also accepts envy's place as the root of sin in the world, as a telling contrast with the traditional Platonic concept of a god without envy.[94] Basil of Caesarea also connects the passion with the devil and describes it as the most dangerous of sins, again drawing on the Clementine history of envy.[95] While his short sermon *On Envy* "is didactically straightforward [and] theologically and philosophically unsophisticated," there are several motifs worth mentioning. First, Basil expands on the secrecy of envy, which is not due to the envious not thinking much of it (as in Cyprian), but because it so bad as to be unspeakable, which in turn is "the worst feature of this malady," turning this hate and grief and bitterness inward and consuming the envious from within.[96] Basil also distinctively compares the envious to animals or beasts, a motif that occurs throughout this short homily.[97] Basil further augments the old equation of envy with illness. Observing the good fortunes of others is "like so many blows and wounds piercing the envious man to his heart's core."[98] There is no disease (*nosos*) more deadly than envy.[99] This disease is especially pernicious since it is one that the sick most vehemently resist being treated for. While the Scriptures are filled with remedies for envy, the envious "does not call in a doctor for his malady and he is unable to discover a healing remedy."[100] Compared to his predecessors and Greek contemporaries, Basil elaborates on the medical metaphors for the affliction and treatment of this most bitter and secret disease, which complements his rhetorical interest in matters medical in his treatises and especially in his letters, and which he shares with his Coptic contemporary Shenoute, to whose sermons I now turn.[101]

93. Andrew Louth, "Envy as the Chief Sin," StPatr 15.1 (1984): 459, citing *De oratione dominica* 5 and *De vita Moysis* 2.256–263; Jean Daniélou, ed., *Grégoire de Nysse: La vie de Moïse*, 3rd ed., SC 1bis (Paris: Cerf, 2007).

94. Louth, "Envy as the Chief Sin," 459.

95. Basil, *Hom.* 11; Saint Basil, *Ascetical Works*, trans. M. Monica Wagner, CSC (New York: Fathers of the Church, 1950), 463–74 (PG 31.371–86); see discussion by Vasiliki Limberis, "The Eyes Infected by Evil: Basil of Caesarea's Homily, *On Envy*," *HTR* 84 (1991): 163–84.

96. *Hom.* 11.1 (Wagner, PG 31.373).

97. Hinterberger, "Basil of Caesarea," 336 (*Hom.* 11.1, 3, 5).

98. *Hom.* 11.1 (Wagner, PG 31.373).

99. *Hom.* 11.3 (PG 31.376).

100. *Hom.* 11.2 (Wagner, PG 31.373).

101. See the analysis by Hinterberger, "Basil of Caesarea," 324–25; Crislip, "Shenoute's Illness."

Envy and Asceticism

Given how central envy was in Christian thought about conflict in Paul's and Jesus's lives, and how woven into the arc of history in the struggle between the devil and God's people, one might hope that Christianity's political triumph might lead to an extirpation—or at least severe diminishment—of envy. As Eusebius of Caesarea hailed a new polity of joy inaugurated by Constantine's dream, perhaps the devil's envy would slink back into its hole or get stomped by the victorious church. Any such hopes would be severely disappointed.

The writings of Shenoute of Atripe offer rare insight into the experiences and practices of envy in ancient Christian life. Shenoute led a federation of monasteries in Upper Egypt for around eight decades (ca. 385–465). He counseled, disciplined, and preached to the possibly thousands of monks and nuns in the three monasteries, a larger and a smaller men's monastery and a women's monastery in the nearby village. His voluminous writings—rules, homilies, letters, and theological treatises—are fragmentarily preserved in manuscripts from his monastery library, where they were copied and read communally for centuries after his death, until the Coptic language he spoke and wrote in ceased to be used in the Middle Ages.[102] His writings give a very different picture of monastic life compared to the more familiar memories and hagiographical narratives in the *Sayings of the Desert Fathers* or the *Life of Antony*. He addresses all manner of interpersonal problems among his monks, launches fierce polemics against his theological opponents (usually as a partisan of Alexandrian orthodoxy), addresses the monks and laity (including visiting dignitaries) in his sermons, and quite famously involves himself in local political arguments, including violently attacking remnants of the old religious ways.[103]

102. Introductions can be found in Bentley Layton, *The Canons of Our Fathers: Monastic Rules of Shenoute* (Oxford: Oxford University Press, 2014); and David Brakke and Andrew Crislip, *Selected Discourses of Shenoute the Great: Community, Theology, and Social Conflict in Late Antique Egypt* (Cambridge: Cambridge University Press, 2015), 1–25; and Andrew Crislip, "The Red Monastery in Early Byzantine Egypt," in *The Red Monastery Church: Beauty and Asceticism in Upper Egypt*, ed. Elizabeth S. Bolman (New Haven: Yale University Press, 2016), 3–9.

103. The various aspects of his persona as archimandrite are covered in Brakke and Crislip, *Selected Discourses*; on conflicts over gender in his monasteries, see Rebecca Krawiec, *Shenoute and the Women of the White Monastery* (Oxford: Oxford University Press, 2003). On Shenoute in his local political and economic context, see Ariel G. López, *Shenoute and the Uses of Poverty: Rural Patronage, Religious Conflict, and Monasticism in Late Antique Egypt*, Transformation of the Classical Heritage 50 (Oakland: University of California Press, 2013).

While he carries the reputation of a harsh and unremitting ascetic leader, in his role as preacher and pastor Shenoute of Atripe developed a nuanced interest in the emotional experiences of his flock. Envy is a concern in a number of contexts in his writings, rules, short discourses, and homilies. Here I focus on several of his public discourses to monks and laity. In these discourses, Shenoute addresses varied facets of envy in his discussion of asceticism and ethics, especially the frequently thwarted desire to achieve (or at least approach) perfection and sanctity, concerns that his followers brought to him. This is part of a broader post-Constantinian reevaluation of the possibility or impossibility of living without sin in a Christian world and further the relative merits of ascetic and worldly lives. The agonistic character of ancient society did not disappear when the desired good switched from the love of honor to the pursuit of holiness and moral perfection. The questions that drove Augustine and Pelagius in the West were alive in Upper Egypt, here played out in the social lives of ordinary and religious supplicants who brought their concerns to the great abbot. In the cities, villages, and cloisters of Egypt, envy drove many of these problems, and monks and lay alike were consumed by competition, comparison, and resentment.

One might not expect envy and competition to be such a problem in a community devoted to poverty, obedience, celibacy, and uniformity in behavior. What is there to envy? Yet, as we have seen, envy thrives among people who are alike, in status, employment, vocation, and identity, and the higher a society values equality and equity, the more the emotions of envy and resentment tend to thrive.[104] In several *Discourses*, Shenoute speaks to the complexities of ascetic practice, success and failure, and competition and envy, both in his more familiar role as fiery ascetic preacher and in a more pastoral role, counseling monks, clergy, and visiting dignitaries in direct audience with the archimandrite. I focus on three discourses which address three constituencies of Shenoute, the lay aristocracy, his own monks, and the clergy of the Egyptian church at large. These are called by their opening lines according to the system in his own library, *I Answered*, *Truly When I Think*, and *I See Your Eagerness.*

I Answered relates a visit from the provincial military commander Caesarius, who would become a major patron for Shenoute's monastery.[105] Caesarius

104. E.g., explored from various disciplinary perspectives in Schoeck, *Envy*, 2–3, 62, 65, 160, 176, 178.

105. Crislip, "Red Monastery," 6, 8; Paul C. Dilley, "Inscribed Identities: Prosopography of the Red and White Monasteries in the Early Byzantine and Medieval Periods," in Bolman, *Red Monastery Church*, 217–18.

laments, according to Shenoute, that he and his distinguished entourage of dignitaries and city leaders want to do "the works of God," but their "weakness" (*tmntasthenēs*) prevents them. Shenoute praises their eagerness, Coptic *ourot*, which can convey something like gladness (*hilarotēs*) but which here and in the thematically similar sermon *I See Your Eagerness* has more a sense of "zeal," pointing to problems with the competitive and mimetic nature of the ascetic life and Christian practice going back to Paul. While Jesus commands, "Be perfect as your Father is perfect," our Father isn't always around, and certainly not visible, so we must emulate and compete with both our peers and the "model of goodness and justice," that is, the saints of Christian memory and the Bible. But Shenoute is aware of what counselors today call the abstinence violation effect. A risk of such competitive emulation is that in sensing the impossibility of attaining perfection in Christian life one might give up entirely.[106]

Shenoute counsels Caesarius on the requirements of asceticism incumbent on ordinary Christians, drawing on the parables of the sower, the vineyard, and the talents, among others, including one of his own.[107] We each should pray, fast, and remain continent according to our ability.[108] If we cannot bear our cross, then at least we can give to the poor. If we cannot pray without ceasing, then at least we can pray as we are able. Shenoute describes Caesarius as greatly comforted, who then collected soldiers around him and comforted them in turn. In offering this teaching, Shenoute presents himself as of little stature, humbled before the military commander and patron: "I myself collect grapes of gleaning and I toss them into the purse."[109] This short discourse shows how effective Shenoute could be in courting a powerful patron like Caesarius, drawing him into his own chain of spiritual patronage, while at the same time affecting the humility of holy poverty, a classic strategy for avoiding envy. For all Shenoute's high standards of ascetic morality, he publicly presents his church as for all Christians, so long as they try to the best of their ability.

In *Truly When I Think*, the focus shifts to the concerns of his monks, who read the stories of the very nonascetic patriarchs, who marry, have children, drink, and feast, along with the martyrs, whose glory and self-denying righteousness outstrips that of the strictly ascetic yet sinful monks. His monks seem to feel perplexity at this, with which Shenoute commiserates: "Truly,

106. Such a feeling of impotence further leads to envy. According to the political theorist Max Scheler, "resentment can 'never develop without the mediation of a specific feeling of impotence'" (Schoeck, *Envy*, 33).

107. Brakke and Crislip, *Selected Discourses*, 127–28.

108. Brakke and Crislip, *Selected Discourses*, 127.

109. Brakke and Crislip, *Selected Discourses*, 129.

when I think about the fathers of old, I become like one who has not known God. And is it any wonder?" This lament expresses a sort of disillusionment or confusion or hopelessness, maybe the temptation just to give up when comparing oneself to the fathers. They married, had children and grandchildren, and all manner of material wealth. And they received the blessings of God, who instructed them and nourished them, and sent his angels to guard them. And these patriarchs, who lived in wealth to great old age with loving families, also share in the posthumous rewards of martyrs.[110] It is not unfair to wonder, as Shenoute says, "How are these honors and these glories of this quality theirs?"[111] Shenoute's rhetoric voices the envy or indignation of his monks, passions as Aristotle defined them, pain felt at the excessive or inequitable honors or goods bestowed on another. The reason for the patriarchs' desert, Shenoute says, is their sinlessness. They achieved perfection, their worldly comforts notwithstanding, in their faith, love, and hospitality.[112]

But his monks, poor "wretches," they try so hard to achieve ascetic perfection, afflicting themselves with poverty, hunger, thirst, and hardships, uncomfortable clothes, no wine, no meat, their bodies desiccated in the desert.[113] But sadly, Shenoute says, "the manifold sins of the demonic enemy have not dried up within us," and when we reach out with our dried tongues to slake our thirst, it is not water or wine that sates us but another sin of the tongue, a primal, diabolical sin: slander (*katalalei*): "We whisper, we goad, we destroy the heart of others, we envy, we hate, we fight."[114] This short discourse, like *I Answered*, on the pains and dangers of comparison and the expectations of ascetic perfection, points to the prevalence of ancient worry about rivalry and envy (*phthonos*, Coptic *kōh*), especially showing its demonic influence in gossip and slander. Envy and the dangers of emulation in seeking perfection were as much a worry in the monastery and the church as in the village or the Greek polis.

A preface in one manuscript provides a plausible context for the lengthy sermon *I See Your Eagerness*, which elaborates on the rivalry and envy that can burn through a community intent on achieving ascetic perfection, or preventing others from achieving such honors. Shenoute here entertains a mixed audience of "very many clergy" of various ranks ("presbyters, deacons, and

110. Brakke and Crislip, *Selected Discourses*, 134.

111. Brakke and Crislip, *Selected Discourses*, 134.

112. Brakke and Crislip, *Selected Discourses*, 134–35.

113. Brakke and Crislip, *Selected Discourses*, 135.

114. Brakke and Crislip, *Selected Discourses*, 135.

other monastic fathers") and monks who had come from other monasteries, "making up a great crowd."[115] Also present would have been a greater or lesser number of monks from Shenoute's monastery, to attend to the archimandrite, hear his words, and (I presume) make a record of his sermon as he delivered it. As the preface sets the scene, this group of people had come to Shenoute for intercession and advice regarding some unsalutary happenings: disputes, grievances, and enmities among the clergy and monks over "evil matters," including thefts. But Shenoute delayed hearing their complaints for a day, and instead delivered his remarks to the crowd on a Saturday evening, "desiring that there might be calm."

The first eight (manuscript) pages of the sermon itself are lost, but when the text resumes we see Shenoute's interest in the behaviors of those who have been entrusted with high offices in the church, of which he includes himself: "We all take pride in God's high offices and holy places."[116] In a trope that emerges as a main theme in the sermon, pride (*šoušou*, probably Greek *hyperēphania*) comes before a fall; we don't know what will befall us when we are called to account before God. Shenoute deems it likely that "most of us" will be put to shame and grieved, to mourn and weep on that day, whatever our titles. Holding such offices is like being entrusted with goods (along the lines of the parable of the talents): One must be a faithful steward of what has been entrusted to him, or he will be punished.[117]

This sermon must have been confrontational to the assembled clergy and elder monks, especially given his opening words (which we find only in a list of incipits preserved in his monastery library): "I see your eagerness," *ourot*, which could speak to the crowd's good spirits, or more likely, their ambition or zeal for honor.[118] It is plausible, as the manuscript preface claims, that many left the monastery at once, though whether out of shame (as the preface says) or indignation is unknown. But still, Shenoute includes himself in the condemnation: We shame "the good among us who do good," but we do evil. "Oh, it is very clear that we are lovers of sin!"[119] Those who claim excellence, purity, and perfection are especially at risk of shame. Being part of the holy community and having rank and title have little predictive value of one's ascetic and moral perfection.

115. Brakke and Crislip, *Selected Discourses*, 91.
116. Brakke and Crislip, *Selected Discourses*, 91.
117. Brakke and Crislip, *Selected Discourses*, 92.
118. Since the beginning of the work is lost, it is hard to say.
119. Brakke and Crislip, *Selected Discourses*, 92, altered.

As in *Truly When I Think*, the patriarchs are useful moral exemplars for thinking about Christian asceticism. Noah "became righteous and without sin" while surrounded by utterly sinful people. Lot "became sinless" though living in sin city, and Daniel and his companions did not sin (and maintained an ascetic diet) though in the heart of godless Babylon. In contrast, the assembled clergy "dwell with the saints among us" and speak of God and his angels and the martyrs and Christ, yet "perform things that are abominable to God."[120] Shenoute describes a reverse of the Christian empire of joy proclaimed by Constantine and Eusebius: Christians surrounded by saints do nothing but sin in their demonic emotions. After a lacuna in the manuscript, Shenoute recalls Judas as a model for his audience, who had "an honorable title" (of apostle) and was surrounded by the holiest of saints and Christ himself, none of which did him any good.[121] It is difficult to know one's own perfection or failure. The clergy and monks in his audience, he says, are criticized for not knowing God or his law, but they just get angry as "[they] perform the works of godlessness."[122] We are to imagine the contrasting experience of the patriarchs, who were also attacked for their behaviors but stood firm and lived without sin in perfection.

As is common in his writings, Shenoute remains vague on the exact nature of the shortcomings of the clergy and monks who have come for his guidance, in part to resolve issues of thefts. According to his *Life*, Shenoute was believed to have the power of clairvoyance, to find lost or stolen items, a power that he shared with his predecessor Pachomius and others in the Egyptian monastic tradition.[123] At the close of the sermon Shenoute defends his real aim as not to reveal the location of hidden items but to reveal the location and nature of sins, hidden by the devil.[124] The very hiddenness of the sins, described in his usual language of pollution and defilement, gives a clue to the nature of his distinguished audience's failure to reach the perfection of the patriarchs. Their pollution is a sin that thrives in secrecy and sublimation: envy.

120. Brakke and Crislip, *Selected Discourses*, 92.

121. Brakke and Crislip, *Selected Discourses*, 93.

122. Brakke and Crislip, *Selected Discourses*, 93.

123. See Jennifer Wees, "False Prophets Are False Fathers: Clairvoyance in the Career of Shenoute of Atripe," in *L'Evangile selon Thomas et les textes de Nag Hammadi*, ed. Louis Painchaud and Paul-Hubert Poirier (Quebec: Presses de Université Laval, 2007), 635–52; Tudor Sala, "Dismantling Surveillance in Late Antique Corporate Monasticism," PhD dissertation, Yale University, 2011.

124. Brakke and Crislip, *Selected Discourses*, 103–4.

Eleven manuscript pages are lacking after Shenoute contrasts the perfection of the patriarchs with the failure of Judas. But when the text returns, he is in the midst of talking about the sin of Adam and Eve, in the wake of which we flee God's anger due to our sins, of abuse, adultery, coveting, stealing, lying, and the rest.[125] Is this what he is accusing the assembled presbyters and deacons of, violating marriage vows, stealing from the church? He puts a finer point on it, comparing the human being to a pilot bailing water that repeatedly splashes and drips into his boat. The boat is the soul, and the splashes and drips are thoughts (*meeue*).[126] Weaving together passages from the Psalms, Proverbs, and Micah, he traces such "inner thoughts" to "the fall," thoughts of fornication and drunkenness.[127] But the failures of his clerical and monastic audience are not really of sex and wine. Rather this biblical phraseology points to the actual "instruments of combat" among his complainants: envy (*kōh*) and all its related sins, hatred, slander, contempt, mockery, and everything like them.[128] This envy lurks in the shadows, a conceit familiar in ancient discussion of the vice, so horrible that it tends to be sublimated into other accusations against the envied, much like the heathens' accusations against the patriarchs earlier in the sermon. But our "envy and hatred" will be revealed on the day of judgment.[129]

As the envious shrink from admitting the true nature of their inner thoughts, Shenoute too addresses envy by other names, especially theft (*jioue*) and fornication (*porneia*), of which Shenoute speaks throughout his disciplinary writings. One would think that these monks sworn to celibacy and poverty were a particularly dissolute group. Shenoute's sermons in his eighth book of *Canons*, however, make clear that fornication often—perhaps normally—refers to the activities constellated around the ancient emotion of envy: gossip, loose talk, backbiting, and malicious criticism. He frames his condemnation of theft as well in terms of envy and gossip and does not normally describe a theft in detail or identify anything stolen. So, he has said "many times . . . in anger, 'Especially cursed are male and female thieves, people—men and women—because of whose disturbances and murmuring and slander and gossip and excessive talk and illicit deeds we fear to bring others

125. Brakke and Crislip, *Selected Discourses*, 94.
126. Brakke and Crislip, *Selected Discourses*, 95.
127. Brakke and Crislip, *Selected Discourses*, 95.
128. Brakke and Crislip, *Selected Discourses*, 95.
129. Brakke and Crislip, *Selected Discourses*, 95.

into these places.'"[130] Theft serves as shorthand for all manner of slander, gossip, hatred, and envy.[131]

Shenoute further elides the emotional problem of envy with fornication, another favorite topic of the archimandrite's sermons.[132] In his *Canon* 8 (the only more or less complete volume of his works), he again clarifies that when he speaks of fornication he means envy and its siblings, not sexual misbehavior. In one passage he waxes prophetic, calling on his congregants in bitter irony to rejoice and behave like Babylonians.

> For if you had not been satiated with things of light, then the things of darkness and bitter things would not have become sweet for you. . . . So clap your hands and rejoice over yourselves (cf. Ps 46:2), you foolish men and women. Stamp your feet like sons and daughters of Chaldean Babylon. Craft and build for yourselves before the doors of your houses and your workshops, before the doors of your congregations, places of slandering and fault finding and murmuring and disturbance and loose talk: this other form of fornication—as those built for themselves places of fornication in every street, until they were far from God, angering him with their idols. You read and you hear: "Let us not become prideful, provoking one another, envying one another" (Gal 5:26). You are prideful. And you also provoke [envy] and you envy. As for those who are themselves envied at any time in these congregations, who will be left unenvied?

Here Shenoute cleverly brings together envy and its manifestations, the feeling of bitterness, and the accusation of fornication, comparing the famous sexual perversity of ancient Babylon with "this other form of fornication," envy, along with all the self-serving complaints that, like an unstoppable contagion, will spread until everyone has been infected and affected. He evokes the model of Daniel, who remained sinless and ascetically pure amid the temptations of Babylon, while clergy and monks—though satiated with God's light—create their own Babylon in God's house.

A few pages later Shenoute returns to the types of fornication, of the flesh

130. *Many Times I Have Said*, XO 243; Anne Boud'hors, ed., *Le Canon 8 de Chénouté*, 2 vols., Bibliothèque d'études coptes 21.1–2. (Cairo: IFAO, 2013).

131. *Many Times I Have Said*, XO 262, 266–258bis [*sic*].

132. Caroline T. Schroeder, "Prophecy and *Porneia* in Shenoute's Letters: The Rhetoric of Sexuality in a Late Antique Egyptian Monastery," *JNES* 65 (2006): 81–97; and Caroline T. Schroeder, *Monastic Bodies: Discipline and Salvation in Shenoute of Atripe* (Philadelphia: University of Pennsylvania Press, 2007), 24–53.

and of the soul. "Fornication of the flesh is one type of fornication. But as for the fornications of the heart and profligacies, who will be able to proclaim them (all)! The matters of theft, lying, false oaths, envy, hate, conflict, murmuring, scorn, backbiting, disturbances, enmity, hardheartedness. . . . If those who fornicate in the flesh are cursed, those who fornicate in the soul are more cursed."[133] This does not mean that monks did not engage in illicit sexual behavior in the monastery any more than it means that they did not steal. But Shenoute's labeling of envy, hate, gossip, and the rest of these emotionally rivalrous behaviors as *porneia*, and in fact forms of fornication even worse than the polymorphous perversities of the Babylonians, is an important reminder that, for all the scholarly emphasis on sexuality in early Christianity, when Shenoute condemns fornication, or theft, he likely speaks of a very different constellation of passions and misbehaviors, all orbiting envy and its siblings.

This clarifies Shenoute's rhetoric about ascetic failings and clerical pride in *I See Your Eagerness*. He brings in another motif from his *Canon* 8, of the bitter seeming sweet, a trope from his favorite prophets. He clarifies: "I'm talking about the pollutions, the defilements, the fornications of various types," to be found in "the envies, the hatreds, the slanders, the acts of greed, the favoritism in judgment," which have filled the ostensibly holy places.[134]

Envy suffuses the community through criticism, though it takes discernment to distinguish righteous indignation from envy, that of "the saints in God's house" and that of Judas. The saints "find fault" not out of envy but in grief (*etmokh nhēt*), unlike "those whose hearts are full of evil and hostility toward one another for no reason."[135] But having an office, a title, vestments, or a gift (*charis*) does little to spare the soul from the evil spirit, as they all did Judas no good, now in hell for his "theft and betrayal," by which Shenoute means the hostility and criticism of *phthonos*. As discussed above, the hostility of Judas's envy came to a head over a meal, which Shenoute alludes to and sees reenacted in his own community: "We sit at a single table. I eat bread with you; your hand is in the bowl with me. We live together in the holy places."[136] For Shenoute, the envy-abating power of meals included sharing ordinary food and the Eucharist, both major disciplinary interests of his and both sources of conflict in his overlapping communities of monastery and church.[137] Such

133. *Many Times Have I Said*, XO 268–269.
134. Brakke and Crislip, *Selected Discourses*, 97.
135. Brakke and Crislip, *Selected Discourses*, 96.
136. Brakke and Crislip, *Selected Discourses*, 96.
137. Bentley Layton, "Social Structure and Food Consumption in an Early Christian

communal meals, sacred and ordinary, provided ample opportunity for interpersonal conflicts to erupt in criticism, blame, and resentment.[138]

The danger of envy and slander to perfection and fulfillment of the Christian life may also be seen in his earlier discussion of the pride of authorities and office holders.[139] Reflecting on Galatians 5:26, Shenoute connects pride with envy, as the prideful both envy others and provoke others' envy. Such leaders are all peace and love outwardly but inwardly full of hostilities.[140] We ask after each other's health, but it is "hypocritically with a false love," that is, "a love compounded with envy and hate," an observation especially poignant for Shenoute, given his chronic and contentious ill health.[141] Shenoute points to the dark delight in others' suffering (deeply submerged in the psyche) and the power of the evil eye to bring misfortune on one's peers and rivals. Best not to ask about another's health at all, Shenoute says. While the unclean in the church are prone to all sorts of sin, favoritism and hypocrisy, for example, their motivation lies in an underlying envy: Shenoute compares them to "someone who would stop up a spring of water," a paradigmatic example of envy, ancient and modern, to spitefully destroy the good of another, even a shared good, just to ensure that no one else undeservedly benefits.[142]

Shenoute diagnoses the conflict between the more senior and junior clergy as the inheritance of humanity's primal envy. In a drive for honor and avoidance of shame we are pained (*mkah nhēt*; cf. *lypē*) when others do good or speak the words of God, "as if to say there is no other person like us. It is on account of this that all envy exists."[143] Shenoute then draws on 1 Clement, which traces a lineage of envy from Cain and Abel, Isaac, Joseph, Paul, and Roman Christians. For Shenoute, the marvel is that envy has not abated in a Christian empire: "But it is rather all the more a marvel that we are envious of one another, and we cause one another to suffer, and we hand one another over to death, even though we have the one and the same God!"[144]

Shenoute ties backbiting and envy to ascetic comparison and competition in a number of ways. The models for perfection are certainly before the eyes

Monastery: The Evidence of Shenoute's *Canons* and the White Monastery Federation A.D. 385–465," *Le Muséon* 115 (2002): 25–55; Schroeder, *Monastic Bodies*.

138. Barton, *Sorrows of the Ancient Romans*, 109.

139. Brakke and Crislip, *Selected Discourses*, 91–92.

140. Brakke and Crislip, *Selected Discourses*, 95.

141. Brakke and Crislip, *Selected Discourses*, 95; Crislip, "Shenoute's Illness."

142. Brakke and Crislip, *Selected Discourses*, 97.

143. Brakke and Crislip, *Selected Discourses*, 98.

144. Brakke and Crislip, *Selected Discourses*, 99.

of the monks and the clergy in the models of the patriarchs and prophets, whose sinlessness in the midst of pollution should be understood as achievable goals for the Christian. They would have been before their eyes literally, if they could see the dramatic paintings covering the walls and domes of his churches, now restored in the church of the smaller men's monastery in his confederation.[145] The stumbling block for this perfection is envy, which entered the world through Satan and can be traced through sacred history through the martyrs.[146] Through envy, even the most august of clerics and ascetics undercut the good deeds and words of others, maliciously criticizing the holy, praising the bad, stopping up wells so that no one can drink. The presbyters, deacons, and senior monks in the audience think of themselves as patriarchs, but they are really just so many latter-day Judases. But as in his short discourse to Caesarius, an absolute perfection is not required. Rather, whatever your vow, be sure to keep it.[147] That way the heathen will have no reason for malicious talk, gossip, and resentment of their own against Christian hypocrisy.

Conclusion

Shenoute's disappointment is palpable that even in a Christian empire, living among the ostensibly pious and ascetic, envy had not gone the way of the old gods but still spread through church, monastery, and village like mange through a flock. While an emotion like anger could seem to an ancient like some sort of madness or *mania*, envy was demonic, a connection that predated the rise of Christianity in Jewish and Greek traditions alike. More than any of the emotions in this book, Christians saw envy as primal, the basic cause of evil and death in the world as well as a primary driver of conflict in society, from the village to the city, from the imperial court to the monastery. Very early in the Christian literary tradition, authors identified envy as a driver of conflict, including among Paul's joyful community in Philippi, and even the arrest and crucifixion of Jesus. And while this has not been a major scholarly interest in early Christianity, the early Christians themselves were deadly serious about the continuing presence of envy in their communities and the deadly threat it posed.

145. Fully documented in Bolman, *Red Monastery Church.*

146. The beginning of Shenoute's exegesis of Gen 2–3 is lost; it is possible that he discusses Satan's envy there, a concept well-known from Wis 2:24.

147. Brakke and Crislip, *Selected Discourses*, 100.

Envy provides a valuable case study in early Christian emotions, given how different the general assumptions about the emotion were in the ancient world compared to its more harmless and acquisitive connotations today, for the few who actually give envy any thought at all. Early Christian reflections on envy can, perhaps, help to excavate some emotional practices in the contemporary world that are kept hidden, or tend to be associated with other developments in technology and global capitalism. Comparison and competition, resentment and spite, slander, whispering, malicious speech, and ostracism—they are quite current and harmful features of our society as well, not to mention the sort of spoiling, nihilistic drive to stop up the springs, as Shenoute puts it. Ancient envy differs from modern emotional concepts but may still have much to teach us about our own complex and often unexamined emotional lives.

Conclusion
(and a Few Notes on Love)

I began this book reflecting on the place of love in my churchgoing youth and love's centrality for Christian life and identity in the first generations of Christianity, which still holds in the modern world. Love as a distinctively Christian emotion, more than any other, has received sustained attention since the time of the early Church, and thinking about love certainly has dominated Christian theology and ethics in the twentieth and twenty-first centuries.[1] Love, as emotion and practice, still defines the perception of Christianity among Christians and non-Christians alike. Surely from week to week in a typical Christian church, it is love among all feelings that will appear most frequently in sermons and hymns. Critics of Christian ethics and politics will also focus on love as the site of alleged hypocrisy among the faithful, who fail to show the love to others that Jesus commands, a command which now often resolves to "love everyone, no matter what," or simply to "be kind." And Christian influence on society at large may be felt in conceptions of love, framed ethically, artistically, and institutionally. Among the more iconic images of postwar American art is Robert Indiana's instantly recognizable "LOVE" sculpture, reproduced in countless iterations around the world, carrying a distinctly Christian and Johannine emotionality into the spaces of multicultural progressivism (and corporate marketing). Countless service institutions worldwide call themselves "Caritas." It would give a more powerfully affective intensity were they simply to be called "Love." And who could forget the ethical axiom of vacation

1. Among the most influential treatments are Anders Nygren, *Agape and Eros*, trans. Philip S. Watson (Philadelphia: Westminster, 1953); and C. S. Lewis, *The Four Loves* (New York: Harcourt Brace Jovanovich, 1960).

homes everywhere, to live, laugh, love. As the old garage rock hit says, love is all around.

Love's ubiquity and shape-shifting makes it both an irresistibly desirous topic of study and a uniquely unwieldy emotion to cover in the form I have undertaken in this book, as I have traced some of the major shifts in emotional thinking and practice over some centuries in relatively short order. As my thinking in this book developed, through reading and writing, my hopes faltered of offering an overview of attitudes toward love among early Christians in a reasonably sized chapter. If God is indeed love, then I came to empathize with the aeon Sophia's desire to truly know the Father, as my own ambition to maintain some grasp on love turned to distress, fear, consternation, and ignorance. This mix of ancient feelings—which had always seemed to me a curious set—conveys well what it is like to desire to fully know something that is beyond one's finite grasp. The Valentinian Ptolemy had some psychological insight here, and I've come to appreciate why bishop Irenaeus felt so intent on detecting and overthrowing his influence in Christian life.

Psychologists and ethicists reflect a similar dynamic in trying to figure out just what love is, sometimes abandoning or even denying its relevance. Compared to the other emotions covered in this volume, emotion scientists have focused less on love, and the efforts of the few who have taken it on "have not germinated a thriving study of love within affective sciences," for some of the reasons gestured toward above. "For emotion scientists, who by definition favor the study of momentary phenomena, love may well seem too large, too all-encompassing, if not too pop culture."[2] Love comprises a number of intersecting concepts and practices. When we speak of love it often connotes intense desire, especially sexual but also "the powerful *bonds* people hold with a select few and the *intimacy* that grows between them, [and] the *commitments* to loyalty and faithfulness." The same profession of love (e.g., I love you, I love my country, I love Buckeye football) "can point to any or all of the above."[3] Love can also function as an emotive par excellence, testing the accuracy of an emotional concept, bringing about the state by its very utterance, even creating a new world, as many who have stumbled through a first "I love you" can attest. One's world is fundamentally changed by those three syllables, and there is no going back.

2. Barbara L. Fredrickson, "Love: Positivity Resonance as a Fresh, Evidence-Based Perspective on an Age-Old Topic," in *Handbook of Emotions*, ed. Lisa Feldman Barrett, Michael Lewis, and Jeannette M. Haviland-Jones, 4th ed. (New York: Guilford, 2016), 847.

3. Frederickson, "Love," 847.

In fact, unlike the other emotions covered here, specialists in psychology and beyond are still divided on whether love should count as an emotion at all or whether "love is not actually a single emotional state."[4] A recent philosophical introduction to love claims flatly, "Contrary to what is often assumed, love is not an emotion," while another leader in the philosophy of emotion declares that "love is an emotion, nothing else."[5] Even those who accept love as an emotion place its polymorphous complexity at the center of analysis, to taxonomize it. Love, for example, is either "passionate" or "companionate," feelings with different evolutionary origins and qualia (what it's like to feel it). In one perspective, passionate love describes an experience, an emotion per se, while companionate love characterizes a relationship, the bonds between individuals and community.[6] Both of these aspects of love help to account for its centrality for early Christians in thinking about how it felt to be a Christian and what it meant to be a church and to claim a relationship with God.

While I have not addressed love systematically, it has made itself felt in various parts of the book. Joy, as ancients describe it, overlaps experientially with love, both connected in an emotional sequence. Christians speak of love and joy as linked, as in the *Gospel of Truth*, to take just one example.[7] As a phenomenon, that is, the feelings of joy, the affective responses of pleasure, intensity, elation, and transcendence just as easily describe emotional feelings of love, not to mention bodily acts of love.[8] Love flows alongside sadness, whether in Paul's Corinthian letters or in the reflections of weepy Augustine, who more than anyone came to shape a distinctive understanding of love for the western Christian tradition.[9] Love, passionate and companionate, exists in duality with loss: "The more we become attached to [things we love], and the more we invest in them, the greater our sense of loss will be when they

4. Frederickson, "Love," 848.

5. Ronald de Sousa, *Love: A Very Short Introduction* (Oxford: Oxford University Press, 2015), 3; Robert C. Solomon, *Love: Emotion, Myth, and Metaphor* (Garden City, NY: Doubleday, 1981), 86.

6. Elaine Hatfield and Richard Rapson, "Love and Attachment Processes," in *Handbook of Emotions*, ed. Michael Lewis and Jeannette M. Haviland (New York: Guilford, 1993), 595–604.

7. Also, for Paul see David E. Fredrickson, *Eros and the Christ: Longing and Envy in Paul's Christology* (Minneapolis: Fortress, 2013), 26.

8. Frederickson, "Love," 849.

9. Augustine of Hippo, *Late Have I Loved Thee: Selected Writings of Saint Augustine on Love*, ed. John F. Thornton and Susan B. Varenne, Vintage Spiritual Classics (New York: Vintage, 2006). His selected writings on love run 409 pages.

are gone."[10] An old psychoanalytic theory suggests that we cry at a wedding not because we are happy, but because we know, deep down, that the happy couple's love will end, in the pain and grief of death (or divorce). But through the grief to which we are fated, the feelings of love like no other emotion can transcend death, a love that can bring joy or further pain.[11] Love further is an antidote to disgust, if not so much as a feeling than an acknowledgment of a bond that transcends a sense of self-preservation. And as psychologists trace the origin of love as an emotion to the attachment process between infant and mother, felt as exultation, union, security, transcendence, and well-being, love—as feeling and relationship—is implicated as a target of the primordial emotion of envy, the devil's desire to ruin the bond between humanity and God.[12] The presence of love, or in the case of anger its threatening lack, runs through early Christian emotional discourse as a whole.

Several aspects of love touch on the themes that recur throughout the early Christian approaches to defining, experiencing, and managing emotions. As I have discussed, some early Christ followers, John and Paul most explicitly, conceived of love as "the binding force of a brotherhood of believers in Christ . . . the practice, attitude and art of being together as members of one 'body of the Spirit.'"[13] It is the sine qua non of being a Christian. Without it, there is no point; without it, there is death.[14] Love makes Christians who they are as individuals and members of a corporate body, a feeling by which they know one another and will be known by outsiders, the most fundamental component of a Christian identity. Such Christian teachings on love have become so commonplace in theology, worship, and Christianese ways of speaking it is easy to overlook how radical this must have sounded in the first generations of Christianity. It is not too much to say that "the value of love had never before been so extravagant."[15]

Ancient Greeks and Romans devoted symposium speeches and countless lines of poetry to exploring the nature of love. Christians differed in their ap-

10. Tom Inglis, *Love* (London: Routledge, 2013), 91.

11. Inglis, *Love*, 91–92; and the classic analysis of Sigmund Freud, "Mourning and Melancholia," in *Standard Edition of the Complete Works of Sigmund Freud*, vol. 14, ed. and trans. James Strachey (London: Hogarth, 1957 [1917]).

12. "Envy, the antipode of longing [a type of love], . . . was universally recognized as the chief vice of the gods and goddesses of death" (Frederickson, *Eros and the Christ*, 96). For non-Freudian discussion of the mother-infant attachment process see Hatfield and Rapson, "Love and Attachment," 2nd ed., 659–60.

13. Simon May, *Love: A History* (New Haven: Yale University Press, 2011), 86.

14. May, *Love*, 87; 1 Cor 13:3; 1 John 3:14.

15. May, *Love*, 86.

proach by their attention to the power of words, rejecting old concepts and adopting new ones as part of their conversion of emotions. The distinctive Christian vocabulary of love has been a persistent interest among theologians, most notably Anders Nygren, whose *Agape and Eros* entered the Anglophone world in the 1930s and would influence Christian love-speak well beyond seminaries and pulpits.[16] I remember in one of my first weeks at college, some of the resident assistants in my dorm organized a session on "the three kinds of love" (RA's at my state school were overwhelmingly evangelical in several senses). They had collage posters depicting what I would come to know as Nygren's typology of *erōs*, *philia*, and *agapē*. I remember thinking, who would want to learn about that?

Nygren's influence goes far beyond Protestant Bible clubs. The psychoanalyst Julia Kristeva, influential among affect theorists and biblical scholars alike, takes Nygren's typology of Christian love as a reliable starting point for her reflections on a biblical psychology of love, which of course goes in very different directions.[17] Nygren understands *agapē* as a distinctive and new feeling, "a higher kind of love" (than mere *erōs*), which "loves—and *creates value* in its object," a love which descends from God toward a humanity that is otherwise unlovable in our utter depravity.[18] Sadly, for all its influence, and a reason why the history of early Christian love needs rethinking (and is beyond the scope of this book), Nygren's theology of Christian *agapē* is fundamentally unsound on every level, methodology, philology, and theology.[19] His conception of *agapē* would be quite unfamiliar to early Christian theologians, as it quite obviously assumes a priori the truth of Lutheran theology.[20] One Norwegian critic puts it with ironic understatement: "One might ask, if we do not buy [Nygren's] intuition-methodology, from where could Nygren have got his fundamental motif [of *agapē*]? It is probably not an unreasonable guess that he found it in some of the basic ideas of the Lutheran reformation, the *sola fide* and the *sola gratia*."[21] Such an approach to love is correct, however, in identifying the lan-

16. Summarized by Nancy M. Martin and Joseph Runzo, "Love," in *The Oxford Handbook of Religion and Emotion*, ed. John Corrigan (Oxford: Oxford University Press, 2008), 317–18.

17. Julia Kristeva, *Tales of Love*, trans. Leon S. Roudiez (New York: Columbia University Press, 1987), 139.

18. Martin and Ruzno, "Love," 317; second quote from Nygren, *Agape and Eros*, 210.

19. Torstein Theodor Tollefsen, "Eros and Agape—a Critique of Anders Nygren," in *Love - Ancient Perspectives*, ed. Kari Grødum et al. (Oslo: Cappelen Damm Akademisk, 2021), 17–29. Also see Fredrickson, *Eros and the Christ*, 6.

20. Tollefsen, "Eros and Agape," 25.

21. Tollefsen, "Eros and Agape," 25. See also Werner G. Jeanrond, *A Theology of Love* (London: Continuum, 2010), 27–30.

guage of love and the conceptual transformation of love as sites of important historical change in early Christianity.

Love was also a form of practice, as were other emotional complexes for early Christians. These practices played out in the cognition and management of emotions, feelings, and thoughts, and also formed components of ritual acts and the embodied interactions of Christians in communal settings. Christians embraced a praxis of *agapē* even more literally than in other emotions. By the end of the first Christian century, they called one of their principal rituals, very simply, "love." This love (normally translated "love feast") first appears in one of the passages discussed above, in Jude's slander of other Christians as disgusting "blemishes on your loves (*agapais*)" (Jude 12).[22] Christians further distinguished themselves ritually by insisting on kissing one another—and thus incurring accusations of disgusting sexual impropriety from outsiders—with a holy kiss (*philēma hagion*) or a kiss of love (*philēma agapēs*).[23] The praxis of love can make the study of this emotion especially complex, as scholars are quite willing to expand beyond the usual semantics of love (*agapē* et al.) into compassion (*splanchna*, *compassio* et al.) or pity (*eleos*).[24] There are good reasons for this, but it casts the net for love language and love practice quite a bit wider than I have tried to do in this volume. Other scholars have further expanded the scope of ancient Christian love by unearthing hidden feelings of *erōs*, which continued to shape the Christian self as an emotional and passionate counterpoint to *agapē*.[25]

Last, Christians could see love as a power that held the world together, structured reality, and manifested itself as a very felt process of embodiment. I have noted several times the claim from cognitive scientists of the psychological construction perspective that we do not just perceive but create the world we live in by our emotions. Christians took this further, sometimes understanding the cosmos itself as created and structured by emotions, as Ptolemy traced the created order to the aeon Sophia's painful passions, Origen traced it to a satiety or disgust among the primordial minds, or others speculated on the anger or envy that caused this material creation and structured it

22. Everett Ferguson, "Agape Meal," *ABD* 1:90–91.

23. William Klassen, "Kiss (NT)," *ABD* 4:89–92.

24. E.g., F. Scott Spencer, *Passions of the Christ: The Emotional Life of Jesus in the Gospels* (Grand Rapids: Baker Academic, 2021), 171–228; Susan Wessel, *On Compassion, Healing, Suffering, and the Purpose of the Emotional Life*, Reading Augustine (New York: Bloomsbury Academic, 2020); Susan Wessel, *Passion and Compassion in Early Christianity* (Cambridge: Cambridge University Press, 2016).

25. Burrus, *Sex Lives of Saints.*

from the stars down to the feelings of ordinary humans. Christians could see love also in the very nature of the universe. Paul and John would "establish love as the fundamental principle of the moral universe."[26] And not just the moral universe. Christians were not alone in "[wondering] whether love might actually explain the nature of the entire universe. Might it be, they wondered in amazement, that what holds the cosmos together is the same force that binds lover to beloved and ties friends fast?"[27] To take love as a cosmic force of attraction transforms what it means to say that God is love or that God sent his son into the world out of love, from a theological postulate to a law of physics. And to take seriously the physical experience of love, which was a physiological process both pleasurable and painful, even unto death, further reframes what it means to share in the passions of Christ and the emotions of the community.[28]

Love, thus, like the other emotional constellations covered in this book, has a history. It entails an experience very different from modern expectations and conventions but familiar enough to be intelligible. Here, even more than in the previous chapters, I have offered but an introduction (here quite a sketchy one) to some of the persistent themes and problems in the study of early Christian emotions. In the book as a whole, I have left out far more than I could include. My hope is that by offering such a survey of emotions over the first four Christian centuries, I might invite others to engage with the various trajectories of emotions history and the current psychology of emotion to continue a dialogue about the experience and management of emotion across times, geography, and genre, crossing boundaries of Bible and patristics, Christian and pagan, Greek, Latin, and beyond, to work toward a collaborative and comprehensive history of the conversion of emotions that Christianity wrought in the ancient world and ancient self.

26. May, *Love*, 85.

27. Frederickson, *Eros and the Christ*, 6, whose masterful rereading of longing (*pothos*) in Paul I follow.

28. See, for example, the important discussion in Frederickson, *Eros and the Christ*, 23–26, 35, 37–39, 46.

Acknowledgments

The ideas explored in this book coalesced over a decade, and I owe a debt to many others for the support and dialogue afforded to me to develop them.

Virginia Commonwealth University, my institutional home, has provided generous support for my research, including a Presidential Research Initiative Program grant and research support through the Blake Chair in the History of Christianity, which I have held since 2008.

I had the opportunity to research and teach at the University of Helsinki in 2018–2019 through the Fulbright Scholar Program and Fulbright Finland, along with research leave from VCU. The Faculty of Theology, with special support from Ismo Dunderberg, provided a rich environment for working on emotion in early Christianity, and I presented early versions of several portions of this book at symposia that year. During that year, Stephen Barton of the University of Durham reached out to me with encouragement and offprints, which inspired me to engage more directly with first-century Christian sources than I have in my previous publications.

I have presented many of the ideas in this book at conferences over the years, at the Society of Biblical Literature Annual and International Meetings, at the North American Patristics Society, the Virginia Early Christian Studies Seminar, and the International Conference on Patristics at Oxford, and I am grateful for the spirited critique I have received through these events.

Portions of chapters 1 and 6 were published in earlier versions, and I thank Lockwood Press and Peeters Press for permissions to rework that material for this project.

"Disgust in Early Christianity: The New Testament and Its Early Reception." *Biblica* 102 (2021): 593–617. Used by permission of Peeters Press.

"Emotion Words in Coptic: Reflections on the Evidence from Shenoute the Great." *Journal of the Canadian Society for Coptic Studies* 10 (2018): 45–57. Used by permission of Lockwood Press.

I further thank Twin Oaks Indexing for preparing the indexes.

The editorial process at Eerdmans has been a great pleasure, and I am grateful to Trevor Thompson and Jenny Hoffman (on the acquisitions and production sides) and their teams for their professionalism and scholarly care.

Finally, I am eternally grateful for the love, forbearance, and joy from my family—my wife, Heather, and my daughters, Grace and Renna—who remind me how fortunate, even happy, I am to be able to do this, and who help me keep it all in perspective.

Works Cited

Achtemeier, Paul J. "The First Letter of Peter." Pages 2060–61 in *Harper Collins Study Bible*. San Francisco: HarperSanFrancisco, 2006.

Ahmed, Sarah. *The Cultural Politics of Emotion*. 2nd ed. Edinburgh: Edinburgh University Press, 2014.

———. *The Promise of Happiness*. Durham, NC: Duke University Press, 2010.

Alicke, Mark D., and Ethan Zell. "Social Comparison and Envy." Pages 73–93 in *Envy: Theory and Research*. Edited by Richard H. Smith. Oxford: Oxford University Press, 2008.

Ambrose of Milan. *Hexameron, Paradise, and Cain and Abel*. Translated by John J. Savage. FC 42. New York: Fathers of the Church, 1961.

Anderson, Robert E. "Envy and Jealousy." *American Journal of Psychotherapy* 56 (2002): 455–79.

Apostolic Fathers. Edited and translated by Bart Ehrman. 2 vols. LCL. Cambridge, MA: Harvard University Press, 2003.

Aristotle. *On Rhetoric*. Translated by George A. Kennedy. New York: Oxford University Press, 1991.

Arockiam, Michaelsami. *The Concept of Joy in the Johannine Literature*. Delhi: ISPCK, 2002.

Attridge, Harold W. "An 'Emotional' Jesus and Stoic Tradition." Pages 77–92 in *Stoicism in Early Christianity*. Edited by Tuomas Rasimus, Troels Engberg Pedersen, and Ismo Dunderberg. Grand Rapids: Baker Academic, 2010.

Attridge, Harold W., ed. *Nag Hammadi Codex I (The Jung Codex)*. NHS 22. Leiden: Brill, 1985.

Augustine of Hippo. *De civitate Dei: Books XIII and XIV*. Edited and translated by P. G. Walsh. Liverpool: Liverpool Classical Texts, 2017.

———. *Late Have I Loved Thee: Selected Writings of Saint Augustine on Love*. Edited by John F. Thornton and Susan B. Varenne. Vintage Spiritual Classics. New York: Vintage, 2006.

Baltussen, Han. "Labelling Pain: Early Greek Concepts from Homer to the Hellenistic Era." Pages 12–43 in *Pain Narratives in Greco-Roman Writings: Studies in the Representation of Physical and Mental Suffering*. Edited by Jaqueline R. Clark, Daniel King, and Han Baltussen. Studies in Ancient Medicine 58. Leiden: Brill, 2023.

Barbalet, Jack. "Weeping and Transformations of Self." *Journal for the Theory of Social Behavior* 35 (2005): 125–41.

Barclay, John M. G. *Pauline Churches and Diaspora Jews*. WUNT 275. Tübingen: Mohr Siebeck, 2011.

Barnes, Timothy. *Constantine: Dynasty, Religion and Power in the Later Roman Empire*. Chichester: Wiley-Blackwell, 2014.

Barr-Zisowitz, Carol. "'Sadness': Is There Such a Thing?" Pages 612–18 in *Handbook of Emotions*. 2nd ed. Edited by Michael Lewis and Jeannette M. Haviland-Jones. New York: Guilford, 2000.

Barrett, Lisa Feldman. "Are Emotions Natural Kinds?" *Perspectives on Psychological Science* 1 (2006): 28–58.

———. "The Conceptual Act Theory: A Precis." *Emotion Review* 6 (2014): 292–97.

———. "Emotions Are Real." *Emotions* 12 (2012): 413–29.

———. *How Emotions Are Made: The Secret Life of the Brain*. Boston: Houghton Mifflin Harcourt, 2017.

———. "Psychological Construction: The Darwinian Approach to the Science of Emotion." *Emotion Review* 5 (2013): 379–89.

———. "The Theory of Constructed Emotion: An Active Inference Account of Interoception and Categorization." *Social Cognitive and Affective Neuroscience* 12 (2017): 1–23.

———. "Was Darwin Wrong About Emotional Expressions?" *Current Directions in Psychological Science* 20 (2011): 400–406.

Barrett, Lisa Feldman, Michael Lewis, and Jeannette M. Haviland-Jones, eds. *Handbook of Emotions*. 4th ed. New York: Guilford, 2016.

Barrett, Lisa Feldman, and James A. Russell. "An Introduction to Psychological Construction." Pages 1–17 in *The Psychological Construction of Emotion*. Edited by Lisa Feldman Barrett and James A. Russell. New York: Guilford, 2014.

Barrett, Lisa Feldman, Kristen A. Lindquist, Eliza Bliss-Moreau, Seth Duncan, Maria Gendron, Jennifer Mize, and Lauren Brennan. "'Of Mice and Men': Natural Kinds of Emotions in the Mammalian Brain? A Response to Panskepp and Izard." *Perspectives on Psychological Science* 2 (2007): 297–312.

Barrett, Lisa Feldman, and James A. Russell, eds. *The Psychological Construction of Emotion*. New York: Guilford, 2014.

Barton, Carlin A. *The Sorrows of the Ancient Romans: The Gladiator and the Monster*. Princeton: Princeton University Press, 1993.

Barton, Stephen C. "'Be Angry but Do Not Sin' (Ephesians 4:26a): Sin and the Emotions in the New Testament with Special Reference to Anger." *Studies in Christian Ethics* 28 (2015): 21–34.

———. "Eschatology and the Emotions in Early Christianity." *JBL* 130 (2011): 571–91.

———. "Spirituality and the Emotions in Early Christianity: The Case of Joy." Pages 173–93 in *The Bible and Spirituality: Exploratory Essays in Reading Scripture Spiritually*. Edited by Andrew T. Lincoln, J. Gordon McConville, and Lloyd F. Pietersen. Eugene, OR: Cascade, 2013.

Basil. *Ascetical Works*. Translated by M. Monica Wagner, CSC. New York: Fathers of the Church, 1950.

Bauer, Walter, William F. Arndt, F. Wilbur Gingrich, and Frederick W. Danker. *Greek-English Lexicon of the New Testament and Other Early Christian Literature*. 3rd ed. Chicago: University of Chicago Press, 2000.

Beatty, Andrew. *Emotional Worlds: Beyond an Anthropology of Emotion*. Cambridge: Cambridge University Press, 2019.

Beecher, Marguerite, and Willard Beecher. *The Mark of Cain: An Anatomy of Jealousy*. New York: Harper & Row, 1971.

Bellet, Benjamin W., Payton J. Jones, and Richard J. McNally, "Trigger Warning: Empirical Evidence Ahead." *Journal of Behavior Therapy and Experimental Psychiatry* 61 (2018): 134–41.

Ben-Ze'ev, Aaron. "Aristotle on the Fortune of Others." Pages 84–103 in *Envy, Spite and Jealousy: The Rivalrous Emotions in Ancient Greece*. Edited by David Konstan and N. Keith Rutter. Edinburgh Leventis Studies 2. Edinburgh: Edinburgh University Press, 2003.

Berlant, Lauren. *Cruel Optimism*. Durham, NC: Duke University Press, 2011.

Best, Stephen, and Sharon Marcus. "Surface Reading: An Introduction." *Representations* 108 (2009): 1–21.

Bittencourt, Thiago. "Righteous or Dangerous? An Investigation of Ὀργίζεσθε in Ephesians 4:26a." *Southeastern Theological Review* 13 (2022): 25–39.

Black, David Alan. "Jesus on Anger: The Text of Matthean 5:22a Revisited." *NovT* 30 (1988): 1–8.

Blair, Elaine. "The Power of Enraged Women." *New York Times*, September 27, 2018.

Bloomquist, L. Gregory. "Subverted by Joy: Suffering and Joy in Paul's Letter to the Philippians." *Interpretation* 61 (2007): 270–82.

Blowers, Paul M. "Envy's Narrative Scripts: Cyprian, Basil, and the Monastic Sages on the Anatomy and Cure of the Invidious Emotions." *Modern Theology* 25 (2009): 21–43.

Boddice, Rob. "Anger." Video Lecture. George Mason University Library, September 2023, https://doi.org/10.13021/MARS/8690.

———. *The History of Emotions*. Manchester: University of Manchester Press, 2018.

———. *A History of Feelings*. London: Reaktion, 2019.

Boddice, Rob, and Mark Smith. *Emotion, Sense, Experience*. Cambridge Elements: Histories of Emotions and the Senses. Cambridge: Cambridge University Press, 2020.

Bongie, Elizabeth Bryson, trans. *The Life and Regimen of the Blessed and Holy Teacher, Syncletica*. Toronto: Peregrina, 1995.

Boquet, Damien, and Piroska Nagy. *Medieval Sensibilities: A History of Emotions in the Middle Ages*. Translated by Robert Show. Cambridge: Polity, 2018.

Boring, M. Eugene. *Mark: A Commentary*. Louisville: Westminster John Knox, 2006.

Boud'hors, Anne, ed. *Le Canon 8 de Chénouté*. 2 vols. Bibliothèque d'études coptes 21.1–2. Cairo: IFAO, 2013.

Boudon-Millot, Véronique, and Jacques Jouanna, with Antoine Pietrobelli. *Galien: Ne pas se chagriner*. Paris: Les Belles Lettres, 2010.

Bowlby, John. *Loss: Sadness and Depression*. New York: Basic, 1980.

Brakke, David. *The Gospel of Judas*. AB 45. New Haven: Yale University Press, 2022.

Brakke, David, and Andrew Crislip. *Selected Discourses of Shenoute the Great: Community, Theology, and Social Conflict in Late Antique Egypt*. Cambridge: Cambridge University Press, 2015.

Bremmer, Jan. "Pseudo-Clementines: Texts, Dates, Places, Authors, and Magic." Pages 1–23 in *The Pseudo-Clementines*. Edited by Jan Bremmer. SECA 10. Leuven: Peeters, 2010.

Brennan, Teresa. *The Transmission of Affect*. Ithaca, NY: Cornell University Press, 2004.

Brinkema, Eugenie. *The Forms of the Affects*. Durham, NC: Duke University Press, 2014.

Brown, Raymond E. *The Gospel According to John (XIII–XXI)*. AB 29A. New York: Doubleday, 1970.

Buch-Hansen, Gitte. "The Emotional Jesus: Anti-Stoicism in the Fourth Gospel?" Pages 93–114 in *Stoicism in Early Christianity*. Edited by Tuomas Rasimus, Troels Engberg Pedersen, and Ismo Dunderberg. Grand Rapids: Baker Academic, 2010.

Buell, Denise. *Why This New Race: Ethnic Reasoning in Early Christianity*. New York: Columbia University Press, 2005.

Bulman, Patricia. *Phthonos in Pindar*. Berkeley: University of California Press, 1992.

Bunge, Gabriel. *Dragon's Wine and Angel's Blood: The Teachings of Evagrius Ponticus on Anger and Meekness*. Crestwood, NY: St. Vladimir's Seminary Press, 2010.

Burrus, Virginia. *Early Christian Ecopoetics: Cosmologies, Saints, Things*. Philadelphia: University of Pennsylvania Press, 2019.

———. *Saving Shame: Martyrs, Saints, and Other Abject Subjects*. Philadelphia: University of Pennsylvania Press, 2011.

———. *The Sex Lives of Saints: An Erotics of Ancient Hagiography*. Philadelphia: University of Pennsylvania Press, 2004.

Burton, Robert. *The Anatomy of Melancholy*. New York: New York Review Books, 2001.

Burton-Christie, Douglas. "Evagrius on Sadness." *Cistercian Studies Quarterly* 44 (2009): 395–409.

Buswell, Robert E., Jr., and Donald Lopez Jr., eds. *The Princeton Dictionary of Buddhism*. Princeton: Princeton University Press, 2014.

Butler, Cuthbert, ed. *The Lausiac History of Palladius*. 2 vols. TS 6. Cambridge: Cambridge University Press, 1898.

Butler, Judith. *Precarious Life: The Powers of Mourning and Violence*. London: Verso, 2004.

Cairns, Douglas. "*koros* (κόρος)." Pages 751–52 in *The Encyclopedia of Greek Tragedy*. Edited by Hanna M. Roisman. Oxford: Wiley-Blackwell, 2014.

Calasso, Roberto. *The Marriage of Cadmus and Harmony*. New York: Knopf, 1993.

Cameron, Averil. *Christianity and the Rhetoric of Empire*. Sather Classical Lectures 55. Berkeley: University of California Press, 1991.

Cameron, Averil, and Stuart G. Hall. *Eusebius: Life of Constantine*. Oxford: Clarendon, 1999.

Carlson, Donald H. *Jewish-Christian Interpretation of the Pentateuch in the Pseudo-Clementine Homilies*. Minneapolis: Fortress, 2013.

Casey, Nell, ed. *Unholy Ghost: Writers on Depression*. New York: William Morrow, 2001.

Casey, R. P. *The Excerpta ex Theodoto of Clement of Alexandria: Edited with Translation, Introduction, and Notes*. SD 1. London: Christophers, 1934.

Castelli, Elizabeth. "Mortifying the Body, Curing the Soul: Beyond Ascetic Dualism in the Life of Saint Syncletica." *Differences* 4 (1992): 143–53.

Castelli, Elizabeth, trans. "Pseudo-Athanasius, *The Life and Activity of the Holy and Blessed Teacher Syncletica*." Pages 265–311 in *Ascetic Behavior in Greco-Roman Activity: A Sourcebook*. Edited by Vincent L. Wimbush. Minneapolis: Fortress, 1990.

Chaniotis, Angelos, ed. *Unveiling Emotions: Sources and Methods for the Study of Emotions in the Greek World*. Stuttgart: Franz Steiner Verlag, 2012.

Charlesworth, James H., ed. *Old Testament Pseudepigrapha*. 2 vols. New York: Doubleday, 1983, 1985.

Chiapparini, Giuliano. "Irenaeus and the Gnostic Valentinus: Orthodoxy and Heresy in the Church of Rome Around the Middle of the Second Century." *ZAC* 18 (2013): 95–119.

Choat, Malcom, and Rachel Yuen-Collingridge. "The Egyptian Hermas: The Shepherd in Egypt Before Constantine." Pages 191–212 in *Early Christian Manuscripts: Examples of Applied Methods and Approach*. Edited by T. J. Kraus and T. Nicklas. TENTS 5. Leiden: Brill, 2010.

Claasens, L. Juliana. "From Fear's Narcissism to Participatory Imagination: Disrupting Disgust and Overcoming the Fear of Israel's *Ḥerem* Laws." Pages 77–96 in *Mixed Feelings and Vexed Passions: Exploring Emotions in Biblical Literature*. Edited by F. Scott Spencer. RBS 90. Atlanta: SBL Press, 2017.

Clark, Elizabeth A. *The Origenist Controversy: The Cultural Construction of an Early Christian Debate*. Princeton: Princeton University Press, 1992.

Clement of Alexandria. *Exhortation to the Greeks*. LCL. Cambridge, MA: Harvard University Press, 1919.

Clements, Niki Kasumi. "Emotions and Ascetic Formation in John Cassian's *Collationes*." StPatr 83 (2017): 251–69.

Clough, Patricia Ticineto. Introduction to *The Affective Turn: Theorizing the Social*. Edited by Patricia Ticineto Clough with Jean Halley. Durham, NC: Duke University Press, 2007.

Cobb, Stephanie L. *Divine Deliverance: Pain and Painlessness in Early Christian Martyr Texts*. Oakland: University of California Press, 2016.

———. *Dying to Be Men: Gender and Language in Early Christian Martyr Texts*. New York: Columbia University Press, 2008.

Connolly, William. *Capitalism and Christianity: American Style*. Durham, NC: Duke University Press, 2008.

Conze, Edward. *Buddhist Meditation*. London: Routledge, 2008.

Cook, Patrick. "Lactantius on the Death of Galerius: A Re-Reading of *De Mortibus Persecutorum* 33." *VC* 73 (2019): 385–403.

Coon, Lynda L. *Sacred Fictions: Holy Women and Hagiography in Late Antiquity*. Philadelphia: University of Pennsylvania Press, 1997.

Crislip, Andrew. "The Ascetic Construction of Emotions: *Lupe* and *Akedia* in the Works of Evagrios of Pontos." Pages 240–65 in *Managing Emotion in Byzantium: Passions, Affects and Imaginings*. Edited by Margaret Mullett and Susan Ashbrook Harvey. London: Routledge, 2023.

———. "Disgust in Early Christianity: The New Testament and Its Early Reception." *Biblica* 102 (2021): 593–617.

———. "Emotions in Eden and After: Ancient Jewish and Christian Perspectives on Genesis 2–4." *JBRec* 6 (2019): 97–133.

———. "Emotion Words in Coptic: Reflections on the Evidence from Shenoute the Great." *Journal of the Canadian Society for Coptic Studies* 10 (2018): 45–57.

———. "Envy and Anger at the World's Creation and Destruction in the *Treatise Without Title 'On the Origin of the World'* (NHC II,5)." *VC* 65 (2011): 285–310.

———. "Pain, Emotion, and Identity in Early Christianity." *Journal of Early Christian History* 12 (2022): 27–51.

———. "The Red Monastery in Early Byzantine Egypt." Pages 3–9 in *The Red Monastery Church: Beauty and Asceticism in Upper Egypt*. Edited by Elizabeth S. Bolman. New Haven: Yale University Press, 2016.

———. "Resurrection, Emotion, and Embodiment in Egyptian Monastic Literature." Pages 144–69 in *Unity of Body and Soul in Patristic and Byzantine Thought*. Edited by Anna Usacheva, Jörg Ulrich, and Siam Bhayro. Contexts of Ancient and Medieval Anthropology 1. Leiden: Brill, 2021.

———. "Shenoute of Atripe on Christ the Physician and the Cure of Souls." *Le Muséon* 122 (2009): 265–95.

———. "Shenoute's Illness." Pages 207–18 in *The Rediscovery of Shenoute*. Edited by Anne Boud'hors, with David Brakke, Andrew Crislip, and Samuel Moawad. OLA 310. Leuven: Peeters, 2022.

———. "*The Shepherd of Hermas* and Early Christian Emotional Formation." StPatr 83 (2017): 231–50.

———. "The Sin of Sloth or the Illness of the Demons? The Demon of Acedia in Early Christian Monasticism." *HTR* 98 (2005): 143–69.

———. "Syncletica." *Brill Encyclopedia of Early Christianity*. Leiden: Brill, 2024.

———. *Thorns in the Flesh: Illness and Sanctity in Late Ancient Christianity*. Philadelphia: University of Pennsylvania Press, 2013.

Crum, Alia J., William R. Corbin, Kelly D. Brownell, and Peter Salovey. "Mind Over Milkshakes: Mindsets, Not Just Nutrients Determine Ghrelin Response." *Health Psychology* 30 (2011): 424–29.

Csikszentimihalyi, Mihalyi. *Finding Flow: The Psychology of Engagement with Everyday Life*. New York: Basic, 1997.

Curtis, Valerie. *Don't Look, Don't Touch, Don't Eat: The Science Behind Revulsion*. Chicago: University of Chicago Press, 2013.

Cvetkovich, Ann. *Depression: A Public Feeling*. Durham, NC: Duke University Press, 2012.

Czachesz, István, and Risto Uro, eds. *Mind, Morality and Magic: Cognitive Science Approaches in Biblical Studies*. London: Routledge, 2014.

Damasio, Antonio. *The Feeling of What Happens*. New York: Mariner, 2000.

Dancyger, Lilly, ed. *Burn It Down: Women Writing About Anger*. New York: Seal, 2019.

Daniélou, Jean, ed. *Grégoire de Nysse: La vie de Moïse*. 3rd ed. SC 1bis. Paris: Cerf, 2007.

Davies, William. *The Happiness Industry: How the Government and Big Business Sold Us Well-Being*. London: Verso, 2015.

De Sousa, Ronald. *Love: A Very Short Introduction*. Oxford: Oxford University Press, 2015.

DeWall, Nathan, Geoff Macdonald, Gregory D. Webster, et al. "Acetaminophen Reduces Social Pain: Behavioral and Neural Evidence." *Psychological Science* 21 (2010): 931–37.

Dickie, M. W. "Envy." *ABD* 2:530.

Didion, Joan. *The Year of Magical Thinking*. New York: Knopf, 2005.

Dilley, Paul. "Inscribed Identities: Prosopography of the Red and White Monasteries in the Early Byzantine and Medieval Periods." Pages 217–29 in *The Red Monastery Church: Beauty and Asceticism in Upper Egypt*. Edited by Elizabeth S. Bolman. New Haven: Yale University Press, 2016.

———. *Monasteries and the Care of Souls in Late Antique Christianity: Cognition and Discipline*. Cambridge: Cambridge University Press, 2017.

Dixon, Thomas. "'Emotion': The History of a Keyword in Crisis." *Emotion Review* 4 (2012): 338–44.

———. *From Passions to Emotions: The Creation of a Secular Category*. Cambridge: Cambridge University Press, 2006.

Djokoto, Vivian Afi, and Sumie Okazuki. "Happiness in the Eye and Heart: Somatic Referencing in West African Emotion Lexica. *Journal of Black Psychology* 32 (2006): 117–40.

Donaldson, Terence L. *Gentile Christian Identity from Cornelius to Constantine*. Grand Rapids: Eerdmans, 2020.

Driscoll, Jeremy. "Penthos and Tears in Evagrius Ponticus." *Studia Monastica* 36 (1994): 147–63.

Dunderberg, Ismo. *Beyond Gnosticism: Myth, Lifestyle, and Society in the School of Valentinus*. New York: Columbia University Press, 2009.

———. *Gnostic Morality Revisited*. WUNT 347. Tübingen: Mohr Siebeck, 2015.

———. "The School of Valentinus." Pages 64–99 in *A Companion to the Second-Century Christian 'Heretics.'* Edited by Antti Marjanen and Petri Luomanen. VCSup 76. Leiden: Brill, 2005.

Dunn, James, D. G. *Neither Jew nor Greek: A Contested Identity*. Grand Rapids: Eerdmans, 2015.

Dyduch-Hazar, and Vanessa Mitschke. "Affective Preferences in Benign Masochism." *Journal of Research in Personality* 107 (2023): 104429.

Eagleton, Terry. "The Excitement of the Stuff." *London Review of Books* 46.19 (October 10, 2024): 27–28.

Ehrman, Bart D. *Jesus: Apocalyptic Prophet of the New Millennium*. New York: Oxford, 1999.

Eidinow, Esther. *Envy, Poison, and Death: Women on Trial in Classical Athens*. Oxford: Oxford University Press, 2016.

Ekman, Paul, and W. V. Friesen. *Pictures of Facial Affect*. Palo Alto, CA: Consulting Psychologists Press, 1976.

Elliott, Matthew. *Faithful Feelings: Rethinking Emotion in the New Testament*. Grand Rapids: Kregel Academic, 2006.

Eng, David, and David L. Kazanjian, eds. *Loss: The Politics of Mourning*. Berkeley: University of California Press, 2002.

Engberg-Pedersen, Troels. *Paul on Identity: Theology as Politics*. Minneapolis: Fortress, 2021.

Epstein, Joseph. *Envy*. New York: Oxford University Press, 2003.

Esler, Philip F. "Group Norms and Prototypes in Matthew 5.3–12: A Social Identity Interpretation of the Matthaean Beatitudes." Pages 147–71 in *T&T Clark Handbook to Social Identity in the New Testament*. Edited by J. Brian Tucker and Coleman A. Baker. London: Bloomsbury, 2014.

———. "An Outline of Social Identity Theory." Pages 12–39 in *T&T Clark Handbook to Social Identity in the New Testament*. Edited by J. Brian Tucker and Coleman A. Baker. London: Bloomsbury, 2014.

Evagrius of Pontus. *Talking Back: Antirrhêtikos*. Translated by David Brakke. CS 220. Collegeville, MN: Liturgical Press, 2009.

Evans, Craig A. *Mark 8:27–16:20*. WBC 34B. Nashville: Thomas Nelson, 2000.

Ferguson, Everett. "Agape Meal." *ABD* 1:90–91.

Fitzgerald, John T., ed. *Passions and Moral Progress in Greco-Roman Thought*. London: Routledge, 2008.

Fitzmeyer, Joseph A., SJ. *First Corinthians*. AB 32. New Haven: Yale University Press, 2008.

Fox, Sherry C. "Health in Hellenistic and Roman Times: The Case Studies of Paphos, Cyprus and Corinth, Greece." Pages 59–82 in *Health in Antiquity*. Edited by Helen King. New York: Routledge, 2005.

Frank, Georgia. *The Memory of the Eyes: Pilgrims to Living Saints in Late Antiq-*

uity. Transformation of the Classical Heritage 30. Berkeley: University of California Press, 2000.

———. *Unfinished Christians: Ritual Objects and Silent Subjects in Late Antiquity*. Philadelphia: University of Pennsylvania Press, 2023.

Franklin, Samuel S. *The Psychology of Happiness: A Good Human Life*. Cambridge: Cambridge University Press, 2010.

Frawley, Ashley. *Significant Emotions: Rhetoric and Social Problems in a Vulnerable Age*. London: Bloomsbury Academic, 2023.

Fredrickson, Barbara L. "Love: Positivity Resonance as a Fresh, Evidence-Based Perspective on an Age-Old Topic." Pages 847–58 in *Handbook of Emotions*. Edited by Lisa Feldman Barrett, Michael Lewis, and Jeannette M. Haviland-Jones. 4th ed. New York: Guilford, 2016.

Fredrickson, David E. "Envious Enemies of the Cross of Christ (Philippians 3:18)." *Word & World* 28 (2008): 22–28.

———. *Eros and the Christ: Longing and Envy in Paul's Christology*. Minneapolis: Fortress, 2013.

———. "'Through Many Tears' (2 Cor 2:4): Paul's Grieving Letter and the Occasion of 2 Corinthians 1–7." Pages 161–79 in *Paul and Pathos*. Edited by Thomas H. Olbricht and Jerry L. Sumney. SymS 16. Atlanta: SBL Press, 2001.

Freud, Sigmund. "Mourning and Melancholia." Pages 237–58 in *Standard Edition of the Works of Sigmund Freud*. Vol. 14. Edited and translated by James Strachey. London: Hogarth, 1957 (1917).

Frevert, Ute. *Emotions in History: Lost and Found*. Budapest: Central European University Press, 2011.

Fulkerson, Laurel. *No Regrets: Remorse in Classical Antiquity*. Oxford: Oxford University Press, 2013.

Fulton, Rachel. *From Judgment to Passion: Devotion to Christ and the Virgin Mary, 800–1200*. New York: Columbia University Press, 2002.

Gemünden, Petra von. *Affekt und Glaube: Studien zur Historischen Psychologie des Früjudentums und Urchristentums*. NTOA/SUNT 73. Göttingen: Vandenhoeck & Ruprecht, 2009.

Gendron, Maria, and Lisa Feldman Barrett. "Reconstructing the Past: A Century of Ideas About Emotion in Psychology." *Emotion Review* 1 (2009): 316–39.

Gendron, Maria, Kristen A. Lindquist, Lawrence Barsalou, and Lisa Feldman Barrett. "Emotion Words Shape Emotion Percepts." *Emotion* 12 (2012): 314–25.

Gertsman, Elina, ed. *Crying in the Middle Ages: Tears of History*. London: Routledge, 2012.

Gilhus, Ingvild Sælid. "'Tears Flowed from His Eyes Unceasingly': Weeping and Total Devotion in Egypt in Late Antiquity." *Religion* 53 (2023): 116–34.

———. "Why Did Jesus Laugh? Laughter in Biblical-Demiurgical Texts." Pages 123–40 in *Humor and Religion: Challenges and Ambiguities*. Edited by H. Geybels and H. W. Van. London: Bloomsbury, 2013.

Goehring, James E. *Ascetics, Society, and the Desert: Studies in Early Egyptian Monasticism*. Harrisburg, PA: Trinity International, 1999.

———. "The First Sahidic *Life of Pachomius*." Pages 19–33 in *Religions of Late Antiquity in Practice*. Edited by Richard Valantasis. Princeton: Princeton University Press, 2000.

Goldie, Peter. "Emotion." *Philosophy Compass* 2.6 (2007): 928–38.

Goldstone, Matthew. "Murder, Anger, and Altars: The First Matthean Antithesis in Light of Exodus 21:14 and Its Early Rabbinic Interpretation." *NovT* 59 (2017): 339–54.

Görgemanns, Herwig, and Heinrich Karpp. *Origenes vier bücher von den Prinzipien*. Texte zur Forschung 24. Darmstadt: Wissenschaftliche Buchgesellschaft, 1976.

Graiver, Inbar. *Asceticism of the Mind*. PIMS Texts and Studies 213. Toronto: PIMS, 2018.

Graver, Margaret. "Anatomies of Joy: Seneca and the *Gaudium* Tradition." Pages 123–42 in *Hope, Joy, and Affection in the Classical Tradition*. Edited by Ruth R. Caston and Robert A. Kaster. Oxford: Oxford University Press, 2016.

———. *Stoicism and Emotion*. Chicago: University of Chicago Press, 2007.

Griffiths, Paul E. *What Emotions Really Are*. Chicago: University of Chicago Press, 1997.

Gross, Daniel L. *The Secret History of Emotion: From Aristotle's "Rhetoric" to Modern Brain Science*. Chicago: University of Chicago Press, 2006.

Grundeken, Mark. *Community Building in the Shepherd of Hermas: A Critical Study of Some Key Aspects*. VCSup 131. Leiden: Brill, 2015.

Gunderson, Jamie. "The Super Foul Apostles: Sexual Impropriety, Disgust, and Stinky Affective Histories in 2 Cor. 11:2–4." *BibInt* 30 (2022): 578–99.

Hagedorn, Anselm C., and Jerome H. Neyrey. "'It Was Out of Envy That They Handed Jesus Over' (Mark 15.10): The Anatomy of Envy and the Gospel of Mark." *JSNT* 69 (1998): 15–56.

Haidt, Jonathan. *The Righteous Mind: Why Good People Are Divided by Politics and Religion*. New York: Pantheon, 2012.

Harkins, Angela Kim. *An Embodied Reading of the Shepherd of Hermas: The Book of Visions and Its Role in Moral Formation*. Sheffield: Equinox, 2023.

Harl, Marguerite. "Recherches sur l'origénisme d'Origène: La satiété (κόρος) de la contemplation comme motif de la chute des âmes." StPatr 8 (1966): 373–405.

Harper Collins Study Bible. San Francisco: Harper San Francisco, 2006.

Harrill, J. Albert. "Cannibalistic Language in the Fourth Gospel and the Greco-Roman Polemics of Factionalism." *JBL* 127 (2008): 133–58.

Harrington, Mary. "Wealthy White Women Turn to 'Rage Rituals' in the Woods." *Unherd*, May 13, 2024.

Harris, William V. "The Rage of Women." Pages 121–43 in *Ancient Anger: Perspectives from Homer to Galen*. Edited by Susanna Braund and Glenn W. Most. Cambridge: Cambridge University Press, 2004.

———. *Restraining Rage: The Ideology of Anger Control in Classical Antiquity*. Cambridge, MA: Harvard University Press, 2001.

Harrison, Thomas. "The Cause of Things: Envy and the Emotions in Herodotus." Pages 143–63 in *Envy, Spite and Jealousy: The Rivalrous Emotions in Ancient Greece*. Edited by David Konstan and N. Keith Rutter. Edinburgh Leventis Studies 2. Edinburgh: Edinburgh University Press, 2003.

Harvey, Susan Ashbrook. *Scenting Salvation: Ancient Christianity and the Olfactory Imagination*. Transformation of the Classical Tradition 42. Berkeley: University of California Press, 2006.

Hatch, Edwin, and Henry A. Redpath. *A Concordance to the Septuagint*. 2 vols. Oxford: Clarendon, 1897.

Hatfield, Elaine, and Richard L. Rapson. "Emotional Contagion: Religious and Ethnic Hatreds and Global Terrorism." Pages 129–43 in *The Social Life of Emotions*. Edited by Larissa Z. Tiedens and Colin Wayne Leach. Cambridge: Cambridge University Press, 2004.

———. "Love and Attachment Processes." Pages 595–604 in *Handbook of Emotions*. Edited by Michael Lewis and Jeannette M. Haviland. New York: Guilford, 1993.

Hausherr, Irénée, SJ. *Penthos: The Doctrine of Compunction in the Christian East*. Translated by Anselm Hufstader, OSB. CS 53. Kalamazoo, MI: Cistercian Publications, 1982.

Haybron, Daniel M. *Happiness: A Short Introduction*. Oxford: Oxford University Press, 2013.

Healy, Patrick. "Joy Is Not a Strategy." *The New York Times*, August 23, 2024.

Helderman, Jan. *Die Anapausis im Evangelium Veritatis: Eine vergleichende Untersuchung des valentinianisch-gnostischen Heilsgutes der Ruhe im Evangelium Veritatis und in anderen Schriften der Nag Hammadi-Bibliothek*. NHS 18. Leiden: Brill, 1984.

Helm, Paul. "Augustine's Griefs." Pages 147–60 in *Augustine's Confessions: Critical Essays*. Edited by William E. Mann. Lanham, MD: Rowman & Littlefield, 2006.

Herion, Gary A. "Wrath of God (OT)." *ABD* 6:989–96.

Hermann, F. G. "φθόνος in the World of Plato's Timaeus." Pages 53–83 in *Envy, Spite and Jealousy: The Rivalrous Emotions in Ancient Greece*. Edited by David Konstan and N. Keith Rutter. Edinburgh Leventis Studies 2. Edinburgh: Edinburgh University Press, 2003.

Hinterberger, Martin. "Basil of Caesarea and Gregory of Nazianzus Speaking About Anger and Envy." StPatr 83 (2017): 313–31.

Hitz, Zena. *Lost in Thought: The Hidden Pleasures of the Intellectual Life*. Princeton: Princeton University Press, 2020.

Hochschild, Arlie. *The Managed Heart: Commercialization of Human Feeling*. Updated with new preface. Berkeley: University of California Press, 2012.

Hockey, Katherine M. *The Role of Emotion in 1 Peter*. SNTSMS 173. Cambridge: Cambridge University Press, 2019.

Holl, Karl, ed. *Epiphanius. Ancoratus und Panarion (Haereses 1–33)*. GCS 25. Leipzig: Hinrichs, 1915.

Horrell, David G. *Becoming Christian: Essays on 1 Peter and the Making of Christian Identity*. LNTS 394. London: Bloomsbury T&T Clark, 2013.

———. *Ethnicity and Inclusion: Religion, Race, and Whiteness in Constructions of Jewish and Christian Identities*. Grand Rapids: Eerdmans, 2020.

———. *The Social Ethos of the Corinthian Correspondence: Interests and Ideology from 1 Corinthians to 1 Clement*. Edinburgh: T&T Clark, 1996.

Horwitz, Allan V. *DSM: A History of Psychiatry's Bible*. Baltimore: Johns Hopkins University Press, 2021.

Horwitz, Allan V., and Jerome C. Wakefield. *The Loss of Sadness: How Psychiatry Transformed Normal Sorrow into Depressive Disorder*. New York: Oxford University Press, 2007.

Houghtaling, Adam Brent. *This Will End in Tears: The Miserabilist Guide to Music*. New York: It Books, 2012.

Hunt, Hannah. *Joy-Bearing Grief: Tears of Contrition in the Writings of the Early Syrian and Byzantine Fathers*. The Medieval Mediterranean 57. Leiden: Brill, 2004.

Hunt, Lynn. "The Self and Its History." *AHR* 119 (2014): 1576–86.

Inglis, Tom. *Love*. London: Routledge, 2013.

Irenaeus of Lyons. *Against the Heresies*. ACW 55. Translated by Dominic J. Unger. New York: Paulist, 1992.

Jacobs, Nicholas F. "New Book on Rural America Started with a False Conclusion, Then Looked for Evidence." *The Daily Yonder*, April 6, 2024.

Jacobs, Nicholas F., and Daniel M. Shea. "The Truth About 'White Rural Rage.'" *Unherd*, April 6, 2024.

Jamison, Leslie. "I Used to Insist I Didn't Get Angry. Not Anymore." *New York Times*, January 17, 2018.

Jeanrond, Werner G. *A Theology of Love*. London: Continuum, 2010.

Jenott, Lance. *The Gospel of Judas*. STAC 64. Tübingen: Mohr Siebeck, 2011.

Jensen, Robin Margaret. *Face to Face: Early Portraits of the Divine in Early Christianity*. Minneapolis: Fortress, 2005.

Jew, Ian Y. S. *Paul's Emotional Regime: The Social Function of Emotion in 1 Thessalonians and Philippians*. LNTS 629. New York: T&T Clark, 2021.

John Cassian. *The Institutes*. Translated by Boniface Ramsay, OP. ACW 58. New York: Newman, 2000.

Johnson, Luke Timothy. "James 3:13–4:10 and the *Topos* ΠΕΡΙ ΦΘΟΝΟΥ." *NovT* 25 (1983): 326–47.

Jones-Smith, Elsie. *Theories of Counseling and Psychotherapy: An Integrative Approach*. 3rd ed. Thousand Oaks, CA: SAGE, 2021.

Jordaan, Gert J. C. "The Joy of Seeing Christ: A Thematic Study of Joy in the Gospel of John." *In die Skriflig* 49(2), Art. 1968.

Karant-Nunn, Susan C. *The Reformation of Feeling: Shaping the Religious Emotions in Early Modern Germany*. Oxford: Oxford University Press, 2010.

Karp, David A. *Speaking of Sadness: Depression, Disconnection, and the Meanings of Illness*. 2nd ed. New York: Oxford University Press, 2016.

Kaster, Robert A. *Emotion, Restraint, and Community in Ancient Rome*. Oxford: Oxford University Press, 2005.

Kazen, Thomas. "Disgust in Body, Mind, and Language: The Case of Impurity in the Hebrew Bible." Pages 97–116 in *Mixed Feelings and Vexed Passions: Exploring Emotions in Biblical Literature*. RBS 90. Atlanta: SBL Press, 2017.

———. *Emotions in Biblical Law: A Cognitive Science Approach*. Sheffield: Sheffield Phoenix, 2011.

———. *Jesus and Purity Halakhah: Was Jesus Indifferent to Purity?* Stockholm: Almqvist & Wiskell, 2002.

Kelhoffer, James A. "Suppressing Anger in Early Christianity: Examples from the Pauline Tradition." *GRBS* 47 (2007): 309–25.

Kelley, Nicole. *Knowledge and Religious Authority in the Pseudo-Clementines: Situating the "Recognitions" in Fourth Century Syria*. WUNT 2/213. Tübingen: Mohr Siebeck, 2006.

Kelly, Daniel. *Yuck! The Nature and Moral Significance of Disgust*. Cambridge, MA: MIT Press, 2011.

Keuls, Eva C. *The Reign of the Phallus: Sexual Politics in Ancient Athens*. Berkeley: University of California Press, 1985.

King, Helen. "The Early Anodynes: Pain in the Ancient World." Pages 51–62 in

The Management of Pain: The Historical Perspective. Edited by R. Mann. Carnforth, UK: Parthenon, 1988.

Kittel, Gerhard, and Gerhard Friedrich, eds. *Theological Dictionary of the New Testament*. Translated by Geoffrey W. Bromley. 10 vols. Grand Rapids: Eerdmans, 1964–1976.

Klassen, William. "Kiss (NT)." *ABD* 4:89–92.

Klawans, Jonathan. *Purity, Sacrifice, and the Temple: Symbolism and Supersessionism in the Study of Ancient Judaism*. New York: Oxford University Press, 2006.

Klein, Melanie. *Envy and Gratitude and Other Works 1946–1963*. New York: Free Press, 1975.

Kleinman, Arthur, and Joan Kleinman. "Somatization: The Interconnections in Chinese Society Among Culture, Depressive Experiences, and the Meanings of Pain." Pages 429–90 in *Culture and Depression: Studies in the Anthropology and Cross-Cultural Psychiatry of Affect and Disorder*. Edited by Arthur Kleinman and Byron Good. Berkeley: University of California Press, 1985.

Knust, Jennifer. "Who's Afraid of Canaan's Curse? Genesis 9:18–29 and the Challenge of Reparative Reading." *BibInt* 22 (2014): 388–413.

Knuuttila, Simo. *Emotions in Ancient and Medieval Philosophy*. Oxford: Clarendon, 2004.

Kok, Michael. "Does Mark Narrate the Pauline *Kerygma* of 'Christ Crucified'? Challenging an Emerging Consensus on Mark as a Pauline Gospel." *JSNT* 37 (2014): 139–60.

Konstan, David. "Aristotle on Anger and the Emotions: The Strategies of Status." Pages 99–120 in *Ancient Anger: Perspectives from Homer to Galen*. Edited by Susanna Braund and Glenn W. Most. Cambridge: Cambridge University Press, 2004.

———. *The Emotions of the Ancient Greeks: Studies in Aristotle and Classical Literature*. Toronto: University of Toronto Press, 2004.

Konstan, David, and N. Keith Rutter, eds. *Envy, Spite and Jealousy: The Rivalrous Emotions in Ancient Greece*. Edinburgh Leventis Studies 2. Edinburgh: Edinburgh University Press, 2003.

Korsmeyer, Carolyn. *Savoring Disgust: The Foul and the Fair in Aesthetics*. Oxford: Oxford University Press, 2018.

Kotrosits, Maia. *The Lives of Objects: Material Culture, Experience, and the Real in Early Christianity*. Chicago: University of Chicago Press, 2020.

———. *Rethinking Early Christian Identity: Affect, Violence, and Belonging*. Minneapolis: Fortress, 2015.

Kraftchick, Steven. "Πάθη [*Pathē*] in Paul: The Emotional Logic of 'Original Argument.'" Pages 39–68 in *Paul and Pathos*. Edited by Thomas H. Olbricht and Jerry L. Sumney. SymS 16. Atlanta: SBL Press, 2001.

Krawiec, Rebecca. *Shenoute and the Women of the White Monastery*. Oxford: Oxford University Press, 2003.

Kristeva, Julia. *Tales of Love*. Translated by Leon S. Roudiez. New York: Columbia University Press, 1987.

Krueger, Derek. *Writing and Holiness: The Practice of Authorship in the Early Christian East*. Philadelphia: University of Pennsylvania Press, 2004.

Lasine, Stuart. *Divine Envy, Jealousy, and Vengefulness in Ancient Israel and Greece*. London: Routledge, 2023.

Lateiner, Donald. "Evoking Disgust in the Latin Novels of Petronius and Apuleius." Pages 203–234 in *The Ancient Emotion of Disgust*. Edited by Donald Lateiner and Dimos Spatharas. Oxford: Oxford University Press, 2016.

Lateiner, Donald, and Dimos Spatharas, eds. *The Ancient Emotion of Disgust*. Oxford: Oxford University Press, 2016.

Lawlor, Clark. *From Melancholia to Prozac: A History of Depression*. Oxford: Oxford University Press, 2012.

Layton, Bentley. *The Canons of Our Fathers: Monastic Rules of Shenoute*. Oxford: Oxford University Press, 2014.

———. "Social Structure and Food Consumption in an Early Christian Monastery: The Evidence of Shenoute's *Canons* and the White Monastery Federation A.D. 385–465." *Le Muséon* 115 (2002): 25–55.

Layton, Bentley, with David Brakke. *The Gnostic Scriptures*. 2nd ed. New Haven: Yale University Press, 2021.

Leach, Colin Wayne. "Envy, Inferiority, and Injustice: Three Bases of Anger About Inequality." Pages 94–116 in *Envy: Theory and Research*. Edited by Richard H. Smith. Oxford: Oxford University Press, 2008.

Leader, Darian, and David Corfield. *Why People Get Sick: Exploring the Mind-Body Connection*. New York: Pegasus, 2008.

Légasse, Simon. *L'Antipaulinisme sectaire au temp des pères de l'église*. CRB 47. Paris: Gabalda, 2000.

Lewis, C. S. *The Four Loves*. New York: Harcourt Brace Jovanovich, 1960.

Leyerle, Blake. *The Narrative Shape of Emotion in the Preaching of John Chrysostom*. Christianity in Late Antiquity 10. Oakland: University of California Press, 2020.

———. "Refuse, Filth, and Excrement in the Homilies of John Chrysostom." *Journal of Late Antiquity* 2 (2009): 337–56.

Leys, Ruth. *The Ascent of Affect: Genealogy and Critique*. Chicago: University of Chicago Press, 2017.

———. *From Guilt to Shame: Auschwitz and After*. Princeton: Princeton University Press, 2007.

———. *Trauma: A Genealogy*. Chicago: University of Chicago Press, 2000.

———. "The Turn to Affect: A Critique." *Critical Inquiry* 37 (2011): 434–72.

Lieu, Judith M. *Christian Identity in the Jewish and Graeco-Roman World*. Oxford: Oxford University Press, 2004.

———. *Neither Jew nor Greek? Constructing Early Christian Identity*. London: T&T Clark, 2016.

Limberis, Vasiliki. "The Eyes Infected by Evil: Basil of Caesarea's Homily, *On Envy*." *HTR* 84 (1991): 163–84.

Lipsett, B. Diane. *Desiring Conversion: Hermas, Thecla, Asenath*. New York: Oxford University Press, 2011.

López, Ariel G. *Shenoute and the Uses of Poverty: Rural Patronage, Religious Conflict, and Monasticism in Late Antique Egypt*. Transformation of the Classical Heritage 50. Oakland: University of California Press, 2013.

Louth, Andrew. "Envy as the Chief Sin." StPatr 15.1 (1984): 458–60.

———. "Evagrios on Anger." StPatr 47 (2010): 179–85.

Lukianoff, Greg, and Jonathan Haidt. *The Coddling of the American Mind: How Good Intentions and Bad Ideas Are Setting Up a Generation for Failure*. New York: Penguin, 2018.

Lumley, Mark A., Jay L. Cohen, George S. Borszcz, et al. "Pain and Emotion: A Biopsychosocial Review of Recent Research." *Journal of Clinical Psychology* 67.9 (2011): 942–68.

Lundhaug, Hugo, and Lance Jenott. *The Monastic Origins of the Nag Hammadi Codices*. STAC 97. Tübingen: Mohr Siebeck, 2015.

Luomanen, Petri. "The Sociology of Knowledge, the Social Identity Approach, and the Cognitive Science of Religion." Pages 199–229 in *Explaining Christian Origins: Contributions from Cognitive and Social Science*. Edited by Petri Luomanen, Ilkka Pyysiänen, and Risto Uro. BibInt 89. Leiden: Brill, 2007.

Luomanen, Petri, Ilkka Pyysiänen, and Risto Uro, eds. *Explaining Christian Origins: Contributions from Cognitive and Social Science*. BibInt 89. Leiden: Brill, 2007.

Lutz, Catherine A. *Unnatural Emotions: Everyday Sentiments on a Micronesian Atoll and Their Challenge to Western Theory*. Chicago: University of Chicago Press, 1988.

MacDonald, Nathan. "Is There Happiness in the Talmud?" Pages 57–73 in *The Bible and the Pursuit of Happiness: What the Old and New Testaments Teach Us About the Good Life*. Edited by Brent Strawn. New York: Oxford University Press, 2021.

Magness, Jodi. "'They Shall See the Glory of the Lord' (Isa 35:2): Eschatological

Perfection and Purity at Qumran and in Jesus' Movement." *Journal for the Study of the Historical Jesus* 14 (2016): 99–119.

Malesic, Jonathan. *The End of Burnout: Why Work Drains Us and How to Build Better Lives*. Oakland: University of California Press, 2022.

Marchal, Joseph A. "The Disgusting Apostle and a Queer Affect Between Epistles and Audiences." Pages 113–40 in *Reading with Feeling: Affect Theory and the Bible*. Edited by Fiona C. Black and Jennifer L. Koosed. Atlanta: SBL Press, 2019.

Marcus, Joel. *Mark 8–16*. AB 27. New Haven: Yale University Press, 2009.

———. "Mark—Interpreter of Paul." *NTS* 46 (2000): 473–87.

Martin, Dale. *The Corinthian Body*. New Haven: Yale University Press, 1995.

Martin, Nancy M., and Joseph Runzo. "Love." Pages 310–32 in *The Oxford Handbook of Religion and Emotion*. Edited by John Corrigan. Oxford: Oxford University Press, 2008.

Massumi, Brian. "The Autonomy of Affect." *Cultural Critique* 31 (1995): 83–109.

Mathewes, Charles. "Toward a Theology of Joy." Pages 63–95 in *Joy and Human Flourishing: Essays on Theology, Culture, and the Good Life*. Edited by Miroslav Volf and Justin E. Crisp. Minneapolis: Fortress, 2015.

Matt, Susan. "Recovering Emotion from Visual Culture." Pages 18–28 in *Reading Roman Religion: Visual and Textual Interpretation*. Edited by Hedvig von Ehrenheim and Marina Prusac-Lindhagen. Acta Instituti Romani Regni Sueciae 4.64. Stockholm: Svenska Institut I Rom, 2020.

May, Simon. *Love: A History*. New Haven: Yale University Press, 2011.

McMahon, Darrin M. *Happiness: A History*. New York: Grove, 2006.

Meeks, Wayne A. *The First Urban Christians: The Social World of the Apostle Paul*. 2nd ed. New Haven: Yale University Press, 2003.

Mena, Peter Anthony. "Scenting Saintliness: The Ailing Body, Chicana Feminism, and Communal Identity in Ancient Christianity." *Journal of Feminist Studies in Religion* 33 (2017): 5–20.

Meyer, Marvin, ed. *The Nag Hammadi Scriptures*. New York: Harper One, 2007.

Meyer, Robert T., trans. *Palladius: The Lausiac History*. ACW 34. New York: Paulist, 1965.

Miller, William Ian. *An Anatomy of Disgust*. Cambridge, MA: Harvard University Press, 1998.

Mirguet, Françoise. *An Early History of Compassion: Emotion and Imagination in Hellenistic Judaism*. Cambridge: Cambridge University Press, 2017.

———. "What Is an 'Emotion' in the Hebrew Bible? An Experience That Exceeds Most Contemporary Concepts." *BibInt* (2016): 442–65.

Moerman, Daniel. *Meaning, Medicine, and the 'Placebo Effect.'* Cambridge: Cambridge University Press, 2002.

Moore, Stephen D. "Retching on Rome: Vomitous Loathing and Visceral Disgust in Affect Theory and the Apocalypse of John." *BibInt* 22 (2014): 503–526.

———. "Why the Johannine Jesus Weeps at the Tomb of Lazarus." Pages 287–309 in *Mixed Feelings and Vexed Passions: Exploring Emotions in Biblical Literature*. Edited by F. Scott Spencer. RBS 90. Atlanta: SBL Press, 2017.

Morrice, William. *Joy in the New Testament*. Grand Rapids: Eerdmans, 1985.

Morris, Jonathan. *God Wants You Happy: From Self-Help to God's Help*. New York: Harper One, 2011.

Moynihan, Michael. "Jane Goodall's Troubling, Error-Filled New Book, 'Seeds of Hope.'" *Daily Beast*, March 26, 2013 (updated July 11, 2017).

Muehlenberg, Ellen. "The Legend of Arius' Death: Imagination, Space and Filth in Late Ancient Historiography." *Past and Present* 227 (2015): 3–29.

Murphy, Edwina. "Imitating the Devil: Cyprian on Jealousy and Envy." *Scrinium* 14 (2018): 75–91.

Nasrallah, Laura Salah. *Archaeology and the Letters of Paul*. Oxford: Oxford University Press, 2019.

———. "Grief in Corinth: The Roman City and Paul's Corinthian Correspondence." Pages 109–39 in *Contested Spaces: Houses and Temples in Roman Antiquity*. Edited by David Balch and Annette Weissenrieder. WUNT 285. Tübingen: Mohr Siebeck, 2012.

Neu, Jerome. *A Tear Is an Intellectual Thing: The Meanings of Emotion*. New York: Oxford University Press, 2000.

Newton, Hannah. *Misery to Mirth: Recovery from Illness in Early Modern England*. Oxford: Oxford University Press, 2018.

Neyrey, Jerome H. *2 Peter, Jude*. AB 37C. New Haven: Yale University Press, 1993.

Ngai, Sianne. *Ugly Feelings*. Cambridge, MA: Harvard University Press, 2007.

Nussbaum, Martha C. *From Disgust to Humanity: Sexual Orientation and Constitutional Law*. Oxford: Oxford University Press, 2010.

———. *Hiding from Humanity: Disgust, Shame, and the Law*. Princeton: Princeton University Press, 2004.

———. *The Therapy of Desire: Theory and Practice in Hellenistic Ethics*. Martin Classical Lectures 2/2. Princeton: Princeton University Press, 1994.

Nygren, Anders. *Agape and Eros*. Translated by Philip S. Watson. Philadelphia: Westminster, 1953.

Oaten, Megan, Richard J. Stevenson, Mark A. Williams, Anina N. Rich, Marina Butko, and Trevor I. Case. "Moral Violations and the Experience of Disgust and Anger." *Frontiers in Behavioral Neuroscience* 12 (2018): Article 179.

Oosterwijk, Suzanne, Kristen A. Lindquist, Morenikeji Adebayo, and Lisa Feldman Barrett. "The Neural Representation of Typical and Atypical Experiences of Negative Images: Comparing Fear, Disgust and Morbid Fascination." *Social Cognitive and Affective Neuroscience* 11 (2016): 11–22.

Oppel, Catherine. "'Why, My Soul, Are You Sad?': Augustine's Opinion on Sadness in the *City of God* and an Interpretation of His Tears in the *Confessions*." *Augustinian Studies* 35 (2004): 199–204.

Origen. *An Exhortation to Martyrdom, Prayer and Selected Works*. Translated by Rowan A. Greer. Mahwah, NJ: Paulist, 1979.

Osiek, Carolyn. *Rich and Poor in the Shepherd of Hermas: An Exegetical-Social Investigation*. CBQMS 15. Washington, DC: Catholic University of America Press, 1983.

———. *The Shepherd of Hermas*. Hermeneia. Minneapolis: Fortress, 1999.

Paffenroth, Kim. "Tears of Grief and Joy: *Confessions* Book 9: Chronological Sequence and Structure." *Augustinian Studies* 28 (1997): 141–54.

———. "The Young Augustine: Lover of Sorrow." *Downside Review* 118 (2000): 221–30.

Pagels, Elaine. "The Rage of Angels." Pages 235–44 in *Rage, Power, and Aggression*. Edited by Robert A. Glick and Steven P. Roose. New Haven: Yale University Press, 1993.

Pagels, Elaine, and Karen King. *Reading Judas: The Gospel of Judas and the Shaping of Christianity*. New York: Viking, 2007.

Parrott, W. Gerrod, and Patricia M. Rodriguez Mosquera. "On the Pleasures and Displeasures of Being Envied." Pages 117–32 in *Envy: Theory and Research*. Edited by Richard H. Smith. Oxford: Oxford University Press, 2008.

Parsenios, George L. *Departure and Consolation: The Johannine Farewell Discourses in the Light of Greco-Roman Literature*. NovTSup 117. Leiden: Brill, 2005.

Pellegrini, Ann. "'Signaling Through the Flames': Hell House Performance and Structures of Religious Feeling." *American Quarterly* 59 (2007): 911–35.

Pile, Steve. "Emotions and Affect in Recent Human Geography." *Transactions of the Institute of British Geographers* n.s. 35 (2010): 5–20.

Plamper, Jan. "The History of Emotions: An Interview with William Reddy, Barbara Rosenwein, and Peter Stearns." *History and Theory* 40 (2010): 237–65.

———. *The History of Emotions: An Introduction*. Translated by Keith Tribe. Oxford: Oxford University Press, 2015.

Poirier, Michel. *Cyprien de Carthage: La jalousie et l'envie*. SC 519. Paris: Cerf, 2008.

Potkay, Adam. *The Story of Joy: From the Bible to Late Romanticism*. Cambridge: Cambridge University Press, 2007.

Protasi, Sara. *The Philosophy of Envy*. Cambridge: Cambridge University Press, 2021.

Raichle, Marcus E., and Debra A. Gusnard. "Appraising the Brain's Energy Budget." *Proceedings of the National Academy of Sciences* 99 (2002): 10237–39.

Ramanathan, Lavanya, and Christian Paz. "Democrats' Vibes Are Excellent. Can They Turn That into Votes? The Vibe Shift Explained." *Vox*, September 1, 2024.

Ramelli, Ilaria L. E., and David Konstan. "The Use of XAPA in the New Testament and Its Background in Hellenistic Moral Philosophy." *Exemplaria Classica: Journal of Classical Philology* 14 (2010): 185–204.

Rebillard, Éric. *Christians and Their Many Identities: North Africa, 200–450 CE.* Ithaca, NY: Cornell University Press, 2012.

———. *Greek and Latin Narratives About the Ancient Martyrs.* Oxford: Oxford University Press, 2017.

Reddy, Sumathi. "Anger Does a Lot More Damage to Your Body Than You Realize." *Wall Street Journal*, May 24, 2024.

Reddy, William M. *The Navigation of Feeling: A Framework for the History of Emotions.* Cambridge: Cambridge University Press, 2001.

Rehm, Bernhard, ed. *Die Pseudoklementinen I: Homilien.* GCS 42. Berlin: Akademie, 1969.

Reingold, Olivia. "I Went to Karen Summer Camp." *The Free Press*, May 27, 2024.

Reuling, Hanneke. *After Eden: Church Fathers and Rabbis on Genesis 3:16–21.* Jewish and Christian Perspectives Series 10. Leiden: Brill, 2006.

Rhee, Helen. *Illness, Pain, and Health Care in Early Christianity.* Grand Rapids: Eerdmans, 2022.

Rieff, Philip. *The Triumph of the Therapeutic: Uses of Faith After Freud.* New York: Harper & Row, 1966.

Rogers, Katie. "Harris Used to Worry About Laughing. Now Joy Is Fueling Her Campaign." *The New York Times*, August 9, 2025. Updated August 19, 2024.

Rosenwein, Barbara H. *Anger: The Conflicted History of an Emotion.* New Haven: Yale University Press, 2020.

———. "Angers Past and Present." *Emotions: History, Culture, Society* 4 (2020): 35–38.

———. *Emotional Communities in the Early Middle Ages.* Ithaca, NY: Cornell University Press, 2006.

———. *Generations of Feeling: A History of Emotions, 600–1700.* Cambridge: Cambridge University Press, 2016.

Rosenwein, Barbara H., and Riccardo Cristiani. *What Is the History of Emotions?* Cambridge: Polity, 2018.

Rothschild, Claire K. "*Horror Vacui*: Welborn's 'Retrospect on the Challenge to a Consensus on the Date of 1 Clement.'" *BR* 65 (2020): 104–13.

Rothschild, Claire K., and Trevor Thompson. "Galen: 'On the Avoidance of Grief.'" *Early Christianity* 3 (2011): 110–29.

Rothschild, Claire K., and Trevor Thompson, eds. *Galen's "De indolentia."* STAC 88. Tübingen: Mohr Siebeck, 2014.

Rotman, Joshua, Jasmine M. Dejesus, and Emily Gerdin. "The Social Origins of Disgust." Pages 27–52 in *The Moral Psychology of Disgust*. Edited by Nina Strohminger and Victor Kumar. London: Rowman & Littlefield International, 2018.

Roukema, Riemer. "Origen on the Origin of Sin." Pages 201–11 in *The Evil Inclination in Early Judaism and Christianity*. Edited by James Aitken, Hector M. Patmore, and Ishay Rozen-Zvi. Cambridge: Cambridge University Press, 2021.

Rousseau, Adelin, and Louis Doutreleau, trans. *Irénée de Lyon, Contre les hérésies, Livre 1*. Vol. 2. SC 254. Paris: Cerf, 1979.

Rousseau, Philip. *Pachomius: The Making of a Community in Fourth-Century Egypt*. Berkeley: University of California Press, 1985.

Rozin, Paul. "Food for Thought: Paul Rozin's Research and Teaching at Penn." *Penn Arts and Sciences*, Fall 1997.

Rozin, Paul, Jonathan Haidt, and Clark McCauley. "Disgust." Pages 815–34 in *Handbook of Emotions*. 4th ed. Edited by Lisa Feldman Barrett, Michael Lewis, and Jeannette M. Haviland-Jones. New York: Guilford, 2016.

———. "Disgust." Pages 757–76 in *Handbook of Emotions*. 3rd ed. Edited by Michael Lewis, Jeannette M. Haviland-Jones, and Lisa Feldman Barrett. New York: Guilford, 2008.

———. "Disgust: The Body and Soul Emotion." Pages 429–51 in *Handbook of Cognition and Emotion*. Edited by Tim Dalgleish and Mick J. Powers. New York, Wiley, 1999.

Rozin, Paul, Lilly Guillot, Katrina Fincher, Alexander Rozin, and Eli Tsukayama. "Glad to Be Sad, and Other Examples of Benign Masochism." *Judgment and Decision Making* 8 (2013): 439–47.

Rubin, Miri. *Emotion and Devotion: The Meaning of Mary in Medieval Religious Cultures*. Budapest: Central European University Press, 2009.

Russell, James A. "The Greater Constructionist Project for Emotion." Pages 429–47 in *The Psychological Construction of Emotion*. Edited by Lisa Feldman Barrett and James A. Russell. New York: Guilford, 2014.

———. "My Psychological Constructionist Perspective, with a Focus on Conscious Affective Experience." Pages 183–208 in *The Psychological Construction of Emotion*. Edited by Lisa Feldman Barrett and James A. Russell. New York: Guilford, 2014.

Sadowsky, Jonathan. *The Empire of Depression: A New History*. Cambridge: Polity, 2023.

Sagnard, François M.-M. *La Gnose valentinienne et le témoignage de Saint Irénée*. Paris: Librairie philosophique J. Vrin, 1957.

Sala, Tudor. "Dismantling Surveillance in Late Antique Corporate Monasticism." PhD diss., Yale University, 2011.

Sanders, Ed. *Envy and Jealousy in Classical Athens: A Socio-Psychological Approach*. Oxford: Oxford University Press, 2014.

Schaefer, Donovan O. *The Evolution of Affect Theory: The Humanities, the Sciences, and the Study of Power*. Cambridge Elements: Histories of Emotions and the Senses. Cambridge: Cambridge University Press, 2019.

———. *Religious Affects: Animality, Evolution, and Power*. Durham, NC: Duke University Press, 2015.

Schaffner, Anna Katarina. *Exhaustion: A History*. New York: Columbia University Press, 2016.

Schaller, Tom, and Paul Waldman. *White Rural Rage: The Threat to American Democracy*. New York: Random House, 2024.

Scheer, Monique. "Are Emotions a Kind of Practice (and Is That What Makes Them Have a History)? A Bourdieuian Approach to Understanding Emotion." *History and Theory* 51 (2012): 193–220.

Schellenberg, Ryan S. *Abject Joy: Paul, Prison, and the Art of Making Do*. Oxford: Oxford University Press, 2021.

Scheve, Christian von, and Mikko Salmela, eds. *Collective Emotions: Perspectives from Psychology, Philosophy, and Sociology*. Oxford: Oxford University Press, 2014.

Schimmel, Solomon. "Envy in Jewish Thought and Literature." Pages 17–38 in *Envy: Theory and Research*. Edited by Richard H. Smith. Oxford: Oxford University Press, 2008.

Schnall, Simone, Jonathan Haidt, Gerald L. Clore, and Alexander H. Jordan. "Disgust as Embodied Moral Judgment." *Personality and Social Psychology Bulletin* 34 (2008): 1096–1109.

Schoeck, Helmut. *Envy: A Theory of Social Behaviour*. Translated by Michael Glenny and Betty Ross. New York: Harcourt, Brace & World, 1966.

Schroeder, Caroline T. *Monastic Bodies: Discipline and Salvation in Shenoute of Atripe*. Philadelphia: University of Pennsylvania Press, 2007.

———. "Prophecy and *Porneia* in Shenoute's Letters: The Rhetoric of Sexuality in a Late Antique Egyptian Monastery." *JNES* 65 (2006): 81–97.

Sedgwick, Eve Kosovsky. *Epistemology of the Closet*. Berkeley: University of California Press, 1990.

———. "Paranoid Reading and Reparative Reading, or, You're So Paranoid, You Probably Think This Essay Is About You." Pages 123–52 in *Touching Feel-*

ing: Affect, Pedagogy, Performativity. Edited by Eve Kosovsky Sedgwick. Durham, NC: Duke University Press, 2003.

Seigworth, Gregory J., and Melissa Gregg. "An Inventory of Shimmers." Pages 1–25 in *An Affect Theory Reader*. Edited by Gregory J. Seigworth and Melissa Gregg. Durham, NC: Duke University Press, 2010.

Shantz, Colleen. "Emotion, Cognition, and Social Change: A Consideration of Galatians 3:28." Pages 251–69 in *Mind, Morality, and Magic: Cognitive Science Approaches in Biblical Studies*. Edited by István Czachesz and Risto Uro. London: Acumen, 2014.

———. "'I Have Learned to Be Content': Happiness According to St. Paul." Pages 187–201 in *The Bible and the Pursuit of Happiness: What the Old and New Testaments Teach Us About the Good Life*. Edited by Brent Strawn. New York: Oxford University Press, 2021.

———. *Paul in Ecstasy: The Neurobiology of the Apostle's Life and Thought*. Cambridge: Cambridge University Press, 2009.

Shinall, Myrick C., Jr. "The Social Condition of Lepers in the Gospels." *JBL* 137 (2018): 915–34.

Shorter, Edward. *How Everyone Became Depressed: The Rise and Fall of the Nervous Breakdown*. New York: Oxford University Press, 2013.

Siegel, Erika H., Jolie B. Wormwood, Karen S. Quigley, and Lisa Feldman Barrett. "Seeing What You Feel: Affect Drives Visual Perception of Structurally Neutral Faces." *Psychological Science* 29 (2018): 495–503.

Siegel, Jeremy. "Why the Harris-Walz Campaign Is Talking About Joy, According to a Political Science Professor." *GBH*, August 7, 2024.

Sinkewicz, Robert E. *Evagrius of Pontus: The Greek Ascetic Corpus*. Oxford: Oxford University Press, 2003.

Smail, Daniel Lord. *On Deep History and the Brain*. Berkeley: University of California Press, 2007.

Smith, J. Warren. *Passion and Paradise: Human and Divine Emotion in the Thought of Gregory of Nyssa*. New York: Crossway, 2004.

Smith, Richard H., David J. Y. Combs, and Stephen M. Thielke. "Envy and the Challenges to Good Health." Pages 290–314 in *Envy: Theory and Research*. Edited by Richard H. Smith. Oxford: Oxford University Press, 2008.

Solevåg, Anna Rebecca. *Negotiating the Disabled Body: Representations of Disability in Early Christian Texts*. ECL 23. Atlanta: SBL Press, 2018.

Solomon, Robert C. *Love: Emotion, Myth, and Metaphor*. Garden City, NY: Doubleday, 1981.

Sorabji, Richard. *Emotion and Peace of Mind: From Stoic Agitation to Christian Temptation*. Oxford: Oxford University Press, 2000.

Soyars, Jonathan E. *The Shepherd of Hermas and the Pauline Legacy*. NovTSup 176. Leiden: Brill, 2019.

Spencer, F. Scott. "Getting a Feel for the 'Mixed' and 'Vexed' Study of Emotions in Biblical Literature." Pages 1–41 in *Mixed Feelings and Vexed Passions: Exploring Emotions in Biblical Literature*. Edited by F. Scott Spencer. RBS 90. Atlanta: SBL Press, 2017.

———. *Passions of the Christ: The Emotional Life of Jesus in the Gospels*. Grand Rapids: Baker Academic, 2021.

Spencer, F. Scott, ed. *Mixed Feelings and Vexed Passions: Exploring Emotions in Biblical Literature*. RBS 90. Atlanta: SBL Press, 2017.

Stark, Rodney. *The Rise of Christianity*. Princeton: Princeton University Press, 1996. Repr., New York: Harper One, 1997.

Stearns, Peter N. "Modern Patterns of Emotions History." Pages 17–40 in *Doing Emotions History*. Edited by Peter N. Stearns and Susan J. Matt. Urbana: University of Illinois Press, 2014.

Stearns, Peter N., and Carol Z. Stearns. *Anger: The Struggle for Emotional Control in America's History*. Chicago: University of Chicago Press, 1986.

———. "Emotionology: Clarifying the History of Emotions and Emotional Standards." *AHR* 90 (1985): 813–36.

Stephens, Randall. *The Devil's Music: How Christians Inspired, Condemned, and Embraced Rock 'n' Roll*. Cambridge, MA: Harvard University Press, 2018.

Stewart, Columba. "Evagrius Ponticus and the 'Eight Generic *Logismoi*.'" Pages 3–34 in *In the Garden of Evil: The Vices and Culture in the Middle Ages*. Edited by Richard Newhauser. PIMS 18. Toronto: University of Toronto Press, 2005.

———. "Evagrius Ponticus on Prayer and Anger." Pages 65–81 in *Religions of Late Antiquity in Practice*. Edited by Richard Valantasis. Princeton: Princeton University Press, 2000.

Stowers, Stanley K. *Letter Writing in Greco-Roman Antiquity*. Louisville: Westminster John Knox, 1986.

Straw, Carole. "Gregory, Cassian, and the Cardinal Vices." Pages 35–58 in *In the Garden of Evil: The Vices and Culture in the Middle Ages*. Edited by Richard Newhauser. PIMS 18. Toronto: University of Toronto Press, 2005.

Strawn, Brent, ed. *The Bible and the Pursuit of Happiness: What the Old and New Testaments Teach Us About the Good Life*. New York: Oxford University Press, 2021.

Stroumsa, Guy. "Christ's Laughter: Docetic Origins Revisited." *JECS* 12 (2004): 267–88.

———. "Les martyrs chrétiens et l'inversion des émotions." Pages 167–81 in *Violentes émotions: approaches comparatistes*. Edited by Philippe Borgeaud and Anne-Caroline Rendu Loisel. Geneva: Librairie Droz, 2009.

Styron, William. *Darkness Visible: A Memoir of Madness*. New York: Random House, 1990.

Taylor, Joshua. "History of Hymns: 'They'll Know We Are Christians by Our Love.'" *Discipleship Ministries*, June 26, 2019. https://www.umcdiscipleship.org/articles/history-of-hymns-theyll-know-we-are-christians-by-our-love.

Taylor, Walter F., Jr. "The Family That Eats Together . . . : 1 Corinthians 11:17–34 from a Mediterranean Perspective." Pages 101–30 in *Exploring Biblical Kinship: Festschrift in Honor of John J. Pilch*. Edited by Joan C. Campbell and Patrick J. Hartin. CBQMS 55. Washington, DC: Catholic Biblical Association, 2016.

Thomassen, Einar. *The Spiritual Seed: The Church of the 'Valentinians.'* NHMS 60. Leiden: Brill, 2006.

Thomassen, Einar, and Marvin Meyer. "The Gospel of Truth." Pages 31–48 in *The Nag Hammadi Scriptures*. Edited by Marvin Meyer. New York: Harper One, 2007.

Thompson, Marianne Meye. "Reflections on Joy in the Bible." Pages 17–39 in *Joy and Human Flourishing: Essays on Theology, Culture, and the Good Life*. Edited by Miroslav Volf and Justin E. Crisp. Minneapolis: Fortress, 2015.

Thorsteinsson, Runar. "The Role of Morality in the Rise of Roman Christianity." Pages 139–57 in *Exploring Early Christian Identity*. Edited by Bengt Holmbert. WUNT 226. Tübingen: Mohr Siebeck, 2008.

Tite, Philip L. *Valentinian Ethics and Paranetic Discourse: Determining the Social Function of Moral Exhortation in Valentinian Christianity*. NHMS 67. Leiden: Brill, 2009.

Tollefsen, Torstein Theodor. "Eros and Agape—a Critique of Anders Nygren." Pages 17–29 in *Love—Ancient Perspectives*. Edited by Kari Grødum, Henny Fiske-Hägg, John Kaufman, Torstein Theodor Tollefsen. Oslo: Cappelen Damm Akademisk, 2021.

Tomkins, Silvan. *Shame and Its Sisters: A Silvan Tomkins Reader*. Edited by Eve Kosofsky Sedgwick and Adam Frank. Durham, NC: Duke University Press, 1995.

Torchia, Joseph. "Satiety and the Fall of Souls in Origen's *De principiis*." StPatr 18.3 (1989): 455–62.

Tracy, Jessica. "Find Something Morally Sickening? Take a Ginger Pill." *Aeon*, February 21, 2020.

Traister, Rebecca. *Good and Mad: The Revolutionary Power of Women's Anger*. New York: Simon & Schuster, 2019.

Travis, Stephen H. "Wrath of God (NT)." *ABD* 6:996–98.

Trepany, Charles. "Women Are Paying Big Money to Scream, Smash Sticks in the Woods. It's Called a Rage Ritual." *USA Today*, May 8, 2024; updated May 28, 2024.

Van Nuffelen, Peter. "The *Life of Constantine*: The Image of an Image." Pages 133–49 in *Eusebius of Caesarea: Tradition and Innovations*. Edited by Aaron Johnson and Jeremy Schott. Washington, DC: Center for Hellenic Studies, 2013.

Veilleux, Armand. *Pachomian Koinonia*. 3 vols. CS 45–47. Kalamazoo, MI: Cistercian, 1980–1982.

Vidaillet, Bénédicte. "Psychoanalytic Contributions to Understanding Envy: Classic and Contemporary Perspectives." Pages 267–89 in *Envy: Theory and Research*. Edited by Richard H. Smith. Oxford: Oxford University Press, 2008.

Vingerhoets, Ad. *Why Only Humans Weep: Unraveling the Mysteries of Tears*. Oxford: Oxford University Press, 2013.

Vivian, Tim, trans. *Four Desert Fathers: Pambo, Evagrius, Macarius of Egypt, and Macarius of Alexandria*. Crestwood, NY: St. Vladimir's Seminary Press, 2004.

Walcot, Peter. *Envy and the Greeks: A Study of Human Behaviour*. Warminster: Aris & Philips, 1978.

Wallace, Daniel B. "ΟΡΓΙ΄ΖΕΣΘΕ in Ephesians 4:26a: Command or Condition?" *Criswell Theological Review* 3 (1989): 353–72.

Ward, Ronald A. *Commentary on 1 & 2 Thessalonians*. Waco, TX: Word, 1973.

Ware, Kallistos. "'An Obscure Matter': The Mystery of Tears in Orthodox Spirituality." Pages 242–54 in *Holy Tears: Weeping in the Religious Imagination*. Edited by Kimberley Christine Patton and John Stratton Hawley. Princeton: Princeton University Press, 2005.

Watters, Ethan. *Crazy Like Us: The Globalization of the American Psyche*. New York: Free Press, 2010.

Webb, Christian A., and Diego A. Pizzagalli. "Sadness and Depression." Pages 859–70 in *Handbook of Emotions*. 4th ed. Edited by Lisa Feldman Barrett, Michael Lewis, and Jeannette M. Haviland-Jones. New York: Guilford, 2016.

Wees, Jennifer. "False Prophets Are False Fathers: Clairvoyance in the Career of Shenoute of Atripe." Pages 635–52 in *L'Evangile selon Thomas et les textes de Nag Hammadi*. Edited by Louis Painchaud and Paul-Hubert Poirier. Quebec: Presses de Université Laval, 2007.

Welborn, L. L. "Jealousy, Envy, Strife, and Discord in First Clement." *Journal of Beliefs and Values* 38 (2017): 173–79.

———. "Paul and Pain: Paul's Emotional Therapy in 2 Corinthians 1.1–2.13; 7.15–16 in the Context of Ancient Psychagogic Literature." *NTS* 57 (2011): 547–70.

———. "Retrospect on the Challenge to a Consensus on the Date of 1 Clement." *BR* (2020): 95–103.

———. *The Young Against the Old: Generational Conflict in 1 Clement*. Lanham, MD: Lexington/Fortress Academic, 2018.

Wendt, Heidi. "Secrecy as Pauline Influence on the Gospel of Mark." *JBL* 140 (2021): 579–600.

Wenzel, Siegfried. *The Sin of Sloth: Acedia in Medieval Thought and Literature*. Chapel Hill: University of North Carolina Press, 1960.

Wessel, Susan. *On Compassion, Healing, Suffering, and the Purpose of the Emotional Life*. Reading Augustine. New York: Bloomsbury Academic, 2020.

———. *Passion and Compassion in Early Christianity*. Cambridge: Cambridge University Press, 2016.

Wetzel, James. *Augustine and the Limits of Virtue*. Cambridge: Cambridge University Press, 1992.

White, L. Michael. "The Pathology and Cure of Grief (λύπη): Galen's *De indolentia* in Context." Pages 221–49 in *Galen's "De intolentia."* Edited by Claire K. Rothschild and Trevor Thompson. STAC 88. Tübingen: Mohr Siebeck, 2014.

Williams, Frank, trans. *The "Panarion" of Epiphanius of Salamis*. 2nd ed. NHMS 63. Leiden: Brill, 2009.

Williams, Peter J. "An Examination of Ehrman's Case for ὀργισθείς in Mark 1:41." *NovT* 54 (2012): 1–12.

Wilson, Eric G. *Against Happiness: In Praise of Melancholy*. New York: FSG, 2008.

Winkelmann, Friedhelm. *Eusebius Werke*. Vol. 1/1. GCS 55. Berlin: Akademie, 1975.

Wipszycka, Ewa. *The Second Gift of the Nile: Monks and Monasteries in Late Antique Egypt*. Translated by Damian Jasińsky. Supplements to the Journal of Juristic Papyrology. Warsaw: University of Warsaw, 2018.

Wormwood, Jolie Baumann, Erika H. Siegel, Justin Kopec, and Karen S. Quigley. "You Are What I Feel: A Test of the Affective Realism Hypothesis." *Emotion* 19 (2019): 788–98.

Wright, David P., and Richard N. Jones. "Leprosy." *ABD* 4:277–82.

Wright, N. T. "Joy: Some New Testament Perspectives and Questions." Pages 39–61 in *Joy and Human Flourishing: Essays on Theology, Culture, and the Good Life*. Edited by Miroslav Volf and Justin E. Crisp. Minneapolis: Fortress, 2015.

Yarbro Collins, Adela. *Mark: A Commentary*. Hermeneia. Minneapolis: Fortress, 2007.

Young, Molly. "How Disgust Explains Everything." *New York Times*, June 15, 2023; revised from December 27, 2021.

Young, Steve. "Being a Man: The Pursuit of Manliness in The Shepherd of Hermas." *JECS* 2 (1994): 237–55.

Yu, Zhaoliang, Persefoni Bali, Myron Tsikandilakis, and Eddie M. W. Tong. "'Look Not at What Is Contrary to Propriety': A Meta-Analytic Exploration of the

Association Between Religiosity and Sensitivity to Disgust." *British Journal of Social Psychology* 61 (2022): 279–99.

Zadra, Jonathan R., and Gerard L. Clore. "Emotion and Perception: The Role of Affective Information." *WIREs Cognitive Science* 2 (2011): 676–85.

Zetterholm, Karin Hedner, Anders Runesson, Cecilia Wassén, and Magnus Zetterholm, eds. *Negotiating Identities: Conflict, Conversion, and Consolidation in Early Judaism and Christianity (200 BCE–600 CE)*. Lanham, MD: Lexington Books/Fortress Academic, 2022.

Index of Names and Subjects

Index of Scripture